Palestinian Christians and the Old Testament

Palestinian Christians and the Old Testament

History, Hermeneutics, and Ideology

Will Stalder

Fortress Press
Minneapolis

PALESTINIAN CHRISTIANS AND THE OLD TESTAMENT

History, Hermeneutics, and Ideology

Copyright © 2015 Fortress Press. All rights reserved. Except for brief quotations in critical articles or reviews, no part of this book may be reproduced in any manner without prior written permission from the publisher. Visit http://www.augsburgfortress.org/copyrights/ or write to Permissions, Augsburg Fortress, Box 1209, Minneapolis, MN 55440.

Cover design: Alisha Lofgren

Library of Congress Cataloging-in-Publication Data is available

Paperback ISBN: 978-1-4514-8214-0

Hardcover ISBN: 978-1-4514-9975-9

eBook ISBN: 978-1-4514-9675-8

The paper used in this publication meets the minimum requirements of American National Standard for Information Sciences — Permanence of Paper for Printed Library Materials, ANSI Z329.48-1984.

Manufactured in the U.S.A.

This book was produced using PressBooks.com, and PDF rendering was done by PrinceXML.

To my dear, my wife, and best friend: Courtney!

אני לדודי ודודי לי

Without you, this would have been impossible! Thank you!

Ich liebe dich! Je t'aime!

Contents

Preface ix

Abbreviations xiii

Introduction xvii

Part I. Palestinian Christians and the Old Testament: Hermeneutics

1. The Elements of Palestinian Christian Hermeneutics of the Old Testament   3

Part II. Palestinian Christians and the Old Testament: History

2. Palestinian Christianity and the Dawn of Zionism   79

3. Palestinian Christianity and the "Promise" of a Jewish Homeland   137

4. Palestinian Christianity and the "Catastrophe" of the Modern State of Israel   175

Part III. Palestinian Christians and the Old Testament: Ideology

5. Perspectives on Palestinian Christian Hermeneutics of the Old Testament — *201*

6. A Prescription for a Palestinian Christian Hermeneutic of the Old Testament — *243*

Conclusion — *323*
Bibliography — *343*
Index — *395*

Preface

Welcome
أهلا و سهلا
ברוכים הבאים

It was a 2001 trip to Israel and Palestine that challenged the very core of my political and theological presuppositions about the land of Israel and Palestine and its people. Interactions with Palestinian Christians in Bethlehem and the Galilee and conversations with Jewish friends in Jerusalem set the stage for a decade of intellectual and spiritual soul-searching. During this time I finished seminary at Gordon-Conwell Theological Seminary (MDiv), moved to Scotland to do youth work, trained for the Ministry of Word and Sacrament with the Church of Scotland, and studied at the University of Aberdeen (MLitt in Jewish Studies and a PhD in Divinity). Still the question stirred in my mind: "How could my friends in both worlds, Palestinian and Israeli, be reconciled?" Subsequent trips to the Middle East in 2002, 2005, 2006, and 2007 only solidified my interest and concern, and with the encouragement and support of a surprising number of people I started looking at Palestinian Christians and the Old Testament. The topic allowed me to explore my interests in

Old Testament/Hebrew Bible, Jewish Studies, and Arab Christianity. In November 2012 I graduated from the University of Aberdeen, and the present book is an adaptation of my PhD dissertation. The topic was never just an academic exercise, but the discipline and rigor of the academy allowed me the space and (I hope) intellectual objectivity to explore issues that were close to my heart. In many ways writing the dissertation and editing it for publication has been a very difficult exercise, as I have tried to walk the fine line between conflicting opinions and heated (to say the least) social and political realities. Nevertheless, I hope that this present work, like my dissertation before it, succeeds in providing more understanding of the issues at hand and the resources by which the respective parties may "welcome" each other with open arms. With this in mind, I present to the reader the present work.

However, before I continue I would like to thank those groups of people to whom I am extremely indebted regarding this project. To my family: Courtney, Auggie, and Liesel; Mom and Dad; Phil and Lynn. To my friends: Aaron and Louise, Mark, B-house and Jennifer. To my supervisor: Professor Joachim Schaper, who tirelessly and enthusiastically supported and guided my research over the last number of years. To my examiners: Lena-Sofia Tiemeyer and Lester Grabbe for their feedback. To the masters and secretaries of Christ's College (University of Aberdeen) for their support and the Ministries Council (Church of Scotland) for allowing me to delay my training for ministry to complete the PhD. To the funding bodies that supported me financially: the Ferguson Bequest Fund and Friends of St. Andrew's Jerusalem. To the following archives and archivists for their help in accessing the relevant information: Church Missionary Society Archives at University Library, Special Collection, Birmingham (Ken Osborne); St. Antony's College, Oxford: Middle East Centre Archive (Debbie Usher); and SOAS Archive–School of

Oriental and African Studies, University of London. To the United Nations Publications Board for permission to reproduce one of its maps in this publication. To countless pastors, priests, and ministers, family and friends, colleagues, lecturers, and strangers, whose kindness and generosity have probably long been forgotten but whose conversations and welcome I will not quickly forget: my extended family, the Franks, Arthurs, Cowies, Dicksons, Gibsons, Merchants, Mansons, Naim Ateek, Mitri Raheb, Munther Isaac, Yohanna Katanacho, Tony Maalouf, Moyna McGlynn, Anthony O'Mahony, Cam and Rinat, Cynthia, Keleigh, Karl-Heinz Ronecker, Sabeel and JUC, and that random group of American tourists who gave me a lift after I missed the last bus to Amman. And last but definitely not least, a big thank you to the secretaries and editors of Fortress Press for agreeing to publish my work and for their help and support in the process. To these and others I have unintentionally forgotten, thank you! May I welcome others as you have welcomed me!

Abbreviations

AB	Anchor Bible
ABCFM	American Board of Commissioners for Foreign Missions
ABD	Anchor Bible Dictionary
ACCSOT	Ancient Christian Commentary on Scripture: Old Testament
ACTA	Analysis of Current Trends in Anti-Semitism
AEEC	Arab Evangelical Episcopal Community
ALJ	*Al-Liqa' Journal*
AnBib	*Analecta Biblica*
ANE	Ancient Near East
BBC	Blackwell Bible Commentary
BC	Michael Prior's, *The Bible and Colonialism: A Moral Critque*
BDB	Brown, Driver, and Briggs. *A Hebrew and English Lexicon of the OT.* Oxford, 1907
BETL	Bibliotheca ephemeridum theologicarum lovaniensium
BFCT	Beiträge zur Förderung christlicher Theologie
BHK	*Biblia Hebraica.* Edited by R. Kittel. Stuttgart, 1905–1906, 1925, 1937, 1951, 1973
BHQ	*Biblia Hebraica Quinta.* Deuteronomy. Edited by Carmel McCarthy. Stuttgart, 2007

BHS	*Biblia Hebraica Stuttgartensia.* Edited by K. Elliger and W. Rudolph. Stuttgart, 1983
Birmingham/UL	University Library, Special Collections Department, Birmingham
BTB	*Biblical Theology Bulletin*
CBQ	*Catholic Biblical Quarterly*
CCC	Catechism of the Catholic Church
CICARWS	Commission on International Church Aid, Refugee and World Service
C M/O	Church Missionary Archives, Original Papers of the Mediterranean and Palestine Mission 1811–1934
CMS	Church Mission Society
CSR	*Christian Scholar's Review*
CUP	Cambridge University Press
DDS	Moshe Weinfeld, *Deuteronomy and the Deuteronomic School*
DLT	Darton Longman and Todd
ELKJ	Evangelisch-Lutherischen Kirche in Jordanien
EMOK	Evangelischen Mittelostkommission
GKC	*Gesenius' Hebrew Grammar.* Edited by E. Kautzsch. Translated by A. E. Cowley. 2d. ed. Oxford, 1910
HALOT	Koehler, L., W. Baumgartner, and J. J. Stamm, *The Hebrew and Aramaic Lexicon of the Old Testament.* 4 vols. Leiden, 1994–1999
HKAT	Handkommentar zum Alten Testament
HUP	Harvard University Press
IB	Interpreter's Bible
IBC	PBC, *The Interpretation of the Bible in the Church*
ICE	International Christian Embassy
ICEJ	International Christian Embassy of Jerusalem
IJSCC	*International Journal for the Study of the Christian Church*
IMC	International Missionary Council

ABBREVIATIONS

ITQ	*Irish Theological Quarterly*
IUP	Indiana University Press
IVP	Intervarsity Press
JAOS	*Journal of the American Oriental Society*
JBL	*Journal of Biblical Literature*
JEM	Jerusalem and East Mission
JES	*Journal of Ecumenical Studies*
JETS	*Journal of Evangelical Theological Studies*
JPS	*Journal of Palestine Studies*
JQR	*Jewish Quarterly Review*
JSOT	*Journal for the Study of Old Testament*
JSOTsup	Journal for the Study of the Old Testament: Supplement Series
JTI	*Journal of Theological Interpretation*
LJS	London Jews Society
LSJ (LSPCJ)	*London Society* for Promoting Christianity amongst the *Jews*
MECC	*Middle East Council of Churches*
MES	*Middle Eastern Studies*
MEQ	*Middle East Quarterly*
MUP	Manchester University Press
NECC	Near East Council of Churches
NEEBII	Near East Ecumenical Bureau for Information and Interpretation
NEST	Near East School of Theology *Theological Review*
NIMEP	New Initiative for Middle East Peace
NRSV	New Revised Standard Vision
OTS	*Old Testament Studies*
OUP	Oxford University Press
PBC	Pontifical Biblical Commission
PBI	Pontifical Biblical Institute

PCHOT	Palestinian Christian Hermeneutic(s) of the Old Testament
PCUSA	Presbyterian Church of the USA
PLT (PTL)	Palestinian Liberation Theology or (Palestinian Theology of Liberation)
PNCC	Palestine Native Church Council (PCC – Palestine Church Council)
QR	*Quarterly Review*
SBL	*Society of Biblical Literature*
SBT	*Studies in Biblical Theology*
SCJR	*Studies in Christian-Jewish Relations*
SICSA	Vidal Sassoon International Center for the Study of Anti-Semitism
SJT	*Scottish Journal of Theology*
SPCK	Society for Promoting Christian Knowledge
TDOT	*Theological Dictionary of the Old Testament*
UN	United Nations
UNEF	United Nations Emergency Force
USM	*The United Secession Magazine*
VT	*Vetus Testamentum*
VTE	Vassal Treaties of Esarhaddon
WBC	Word Biblical Commentary
WCC	World Council of Churches
WCCP	World Conference of Christians for Palestine
ZAW	*Zeitschrift für die alttestamentliche Wissenschaft*

Introduction

"Peacemaking calls for courage, much more so than warfare. It calls for the courage to say yes to encounter and no to conflict: yes to dialogue and no to violence; yes to negotiations and no to hostilities; yes to respect for agreements and no to acts of provocation; yes to sincerity and no to duplicity. All of this takes courage, it takes strength and tenacity."
—Pope Francis[1]

"You must utterly destroy them (place them under the "ban"). Make no treaty with them, and show them no mercy... Break down their altars, smash their sacred stones... burn their idols with fire."
—(Deuteronomy 7:2-3, 5)[2]

No one doubts the existence of the seemingly endemic "cycle of hatred and violence" that exists between Israel and Palestine and that needs to be broken. In the summer of 2014 it only took the kidnapping and murder of three Israeli teenagers and a subsequent retaliation killing to plunge the region into conflict again (i.e., Israel's "Operation Protective Edge," the bombardment and invasion of Gaza), effectively nullifying the unprecedented and laudable efforts of Pope Francis in bringing Israeli and Palestinian presidents together in an invocation for peace. No sooner had Shimon Peres and Mahmoud

---

1. "Pope Francis and the Presidents of Israel and Palestine Invoke Peace," [accessed 24 September 2014]. Online: http://www.news.va/en/news/pope-francis-and-the-presidents-of-israel-and-pale.
2. The translation is the author's own.

Abbas concluded their prayers, kissed each other on the cheek, and planted an olive tree as a sign of ending the "cycle of hatred and violence" than peace was uprooted by yet another outbreak of hostility and war.

This latest clash, whose roots are much deeper and causes more complex than the aforementioned murders, is just one in a series of skirmishes and wars that have plagued the people of Israel and Palestine since the dawn of Zionism and the foundation of the modern state of Israel in particular. The factors behind this conflict have been well rehearsed elsewhere and will not be repeated here.[3] However, what the reader may not be aware of is how this conflict has proved doubly oppressive for Palestinian Christians.

The foundation of the modern state of Israel in 1948 is commemorated by countless Palestinians as a day of "catastrophe." Many Palestinian Christians *also* claim that it was spiritually catastrophic, as the characters, names, events, and places of the Old Testament took on new significance for the newly formed political state and thereby caused vast portions of the text to be abandoned and unusable in their eyes. Suddenly, the text of the Old Testament to which they were devoted and from which they might find help, comfort, and resources for *rapprochement* seemed to be "against them" and, as in the case of Deuteronomy 7, seemed to justify not only their expulsion from the land but their eradication.[4]

One need not look far back into the annals of history to see evidence of this connection being made. In 1995, Israeli Prime Minister Yitzak Rabin was assassinated by Yigal Amir on account of the former's efforts at *rapprochement* with Palestinians. Amir was against the famous Oslo Peace Accords of 1993 on religious grounds,

---

3. For an introduction to the conflict see, for example, James L. Gelvin, *The Israel-Palestine Conflict: One Hundred Years of War* (3d ed. Cambridge: Cambridge University Press, 2014).
4. See Deut 7:2, "You must utterly destroy them [place them under the 'ban']."

seeing Rabin's efforts to promote them as a transgression against the command in Deuteronomy 7 not to make any treaty or covenant with the "inhabitants of the land." For Amir, Rabin was doing just that, and this had to be rectified. The "ban" in Deuteronomy 7 had to be maintained, thought Amir. So, some twenty years ago, he shot and killed Rabin.[5]

This book looks to investigate the problem: How *might* Palestinian Christians read the Old Testament in a context in which biblical texts are routinely read as an endorsement of their suffering? Before any proposals are put forward, however, the book takes extra care to guide the reader through the maze of facts and figures that are germane to the present topic. The first chapter and section (Hermeneutics) outlines the key components that influence a Palestinian Christian reading of the Old Testament. It defines Palestinian Christian identity and looks at what it is to be Palestinian, a Christian in Israel and Palestine, and a Palestinian Christian in particular. It then surveys the work of the following Palestinian Christian leaders and their respective readings of the Old Testament in light of the foundation of the State of Israel: Naim Ateek, Mitri Raheb, Naim Khoury, Yohanna Katanacho, Michel Sabbah, and Atallah Hanna. These leaders come from a variety of religious traditions (Anglican, Lutheran, Baptist, Evangelical, Catholic, and Orthodox) and give the reader an appreciation of the range of opinion and the acerbity of the topic. Almost all these Palestinian Christians view the foundation of the State of Israel as a "catastrophe" for the Palestinian people politically (in the widest sense) and spiritually (including in their reading of the Old Testament). For example, Naim Ateek says: "For most Palestinian Christians, as for

---

5. Cf. Georg Braulik, "Die Völkervernichtung und die Rückkehr Israels ins Verheissungsland: Hermeneutische Bemerkungen zum Buch Deuteronomium," 3–38 in *Deuteronomy and Deuteronomic Literature: Festschrift C. H. W. Brekelmans*, ed. Marc Vervenne and Johan Lust (Leuven: Leuven University Press, 1997), at 3.

many other Arab Christians, their view of the Bible, especially the Hebrew Scriptures, or Old Testament, has been adversely affected by the creation of the State of Israel."[6] Similarly, Mitri Raheb laments:

> The Bible I had heretofore considered to be "for us" had suddenly become against us. It was no longer a consoling message to me but a frightening word. My salvation and that of the world were not the issue in the Bible any longer. The issue was my land, which God had promised to Israel and in which I no longer had a right to live unless it was as a "stranger." The God I had known since my childhood as love had suddenly become a God who confiscated land, waged "holy wars," and destroyed whole peoples."[7]

Kenneth Cragg sums up the problem by saying:

> Arab Christianity and Christian Palestinianism in particular suffer what all other Christianities in the West, in Africa, and in far Asia can escape, namely, the ambiguity between biblical loyalty to Hebrew scriptures as part of Christian heritage and the actualities of contemporary Israel with its enmity to Palestinianism *per se*."[8]

The first chapter then outlines how Palestinian Christians are reading the Old Testament in this context and details the factors that are influencing their understanding of it.

Having sketched the basic elements of *contemporary* Palestinian Christian hermeneutics of the Old Testament (PCHOT), the next section of the book (History) surveys the historical development of Palestinian Christian hermeneutics in the *past* and asks: "To what extent has Palestinian Christian hermeneutics of the Old Testament actually changed since the foundation of the state of Israel, and what have been the deciding factors that have influenced its development?

---

6. Naim Ateek, *Justice and Only Justice: A Palestinian Theology of Liberation* (Maryknoll, NY: Orbis Books, 2002), 77.
7. Mitri Raheb, *I am a Palestinian Christian* (Minneapolis: Fortress Press, 1995), 56.
8. Kenneth Cragg, *The Arab Christian: A History in the Middle East* (Louisville: Westminster John Knox, 1991), 11.

Has the political or religious context in which Palestinian Christians have found themselves governed how they have viewed and interpreted the Old Testament?" Answers to these questions are presented over the next three chapters. Chapters 2–4 look at Palestinian Christianity and its reading of the Old Testament before 1917 (chap. 2), between 1917 and 1948 (chap. 3), and after the foundation of the state of Israel in 1948 (chap. 4). The fourth chapter completes the historical survey and brings the reader back to the question of how Palestinian Christians *might* read the Old Testament in such a context.

The final section (Ideology) is perhaps the most contentious and yet important part of the book, for it seeks to prescribe a way forward for Palestinian Christians that is faithful to all the relevant sources and parties. This requires a vision that is not limited by the cataracts of one's own perspective. It requires openness to the "other(s)" and a willingness to see things from their point of view. This is undoubtedly difficult when one's eye is glued to a lens focused on war. However, if time is taken to adjust the way we see things, rather than cementing the lens in place we might just see a way forward. Chapter 5 gives a panoramic shot of the main non-Palestinian perspectives on how a Palestinian Christian might read the Old Testament. These include the views of Michael Prior: "Reading with the Eyes of the Canaanite," Charles Miller: "Reading with the Eyes of Tradition," and Gershon Nerel: "Reading with the Eyes of Jewish-Christian *fraternité*." On the basis of the strengths and weaknesses of these perspectives the present author outlines his own proposal in Chapter 6 and tests it against an in-depth analysis of the abovementioned text of Deuteronomy 7.

The conclusion brings the entire corpus into view and summarizes each of the sections (Hermeneutics, History, and Ideology) and chapters of the book, critiques them in light of this author's own proposal, and then makes some final suggestions for how Palestinian Christians might read the Old Testament in the future.

Father Pierbattista Pizzaballa, who is the current *Custos* of the Holy Land, admitted to Reuters before the "prayer summit" between Pope Francis, Israeli President Shimon Peres, and Palestinian President Mahmoud Abbas, "No one is presumptuous enough to think peace will break out on Monday...."[9] I do not presume that this book will cause peace to "break out" in Israel and Palestine. However, I do hope it will act in a manner similar to Pope Francis's initiative, namely, "to reopen a road that has been closed for some time; to re-create a desire, a possibility; to make people dream."[10] Rafiq Khoury argues:

> [There are] two types of narratives, two types of memories: the closed ones and the creative ones; memory as prison and memory as prophecy. As a prison, memory could mummify us in a certain place and prevent us from getting out of it. According to that meaning, memory is no more a stimulant, but a paralyzing reality. It paralyzes our vitality and creativity. We ruminate on the past, but we remain unable to imagine the future. We are no more able to invent history. As a prophecy, memory is a stimulant. It helps us, on the basis of our vivid memory, to go forward and invent a new future and a new untold narrative.[11]

I hope the reader will find in the following pages a narrative that is faithful to the realities and memories of the past and also creative and open to a new way of looking at things, a memory that sees a future with the "other." With regard to Palestinian Christians and the Old Testament, the task starts with understanding the text (Hermeneutics), then its reception (History), and finally how its

---

9. William Booth, "Pope Francis hosts Israeli, Palestinian leaders at 'prayer summit,'" *The Washington Post* (June 8, 2014), [accessed 24 September 2014]. Online: http://www.washingtonpost.com/world/pope-francis-hosts-israeli-palestinian-leaders-at-prayer-summit/2014/06/08/b9adc57e-ef48-11e3-bf76-447a5df6411f_story.html.
10. Ibid.
11. In Mitri Raheb, *Faith in the Face of Empire: The Bible through Palestinian Eyes* (Maryknoll: Orbis Books, 2014), 20.

meaning has been or can still be manipulated in an effort to "imprison" or "mummify" a particular understanding of the past and/or reality that silences or negates the memory of the "other" (Ideology). I hope this book will equip the interested reader to see beyond her or his own natural field of view and envision a future in which Palestinian Christians read the Old Testament not at odds against the "other" or in tension with what Cragg calls the "actualities of contemporary Israel with its enmity to Palestinianism *per se*," but in concert with them: unpacking, interpreting, and writing a new "narrative" that future generations might one day read with their own eyes.[12]

Will Stalder
Methlick
Aberdeenshire, Scotland
24 September 2014

---

12. Cragg, *Arab Christian*, 11. For a review of relevant literature and a description of the unique way in which the present work contributes to the discussion of Palestinian Christians, see William Andrew Stalder, "Palestinian Christians and the Old Testament: Hermeneutics, History, and Ideology." Ph.D. diss., University of Aberdeen, 2012.

PART I

Palestinian Christians and the Old Testament: Hermeneutics

1

The Elements of Palestinian Christian Hermeneutics of the Old Testament

The reader will at once recognize the inherent complexity of the title, "Palestinian Christian Hermeneutics of the Old Testament." It contains at least four aspects. The first, and the foundation of the present discussion, is the question of hermeneutics, or as more generally described, the "art of understanding."[1] The second facet of the title qualifies the task of hermeneutics and limits its scope to the understanding of a given text, namely, in this case, one in the Old Testament. This is further qualified by the interpretation of the Old Testament from a Christian perspective, and if that were not multi-faceted enough, the Christian hermeneutics of the Old Testament under consideration here is modified by yet another factor, namely,

---

1. Hermeneutics can have two dimensions. "Used in a narrower sense, hermeneutics can refer to the method and techniques used to interpret a text. In a wider sense, it can refer to the conditions which make understanding possible and even to the process of understanding as a whole." Bernard C. Lategan, "Hermeneutics," *ABD* 3: 149.

a class of individuals and communities commonly identified as "Arab Christians" who live in Israel and Palestine. As the title states, this chapter examines Palestinian Christian hermeneutics of the Old Testament (PCHOT).

Each of the aforementioned components has a significant bearing on PCHOT and thereby warrants a brief explanation. As intimated above, hermeneutics is generally referred to as the "art of understanding."[2] It is the necessary mediation between two stages of communication, namely, "the art of presenting one's thoughts correctly" and "the art of communicating someone else's utterance to a third person."[3] Without this intermediate stage, "the art of understanding another person's utterance correctly," all communication fails.[4] "Misunderstanding" persists and accurate explication (*das Auslegen*) is impossible.[5] However, the possibility of "understanding" is not beyond reach. One must pay attention to the "grammatical" and "psychological" dimensions of an utterance.[6] Even if someone adopts the "more strict practice" and "assumes that misunderstanding results as a matter of course," as opposed to adopting a "more lax practice" and "assum[ing] that understanding results as a matter of course," understanding is still possible and indeed open to all.[7] As Schleiermacher contends, "The successful practice

---

2. Hermeneutics is a field in its own right. For a general introduction to the issues and relevant personalities see Werner Jeanrond, *Theological Hermeneutics: Development and Significance* (London: MacMillan, 1991); Bernard C. Lategan, "Hermeneutics," *ABD* 3: 149–54; Richard E. Palmer, *Hermeneutics: Interpretation Theory in Schleiermacher, Dilthey, Heidegger, and Gadamer* (Evanston: Northwestern University Press, 1969).
3. Friedrich Schleiermacher, *Hermeneutics and Criticism: And Other Writings*, trans. and ed. Andrew Bowie (Cambridge: Cambridge University Press, 1998), 5.
4. Schleiermacher, *Hermeneutics and Criticism*, 5.
5. Schleiermacher, *Hermeneutics and Criticism*, 11, 22.
6. Schleiermacher explains, "As every utterance has a dual relationship, to the totality of language and to the whole thought of its originator, . . . all understanding also consists of the two moments, of understanding the utterance as derived from language, and as a fact in the thinker." Schleiermacher refers to the former as "grammatical" and the latter as "psychological." Ibid., 8–10.
7. Ibid., 21–22.

of the art depends on the talent for language and the talent for knowledge of individual people," but as "these talents (to a certain extent) are universal gifts of nature, hermeneutics is a universal activity."[8] "Understanding" is therefore universally possible, and this is true even for the text of the Old Testament. It is "in essence the same whether the text be a legal document, a religious scripture, or a work of literature."[9]

Hermeneutics of the Old Testament proceeds from the above definition of hermeneutics. Understanding an Old Testament text requires one to inquire into the "grammatical" and "psychological" basis of its composition. One must first determine the "language area which is common to the author and his original audience" and then find out the "sense of every word in a given location" by looking at the text's immediate literary context.[10] This is the "grammatical" side of Old Testament hermeneutics, and the "psychological" side is not far removed from it. It builds on what was established by "grammatical" interpretation and asks about the "principle" that moved an author to write.[11] This is evidenced by looking at "the basic characteristics of the composition," which betray the author's individuality or originality.[12]

This way of looking at the Old Testament is not far removed from the classic historical-critical method, which "endeavour(s) to interpret any passage according to the natural sense of the words ('grammatical') and according to the possible meaning of the author in his or her own time ('historical')."[13] This method governed Old

---

8. Ibid., 11–12.
9. Palmer, *Hermeneutics*, 84. Cf. Schleiermacher, *Hermeneutics and Criticism*, 16–20. As Schleiermacher puts it, "[E]ven if the writers were dead tools, the Holy Spirit could only have spoken through them in the way they themselves would have spoken." Ibid., 17.
10. Ibid., 30, 44.
11. Ibid., 90.
12. Ibid.
13. David C. Clines, "Methods in Old Testament Study," 25–48 in *Beginning Old Testament Study*, ed. John Rogerson (London: SPCK, 1998), at 29.

Testament hermeneutics for much of the nineteenth and twentieth centuries.[14] Since then there has been what some describe as a "hermeneutical revolution" in the way the Old Testament is interpreted.[15] Methods now abound,[16] and some scholars believe this will help "contribute to a brave new world of kaleidoscopic biblical readings" in which "the future will be a paradise of different readings with none privileged and all equally valid."[17] This sentiment, however, is not universally received, not least by the present author.[18] How, then, should one interpret the Old Testament? For now it suffices to show that there is a proliferation of methods prescribing how the Old Testament should be understood. Moreover, this cornucopia of options does not diminish when one inquires into the nature of Christian hermeneutics of the Old Testament.[19] As Bernhard Anderson writes, "Once the Church decided that the Old Testament must be retained in the Christian canon it committed itself to a major hermeneutical problem: what is the nature of the relationship between the Testaments?"[20] Some scholars rightly argue that the relationship between the Old and New Testaments "must begin with the premise that each speaks from its own complete integrity."[21] As Jon Levenson puts it, "Christianity is not the historical

---

14. For an overview of the history of Old Testament study see John Rogerson, "An Outline of the History of Old Testament Study," 6–24 in *Beginning Old Testament Study*.
15. Francis Watson, ed., *The Open Secret: New Directions for Biblical Studies?* (London: SCM, 1993), 2.
16. See, for example, the variety of methods outlined in John Barton, ed., *The Cambridge Companion to Biblical Interpretation*.
17. Watson, *Open Secret*, 2.
18. The reasons for this will become evident in subsequent chapters.
19. Not least among the issues are the different versions of the Old Testament Christians use. Traditionally, the Orthodox Church uses the Septuagint (LXX), Roman Catholics use the Vulgate, and Protestants use the Hebrew Bible. For an introduction to the various versions of the Old Testament see Ernst Würthwein, *The Text of the Old Testament: An Introduction to the Biblia Hebraica* (trans. Erroll F. Rhodes; London: SCM, 1980).
20. Bernhard W. Anderson, ed., *The Old Testament and Christian Faith* (London: SCM, 1964), 4.
21. Jon D. Levenson, *The Hebrew Bible, the Old Testament, and Historical Criticism* (Louisville: Westminster John Knox, 1993), 83.

context for a single religious idea in the Hebrew Bible, the latest of whose writings predate the earliest Christian material by a full two centuries."[22] Thus any Christian hermeneutic of the Old Testament must first seek to understand the Old Testament on its own terms. The question remains, however, "what is the relationship between the Old and New Testament and the religious ideas contained therein?" As Rudolf Bultmann writes, "The question . . . can be asked in such a manner that the Old and New Testaments are considered as sources for reconstructing the religion of Israel and the religion of primitive Christianity."[23] The fact that these two religious histories are both present in the Christian canon begs the question of the relationship between the two religions. It is clear that they stand in historical continuity with each other, but that does not answer the question whether the connection between the "religion of Israel" and the "religion of primitive Christianity" should be described as a "historical development" marked by "progress" or "decadence."[24] As Levenson puts it,

> To say that the Hebrew Bible has complete integrity over against the New Testament is to cast grave doubt upon the unity of the Christian Bible. . . . [but] for Christians to say the New Testament adds nothing essential to the Hebrew Bible is on the order of Marxists saying that they have no objection to leaving the means of production in the hands of capitalists: the assertion belies the speaker's announced identity.[25]

This is the challenge of Christian hermeneutics of the Old Testament: interpreting the Old Testament on its own terms and recognizing the continuing integrity and viability of the Old Testament as a religious text without being unfaithful to one's own Christian tradition.[26]

---

22. Ibid., 39.
23. Rudolf Bultmann, "The Significance of the Old Testament for the Christian Faith," 8–35 in *The Old Testament and the Christian Faith*, ed. Bernhard Anderson (London: SCM, 1964), at 8.
24. Ibid.
25. Levenson, *The Hebrew Bible*, 101.

The present discussion, however, is not limited to evaluating hermeneutics, hermeneutics of the Old Testament, or even Christian hermeneutics of the Old Testament. It seeks to describe the nature of Palestinian Christian hermeneutics of the Old Testament. Hence we need to begin by outlining the nature of Palestinian Christian identity, after which we will identify and describe six contemporary Palestinian Christians and their understanding of the Old Testament.

Palestinian Christian Identity

Is there such a thing as a Christian Palestinian or Palestinian Christian? Can a Christian understand himself or herself as a Palestinian? Can a Palestinian be simultaneously a Christian, and if so, how? Who are these Christian Palestinians? Where do they come from? What do they think? How do they define themselves? What are their distinctive characteristics and their problems? What determines their identity?[27]

So Mitri Raheb opens a Pandora's box filled with the "questions of identity" Palestinian Christians face. These questions are not dissimilar to the wider issues of Arab Christian identity, but there are matters peculiar to Palestinian Christians that need to be explained.[28]

---

26. In addition to this, Christian hermeneutics of the Old Testament has also been profoundly influenced by the Holocaust and the foundation of the state of Israel. See Bruce D. Marshall, "Christ and the Cultures: the Jewish People and Christian Theology," 81–100 in *The Cambridge Companion to Christian Doctrine*, ed. Colin Gunton (Cambridge: Cambridge University Press, 1997), at 81. Cf. Tod Linafelt, ed., *Strange Fire: Reading the Bible after the Holocaust* (Sheffield: Sheffield Academic Press, 2000).
27. Mitri Raheb, *I am a Palestinian Christian* (Minneapolis: Fortress Press, 1995), 3.
28. Kenneth Cragg introduces the complexity of Arab Christianity well when he says that the term "Arab Christian . . . has to do with an identity the elements of which are often thought to be dissociated. Arabism is so deeply involved in being Muslim, for reasons inherent in Islamic history, that it is thought to belong exclusively to that faith and culture. Yet 'Christian' was a descriptive of Arabs centuries before Islam, and there has been a Christian Arabism, an Arab Christianity, throughout the Muslim centuries since Muḥammad's day. The Muslim dominance of Arabness, however, from the beginning brought a tension and a tribulation into that Arab Christian existence under which it has labored and survived." Cragg, *Arab Christian*, ix. For further information on Arab Christianity and identity see also Joseph Maïla, "The Arab

The following section will unravel the entangled complexity of being a Palestinian Christian by defining what it means to be Palestinian, what it means to be Christian in Israel and Palestine, and finally what it means to be Palestinian Christian.

What Does It Mean to be Palestinian?

Most Palestinians distinguish themselves by their national identity.[29] As Bernard Lewis explains, the term "nation" can be used "without its connotations of territory or sovereign statehood."[30] He adds, "In this sense, a nation means a group of people held together by a common language, belief in a common descent and in a shared history and destiny."[31] Most of the time this group of people would "inhabit a contiguous territory" and "enjoy sovereign independence in their own name."[32] However, this is not always the case. As Edward Said argues, Palestinians still identify themselves as a nation in spite of the fact they have no nation-state. He writes: "Despite the fact that we are geographically dispersed and fragmented, despite the fact that we are without a territory of our own, we have been united as a people largely because of the Palestinian idea," namely the idea of a Palestinian state.[33]

Christians: From the Eastern Question to the Recent Political Situation of the Minorities," 25–47 in *Christian Communities in the Arab Middle East: The Challenge of the Future,* ed. Andrea Pacini (Oxford: Clarendon Press, 1998); George Sabra, "Two Ways of Being a Christian in the Muslim Context of the Middle East," *Islam and Christian–Muslim Relations* 17 (2006): 43–53; David Thomas, "Arab Christianity," 1–22 in *The Blackwell Companion to Eastern Christianity,* ed. Ken Parry (Oxford: Blackwell, 2007); Antonie Wessels, *Arab and Christian?: Christians in the Middle East* (Kampen: Pharos, 1995).

29. It is important to note that there are Palestinians who are Israeli citizens. In this case they are ethnically Palestinian but politically citizens of Israel. This group of Palestinians is known as Arab-Israelis. It is also important to note that for many Arab-Israelis the fact that they are not "nationally" Palestinian has more to do with geography than with affinity.
30. Bernard Lewis, *The Multiple Identities of the Middle East* (New York: Schocken Books, 1998), 81.
31. Ibid.
32. Ibid.
33. Edward Said, *The Question of Palestine* (New York: Vintage Books, 1979), x.

Where did this "Palestinian idea" come from? Three key factors are responsible for the rise of Palestinian nationalism: Arab nationalism, the political fragmentation of the Middle East after World War I, and the foundation of the state of Israel in 1948.[34] Rosemary Radford Ruether claims that Arab nationalism "emerged out of the colonial fragmentation of the region."[35] This is not true, however, as Arab nationalism preceded the disintegration of the Ottoman Empire. It certainly intensified after World War I, for Britain and France had "promised self-determination and ultimate independence to the Arab peoples who now came under their rule."[36] When the Levant was split between France and Britain, subdivided into separate mandates, and the aforementioned promise of statehood for the Arab people was not kept, it certainly exacerbated the Arab national cause but it most certainly did not create it. It would be more accurate to say that Palestinian nationalism emerged in the wake of the "colonial fragmentation of the region."[37]

Palestinian nationalism arose out of and solidified in its struggle against the British administration, Zionism, and the establishment of the state of Israel.[38] Of particular importance was the British administration's declaration that those who lived in the land of Palestine were to be referred to as "non-Jewish communities in Palestine." Rashid Khalidi points out:

---

34. For more information on the political context of Palestinian Christianity, see the relevant sections in chapters 2, 3, and 4.
35. Rosemary Radford Ruether and Herman J. Ruether, *The Wrath of Jonah: The Crisis of Religious Nationalism in the Israeli-Palestinian Conflict* (Minneapolis: Fortress Press, 2002), 95. They also claim (p. 95) that "nationalism was itself Western, not an Arab idea, imported to the region in the late nineteenth century."
36. Bernard Lewis, *The Middle East: A Brief History of the Last 2,000 Years* (New York: Scribner, 2003), 343.
37. Ruether and Ruether, *Wrath of Jonah*, 95.
38. Rashid Khalidi lists three main obstacles hindering Palestinian national expression: the external powers of Britain and the United states, the Zionist movement, and internal factors within Palestinian society. Rashid Khalidi, *Palestinian Identity: The Construction of Modern National Consciousness* (New York: Columbia University Press, 1997), 24–26.

> [This] . . . negation was an important prerequisite both for the denial of self-determination to the Palestinians, and for the British decision to favor Zionism: for if the Palestinians had no determined identity, they were unworthy of self-determination, or at least less worthy than the Jews, who clearly had a determined identity, now being posed in national rather than religious terms.[39]

As a result Palestine could easily be described as a "land without a people for a people without a land."[40] The Palestinian people could be ignored and the way opened for the foundation of a Jewish state. The countless skirmishes between the Palestinian people, the British administration, and the growing Jewish population betray the nascent nationalism that was growing among Palestine's native population.

The establishment of the state of Israel and the "catastrophe" (*al-Nakba*) it meant for many Palestinians undoubtedly helped solidify Palestinian national identity, but it did not generate it. As Khalidi writes:

> Were a basic core sense of national identity not already in place among key segments of the Palestinian people, the catastrophic shock of these events might have been expected to shatter the Palestinian people, eventually leading to their full absorption into the neighboring Arab countries. This indeed was what many of their opponents hoped would happen.[41]

---

39. Khalidi, *Palestinian Identity*, 23.
40. For a history of this infamous slogan see Diana Muir, "A Land without a People for a People without a Land," *Middle East Quarterly* 15, no. 2 (Spring 2008): 55–62. A version of the phrase first appeared in 1843 in connection with the Church of Scotland minister Alexander Keith, who wrote that the Jews are "a people without a country; even as their own land, as subsequently to be shown, is in a great measure a country without a people." Alexander Keith, *The Land of Israel according to the Covenant with Abraham, with Isaac, and with Jacob* (Edinburgh: William Whyte, 1843), 43. A year later *The United Secession Magazine* reviewed Keith's book and wrote with regard to the land and the Jews that they are a "land without a people, and a people without a land." Review of Alexander Keith, *The Land of Israel according to the Covenant with Abraham, with Isaac, and with Jacob*. *United Secession Magazine* 1 (April 1844): 189. This phrase was taken up and popularized in large measure by Christian and Jewish Zionists.
41. Khalidi, *Palestinian Identity*, 22.

Regardless of the reasons why Palestinian nationalism did not materialize in a state of its own, the above shows that Palestinians did exist in the land with a certain degree of corporate and national identity prior to the establishment of the nation of Israel.

Palestinian identity is clearly informed by a national consciousness, but to what extent is this national identity held together by ethnicity, language, or religion? Bernard Lewis states that "the first, primal and indelible mark of identity is race."[42] In the Middle East and for Palestinians, however, race is not a major distinguishing "mark of identity." Ali Qleibo argues:

> Throughout ancient and modern history, the land of Palestine has been a veritable melting pot wherein diverse peoples and civilizations succeeded one another. As each civilization waned and lost its hold, its heritage was assimilated within the civilization that followed. Modern Palestinian cultural identity has taken shape under the influence of the various civilizations that reigned over the land of Palestine.[43]

The fact, then, that Palestinians have emerged from a proverbial cauldron of cultures and are called "Palestinian" has little to do with any one ethnicity and even less to do with ancient Philistines.[44] What

---

42. Lewis, *Multiple Identities*, 40.
43. In Raheb, *I am a Palestinian Christian*, 14. Qleibo also adds that there is therefore "no specific ideal body type for the Palestinians that would distinguish them from the Europeans on the other side of the Mediterranean, be they Greeks, Italians, Southern-French or Spanish. Palestinian complexion ranges from olive tan to blue-white. . . . The highly diverse pool that the different peoples who inhabited Palestine bequeathed us is reflected in the marked absence of a single Palestinian physical type." In Raheb, *I am a Palestinian Christian*, 13.
44. Bernard Lewis rightly details that, in response to the Bar-Kokhba revolt in 135 CE, the Romans not only exiled a portion of the population but "obliterated the historic nomenclature of the Jews. . . . Jerusalem was [therefore] renamed Aelia Capitolina, and a temple to Jupiter [was] built on the site of the destroyed Jewish Temple. The names Judea and Samaria were abolished, and the country renamed Palestine, after long-forgotten Philistines." Lewis, *Middle East*, 31. The renaming of Judea and Samaria after the failed Bar-Kokhba revolt had less (if anything at all) to do with the connection with the ancient Philistines than with Roman disgust and the suppression of the Jewish revolts. Furthermore, the fact that Palestine and Philistine is the same word in Arabic is rather unfortunate for Palestinian Christians.

distinguishes Palestinians from other nationalities is not their race but their connection to the land.

To what extent then is Palestinian identity held together by language and religion? As Arabic is the mother tongue for Palestinians, they cannot be distinguished from other Arab nations on the basis of their language.[45] What sets Palestinians apart is their connection to the land. This relationship to the land embraces the Palestinian religious communities that live in it, namely, Muslims and Christians, all of whom have shared in the same national ideal of self-determination and self-governance and the same struggle with occupation and land. From the outset of the Arab Awakening, and in particular during the British Mandate, the majority of Christians and Muslims united within the emerging "Palestinian Arab National Movement."[46] The extent to which this collaboration has broken down in the subsequent *intifada*s has no doubt been exacerbated by the rise of Islamic fundamentalism.[47] Whether Islamic fundamentalism is the primary or secondary cause of this rift is debatable.[48] Whatever the case, many Palestinian Christians are finding themselves marginalized as they struggle against the same adversary.

---

45. Some case could be made that the Arabic spoken by Palestinians is much different from Egyptian or Iraqi, etc. The reason for these differences has to do with geography and therefore strengthens my argument that Palestinian identity is distinguished primarily by its connection to a particular land.
46. Anthony O'Mahony, "Palestinian Christians: Religion, Politics and Society c. 1800–1948," 9–55 in *Palestinian Christians: Religion, Politics and Society in the Holy Land*, ed. idem (London: Melisende, 1999), at 41.
47. Naim Ateek mentions that the first *intifada* was "patriotic and nationalist and was not based on religion." Naim Ateek, *A Palestinian Cry for Reconciliation* (New York: Orbis Books, 2008), 6. The second *intifada* and ensuing political turmoil, however, has been clearly marked by religious overtones and has caused a certain degree of tension between the Muslim and Christian communities.
48. Naim Ateek suspects Israel as the primary cause of this rift. He writes: "Some Palestinians, including myself, immediately suspected that Israel was attempting to interject religion into the conflict in order to shatter the national unity and solidarity of the Palestinians." Ateek, *Palestinian Cry*, 7.

What, then, does it mean to be Palestinian? Palestinians are a community that is religiously, ethnically, and politically diverse and yet at the same time is for the most part united around its connection to the land, namely, its national identity.

What Does It Mean to be a Christian in Israel and Palestine?

When asked by a cardinal during an address to the Roman Catholic superiors general in Rome in 1986 whether he was in communion with Rome, Elias Chacour, who is now Metropolitan of the Melkite Catholic Diocese of Akka, Haifa, Nazareth, and all of Galilee, responded:

> Your Eminence . . . you are a prince of the holy church of God and do not yet know that I am not in communion with Rome? It is rather Rome who is in communion with me! Nothing began in Rome. Everything began in Galilee. I want you to know, Eminence, that the pope is sitting over there in that high building because of me. I am not here because of the pope. We in Galilee believed what happened in our streets and our villages, and we came to Rome to tell you about Jesus Christ, to give you the message, to give you Christ himself.[49]

The above exchange between the then Melkite priest and a Roman cardinal raises the question: "What does it mean to be a Christian in Israel and Palestine?" Does being a Christian mean being indigenous to the land or being a beneficiary of Western missionary work? The former Latin Patriarch of Jerusalem, Michel Sabbah, rightly states that as "Christians in the Holy Land, we are a small Church. We are the Mother Church, where every Christian was born, where all Christians have their roots. . . ."[50] This is the first point of what it

---

49. Elias Chacour, *We Belong to the Land: The Story of a Palestinian Israeli Who Lives for Peace and Reconciliation* (San Francisco: Harper, 1992), 174.
50. Michel Sabbah, "Christian Identity in the Holy Land," 9–16 in *Palestinian Christians: The Holy Land Guardians* (Jerusalem: Laity Committee in the Holy Land, 2006), at 9.

means to be a Christian in Israel and Palestine: it means seeing oneself as part of the "Mother Church."[51]

The second characteristic, which Sabbah touched upon above, is that the Christian Church in Palestine and Israel is small. Raed Abdul-Masih rightly notes that "Christianity hasn't been the majority (religion) in the Holy Land except for a relatively brief period of time: from the Constantinian peace (313) until the Arab conquest in 638. . . . Apart from this Byzantine period, the Christians of the Holy Land have always been a minority. . . ."[52]

Besides being just a small minority in Israel and Palestine, the Christian population is also declining.[53] "In British mandated Palestine of 1946 Christians numbered 148,910. At present, the Christian population counts less than 160,000 in both Palestine and Israel."[54] On the surface one sees growth, but it is disproportionate to the population growth as a whole.[55] For example, the Christian population of British-mandated Palestine in 1947 was 7.3 percent of the total of 1,970,000.[56] If, as Soudah states, the Christian population

---

51. As will be seen in subsequent chapters, however, a number of Christian traditions in Israel and Palestine have come about via Western influence, namely, under the auspices of Catholic and Protestant missionary efforts. Nevertheless, most contemporary Christians in the land still see themselves as deriving straight from the time of Christ.
52. Raed Abdul-Masih, *La Iglesia Local de Tierra Santa: 2,000 Años Continuos de Transmisión y Testimonio de la Fe Cristiana* (Jerusalem: RAI: House of Art, 2005), 55–56. Author's translation. Original reads: "El cristianismo en Tierra Santa no ha sido mayoría más que por un periodo relativamente breve: desde la paz constantiniana (313) hasta la conquista árabe en 638. . . . Aparte de este paréntesis bizanto, los cristianos de Tierra Santa han sido siempre minoría."
53. For an alternative perspective see Malcolm Lowe, "The Myth of Palestinian Christianity," accessed 16 July 2012: http://www.gatestoneinstitute.org/2045/palestinian-christianity-myth.
54. Romell Soudah, "Christians in the Holy Land: Across the Political and Economic Divide," 9–37 in *The Sabeel Survey on Palestinian Christians in the West Bank and Israel* (Jerusalem: Sabeel, 2006), at 9.
55. Michel Sabbah notes just one small example to illustrate this point and states, "Bethlehem 50 years ago counted 6,000 Christians out of a population of 8,000. Today it has 12,000 out of a total population of 40,000." Sabbah, "Christian Identity in the Holy Land," 11.
56. Bernard Sabella notes a different source than Romell Soudah. The Christian populations in 1946–1947 vary by 5,910. The sharp decrease could be because of immigration, but it is most likely a statistical discrepancy between sources. The numbers are similar enough to make a justifiable point. Bernard Sabella, "Palestinian Christians: Historical Demographic

of Israel and Palestine is now 160,000, Christians are approximately 1.6 percent out of a total of eleven million.[57] Christians, therefore, are not just a small percentage of the overall population in Israel and Palestine. Their numbers are rapidly shrinking as well.

What are the reasons for the decrease in the Christian population? Charles Sennott argues that there have been spiritual, social, and political pressures that have made life unbearable and fueled a desire for emigration.[58] Spiritually, he notes that a type of "carnival Christianity" from the Western Church has frustrated, neglected, and isolated the Christian community.[59] Westerners visit the shrines but neglect the Christians in the Holy Land and thus make a "mockery of the reality lived by the local community."[60] Socially, the lack of tourism, the limited options for employment, and, as the Latin Patriarch echoes, the general "absence of peace; and [the presence of] injustices and instability" have corroded some of the cohesive social fabric.[61] Politically, Sennott notes that despite the affinity that exists among Palestinians regarding "matters of occupation and land, self-determination and economics, and limited water resources," the Christian community has felt marginalized since the second *intifada*.[62] On the street the second *intifada* came to be known as the "Al-Aqsa Intifada" as religion (Islam in this case) began to be fused with nationalism. As a result the second *intifada* developed overtones of

Developments, Current Politics and Attitudes Towards Church, Society and Human Rights," 39–93 in *The Sabeel Survey*, at 41.
57. "Israel Profile," accessed 3 Aug 2007: http://news.bbc.co.uk/1/hi/world/middle_east/country_profiles/803257.stm; "Palestinian territories profile," accessed 3 Aug 2007: http://www.bbc.co.uk/news/world-middle-east-14630174. As of 2010 the total population of Israel and the Palestinian territories was estimated at 11.7 million. "Israel Profile," accessed 7 Feb 2012; "Palestinian territories profile," accessed 7 Feb 2012.
58. Charles Sennott, *The Body and the Blood: The Holy Land's Christians at the Turn of the Millennium* (Oxford: Public Affairs, 2001).
59. Ibid., 432.
60. Ibid.
61. Sabbah, "Christian Identity in the Holy Land," 11.
62. Sennott, *Body and the Blood*, 352.

being a "Muslim-Jewish" conflict and Christians became alienated and subject to attack as "infidels."[63]

In light of the above circumstances for Christians in Israel and Palestine, the prospect for a future Christian presence in the land appears dismal. Pope Benedict XVI, trying to stem the tide of Christian emigration and encourage the Christians in the land, affirmed that "Christian minorities find it difficult to survive in the midst of such a volatile geopolitical panorama and are often tempted to emigrate. In these circumstances, Christians of all traditions and communities in the Middle East are called to be courageous and steadfast in the power of the Spirit of Christ."[64] Despite these efforts, most Christians in the West suspect that "Christians are going towards death rather than towards life. Others express their fear about the Holy places becoming a museum or a Disneyland."[65]

But in the midst of discouragement many Palestinian Christians are offering words of encouragement. The first Palestinian Latin Patriarch of Jerusalem, Michel Sabbah, has countered the aforementioned pessimism by saying: "A Christian vision of the future is essentially a vision of hope, a hope based on trust in the goodness of God as well as in the basic goodness of all human beings who are God's creatures and children, 'since it is in him that we live, and move, and exist' (Acts 17:28)."[66] Elias Chacour, the person responsible for coining the term "living stones" to refer to the Christians in Israel and Palestine, recently wrote a book called

---

63. Ibid., 377. For example, *Ha'aretz* reported on April 14, 2007 the bombing of a Christian bookstore and two internet cafés in Gaza City. "Heavy external damage was visible at the three stores. At the bookstore, which is funded by American Protestants and known as the Bible Society, a number of books were also burned by the explosion. . . . Palestinian security officials have said they suspect a secret vice squad of Muslim militants." *Bulletin: Associated Christian Press* 451 (March–April, 2007): 25.
64. *Bulletin: Associated Christian Press* 450 (January–February, 2007): 12–13.
65. Sabbah, "Christian Identity in the Holy Land,"11.
66. Michel Sabbah, "Forgotten Christians in the Holy Land?" *Cornerstone* 43 (Jerusalem: Sabeel, Winter 2007), 6.

Faith Beyond Despair: Building Hope in the Holy Land.[67] Each of these individuals, responsible for large portions of the Christian population in Israel and Palestine, are challenging Christians not to turn a blind eye to their struggles but to see beyond them and work toward a future in faith and hope.

In addition to the above characteristics, the Christian community in Israel and Palestine is not just small and decreasing in number; it is also quite "varied." The term "varied" seems to suggest that the Christian community in Israel and Palestine is plagued by division. Raed Abdul-Masih underscores this point and paints one of the most sarcastic and depressing pictures of the Christian community in what he calls "A Minority Divided."

> One of the sad characteristics of the Holy Land is the reality of its divisions. In effect, obvious to the eyes of the most distracted observer upon coming to the place of Jerusalem is a mosaic of confessions and of rites. The Church of the Holy Sepulchre is one typical example of this division. Under the same roof, one encounters Greek Orthodox, Armenian, Syrian, Copts, Latin, yet they certainly do not evoke for the world the diversity of Pentecost. In effect, in the course of the centuries their differences have degenerated into divisions, their traditions into traditionalism, their particularities into particularism, their confessions into confessionalism, their confidence into a lack of confidence toward one another, the withdrawal into distrust and aggression; ignorance has gone so far as to make them seem enemies . . . thus the sociological attitude, foreign to the evangelical spirit and the purifying profundity of the faith.[68]

---

67. Elias Chacour uses "living stones" to differentiate the Christian community from the lifeless stones and shrines Western Christians visit. The Christian community, although connected historically to land and place, are what is living, and they consequently demand attention. Elias Chacour, *Blood Brothers* (New York: Chosen Books, 1984), ix.

68. *Una de las tristes características del cristianismo de Tierra Santa es el hecho de sus divisiones. En efecto, salta a los ojos del observador más distraído hasta qué punto Jerusalém es un mosaico de confesiones y de ritos. La Iglesia del Santo Sepulcro es un ejemplo típico de esta división. Bajo la misma cúpula se encuentran griegos ortodoxos, armenios, sirios, coptos, latinos, sin por esto evocar para nada al mundo la diversidad de Pentecostés. En efecto, en el curso de los siglos, sus diferencias han degenerado en divisiones, sus tradiciones en tradicionalismo, sus particularidades en particularismo, sus confesiones en*

The Latin Patriarch Michel Sabbah also recognizes this division and says: "[W]e are many and divided."[69] However, he goes on to say that "we have to recognize with a feeling of joy and satisfaction that relations between all these Churches are warm and fraternal. ..."[70] This is confirmed by the fact that in recent years there has been an increased display of unity among the Christian traditions, as is evident in the many statements issued by the heads of the churches in Israel and Palestine, and most notably in the recent "Kairos Palestine Document."[71] It seems appropriate to conclude, therefore, that the Christian community in Israel and Palestine is "varied." The term "varied" allows for the reality of tension that exists between the Christian traditions in Israel and Palestine, but it does not have wholly negative connotations; it also allows for the presence of positive relations among the "varied" Christian traditions.

Christians in Israel and Palestine have been described as members of the Mother Church, as small, as shrinking yet living, and as varied: both fragmented and unified. What, then, are the churches/denominations that make up the Christian community in Israel and Palestine? The Christian church(es) in Israel and Palestine are part and parcel of the wider Christian community in the Middle East. Many of the patriarchates, dioceses, and denominations extend beyond the boundaries of Israel and Palestine. It is therefore helpful to draw back

---

confesionalismo, su confianza en sí en desconfianza hacia el otro, el replegarse sobre sí en recelo y agresividad; ignorándose, han llegado a tomarse por enemigos ... así como actitudes sociológicas extrañas para el espíritu evangélico y la profundidad purificadora de la fé. (Abdul-Masih, *La Iglesia Local de Tierra Santa*, 70. Author's translation.)

69. Sabbah, "Christian Identity in the Holy Land," 10.
70. Ibid.
71. See Melanie A. May, *Jerusalem Testament: Palestinian Christians Speak, 1988–2008* (Grand Rapids: Eerdmans, 2010); the Palestinian Kairos Document was issued on December 15, 2009 and is entitled: "A Moment of Truth: A Word of Faith, Hope, and Love, from the Heart of Palestinian Suffering," accessed 10 Feb 2012: http://www.kairospalestine.ps/sites/default/Documents/English.pdf.

for a moment to view the wider Christian church in the Middle East before looking at any one church in Israel and Palestine in detail.

The Christian churches in the Middle East can be and are often divided into four different families: the Oriental Orthodox, the Eastern Orthodox, the Catholic, and the Evangelical/Protestant. In short, the Oriental Orthodox family comprises those churches that rejected to varying degrees the christological statements established by the Council of Chalcedon. The Eastern Orthodox family includes those churches that embraced the decision made at the Council of Chalcedon and yet split away later for a variety of reasons, not least of them the issue of the *filioque*. The official division happened in 1054 when the Eastern Orthodox and Catholic churches sent each other official bulls of excommunication. The Catholic family consists of the Latin or Roman church as well as many Oriental Churches established as a result of Catholic missionary work and Orthodox conversion. These Oriental Catholic or Uniate churches are no doubt often a source of heated tension between the Orthodox and Catholic churches. The Evangelical family is made up of varying Protestant churches, including Anglican, Lutheran, Evangelical, Baptist, and even a growing Messianic Jewish population. The Middle East Council of Churches (MECC) provides a helpful list of these four different families.[72]

---

72. Adapted from O'Mahony, "Introduction" in *Christianity in the Middle East*, 11–12. Cf. "Member Churches," accessed 7 Feb 2012: http://www.mec-churches.org/member_churches/member_churches.htm. There are two key differences between O'Mahony's overview of the Middle East churches and that of the MECC. First, O'Mahony categorizes the Assyrian Church of the East and its Catholic counterpart, the Chaldean Catholic Church, as a separate family; second, he recognizes the Hebrew Catholic Church although it is not a member of the MECC.

1. The Oriental Orthodox Family
   The Armenian Orthodox Church
   The Syrian Orthodox Church
   The Coptic Orthodox Church
   The Ethiopian Orthodox Church

2. The Eastern Orthodox Family
   The Greek Orthodox Patriarchate of Jerusalem
   The Greek Orthodox Patriarchate of Antioch
   The Greek Orthodox Patriarchate of Alexandria

3. The Catholic Family: Six Oriental, one Latin, one Hebrew
   The Latin Patriarchate of Jerusalem (restored in 1847)
   The Greek Catholic Church
   The Maronite Church
   The Syrian Catholic Church
   The Armenian Catholic Church
   The Chaldean Catholic Church
   The Coptic Catholic Church
   The Hebrew Catholic Church

4. The Evangelical and Anglican-Episcopal family
   The Anglican and Episcopal Church (in Jerusalem and the Middle East)
   Various other Protestant churches and denominations such as the Lutheran, Presbyterian, Baptist, Evangelical, Messianic Jews, and others.

All the Christians in Israel and Palestine fall into one of the above families.

Now that we have established both what it means to be a Palestinian and what it means to be a Christian in Israel and Palestine, it is time to ascertain how these identities coalesce when someone is asked, "What does it mean to be a Palestinian Christian?"

What Does It Mean to be a Palestinian Christian?

For some, the combination of the two terms "Palestinian" and "Christian" is inappropriate. When asked in an interview about Palestinian Christians, Johann Lückhoff, then director of the International Christian Embassy (ICE) in West Jerusalem, responded, "They're not really Christians anyway. Christianity for Arabs is just a political commitment."[73] When asked ten years later if his views had changed, he still maintained that "Arab Christians compromise their Christianity regularly when they embrace any of the Palestinian causes," and said, "Promoting the restoration of Israel is the first sign of Arab spirituality."[74] Yohanna Katanacho acknowledges that "some people are surprised by the presence of Christians in Israel and Palestine."[75] In contrast to the ICE, who argue that there is really no such thing as a Palestinian Christian, that is, a Palestinian who is "truly" a Christian, Katanacho unabashedly claims, and rightly, that "Christian Palestinian Arabs" are Christians.[76]

The inability of the West to see the authenticity of Arab (and in this case Palestinian) Christianity is nothing new. Kathleen Christison notes that "in a milieu so strongly perceived by the non-

---

73. Gary Burge, *Whose Land? Whose Promise? What Christians Are Not Being Told about Israel and the Palestinians* (Carlisle: Paternoster Press, 2003), 195. A similar account is also reported by Bishop Munib Younan of the Lutheran Church. "As I was walking once in Jerusalem, I came upon a woman with her church group from the United States visiting the Holy Land. I asked her where she had visited, and she gave me the usual list of places. Then I asked her if she had spoken with any Palestinian Christians, and she was quick to reply: 'No, no, this is a church group. We're not getting political.'" Munib Younan, "Religion and Politics" (lecture given at the WCC General Assembly in Porto Alegre, Brazil, Feb 2006), 1. Accessed 7 Feb 2012: http://www.elcjhl.org/resources/younan/lecturestalks/lectures.asp.
74. Burge, *Whose Land?* 195.
75. Yohanna Katanacho, "Christian Palestinian Arabs: Spreading Hope in the Middle East," 1–2 in *In the Gap: John Stott Ministries Newsletter* (London: John Stott Ministries, Fall 2004).
76. Katanacho, "Christian Palestinian Arabs," 1.

Arab world to be Islamic and therefore alien, Arab Christians have always been the poor relatives of Western Christianity."[77] The unfortunate thing is that little has changed. Christison notes that Western Christians are

> unaware of the uniquely poignant dilemma posed for Arab and particularly Palestinian Christians by the existence of Israel as a Scripture-based Zionist state, for the very scriptures that Christians revere are those in whose name Palestine has been made over into an exclusively Jewish state with little or no room for Palestinians. Western Christians, if they know of their Arab co-religionists at all, are unsympathetic to this unique theological and national dilemma.[78]

It is this dilemma that will be investigated in the remaining chapters of this book. How have Palestinian Christians responded, as an authentic Christian community in Israel and Palestine, not only to the formation of the state of Israel but, moreover, to the text that is used, by both Christians and Jews, to delegitimize their presence in the land? To answer these questions we need to examine Palestinian Christian hermeneutics of the Old Testament.

---

77. Kathleen Christison, "Dilemmas of Arab Christianity" (review of Kenneth Cragg, *Arab Christian*), *JPS* 22, no. 1 (1992): 117–19. Christison adds that Crusaders despised Arab Christians as "*pagani*" and "*barbari*"; they were "subjects for conversion rather than partnership."
78. Ibid.

Palestinian Christian Hermeneutics of the Old Testament

May 16, 2007 marked "Jerusalem Day," the official starting point of a series of summer-long celebrations sponsored by the Israeli government and the Jerusalem municipality commemorating the fortieth anniversary of the reunification of Jerusalem. Banners and signs were placed throughout the city to mark the celebrations. Some signs read, "Something is special, for everything is one." Others, such as the one outside the Jaffa Gate, simply marked the occasion with a special "40" placard. Most common were banners, such as the one illustrated here, that lined the streets of Jerusalem. On one of these banners just outside the German Colony, however, someone had conspicuously written "Occupation" under the word "Reunification."[79]

This is a telling sign of the nature of historical memory. For some, 1967 signals "reunification," but for others it signifies "occupation." Furthermore, 1948 signals "independence" for some but "catastrophe" for others. How then should one remember these events? Shall it be as "independence" or as "catastrophe"? Shall it be as "reunification" or "occupation"? Kenneth Cragg is right to point out that "the historian [then], given the controversies of the story and the passion in events, is very much liable to become the propagandist."[80] He elaborates in his book, *This Year in Jerusalem*:

> Facts themselves, even when satisfactorily established, may still be tendentiously selected or interpreted from prejudice. One can hardly see the history "whole" if one is taking it as an itemized sequence of prosecution and defense. It seems better, therefore, on every account of honesty and hope, to comprehend the whole by letting the partial perspectives of the protagonists present it thus partially than to attempt an elusive impartiality which must punctuate the story with interim verdicts and make the reader's mind a sort of juror's notebook.[81]

Cragg frames his book accordingly. He calls his first chapter "Achievement" to describe the foundation of the state of Israel from a Jewish perspective and titles the second "Tragedy" to indicate the views of many Palestinians. The next few paragraphs will briefly describe the foundation of the state of Israel from a Jewish perspective. The rest of the chapter will then enumerate the views and responses of contemporary Palestinian Christians.

---

79. William Andrew Stalder, "Jerusalem: 40 Years of Reunification/Occupation." Photograph taken on June 24, 2007. © William Andrew Stalder.
80. Kenneth Cragg, *This Year in Jerusalem* (London: DLT, 1982), 2. This dilemma has led some historians to abandon the task of writing a history of Israel. One of them asserts, for example, that "we should not be writing a history *of* Israel at all: it should be the history of all the peoples of Syria/Palestine, or however we denominate the area. By even *trying* to write a history of Israel we are 'privileging' one people and neglecting the others." So argue Keith W. Whitelam and Edward Said: cf. James Barr, *History and Ideology in the Old Testament: Biblical Studies at the End of the Millennium* (Oxford: Oxford University Press, 2000), 61.
81. Cragg, *This Year*, 2.

Without a doubt, the formation of the state of Israel in 1948 was both "achievement" and "tragedy." It achieved not least "A Solution of the Jewish Question," to quote Theodor Herzl's 1896 article in the Jewish Chronicle.[82] The failure of emancipation in Europe signaled for Herzl a need to solve not just a religious issue but primarily one of national concern. For him the Jewish identity was not just religious but political. He wrote: "We are one people—One People. We have honestly striven everywhere to merge ourselves in the social life of surrounding communities, and to preserve only the faith of our fathers. It has not been permitted to us."[83] He therefore requested: "Let the sovereignty be granted us over a portion of the globe large enough to satisfy the requirement of the nation—the rest we shall manage ourselves."[84] In Herzl's mind, therefore, the Jews were a nationality needing and awaiting a homeland. The formation of the state of Israel is consequently a story of "achievement" in the minds of many Jews.

For the Palestinians, however, the story is one of physical and spiritual "tragedy/catastrophe."[85] Physically, some "531 villages were destroyed and 11 urban neighborhoods emptied."[86] Spiritually, the

---

82. Paul R. Mendes-Flohr and Jehuda Reinharz, eds., *The Jew in the Modern World: A Documentary History* (Oxford: Oxford University Press, 1980), 533–38.
83. Ibid., 534.
84. Ibid., 534–35.
85. It is important to note at this juncture that the term Palestinian is broad. In the Middle East there are Palestinians who live in Lebanon, Jordan, Syria, Egypt, Israel, and the West Bank. This book will focus on those Palestinians who live in Israel proper (commonly referred to as Arab-Israelis) and those who live in the West Bank (commonly referred to as Palestinians).
86. Ilan Pappé, "Calling a Spade a Spade: The 1948 Ethnic Cleansing of Palestine," *Cornerstone* 43 (Winter 2007): 10–11. Pappé asserts that the term "Nakba" is no longer satisfactory, writing: "I think it is time to use a different term: 'The Ethnic Cleansing of Palestine.' The term Nakba does not imply directly any reference to who is behind the catastrophe—anything can cause the destruction of Palestine, even the Palestinians themselves. Not so when the term ethnic cleansing is used. It implies direct accusation and reference to culprits, not only in the past but also in the present." Cf. Ilan Pappé, *The Ethnic Cleansing of Palestine* (Oxford: Oneworld Publications, 2007). The rest of this book, however, will use the word "catastrophe," which is the English translation of the Arabic "*Al-Nakba*," the word traditionally used by both Palestinians and Arab-Israelis in reference to the formation of the state of Israel.

establishment of the state of Israel and the ensuing conflicts caused a particular strain on the Palestinian Christian community. This "catastrophe" of faith has been detailed by a number of Palestinian Christians. Naim Ateek, a canon of St. George's Cathedral in Jerusalem and founder of Sabeel, writes: "For most Palestinian Christians, as for many other Arab Christians, their view of the Bible, especially the Hebrew Scriptures, or Old Testament, has been adversely affected by the creation of the state of Israel."[87] Mitri Raheb, who is pastor of the Evangelical Lutheran Christmas Church in Bethlehem, also describes how this change affected him. "The Bible I had heretofore considered to be 'for us' had suddenly become 'against us.'"[88] The characters of the Old Testament "no longer seemed in continuity with Jesus, as they used to be. They were instead placed into a kinship with Menachem Begin and Yitzhak Shamir. Their [Joshua's and David's] conquests were no longer for spiritual values but for land—my land in particular."[89] This is the "catastrophe" of faith for the Palestinian Christian community. Is God "for us" or "against us?" Does God love the Jews more than us? Does the Bible actually warrant the removal of Palestinians from the land? The questions are endless, but they are symptomatic of a "catastrophe" of faith.

The rest of this chapter will investigate to what extent Naim Ateek and Mitri Raheb's sketches are correct. It will ask, in other words, "To what extent is this 'catastrophe of faith' indicative of the wider Palestinian Christian community? And how has it manifested itself in the manner in which contemporary Palestinian Christians read the Old Testament?"[90] Naim Ateek and Mitri Raheb's hermeneutic of the Old Testament will be analyzed first in order to establish a basis from

---

87. Naim Ateek, *Justice and Only Justice: A Palestinian Theology of Liberation* (Maryknoll, NY: Orbis Books, 2002), 77.
88. Raheb, *I am a Palestinian Christian*, 56.
89. Ibid.

which to compare the views of other Palestinian Christians. Then the hermeneutics of Naim Khoury, Yohanna Katanacho, Michel Sabbah, and Atallah Hanna will be examined. These examples will provide a good picture of PCHOT across the breadth of the Christian church in Israel and Palestine.

Naim Ateek: An Anglican Perspective

Naim Ateek was born in Beisan (Beth Shean) in 1937, and he describes his first encounter with Israel as follows: "I had just turned eleven in 1948 when Zionists occupied my hometown, Beisan (Beth Shean). We had no army to protect us. There was no battle, no resistance, no killing; we were simply taken over, occupied, on Wednesday, May 12, 1948."[91] The events surrounding the foundation of the modern state of Israel undoubtedly impacted Naim Ateek's early life and the lives of many Palestinian Christians. However, Ateek argues that it was the events of 1967 that have been "perceived by many Palestinians as a watershed in both the political and religious spheres."[92]

Having received his theological training in the United States, Naim Ateek returned to Israel and was ordained priest on May 21, 1967, just two weeks before the Six Day War.[93] He claims that the Six Day War was one of the two pivotal events that "impacted my ministry politically and theologically and contributed to the

---

90. It should be said that all the Palestinian Christians who will be surveyed in this chapter were born after 1948 except for Ateek and Sabbah. Nevertheless, as will be seen, the foundation of the state of Israel, along with subsequent Arab-Israeli wars and conflicts, are at the forefront of their minds. For information on the development of PCHOT among Palestinian Christians in the years after 1948, see chap. 4.
91. Ateek, *Justice and Only Justice*, 7.
92. Naim Ateek, "The Emergence of a Palestinian Christian Theology," 1–6 in *Faith and the Intifada: Palestinian Christian Voices*, ed. Naim Ateek, Marc Ellis, and Rosemary Radford Ruether (Maryknoll, NY: Orbis Books, 1992), at 1.
93. Naim Ateek, *A Palestinian Christian Cry for Reconciliation* (Maryknoll, NY: Orbis Books, 2008), 4.

emergence of a Palestinian theology of liberation."[94] He says, "Before that time the struggle of Palestinians for their national rights had not seemed to us to be a religious question, but rather a political and a human question. It was out of this [growing] challenge that the need arose for a Palestinian Christian theological response, a Palestinian theology of liberation."[95] It was in this context that Ateek began his ministry and developed the notion of Palestinian Liberation Theology (PLT).

Ateek recounts that the growth of a PLT was "influenced by four distinct factors."[96] First, on a pastoral level, numerous people were imploring their clergy: "Where is God in all this? Why does God allow the confiscation of our land? Why does God allow the occupation and oppression of our people?"[97] Second, these emerging questions demanded a response from the indigenous Palestinian clergy. Ateek argues that "it is we, as Palestinian Christians, who have to define the meaning of this land to us in response to these theological and biblical claims, for it is our lives and also our faith which is threatened."[98] Third, there was the unique dilemma of the Old Testament. Numerous clergy and parishioners began to abandon its use in liturgy and preaching. It seemed to have no relevance to their Christian faith, especially as it was being used as a tool to delegitimize their presence in the land. But as "the Bible is central to our faith," claims Ateek, "so it was essential to work out our Palestinian Christian reading of the Bible. . . ."[99] Fourth, there were the theological questions about how Christ relates to the present historical situation.

---

94. The other key event was the first *intifada*. Ibid., 4–5.
95. Ateek, "Emergence," 3–4.
96. Ibid., 4.
97. Ibid.
98. Ibid.
99. Ibid.

These grassroots questions and biblical and theological reflections eventually gave rise to PLT. In 1989, Naim Ateek penned *Justice and Only Justice: A Palestinian Theology of Liberation*. In March 1990 the First International Symposium on Palestinian Liberation Theology met at Tantur.[100] Demand for further programs and resources by the Palestinian Christian community followed and called for the establishment of a "more permanent center," so that in 1994 Ateek founded Sabeel.[101]

As intimated above, the basic message of PLT is outlined in *Justice and Only Justice*. Ateek argues that the two core issues addressed by PLT are those issues of justice and the Bible.[102] As to justice, he addresses the uncertainty of God's justice in the minds of Palestinian Christians. He links the issue of justice with God's character. "In the Hebrew Scriptures," he says, "God is called the God of justice."[103] He then articulates seven examples of God's justice.

---

100. Its proceedings were compiled in book form in 1992. Rosemary Radford Ruether, "Preface: The Conference and the Book," ix–xiv in *Faith and the Intifada*, at ix. Later symposia have been published by Melisende Press.
101. Naim Ateek, "The Beginning of the Center," *Cornerstone* 1 (Spring 1994): 4–5. *Sabeel*'s purpose statement (published in *Cornerstone* 61 [Winter 2011]: 20) is as follows:

    Sabeel is an ecumenical grassroots liberation theology movement among Palestinian Christians. Inspired by the life and teaching of Jesus Christ, this liberation theology seeks to deepen the faith of Palestinian Christians, promote unity among them, and lead them to act for justice and love.

    Sabeel strives to develop a spirituality based on justice, peace, non-violence, liberation, and reconciliation for the different national and faith communities. The word "Sabeel" is Arabic for "the way" and also a "channel" or "spring" of life-giving water. *Sabeel* also works to promote a more mature accurate international awareness regarding the identity, presence, and witness of Palestinian Christians as well as their contemporary concerns. It encourages individuals and groups from around the world for a just, comprehensive, and enduring peace informed by truth and empowered by prayer and action.
102. These issues are examined in detail in chapters 4 and 5 of Ateek, *Justice and Only Justice*, 74–150.
103. Ibid., 117.

1. Justice is God's measuring line and righteousness is God's plumb line (Isa 28:17).
2. Justice is inherent in God's essence and identified with all God's ways (Deut 32:4).
3. God's justice, righteousness, and kindness are extended to all people on the earth (Jer 9:23-24).
4. God's justice extends beyond the limits of one nation to encompass the whole world (Ps 9:7-9).
5. It is not only humans who should glory in such a God; God himself is exalted in justice (Isa 5:16).
6. The prophets stressed justice and righteousness over sacrifice (Amos 5:22-24).
7. For the prophets, morality and religion were inseparable. The unity between them derived from the very nature of the Creator God (Isa 56:1a, 2a).[104]

After affirming the nature of this just God, Ateek heralds its importance for his audience. He proclaims: "Throughout the Hebrew Scriptures and the New Testament, God shows special concern for the underprivileged, the disadvantaged, and the vulnerable."[105] Furthermore, God's interest, preference, and hope for the poor and the oppressed are authenticated in the death and resurrection of Christ.[106] For Palestinian Christians, this message of justice liberates. For PLT, once justice materializes, prospects for peace blossom and hope for reconciliation finally becomes promising. For now, justice remains the major issue.

Before the second core issue of PLT is addressed, namely, the need to establish a suitable hermeneutic of the Bible, it is appropriate to ask how Ateek's liberation theology compares with other political

---

104. Ibid., 117–18, 201.
105. Ibid., 130.
106. Ibid., 141–42.

readings of the Bible. The following will first detail the nature of political readings of the Bible and evaluate the extent of their equivalence to PLT; then it will compare the thematic correlation between traditional liberation theology and liberation theology in its Palestinian context.

Richard Bauckham writes: "Many Christians have recently been rediscovering the political dimension of the message of the Bible. This is really a return to normality, since the notion that biblical Christianity has nothing to do with politics is little more than a modern Western Christian aberration."[107] Before the modern emergence of political hermeneutics in Latin America in the 1960s and 1970s the study of the Bible was primarily split between the equally non-political readings of the "congregation" and of the "academy."[108] The distinctive characteristics of the three methods of reading the Bible thus noted are aptly clarified in Tim Gorringe's comparison: "Where pietist forms are intended to strengthen the soul's relation with God this [the political reading] asks first and foremost how the text bears on the political and social situation. Where academic forms have often been a variant of studies in ancient history this [the political reading] is concerned primarily about the text's contemporary significance."[109] In other words, political readings of the Bible focus on its significance and relevance to the present unjust or oppressive political and/or social situation.

The typical hermeneutic of political readings of the Bible falls in line with what Clodovis Boff classified as a "correspondence of relationships." This reading works under the assumption that biblical texts are "witness(es) of faith rather than historical records."[110] As

---

107. Richard Bauckham, *The Bible in Politics: How to Read the Bible Politically* (London: SPCK, 1989), 1.
108. Tim Gorringe, "Political Readings of Scripture," 67–80 in *The Cambridge Companion to Biblical Interpretation*, ed. John Barton (Cambridge: Cambridge University Press, 1998), at 74.
109. Ibid., 75.

"witnesses of faith," the biblical texts have particular importance for present faith communities. Boff states that this relevance is to be sought neither in connection with the level of context nor that of message, "but rather on the level of the relationship between context and message on each side respectively."[111] It is this "relationship" between context and message that provides a model for action for later faith communities. In other words, present faith communities can examine the text and ask, "How might we then act in lieu of previous politically-situated faith communities?"

PLT follows the same hermeneutical basis for political readings of the Bible as that proposed by Clodovis Boff. The goal is to make the Bible relevant to a poor and oppressed community. In this venture the biblical texts "witness" an array of possible "relationships" for Christian communities to mirror and follow. In many cases PLT follows suit and looks to biblical texts to provide a "correspondence of relationships" for Christian praxis. It also interprets the political situation directly in relation to a particular biblical story, in what Boff calls a "correspondence of terms."[112] In this way PLT coincides with other political readings of the Bible as defined by Boff.

PLT is distinguished from other political readings of the Bible, and traditional liberation theology in particular, by its theme. In the

---

110. Ibid.
111. Clodovis Boff, "Hermeneutics: Constitution of Theological Pertinency," 9–35 in *Voices from the Margin: Interpreting the Bible in the Third World*, ed. R. S. Sugirtharajah (London: SPCK, 1991), 30.
112. Cf. Gorringe, "Political Readings of Scripture," 68; Boff, "Hermeneutics," 30. There are numerous examples of the same practice in Ateek's writings, especially in articles published in *Cornerstone*. For example, he writes: "The Christmas story according to Matthew . . . includes all the human ingredients for making a modern contemporary political event relevant to people's life in Israel/Palestine. The main actors are still with us and around us. There are the Herods, the chief priests, and the people of Jerusalem. . . . Those of us who live in Jerusalem are conscious of the presence of the Herods today in the form of government leaders and military powers that seek the good of their own people, but not the good of all; a military power that wants to impose its will on people without satisfying the demands for justice." Cf. Naim Ateek, "Herod & the Star," *Cornerstone* 2 (Winter 1994): 1–2.

reading of the Bible, traditional liberation theology places particular emphasis on "the liberation of Israel from bondage in Egypt, the prophet's denunciation of oppression, and Jesus' proclamation of the gospel to the poor and outcast."[113] PLT employs the prophet's call for justice and Jesus' gospel proclamation, but it dissociates itself from the theme of the Exodus. Naim Ateek explains that Palestinians find it difficult to appropriate the Exodus theme because of the way "its message has been abused by both religious Zionists and Christian fundamentalists, who see in it a call for the physical return of the Jews to the land in this century."[114] In *Justice and Only Justice*, Ateek articulates three alternative biblical passages to serve as themes relevant to his Palestinian context:

1. "Naboth and the God of Justice": 1 Kings 21
2. "The Ecstatic Prophets—A Cautious Warning": 1 Kings 22
3. "The Cry of a Refugee—Hope in God": Psalm 42, 43, [115]

In *A Palestinian Christian Cry for Reconciliation*, Ateek finds a prime biblical text and example in the book of Jonah. He acknowledges that he always recognized the inclusive nature of the book of Jonah and admits that he "interpreted the story of Jonah in this light in my first book. [But] since then, after much more reflection, I understand the text in a more radical and revolutionary way."[116] He adds: "For me, the writer of Jonah appears to be the first Palestinian liberation theologian, someone who has written the greatest book in the Old Testament."[117] Jonah has become one of Ateek's governing narratives

---

113. Alister E. McGrath, *Historical Theology: An Introduction to the History of Christian Thought* (Oxford: Blackwell, 2001), 256.
114. Ateek, *Justice and Only Justice*, 86.
115. Ibid., 86–92.
116. Ateek, *A Palestinian Christian Cry*, 71.
117. Ibid.

for his liberation theology, and in this way PLT is certainly distinct from other political readings of the Bible.

Now that we have detailed the nature of Naim Ateek's PLT as it has to do with the issue of justice and having compared it to other political readings of the Bible with regard to method and theme, it is appropriate to return to the second core issue of PLT, namely, establishing an appropriate hermeneutic of the Bible. According to Naim Ateek the principal questions raised by Palestinian Christians concern "whether what is being read in the Bible is the Word of God to them and whether it reflects the nature, will, and purpose of God for them."[118] In other words, Palestinian Christians are looking for an appropriate hermeneutic.[119] For Ateek, Jesus Christ is that hermeneutic. The "word of God" in the Bible should be interpreted by the "Word of God" incarnate in Jesus Christ.[120]

Naim Ateek's hermeneutic affects how he reads the entire Bible. He explains: "From this perspective, the biblical material is not viewed in a horizontal way as having the same authority and the same theological value. What God has done in Christ for the redemption of the world is more authoritative and has greater value for the believer than anything else."[121] Consequently, nationalist and Torah-oriented traditions in the Old Testament are useless for the Christian life,

---

118. Ibid., 79.
119. Naim Ateek acknowledges that this hermeneutic must not substantiate "subjective claims and prejudices" of Jewish Zionists, Christian fundamentalists, *or* Palestinians. "The hermeneutic must ring true of a God whom we have come to know—unchanging in nature and character, dynamically constant rather than fickle and variable, responding to but not conditioned by time, space, or circumstance." Ibid., 79.
120. Ibid., 80. Note the cases chosen by Ateek to delineate his hermeneutic authority. Christ has interpretive primacy over the *word* of God in the Bible as the *Word* of God himself.
121. Ateek does not personally respond to the criticisms of Yohanna Katanacho, but because there is ample resource in Ateek's writings it is justifiable to conjecture how he might respond. The above sentence is therefore framed as such a response. See Naim Ateek, "Putting Christ at the Centre: The Land from a Palestinian Christian Perspective," 55–63 in *The Bible and the Land: An Encounter*, ed. Lisa Loden, Peter Walker and Michael Wood (Jerusalem: Musalaha, 2000), at 56.

whereas portions of the prophetic tradition, which heralds at times a more universalistic understanding of God, prove to be much more authoritative for a Palestinian theology of liberation, since these fall in line with the inclusive nature of God proclaimed by Christ.[122] Old Testament narratives are used, but only as they correspond with what Palestinian Christians have come to know in Christ.[123] Christ, then, is the hermeneutical key. It is his nature and character that measure and regulate all biblical interpretation, even that of the OT.

Naim Ateek's hermeneutic of the Bible, and of the Old Testament in particular, is spelled out even more in his most recent book, *A Palestinian Christian Cry for Reconciliation*. In one chapter, "The Bible and the Land," he dialogues with Walter Brueggemann and Brevard Childs over how the Old Testament should be read.[124] Brueggemann asserts that "Old Testament theology has been characteristically a Christian enterprise . . . whereby Jewish religious claims are overridden in the triumph of Christian claims."[125] Brueggemann disagrees with Brevard Childs that the Old Testament should be read as Christian Scripture, at least not exclusively, as if the Old Testament must bear witness to Jesus Christ alone. He complains that "such a way of presenting the Old Testament proceeds as if the community of Judaism was only an interim community, which existed until the New Testament and then withered into nonexistence and insignificance."[126] According to Brueggemann, a proper hermeneutic of the Old Testament must be "polyphonic."[127] It must allow the

---

122. These three streams of tradition are described by Naim Ateek in *Justice and Only Justice*, 93–100.
123. It is in this light that Ateek uses Jonah as a source of Palestinian liberation theology. He says: "While Jonah truly reflects the genius and climax of Old Testament theology, its theology also approaches most closely that of the New Testament." Ateek, *Palestinian Christian Cry*, 71–72.
124. Ibid., 53–56. Ateek references Walter Brueggemann, *Theology of the Old Testament: Testimony, Dispute, Advocacy* (Minneapolis: Fortress Press, 1997), 729–33. He interacts, however, with Brevard Child's *Biblical Theology of the Old and New Testaments* (London: SCM, 1992) only in connection with Brueggemann's work.
125. Ateek, *Palestinian Christian Cry*, 53.
126. Ibid.

text of the Old Testament to speak on its own, thereby allowing a plurality of possible readings that are inherent in the text. A Christian reading may be one of them, but not to the exclusion of a genuine Jewish reading as well.

Naim Ateek argues against Brueggemann and states that as a Palestinian Christian he must read the Old Testament from a Christian perspective. He declares:

> I maintain that as a Palestinian Christian I read the Old Testament through the lens of my Christian faith. It is a part of my religious heritage and my holy scriptures. It is integrally connected with the witness of the early church of the New Testament. What renders the Old Testament important for me is the presence of the New Testament. The Old Testament alone, without the incarnation and redemption, without its fulfillment in Jesus Christ, would be interesting reading about the history and heritage of the Jewish people but would lack personal religious significance for me.[128]

Ateek does not negate the "polyphonic" character of the Old Testament, but he insists: "The text [the Old Testament] makes most sense when read primarily through the lens of Jesus Christ. In reading it with my Palestinian eyes, I see its meaning and its relevance for my social and political context."[129]

In light of his hermeneutic of the Bible it can be seen that Naim Ateek must read the OT from two perspectives. On the one hand he reads through the lens of Christ, that is, from a Christian perspective. On the other hand he reads the OT from a Palestinian perspective. Any other reading would do injustice to his context. As a result, some have criticized him and the work of the Sabeel Center in Jerusalem as a "source of systematic demonization of the Jewish state."[130] But

---

127. Ibid.
128. Ibid., 53–54.
129. Ibid., 54.
130. Melanie Philips in Barry Horner, *Future Israel: Why Christian Anti-Judaism Must be Challenged* (Nashville: Baker, 2007), 141.

even a cursory look at his writings will show that Naim Ateek does not desire that Israel be "thrown into the sea," and neither do his hermeneutic of the Bible nor his PLT demand such a result. He demands justice, not violence, and he finds in Christ a biblical basis for this theology and hermeneutic.

To conclude: Naim Ateek has undoubtedly been influenced by the foundation of the state of Israel and the ensuing Arab-Israeli conflict. His work developed in a hope of redressing the "catastrophe" of faith that has plagued many Palestinian Christians. In Christ he finds a way to read the Old Testament again, and with his Palestinian Liberation Theology he offers hope and strength for many Palestinian Christians.

Mitri Raheb: A Lutheran Perspective

Mitri Raheb[131] was born in Bethlehem on June 26, 1962.[132] In his book, *I Am a Palestinian Christian*, he relates that the Raheb family has been resident in and around Bethlehem for centuries and his name bears witness to the Christian presence in the Middle East. Raheb is Arabic for "monk," and testifies to the presence and influence of desert monasticism in his family and in Palestine,[133] and his first name, Mitri, recalls in Arabic the name of "Saint Demetrius, a name prevalent in the Greek and Russian Orthodox churches."[134] It was

---

131. This author is aware of the contributions made by Bishop Munib Younan, not least in *Witnessing for Peace: In Jerusalem and the World* (Minneapolis: Fortress Press, 2003). Younan's "theology of *martyria*" is based on both the Old and New Testaments. He hopes that, as a result of providing a testimony and framework for nonviolent Christian witness for justice in the land of Israel and Palestine, dialogue and eventual societal reconciliation might come about among Christians, Muslims, and Jews. This author has chosen to focus on Mitri Raheb, however, not least because his work, *I am a Palestinian Christian*, has more explicitly tackled issues of Old Testament hermeneutics but also because it better relates to the current discussion about the extent to which the foundation of the state of Israel caused a "catastrophe of faith" for the wider Palestinian Christian community.
132. Mitri Raheb, *I Am a Palestinian Christian* (Minneapolis: Fortress Press, 1995), 3.
133. Ibid., 6.
134. Ibid.

through his grandfather, who was also named Mitri, that his family found their way into the Lutheran Church. Born into the Greek Orthodox Church, his grandfather was orphaned and was accepted into a Lutheran orphanage and school founded by Johann Ludwig Schneller.[135] As a result, the younger Mitri Raheb was born and raised in the Lutheran tradition.

Mitri Raheb tells how the Bible was an important part of his upbringing.

> My parents were members of the Evangelical Lutheran congregation in Bethlehem; both were pious Christians. Holy Scripture was not extra or ornamental to them. It was a lifetime occupation, a basic necessity. Bible reading was part of our daily routine at home. We read all of Holy Scripture, the Old as well as the New Testament.[136]

It was during his studies in Germany that Mitri Raheb noticed how the Bible, and the Old Testament in particular, had become politicized, and this realization challenged the way he read it. He notes how the conquests of Joshua and David were "no longer for spiritual values but for land—*my land* in particular."[137] He was suffering from a "catastrophe of faith." Raheb explains:

> The God I had known since my childhood as love had suddenly become a God who confiscated land, waged "holy wars," and destroyed whole peoples. I began to doubt this God. I started to hate this God and quietly became "indignant at God, if not with blasphemy at least with great grumbling."[138]

He notes how some of his theology professors in Germany seemed to have been infused with the "Israel craze" after the Six Day War, but as a Palestinian he "noticed little of Israel's suffering or holiness,

---

135. Ibid., 7.
136. Ibid., 55.
137. Ibid., 56. Emphasis added.
138. Ibid.

even when I heard about the oppression of Jews."[139] So, like Naim Ateek, Mitri Raheb was forced to find a new way to read the Bible in response to the foundation of the state of Israel. The following will outline his assessment of the difficulties Palestinian Christians have faced with interpreting the Old Testament in light of the foundation of Israel and detail the principles he establishes for a proper hermeneutic of the Bible. In conclusion it will examine in detail the significance of his Christ-centered hermeneutic for the Palestinian Christian context.

Mitri Raheb tells how the foundation of the state of Israel has challenged the way Palestinian Christians read the Bible. Until the middle of the twentieth century, he says, "all the churches interpreted the Holy Scripture allegorically or typologically."[140] Reading allegorically, Palestinian Christians would find "deeper meanings" in the Old Testament and apply them to Christ. In a typological interpretation "events and figures sketched in the Old Testament were images and foreshadowings pointing beyond themselves toward the future and the real."[141] Raheb tells how this method of interpretation became irrelevant and obsolete as the Bible was coopted by the political aspirations of the Zionist movement. The foundation of the state of Israel solidified the situation, and the Hebrew Bible became an alien text to Palestinian Christians. He describes the dilemma they faced as they read the Bible. "If they read it allegorically, it did not have much to say to them. If they read it politically, its message was frightening."[142] Palestinian Christians were therefore forced to find new ways to interpret the Bible in their context.

---

139. Ibid.
140. Ibid., 59.
141. Ibid.
142. Ibid.

As a way forward for the Palestinian Christian community in the Israeli-Palestinian context, Raheb presents six hermeneutical principles for interpreting the biblical text.[143] First, "the Bible is God's Word in human words." According to Raheb, the Bible is not really about God but about human experiences of God. As such, it consists simply of "testimonies of faith."[144] These are, consequently, not "objective facts but rather experienced truths."[145] These experiences are not to be eternally fixed, but rather remain permeable so later faith communities can participate in them. Perhaps most significant to the present context, these experiences include both promise and invitation from which Palestinian Christians are not to be excluded.

Second, "The Holy Scripture did not fall from heaven and is not timeless." In this light Raheb contends that the biblical interpreter must recognize that the Bible is "written in history, it is history, it makes history."[146] The first two points emphasize the fact that historical-critical as well as socio-critical questions must be asked. In addition, the third point begs the reader to understand that biblical texts give rise to history; therefore it is imperative that biblical interpreters be aware of theological developments and where they are in relation to this historical continuum.

Third, "the Bible is always contemporary." Raheb says, "The Bible is alive and cannot be preserved in a static form."[147] The Bible is alive because of the Spirit of God's work to apply it in subsequent generations and contexts. Proper application is contingent on God's Spirit. Raheb argues that "one can interpret Scripture correctly in any

---

143. Ibid., 59–64. These principles are found in "A Personal Perspective," the sixth chapter of Raheb's book. A different translation of this chapter can be found in Mitri Raheb, "Biblical Interpretation in the Israeli-Palestinian Context," 109–17 in *Israel and Yeshua*, ed. Torleif Elgvin (Jerusalem: Caspari Center for Biblical and Jewish Studies, 1993).
144. Raheb, *I am a Palestinian Christian*, 59.
145. Ibid., 60.
146. Ibid., 60.
147. Raheb, "Biblical Interpretation," 114.

given context only when one's conscience is illumined by faith and one's reason is permeated by love."[148]

Fourth, "the Bible is a great whole." *Contra* Marcion, Raheb maintains that the Old and New Testaments form a single unit. This unity is "grounded in God's very self, for the God of Israel is the Father of Jesus Christ. It is the one and the same God."[149]

Fifth, "Holy Scripture is the book about a minority." Raheb contends that both the Jewish and Christian communities were minorities in their respective contexts, and for those minorities persecution was often an unfortunate reality. This reality, therefore, framed the Bible's composition. For Raheb the Bible is consequently a book about, by, and for persecuted people.[150] Any hermeneutic that does not take the reality of this persecuted minority into consideration is at risk not only of faulty interpretation but also possibly of devastating application. He concludes that the only possible hermeneutic of the Bible must have the "crucified Lord at its centerpiece."[151]

Sixth, Raheb states that "Law and Gospel are the hermeneutical keys to interpreting the Bible." The distinction between Law and Gospel was also "basic for Luther's understanding of Scripture."[152] But where traditional Lutheran thought equated law with command and gospel with gift, i. e., grace and forgiveness, the concepts of Law and Gospel are politically nuanced in Raheb's perspective. He argues that "Law and Gospel are the two sides of the one righteous God. The God of the Bible is simultaneously the God demanding justice and the God pursuing it."[153] In practical terms, Law and Gospel become

---

148. Raheb, *I am a Palestinian Christian*, 61. Emphasis added.
149. Ibid., 62.
150. Ibid., 62–63.
151. Ibid., 63.
152. Donald K. McKim, "Martin Luther," 212–29 in *Historical Handbook of Major Biblical Interpreters* (ed. Donald K. McKim; Leicester: InterVarsity Press, 1998), at 216.
153. Raheb, *I am a Palestinian Christian*, 63.

God's demand for justice from some and his promise of justice for others.[154]

Of the six principles Mitri Raheb lays out for biblical interpretation, the fifth will be evaluated in greater detail, as it has particular significance for the Palestinian Christian context. On the surface his hermeneutic seems to correspond with Naim Ateek's hermeneutic of the Bible. Both Ateek and Raheb have Christ at the center of their hermeneutical enterprise. Raheb's hermeneutic, however, has an additional dimension. First, Christ is the hermeneutical cornerstone for this form of biblical interpretation. Raheb's understanding is unquestionably Lutheran. For Martin Luther, "the center or core of Scripture is 'what drives Christ' (*was Christum treibet*), that is, what preaches Christ, what promotes or points to Christ."[155] Raheb similarly writes: "Only from this center—and with the aid of this hermeneutical key—can the Bible be understood and interpreted correctly."[156] He examines various themes in the Old Testament, but it is always Christ who informs and illumines the texts with regard to the way they should be interpreted.[157]

Second, Raheb's christological hermeneutics has the crucifixion at its center. As the above survey indicated, the crucified Christ is a hermeneutical buffer against errant interpretation. In other words, the crucified Christ keeps the reader true to the heart of the text and in line with the persecuted community about, by, and to whom the text was written. Furthermore, it helps the reader appreciate how a "persecuted" community and "those deprived of power" might

---

154. Ibid., 64.
155. McKim, "Martin Luther," 216.
156. Raheb, *I am a Palestinian Christian*, 63.
157. This can be seen in Raheb's evaluation of the themes of Election, Land, and Exodus in chaps. 7–9 of his book, pp. 65–91.

interpret the Bible differently than those who "persecute" and are in positions of "power."[158] Raheb explains:

> When a persecuted Christian praying in a catacomb reassures his persecuted brothers of God's proximity and tells them that "God is with us," the same words have different meanings. When an alarmed Christian makes the sign of the cross with his body as a sign of faith in the crucified Lord, and when a Roman soldier engraves the sign of the cross on his helmet as a sign of the triumphant God, the same sign has different meanings. When a Jewish concentration camp survivor speaks of "the promise of land" and an Israeli settler from the United States speaks of "the promise of land," the same words have different meanings.[159]

All this confirms for Raheb that the center of one's hermeneutic must be the crucified Christ.

The significance of Mitri Raheb's central hermeneutic of the crucified Christ is witnessed by its relevance to the Palestinian context. For example, Raheb recalls the following event at the International Center of Bethlehem during the early days of the curfew imposed after the Israeli military invasion of Bethlehem in April 2002:[160]

> Earlier, during the curfew, we announced a competition and solicited paintings on the theme, "Christ in the Palestinian Context." We thought no one would be up to it, yet 16 artists signed on, 60% of them Muslim. All but one of the Muslim artists depicted Christ on the cross. Even though this is totally in opposition to their faith, this is the image they presented. In the midst of this suffering, they said, they could not but think of the suffering Christ, someone who knows what it means to live in a context like this.[161]

---

158. Raheb, "Biblical Interpretation," 115.
159. Ibid., 115–16.
160. For a series of short stories surrounding this time see Mitri Raheb, *Bethlehem Besieged: Stories of Hope in Times of Trouble* (Minneapolis: Fortress Press, 2004).
161. Mitri Raheb, "Christ in the Palestinian Context: A Perspective from Bethlehem," *Church and Society* 94, no. 1 (Sept/Oct 2003): 39–46, at 43–44.

For Raheb the crucified Christ shows compassion. The crucified Christ shows solidarity. The crucified Christ offers hope in the midst of catastrophe. In this hope, Raheb could conclude, "Out of destruction, continuity shall be."[162]

These are the views of two theologians. It remains now to be seen to what extent the wider Palestinian Christian community proffers its hermeneutics of the Old Testament in response to this event as a "catastrophe of faith."

Naim Khoury: A Baptist Perspective

In *A Future for Israel: Christian Arabs Share Their Stories*, Julia Fisher interviews a number of Arab Christians who actually "cherish Israel and the Jewish People."[163] She adds:

> They are a small group of Arab believers; most of them are pastors. They all live in the Middle East; some in Israel, others in the West Bank, others in countries neighbouring Israel. While most have every reason to hate the Jewish people and the nation of Israel, not only have they forgiven everything in the past . . . but through the study of the Scriptures, they come to understand the strategic importance of Israel and the Jewish people in God's plan.[164]

It is in this context that Julia Fisher introduces the reader to Naim Khoury, who is currently the pastor of First Baptist Church in Bethlehem.

Naim Khoury was born in the Old City of Jerusalem in 1951 and was reared in the Greek Orthodox Church. A few days after the Six Day War, Khoury attended a meeting at the YMCA in West Jerusalem and describes how he "found the Lord." "I'd never read

---

162. Ibid., 44.
163. Julia Fisher, *A Future for Israel? Christian Arabs Share Their Stories* (Milton Keynes: Authentic, 2006), 11. Emphasis added.
164. Ibid., 11–12.

the Bible because I'd never had a Bible. So I was ignorant until one night . . . I listened to a preacher from America describe how Jesus Christ died on a cross for me. [And] that night the Holy Spirit grabbed my heart and I could not leave that meeting without making a decision."[165] Khoury's "decision" caused him to leave the Greek Orthodox Church, but in time his entire family followed suit and "came to know the Lord as their personal Saviour."[166]

Naim Khoury's perspective on Israel and the Jewish people came from his avid reading of both the Old and New Testaments. He says that "the more I studied the Bible, the more I discovered the covenant promises God made with Abraham and his people are for ever and ever and ever."[167] In addition to these promises being eternal and thereby irrevocable, they are also to be interpreted literally. Khoury says, "No one can switch or twist it—it's God's word and we have to believe it just as it is written."[168] Therefore, these promises are for "God's chosen people, the Jews, and for Israel, the Promised Land. . . ."[169] Other hermeneutical perspectives are consequently errant and irreconcilable with the "word of God."[170]

Khoury's hermeneutic of the Bible and of the OT in particular is clearly influenced by both Christian fundamentalism and Dispensationalism. James Barr defines this strand of Christian fundamentalism as a "tradition of Protestant Christianity, identified by its strong emphasis on the absolute authority of Scripture, understood to be inspired and infallible."[171] As the Bible is inspired

---

165. Ibid., 92.
166. Ibid., 93.
167. Ibid., 96.
168. Ibid.
169. Ibid., 97.
170. Khoury states that "those who believe in Replacement Theology base their beliefs on what politicians say rather than the word of God." Ibid., 100.
171. There are other characteristics of fundamentalism. Among them are its connection to the evangelical "revivals" of the nineteenth and twentieth centuries and resultant emphasis on "personal experience" in the Christian life. James Barr, "The Fundamentalist Understanding

and infallible, it becomes an authoritative source not only for personal piety but also as a commentary on historical affairs.[172] Unconditional support for the Jewish people and Israel is therefore warranted in Khoury's mind simply because "it's God's word."

There is also a distinctive mark of Dispensationalist thought in Khoury's words.[173] In general, Dispensationalism recognizes different aspects in God's dealings with humankind.[174] C. I. Scofield popularized the following definition of these divine dealings as dispensations[175] when he wrote: "A dispensation is a period of time during which man is tested in respect of obedience to some specific revelation of the will of God. Seven such dispensations are distinguished in Scripture."[176] Charles Ryrie argues, however, that a dispensation is better defined as "a distinguishable economy in the outworking of God's purpose."[177] For Ryrie this definition clarifies that a dispensation refers to more than "periods of time."

Dispensationalism's unique influence on Naim Khoury is seen with regard to the "economies" or "dispensations" in reference to Israel

---

of Scripture," 70–74 in *Conflicting Ways of Interpreting the Bible*, ed. Hans Küng and Jürgen Moltmann (Edinburgh: T & T Clark, 1980), 70.
172. Ibid.
173. Unlike dispensationalists in other parts of the Middle East such as at JETS (Jordan Evangelical Theological Seminary), Khoury is representative of a unique minority who have chosen to adhere strictly to the above viewpoints in a Palestinian context.
174. Dispensationalism is not unique in recognizing different aspects of God's dealings with humankind. Among others, Covenant theology also notes differences.
175. In addition to C. I. Scofield (1843–1921), the modern systematization and promotion of Dispensationalism stems also from John Nelson Darby (1800–1882). Charles Ryrie argues, however, that, despite this modern systematization, Dispensationalist roots go back to the Church Fathers as well as to the likes of Pierre Poiret, Jonathan Edwards, and Isaac Watts. Charles Ryrie, *Dispensationalism Today* (Chicago: Moody Press, 1980), 65–85.
176. Ibid., 22. According to Scofield's notes these seven dispensations are that of Innocence (Eden; Gen 1:28), Conscience (Fall to Flood; Gen 3:23), Human Government (Noah to Babel; Gen 8:21), Promise (Abraham to Egypt; Gen 12:10), Law (Moses to John the Baptist; Exod 19:8), Grace (Church age; John 1:17), and Kingdom (Millennium; Eph 1:10). Vern S. Poythress, *Understanding Dispensationalists* (Grand Rapids: Zondervan, 1987), 21.
177. Ryrie, *Dispensationalism Today*, 29.

and to the church. Charles Ryrie insisted that the *sine qua non* of Dispensationalism was:

1. A dispensationalist keeps Israel and the church distinct . . .
2. This distinction between Israel and the church is born out of a system of hermeneutics that is usually called literal interpretation . . .
3. A third aspect . . . concerns the underlying purpose of God in the world. The covenant theologian, in practice, believes this purpose to be salvation . . . and the dispensationalist says the purpose is broader than that, namely, the glory of God.[178]

Regarding the first point, Lewis Sperry Chafer adds that "the Dispensationalist believes that throughout the ages God is pursuing two distinct purposes: one related to the earth with earthly people and earthly objects involved which is Judaism; while the other is related to heaven with heavenly people and heavenly objectives involved, which is Christianity."[179]

These two distinct purposes of God, one for Israel and one for the church, exist in parallel. They are separate entities. Hence there is a sharp line drawn between the promises made to Israel and promises made to the church. The church is therefore "not presently fulfilling promises made to Israel in the Old Testament that have not yet been fulfilled."[180] Promises made to Israel await fulfillment. Dispensationalism can therefore establish a link between biblical Israel and the modern state of Israel by interpreting its establishment as the fulfillment of prophecy and the keeping of promises.

---

178. Ibid., 43–47.
179. Stephen Sizer, "The Theological Basis of Christian Zionism: On the Road to Armageddon," 59–75 in *Challenging Christian Zionism: Theology, Politics and the Israel-Palestine Conflict*, ed. Naim Ateek, Cedar Duaybis, and Maurine Tobin (London: Melisende, 2005), at 64.
180. In Burge, *Whose Land?*, 237.

With regard to Ryrie's second point, the distinction between Israel and the church emerges out of a hermeneutic of literalism in relation to the Bible, and the Old Testament in particular. One clearly recognizes the effects of this hermeneutic of literalism with regard to Israel and the church in the prophetic genre. For example, Scofield maintained that "not one instance exists of a 'spiritual' or figurative fulfillment of prophecy. . . . Jerusalem is always Jerusalem, Israel is always Israel, Zion is always Zion. . . . Prophecies may never be spiritualized, but are always literal."[181] One should not misconstrue this illustration, however, as communicating that Dispensationalists only interpret the Bible literally. They do, but their hermeneutic is more nuanced. Vern Poythress properly qualifies the understood definition of Dispensationalist hermeneutics by saying:

> The more fundamental element in Scofield's approach is his distinction between Israel and the church. In a manner reminiscent of Darby, Scofield derives from this bifurcation of two peoples of God a bifurcation in hermeneutics. Israel is earthly, the church heavenly. One is natural, the other spiritual. What pertains to Israel is to be interpreted in literalistic fashion. But what pertains to the church need not be so interpreted.[182]

One can more accurately conclude that the distinction between Israel and the church emerges out of a literalist hermeneutics of the Old Testament with reference to Israel.

Finally, since God's underlying purpose in this world is not salvation but his own glory, as Ryrie's third point indicates, there is room for the Dispensationalist to hold in tension God's work with Israel and with the church.

Thus one can clearly see that Khoury's hermeneutic is influenced by fundamentalist and Dispensationalist thought. They lay the

---

181. In Sizer, "The Theological Basis of Christian Zionism," 61.
182. Poythress, *Understanding Dispensationalists*, 23–24.

groundwork for justifying his allegiance to the Jewish people and their settlement in the land. According to Khoury there is a distinction between Israel and the church, but it is not in accordance with Replacement Theology. The church exists, but not at the expense of the people of Israel. Israel continues to exist according to God's own economy, and for those with ears to hear the prophetic references to Israel in the Old Testament literally, the establishment of a modern state of Israel is praised as an achievement. Therefore, in contrast to Ateek and Raheb, he does not see the foundation of the state of Israel as a "catastrophe of faith." In Khoury's mind it is a sign of God's handiwork that encourages him in his faith. Khoury does acknowledge that Israel has been in the wrong on numerous occasions.[183] Nevertheless, he maintains that Palestinian Christians need to persist in their loyalty to Israel and the Jewish people. He writes: "I believe we need to keep standing on the promises of God towards his Jewish people until the day when we see these things fulfilled."[184] As long as Khoury continues to maintain his position, for him the foundation of the state of Israel will not trigger a "catastrophe of faith." It will not adversely affect his reading of the Old Testament. In his view the foundation of the state of Israel will rather be seen as a fulfillment of God's promises in the Old Testament and will thereby support his faith and lend credence to his hermeneutic of the Old Testament.[185]

---

183. Naim Khoury does not detail these occurrences but rather conveys a notion that Israel is persisting in certain "wrongs." Fisher, *Future for Israel?* 97.
184. Ibid. Emphasis added.
185. Khoury's hermeneutic obviously bodes well for his relationship with Israel and equally puts him at odds with other Palestinian Christians. For example, when addressing the Knesset in September 2006, Khoury wedded his unique hermeneutic with the following statement: "I believe the land of Israel is going to prosper . . . the Iranian president cannot touch this land, because it belongs to God's chosen people. And God is going to protect this land, and keep Jerusalem a united city, forever and ever. Because Jerusalem does not belong to Iran, Hamas, Hizbullah, or Syria. It belongs to the state of Israel, and the great king the lord Jesus Christ." Yaakov Lappin, "Christians: We'll Fight for Israel: Evangelical Delegates from around the world arrive at Knesset to express 'love for Israel,'" accessed 7 Feb 2012:

Yohanna Katanacho: An Evangelical Perspective

Bethlehem Bible College is a leading Evangelical school in Palestine.[186] In looking at their statement of faith one might easily equate its view of the Bible with the fundamentalist views of Naim Khoury, for the statement says

> We affirm the divine inspiration, truthfulness and authority of both Old and New Testament scriptures in their entirety as the only written Word of God, without error in all that it affirms and the only infallible rule of faith and practice. We also affirm the power of God's word to accomplish His purpose of salvation. The message of the Bible is addressed to all humanity, for God's revelation in Christ and in Scripture is unchangeable. Through it the Holy Spirit still speaks today. He illuminates the mind of God's people in every culture to perceive its truth freshly through their own eyes and thus discloses to the whole Church the multi-colored wisdom of God.[187]

Although there is a similarity between Naim Khoury's view of the Bible and that of Bethlehem Bible College, they are markedly

---

http://www.ynetnews.com/articles/0,7340,L-3309009,00.html. In relation to other Palestinian Christians he says: "I am a minority amongst a minority! And because of my position I have been harassed a lot by both Muslims and Christians." Julia Fisher notes how the First Baptist Church of Bethlehem has been bombed some fourteen times in the past ten years. Khoury himself has been threatened and was even shot in 2003. In all these things, he states, "the enemy is working to try and silence me. But there is good news—we have victory in Jesus. It is not yet time for me to die! There are many things that need to be accomplished before Jesus comes back again. So I am not going to give up. *I am not going to stop preaching the truth, the whole truth from the word of God, both the Old Testament and the New Testament*" (Fisher, *Future for Israel?* 98; emphasis added). Despite all the harassment, Khoury persists in his position and the division between him and other Palestinian Christians remains.

186. It is important to note that the Anglican and Lutheran churches are historically referred to as Evangelical churches in Israel and Palestine. The Baptist Church is also often placed under the Evangelical umbrella but, as the above illustrates, it can also fall within the category of fundamentalism. The current section has been so labeled to make people aware that there are those who consider themselves Evangelical and yet would not be in the same "camp" as the Baptist and the traditional evangelical churches that are Anglican and Lutheran.

187. "What we Believe," accessed 12 Aug 2007: http://www.bethlehembiblecollege.edu/about/what-we-do. It is interesting to note that the above statement has since changed. It now limits what it says about the Bible to: "We believe the Bible to be the inspired, the only infallible, authoritative Word of God." "What we Believe," accessed 8 Feb 2012: http://www.bethlehembiblecollege.edu/about/what-we-do.

different in the way they interpret the Bible.[188] For people at Bethlehem Bible College, the Bible does not justify the removal of Palestinians from their land.[189] In fact, such interpretations need to be challenged and a proper hermeneutic of the OT established. That such a duty exists in the minds of students and faculty of the school can be seen in the February 10–13, 2009 conference at Bethlehem Bible College at which numerous scholars gathered together to "reflect on questions that rise when the Old Testament is read in the context of Palestinian Christians."[190] Among the key

188. One of the most poignant announcements the Palestinian Evangelical Christian community have made to show their dissent from the fundamentalist line like that of Naim Khoury was in a 1998 open letter to American Christian fundamentalist Jerry Falwell. Some twelve Palestinian Evangelical pastors signed a document stating "We, your brothers and sisters in Christ, prayerfully and in the spirit of love, appeal to you to reexamine your positions regarding Israeli policies in Jerusalem, the West Bank and the Gaza Strip." The fact that there are so many Baptist and other churches typically classified as "fundamentalist" in the above document shows how much Naim Khoury is a minority in the Palestinian Christian community. Even traditional Dispensationalist churches have slightly modified their views in accordance with their Palestinian context. The following Evangelical ministers signed the aforementioned document: Reverend Mus Abu Ali (Bible Baptist Church, Beit Hanina); Reverend Alex Awad (East Jerusalem Baptist Church, Jerusalem); Reverend George Awad (Bible Presbyterian Church, Bethlehem); Reverend Bassam Bannoura (Shepherd Field Baptist Church, Beit Sahour); Reverend Atallah Esawi (Church of God, Aboud); Reverend Naju Issa (Bible Baptist, Jericho); Reverend Munir Kakish (Pentecostal Church, Ramallah); Reverend Ibrahim Mseeh (Local Baptist, Ramallah); Reverend Botrus Mualiem (Church of God, Beit Jala); Reverend Magdi Anwar (Missionary Alliance Church, Jerusalem); Reverend Nizar Tuma (Nazarene Church, Jerusalem); Reverend Nihad Salman (Church of God, Bethlehem). "Letter to Rev. Jerry Falwell," accessed 7 Feb 2012: www.saltfilms.net/issues/openletter.html.
189. For example, Bishara Awad, the president of Bethlehem Bible College, says: "Can one group or faith claim this land for itself alone? Do I, together with the rest of the Palestinians, have any right to live here? Yes, I believe we have religious as well as political rights. The denial to the Palestinians of a continuing right to exist in the land of their ancestors is a crime against God and humanity. I, as a Palestinian, see God on my side because He is just and loving." Bishara Awad, "Speaking from the Heart: The Palestinians and the Land of their Fathers," 177–85 in *The Bible and the Land: An Encounter*, ed. Lisa Loden, Peter Walker and Michael Wood (Jerusalem: Musalaha, 2000), at 184–85.
190. "Reading the Old Testament in Bethlehem," accessed 15 Apr 2009: http://www.comeandsee.com/modules.php?name=News&file=article&sid=974. See also the recent conference put on by Bethlehem Bible College on March 5–9, 2012, "Christ at the Checkpoint: Hope in the Midst of Conflict," accessed 25 April 2012: http://www.christatthecheckpoint.com. Cf. Salim J. Munayer and Lisa Loden, eds., *The Land Cries Out: Theology of the Land in the Israeli-Palestinian Context* (Eugene, OR: Cascade Books, 2012).

scholars present at the conference was the college's Academic Dean, Yohanna Katanacho.

Yohanna Katanacho was born in Jerusalem in 1967. After having received his PhD at Trinity Evangelical Divinity School, he returned to Israel to teach at Bethlehem Bible College. One of the clearest examples of the aforementioned commitment to an Evangelical understanding of the Bible and Palestinian recognition is found in his 2005 article, "Christ is the Owner of Haaretz."[191] Written with a view toward improving Muslim-Christian relations, the essay aims to "analyze popular doctrines [namely those theologies that promote giving Haaretz to the state of Israel] concerning the ownership of Haaretz and then re-represent the biblical teachings throughout salvation history."[192] The opening section of "Christ is the Owner of Haaretz" asks three questions: (1) What are the territorial dimensions of Israel's land? (2) Who is Israel? and (3) How did God give Israel Haaretz?[193] In light of these questions, and the answers proposed, the second section then asks what Haaretz meant before Abraham, between Abraham and Christ, and after Christ.[194]

First, Katanacho asks: "What are the territorial dimensions of Israel's land?" He evaluates the works of Zecharia Kallai, Jeffrey Townsend, and Moshe Weinfeld and concludes that they have "rightly highlighted the territorial diversity of Haaretz in the Old Testament, challenging any notion of fixed borders."[195] The fact that Haaretz in the Old Testament refers to a variety of territories

---

191. Yohanna Katanacho, "Christ is the Owner of Haaretz," *Christian Scholar's Review* 34 (2005): 425–41. "Haaretz" [or ha'aretz] means "the land" in Hebrew.
192. Ibid., 425. There Katanacho states that something needs to be written to better Muslim-Christian relations because "whenever Muslims are troubled by Westerners, there will be Islamic voices that question the loyalty of local Christians. The latter will be compelled to clarify their biblical beliefs, demonstrating that the God of the Bible does not despise Muslims and is not trying to take away their lands."
193. Ibid., 427–33.
194. Ibid., 434–39.
195. Ibid., 429. Emphasis added.

has theological significance for Katanacho. He maintains that the territorial diversity shows that God's redemptive plan is for "the whole world, what we might call 'HaaretzGlobal.'"[196]

Second, Katanacho asks: "Who is Israel?" He cites Gerhard von Rad and evaluates the term "Israel" in the OT and NT, concluding: "biblically, the label 'Israel' has many meanings and is distinct from the label 'Hebrew,' or 'Jew.' A person could be a Hebrew but not Jewish or Israelite—for example, Abraham. One could be a member of Israel and a Hebrew without being Jewish—for example, Samuel."[197] What does it mean, then, to be an Israelite according to the OT? Katanacho concludes that the lineage of the Jewish people is so diverse that Israel cannot justify the claim to the land based on genealogical rights.[198]

Finally, Katanacho queries: "How did God give Israel Haaretz?" He challenges the claim that God gave Israel its land unconditionally and that the formation of the modern state of Israel is the fulfillment of God's promises enumerated in biblical prophecies. He contends that the promises of land were always linked with moral obligations and concludes:

> There is no inheritance without meeting the biblical requirements of justice and righteousness. In view of this teaching, any credible argument for the prophetic place of modern Israel should provide a theological justification for the moral state of Israel and for the dislocation of the 50,000 Christian Palestinian refugees who lost their homes in 1948.[199]

If, as Katanacho claims, the territorial dimensions of Haaretz are too varied, the genealogy of the people of Israel in the OT too mixed to claim certain familial rights to the land, and moral obligations were

---

196. Ibid.
197. Ibid., 430–31.
198. Ibid., 432.
199. Ibid., 433.

always inherent in God's gifting of land, then what can one mean for certain when one speaks of Haaretz?

Katanacho writes that when one speaks of Haaretz one must acknowledge principally that "the ownership of Haaretz cannot be understood without a theology that perceives God as the ultimate creator and owner of the earth (Gen. 1), the one who entrusted it to humanity."[200] In the course of salvation history, he says, there were three basic stages of inheritance, sub-ownership or stewardship of the land. Katanacho argues that the first stage took place before Abraham and saw a shift from "HaaretzGlobal" to "HaaretzLocal," namely "HaaretzJapheth, Ham, and Shem."[201] He contends that this change was the result of sin. In other words, "the real problem is not the plurality of lands, but sin. The former is only a result of the latter. It is the symptom, not the disease. As a result, any effective solutions must address the root of the problem, that is, the curse of Adam when he disobeyed God."[202]

During the second stage, which took place between Abraham and Christ, the problem of sin was being addressed. Katanacho stresses that this is the beauty of the promise given to Abraham in Genesis 12:1-3. "God's intentions were not to formulate fixed borders but to unite the ends of the world under the Abrahamic banner."[203] Under that banner God's blessing to Abraham will have its healing effect for the nations as the blessing extends and percolates from "HaaretzAbrahamic" to "HaaretzGlobal." The blessing, then, as opposed to the grant of land, was God's solution to the real problem, namely, the problem of sin.

---

200. Ibid., 434.
201. Ibid., 435–36.
202. Ibid., 436.
203. Ibid., 437. Katanacho recognizes the "ideological shift" that emerged with the Davidic dynasty. He insists, however, that this never abolished the "global aspect of God's promises."

The final stage takes place after Christ, when Haaretz is "Christified."[204] Christ, therefore, is Katanacho's hermeneutical compass through a contentious maze surrounding Haaretz. He concludes that "in accordance with progressive revelation, Christ is now the owner of Haaretz even if God had entrusted it to Abraham and his descendants in the past. He owns it because he is the Abrahamic seed and the fulfillment of prophecies."[205] Christ, then, is the unambiguous owner of "HaaretzGlobal."

In summary, one can see from the survey of Katanacho's work that his hermeneutic of the OT is influenced first by an Evangelical understanding of Scripture, second by typical Evangelical principles of interpretation, and third by a covenant theological perspective.

Yohanna Katanacho's hermeneutic of the OT is influenced by his Evangelical understanding of the Bible. As Bethlehem Bible College's doctrinal statement says, the Bible is the Word of God. It is inspired, without error, truthful, authoritative, and the only infallible rule for faith and practice. As I. Howard Marshall says:

> What makes the Bible different from other books for us, of course, is that it is *Scripture*, which signifies (among other things) that it possesses authority over its readers, speaking in the language of truth and command. This alone, however, is not what makes the question of what the Bible says all the more important. If it is authoritative, we need to be as sure as possible about what it is that God says to us by way of promise and warning and what we are authoritatively called to believe and to do. Furthermore, there may be ways in which the process of interpretation is also different. If the Bible is a book that is in some sense authored by God, then an appropriate manner of interpretation is required.[206]

---

204. Ibid., 438.
205. Ibid., 439.
206. I. Howard Marshall, *Beyond the Bible: Moving from Scripture to Theology* (Grand Rapids: Baker, 2004), 13.

This view demands that Katanacho discern what the Bible is trying to say, for in doing so one actually discerns the word of God.

Katanacho's hermeneutic of the OT is also influenced by typical Evangelical principles of interpretation. J. I. Packer formulates four such principles.[207]

1. "Biblical passages must be taken to mean *what their human authors were consciously expressing.*" For what the human authors say is what God says.
2. "The *coherence, harmony and veracity* of all biblical teaching must be taken as our working hypothesis in interpretation."
3. "Interpretation involves *synthesizing* what the various biblical passages teach, so that each item taught finds its proper place and significance in the *organism* of revelation as a whole."
4. "*The response for which the text calls* must be made explicit."

In line with the first principle, Katanacho makes an effort to discover authorial intent, for in doing so one discovers what "God says." In accordance with the second principle, he draws attention to what he calls the "intelligentsia of Ancient Israel" and the corresponding coherence of the text they produced.[208] Although he acknowledges the need for diachronic analysis, he demands that the *textus receptus* of the Old Testament be taken into consideration and read as such.[209] In Katanacho's view the biblical text is coherent and true, so it can be understood when read synchronically.[210] In agreement with the

---

207. J. I. Packer, "Understanding the Bible: Evangelical Hermeneutics," 147–60 in idem, *Honouring the Written Word of God* (Carlisle: Paternoster, 1999), quoted in Marshall, *Beyond the Bible*, 26–27.
208. Katanacho, "Christ is the Owner of Haaretz," 429.
209. Ibid. It is not completely clear to what Katanacho is referring when he says *textus receptus*. Most likely he is referencing the Masoretic Text (MT).
210. Although Katanacho does not deny the importance of diachronic readings, he distances himself from the practice of historical criticism and the traditional documentary hypothesis and favors reading the OT synchronically (ibid.). Cf. Yohanna Katanacho, "Approaches to the Bible"

third principle, Katanacho integrates his research in concert with the whole of Scripture. In other words, biblical texts are not interpreted in isolation but in connection with the rest of the biblical narrative. Finally, he calls for a response to the text. For example, he says his "essay provides a biblical framework for questioning any theological system that promotes a higher status for one nation than another, hoping to persuade Muslims to revisit Christianity."[211]

Katanacho's work and understanding of Scripture are also influenced by Covenant Theology. In contrast to Dispensationalism, Covenant Theology does not posit two parallel economies that differentiate between Israel and the church but a single covenant of grace that starts with Abraham, reaches its climax with Christ, and then spreads to the nations and blesses them.[212]

Yohanna Katanacho's context, work, and hermeneutic of the Old Testament are no doubt influenced by the foundation of the modern state of Israel. Israel may not have caused a "catastrophe of faith" in the case of Katanacho but it no doubt raises some serious questions about OT hermeneutics. Katanacho addresses them from an Evangelical perspective, petitioning his constituency to know and understand the Word of God, interpret it rightly, and think of God's working in history and salvation from a Reformed perspective.

(paper presented at ICCJ—Kairos Consultation, Beit Jala, October 27, 2011): 3–4. For an overview of historical-critical and literary approaches see John Barton, "Historical-critical Approaches," 9–20 in *The Cambridge Companion to Biblical Interpretation*; and David Jasper, "Literary Readings of the Bible," 21–34 in the same volume.

211. Katanacho, "Christ is the Owner of Haaretz," 441.
212. Louis Berkhof notes the unity and distinction in the covenant of grace between the Old and New Testaments. He states the following four points. "(1) The covenant of grace, as it is revealed in the New Testament, is essentially the same as that which governed the relation of Old Testament believers to God. (2) The New Testament dispensation differs from that of the Old in that it is universal, that is, extends to the nations. (3) The New Testament dispensation places greater emphasis on the gracious character of the covenant. (4) Finally, the New Testament dispensation brings richer blessings than the Old Testament dispensation." Louis Berkhof, *Systematic Theology* (Edinburgh: Banner of Truth Trust, 1988), 299–300.

Michel Sabbah: A Latin Perspective

Michel Sabbah[213] was born in Nazareth on March 19, 1933.[214] He was ordained a priest in Nazareth shortly after his twenty-second birthday, on June 29, 1955. Throughout his early years of ministry Sabbah moved between educational and ministerial roles. His ministerial duties consisted of youth and parish ministry in Nazareth, Jerusalem, and Amman, Jordan; his educational responsibilities included teaching at the Latin Patriarchal Seminary of Beit Jala, the University of St. Joseph in Beirut, Lebanon, and at a university in Djibouti. He also directed the schools in the patriarchal diocese of Jerusalem and was president of the University of Bethlehem until his commissioning as the first Palestinian Latin Patriarch of Jerusalem. He served as Latin Patriarch from 1987 to 2008.

As the Latin Patriarch of Jerusalem, Michel Sabbah soon became renowned for his ecumenical spirit and his advocacy for the Palestinian people.[215] Geries Khoury notes that as the Latin Patriarch of Jerusalem, Sabbah was a "pioneer in local theology as seen in all his pastoral letters, sermons and especially his pastoral letter "Reading the Bible Today in the Land of the Bible."[216] The remainder of this section will make note of the context of his letter and then survey

---

213. The term Latin refers to the Latin Rite of the Roman Catholic Church and as such distinguishes it (Western Catholicism) from the Eastern Rite of the Roman Catholic Church.
214. Biographical information from "Who's Who: A Directory of Existing National Level Palestinian Christian Figures," 57–58 in *Palestinian Christians: The Holy Land Guardians* (Jerusalem: Laity Committee in the Holy Land, 2006).
215. Sabbah played a key role in the realization of two key programs for the Palestinian community: the Ecumenical Accompaniment in Palestine and Israel (EAPPI) and the Jerusalem Ecumenical Center, Tantur. Mounib Younan, "Al-Liqa' Center's Celebration of HB Patriarch Michel Sabbah's Golden Jubilee," *Al-Liqa' Newsletter* 30 (October 2005): 2. For information about EAPPI and Tantur see http://www.eappi.org and http://www.come.to/tantur.
216. "Al-Liqa' Center's Celebration of HB Patriarch Michel Sabbah's Golden Jubilee," 3. A collection of Sabbah's pastoral letters can be found in Michel Sabbah, *Faithful Witness: On Reconciliation and Peace in the Holy Land* (Hyde Park, NY: New City Press, 2009), 23–60.

and evaluate its content in order to discern its place among other Palestinian Christian hermeneutics of the Old Testament.

"Reading the Bible Today in the Land of the Bible" was written in November 1993 in the promising wake of the Oslo Peace Accords. Michel Sabbah lauds how this "new hope has just been born in the history of our country, opening new perspectives for peace and reconciliation between our two peoples, Jews and Palestinians, and with all of the Arab world. The pursuit of justice will continue, but from now on it will be through collaboration and no longer through confrontation."[217] Sabbah acknowledges that "in the recent past of confrontation, many among you were seized by anguish and assailed by doubts when confronted with the Bible, because it appeared to be directly linked to the difficult situation that we have experienced and the new period of peace which we have to build together."[218] And so Michel Sabbah writes this letter in order that the Christians in his Patriarchal diocese, those he calls "faithful" and who have been "affected by the past conflict," may read and understand the Bible correctly. A proper reading and understanding of the Bible will help his diocese to be loyal to "Church and society."[219] Unfortunately for both sides of the conflict, the period of collaboration Sabbah so applauded soon collapsed back into confrontation, and his letter remains all the more pertinent to the Palestinian Christian community who feel plagued by "catastrophe."

Michel Sabbah outlines his letter in accordance with the questions raised by the Palestinian Christian community. These fall under three categories:

---

217. Sabbah, *Faithful Witness*, 23, §1. Emphasis added.
218. Ibid., 24, §2. Emphasis added.
219. Ibid., 24, §§2, 4. These Christians include mostly Arabic-speaking Catholics but also a small community of Hebrew-speaking Catholics.

1. What is the relationship between the Old and New Testaments?
2. How is the violence attributed to God in the Bible to be understood?
3. What influence do the promises, the gift of land, the election, and the covenant have for relations between Palestinians and Israelis? Is it possible for a just and merciful God to impose injustice or oppression on another people in order to favor the people he has chosen?[220]

Before addressing these vexing questions, however, Sabbah says that there is an even more foundational issue that must be clarified: "We have to explain what the Bible is for the Christian and how it can be understood by him/her."[221] He outlines this section called "What is the Bible?" in four parts.[222]

1. The Bible is the Word of God
2. The Bible is a History of Salvation
3. The Bible is a History of Our Individual and Communal Salvation
4. Christ is the Key for a Christian Reading of the Bible

What follows will focus on this preliminary section as it provides a basis not only for assessing Sabbah's hermeneutic of the Old Testament but also for discerning how he responds to his diocese's "catastrophe of faith." Sabbah first of all asserts that "all of Sacred Scripture is the Word of God."[223] It is a record of the living events of divine revelation to humankind first passed down orally and then in written form. Unlike Mitri Raheb, Sabbah thinks these records are

---

220. Ibid., 27, §8.
221. Ibid., 27, §8.
222. Ibid., 28–39, §§9–32.
223. Sabbah maintains that Sacred Scripture refers to the 39 books of the Old Testament, 27 books of the New Testament, and the 8 Deuterocanonical books. Ibid., 29, §9.

more than "testimonies of faith." They are human words inspired by the Holy Spirit. Quoting Vatican II's *Dei Verbum*, Sabbah explains that "with Him (God) acting in them and through them, they as true authors consigned to writing everything and only those things which he wanted."[224] Sabbah maintains that inspiration does not negate the role of hermeneutics but rather infuses it with significance. In other words, proper biblical interpretation is not only warranted but encouraged in order to discern God's revelation. He explains: "Since God speaks in sacred Scripture through men in human fashion, the interpreter of Sacred Scripture, in order to see clearly what God wanted to communicate to us, should carefully investigate what meaning the sacred writer intended, and what God wanted to manifest by means of their words."[225] Furthermore, Sabbah notes that in order to understand what the divine and human authors wanted to "manifest by means of their words" the biblical interpreter must be attentive to the fact that divine revelation is progressive. Moreover—and this is characteristic of Sabbah's Roman Catholic hermeneutic—the biblical interpreter "can develop a true understanding of Scripture only in communication with the Church, in light of Tradition, and through the living liturgy and progress in Biblical studies. [For] 'sacred tradition and sacred Scripture form one sacred deposit.'"[226]

Second, Sabbah continually emphasizes to the Palestinian Christian community that "the Bible is our history of salvation."[227] Salvation is the "great gift of God, which is liberation."[228] He acknowledges

---

224. The quotation from *Dei Verbum* continues by explaining that "since everything asserted by the inspired authors or sacred writers must be held to be asserted by the Holy Spirit, it follows that the books of Scripture must be acknowledged as teaching solidly, faithfully and without error, that which God wanted put into the sacred writings for the sake of our salvation." Sabbah, *Faithful Witness*, 28–29, §11.
225. Ibid., 29, §12.
226. Ibid., 30, §14. Emphasis added.
227. Ibid., 30, §15. Emphasis added.
228. Ibid.

the economic, political, social, and cultural realities that oppress Palestinians, but he emphasizes that salvation is "above all, liberation from sin and the evil one, in the joy of knowing God and being known by Him, of seeing Him and of being turned over to Him."[229] Salvation is therefore "total liberation" from everything that separates humankind from God.

Sabbah points out that the history of this salvation is between the bookends of "paradise lost" and the "new Jerusalem." Within this framework "the history of salvation passes through a number of vital moments which reveal divine pedagogy dealing with humankind according to its ability to accept and understand His Word."[230] These vital moments, or covenants, detail successive stages of "conversion to God and the process of reconciliation between human beings."[231] They comprise the Covenant with Noah, the Covenant with Abraham, the Sinai Covenant, and the Covenant with David. Subsequent to these covenants there is a period of messianic expectation. "With the coming of Jesus, the times are fulfilled (Mk 1:15), the Kingdom of God has come."[232] Christ institutes a new covenant and gives birth to a new community of people, namely, his church. Sabbah concludes by saying: "The Church convoked by the word of God was indeed prepared in a marvelous way through the history of Israel and in the Old Covenant. Then it was founded in these times that are the final age and manifested by the gift of the Holy Spirit. At the end of times, it will be accomplished and achieved in glory."[233]

Third, Michel Sabbah declares that the "Bible is a history of our individual and communal salvation." In so declaring he invites

---

229. Ibid.
230. Ibid., 31, §16.
231. Ibid.
232. Ibid., 33–34, §22.
233. Ibid., 33–34, §22.

Palestinian Christians to read the Bible not only literally but also spiritually, a characteristically Catholic approach to reading Scripture. In accordance with the *Catechism of the Catholic Church*, the spiritual sense of Scripture expresses the unity of God's plan and therefore allows "not only the text of Scripture but also the realities and events about which it speaks to be signs."[234] It is in this light that Sabbah can say: "The history of God with the Jewish people is the model of the history of God with each of us, as individuals and as peoples."[235] The Bible is therefore a history of both Jewish and Palestinian salvation.

Finally, Sabbah claims that "Christ is the key for a Christian reading of the Bible." As Christ is the covenantal climax to salvation history, so also is Christ the hermeneutical key for reading scripture. This approach takes into account both the "continuity" and the "newness" that exist between the OT and NT and links the two concepts with the person of Christ, who, Sabbah writes, "fulfills" the law, prophets, and writings.[236] He concludes:

> To be a Christian means to believe in Jesus Christ and to accept everything that has been revealed about Him in the New Testament, and the way in which He understood and lived the Revelation of the Old Testament. He is also the key and supreme criterion for understanding the truth of the Bible, not only for everything that was said and done in Israel before His coming, but also for everything that will be done after Him (cf. John 16:7-11). To be Christian is to accept

---

234. *Catechism of the Catholic Church* (Dublin: Veritas, 1994), 117, §31. The *spiritual* reading of Scripture includes three separate senses. The *CCC* defines them as follows:

    1. The *allegorical sense*. We can acquire a more profound understanding of events by recognizing their significance in Christ; thus the crossing of the Red Sea is a sign or type of Christ's victory and also of Christian Baptism.

    2. The *moral sense*. The events reported in Scripture ought to lead us to act justly. As St. Paul says, they were written "for our instruction."

    3. The *anagogical sense* (Greek: *anagōgē*, 'leading'). We can view realities and events in terms of their eternal significance, leading us toward our true homeland: thus the Church on earth is a sign of the heavenly Jerusalem.

235. Sabbah, *Faithful Witness*, 34, §23.
236. Ibid., 36–38, §§26–29, 31.

the whole of the Scriptures, with the consciousness of Jesus, fully aware that He will reveal to us the fullness of the truth.[237]

Michel Sabbah is a distinctive case in the discussion of Palestinian Christian hermeneutics of the Old Testament. On the one hand, like Ateek and Raheb he writes in response to a pastoral reality. He addresses "Reading the Bible Today in the Land of the Bible" to the Palestinian Christian community who are having difficulty reading the Bible because of an atmosphere of "confrontation" that has beleaguered his community. He tells his constituency that the problem is not with the Bible but with those who misuse it. So he admonishes his faithful to remember: "We have already said that if some manipulate the Sacred Scriptures, this is not a reason to abandon our faith in our Scriptures. On the contrary, it is not the Word of God but the manipulation that we must denounce and correct."[238] He hopes his letter and in particular the section "What is the Bible" may "contribute to the new journey towards peace, justice, and reconciliation that has started in our land."[239]

On the other hand, Michel Sabbah's letter is unique in its traditionally Catholic reading of the Bible. He insists on reading the Bible in communion with the church. For Sabbah, Scripture does not stand alone; it stands with Tradition, namely, the "traditional way of interpreting Scripture within the community of faith."[240] In other words, "Scripture could not be allowed to be interpreted in any arbitrary or random way: it had to be interpreted within the context of the historical continuity of the Christian church."[241]

---

237. Ibid., 39, §32.
238. Ibid., 41, §36.
239. Ibid., 60, §64.
240. Alister E. McGrath, *Christian Theology: An Introduction* (2d ed. Oxford: Blackwell, 1997), 219.
241. Ibid. McGrath notes that traditional Catholicism, after the Council of Trent (1545–1563), fell along the lines of a "Dual-Source Theory of Tradition." In this view "'tradition' was understood to be a separate and distinct source of revelation, *in addition to Scripture*." With the Second Vatican Council (1962–1965), however, there seems to be a move toward a "Single-Source

Sabbah maintains that Christ is the hermeneutical key for the reading of Scripture, but unlike Ateek and Raheb he affirms the church as the final guarantor for proper biblical interpretation. Christ and the church are central to Sabbah's hermeneutic of the Old and New Testament.

In conclusion, we can say that, like those of Ateek and Raheb, Michel Sabbah's context, work, and hermeneutic of the Bible and of the Old Testament in particular are definitely affected by the foundation of the state of Israel and the subsequent Arab-Israeli conflicts. It is out of this context that Sabbah writes "Reading the Bible Today in the Land of the Bible" to a community on the verge of a "catastrophe of faith." But his letter and its underlying hermeneutic differ greatly in content and responsibility from those of Ateek and Raheb in one respect. As Latin Patriarch in Jerusalem, Sabbah not only writes from a Catholic perspective in which he must take into account the position of the wider Catholic Church, not least the Catholic position toward the Jewish people in Vatican II's *Nostra Aetate*, but he also writes as one responsible not just for the faith of Palestinian Christians but also for that of a small group that is "Hebrew speaking and is part of the Jewish people or lives in the midst of Jewish people."[242]

Atallah Hanna: A Greek Orthodox Perspective

Theophilos III is currently Patriarch of the Greek Orthodox Church in Jerusalem,[243] whose administrative scope covers "Israel, the

---

Theory of Tradition." It is this view that is highlighted in the 1994 *Catechism of the Catholic Church* and in the above evaluation of Michel Sabbah. One can conclude not only from the Pastoral Letter under discussion but also from the number of references made to Vatican II and *Dei Verbum* that Sabbah adheres to a "Single-Source Theory of Tradition." For McGrath's discussion on the issue of Tradition see *Christian Theology*, 219–23.

242. Sabbah, *Faithful Witness*, 25, §4.
243. The other three ancient patriarchates in the Middle East are Constantinople, Antioch, and Alexandria.

Occupied Palestinian Territories (OPT), and Jordan."[244] Its leadership is predominantly Greek. As Dan McDermott observes, "[T]here has never been an Arab Patriarch of Jerusalem, and out of the nineteen total members of the Holy Synod, only two are Arab—Archbishop Theodosius (also known as Atallah Hanna) and Archbishop Silvestros."[245] The laity, however, are chiefly Arab, as are the "vast majority of lower priests."[246] This has proven to be a bone of contention between the clergy and laity. Questions naturally arise: "whose church is it? does the church belong to the Greek expatriates or to the Arab majority?"[247] It is no wonder that the Palestinian Arab Orthodox community celebrated the ordination of Atallah Hanna as Archbishop Theodosios. Atallah Hanna was born in 1965 in a small village near Haifa called al-Rameh, was ordained as a priest in 1991, and on December 24, 2005, was ordained Archbishop at the Church of the Holy Sepulchre.

Atallah Hanna is a prime example of a fusion between Orthodox fidelity, Palestinian identity, and opposition to the modern state of Israel. In an address entitled "Pentecost and Jerusalem" he says:

> Jerusalem is the city of Pentecost and the city of our faith. The Church of Jerusalem is rightly called "the Mother of all Churches" because the first Church was established in Jerusalem. It is the city of redemption and salvation. . . . We the Christians of Palestine regard ourselves as an integral and inseparable part of the city of Jerusalem. Jerusalem is in our hearts and conscience and we refuse the distortion of its image and character.[248]

---

244. Dan McDermott, "Shaping the Church, Shaping the City," New Initiative for Middle East Peace *Insights* 44 (2006): 44–54, at 48.
245. Ibid., 50.
246. Ibid.
247. Ibid., 49–51. In addition there is the issue of land sales. See Michael Dumper, "Faith and Statecraft: Church-state Relations in Jerusalem after 1948," 56–81 in *Palestinian Christians: Religion, Politics and Society in the Holy Land*, ed. Anthony O'Mahony (London: Melisende, 1999).

When Hanna condemns the "distortion" of Jerusalem's "image and character" he does not name names, but Israel is understood to be the culprit.[249]

Like other Palestinian Christians, Atallah Hanna has obviously been influenced by the foundation of the state of Israel. This was evident in his address, "Pentecost and Jerusalem." Although the address did not supply any explicit statement on how Atallah Hanna interpreted the OT, the following survey of Jewish-Christian dialogue and Orthodox hermeneutics will supply a picture of how he and the Greek Orthodox Church in Israel and Palestine interpret the OT.

The foundation of the state of Israel definitely affected interreligious dialogue between Orthodox Christians and Jews. Some Orthodox Christians have recognized the long history of Christian anti-Semitism and the atrocities of the Holocaust and have responded positively to the idea of interreligious dialogue. George C. Papademetriou, for instance, points out three axioms for the advancement of Orthodox Christian-Jewish dialogue in the introductory chapter of his book, *Essays on Orthodox Christian–Jewish Relations*.[250]

1. Anti-semitism as a sin against God.
2. The incompatibility with the Christian faith of coercive proselytism or forced baptism directed towards the Jews.
3. The reality today of the covenant God made with the Jewish people at Sinai.

---

248. Atallah Hanna, "Pentecost and Jerusalem," 5–7 in *Jerusalem: What Makes for Peace? A Palestinian Christian Contribution to Peacemaking* (ed. Naim Ateek, Cedar Duaybis, and Marla Schrader; London: Melisende, 1997), at 7.
249. Hanna says later: "we absolutely refuse attempts by any part to impose its unilateral control over Jerusalem without taking into consideration the rights, the needs and feelings of others." Ibid.
250. In Petra Heldt, "A Brief History of Dialogue between Orthodox Christians and Jews," *Immanuel* 26/27 (1994): 211–24, at 212.

The foundation of the state of Israel has also become a bone of contention for some Orthodox Christians. As a result, they have responded negatively to the idea of interreligious dialogue with Jews. Petra Heldt makes special note of Metropolitan Georges Khodr as a prime example of such sentiment. "From his 1962 article on 'Church and Mission' to his 1991 article on 'An Orthodox Perspective on Interreligious Dialogue,' he has continued to pursue the replacement theology of old (the claim that the Church has replaced Israel)."[251] As seen in these examples, the measure to which Orthodox Christians respond positively or negatively to the foundation of the state of Israel and accord religious significance to the Jewish people will no doubt influence their hermeneutics of the Old Testament. Before one can evaluate how a Palestinian Arab Orthodox Christian might interpret the OT, however, it is important to outline Orthodox Christian hermeneutics in general.

For the Orthodox tradition scripture is not unique among the forms in which God's Spirit indwells and communicates with the church. There are in fact seven: "Scripture, the seven ecumenical councils, later councils and their dogmatic statements (Orthodoxy's so-called symbolic books), the Fathers, liturgy, canon law, and icons."[252] Scripture is therefore not the sole authority for the Orthodox Christian (*contra* Protestant *sola scriptura*). Nevertheless, scripture is still the "'supreme expression' of God's revelation."[253]

What is the nature of this divine revelation that is found in scripture? *Contra* Raheb, "the Bible is not merely a human record of

---

251. Heldt, "A Brief History of Dialogue," 212. Georges Khodr is Metropolitan in the Greek Orthodox Patriarchate of Antioch and all of the East. His archdiocese is thus outside the boundaries of Israel. This fact may seem to undermine Heldt's reference, but as will be seen in chap. 4, the development of PCHOT after the foundation of the state of Israel, and in particular after 1967, was profoundly influenced by Orthodox Christians in Lebanon.
252. Daniel B. Clendenin, *Eastern Orthodox Christianity: A Western Perspective* (Grand Rapids: Baker, 1997), 108.
253. Ibid., 109.

... divine interventions and deeds. It is a kind of divine intervention itself."[254] It is the "Word of God" in "human words." Moreover, it is a "living reality" in which the "mysterious and miraculous" experiences recorded in the Bible correspond with those in the Orthodox Church.[255]

Similar to the Latin perspective, Orthodox interpretation of the Bible always falls within the community of the church. Elias Oikonomou writes:

> It is not allowed for anyone to interpret Holy Scripture as he likes and to teach it as he likes. For that reason, the Orthodox Church reached a decision in the Quintsextine Council (691 A.D.) and determined that Holy Scripture should be interpreted as understood by the Fathers of the Church.[256]

In other words, "the Church is the proper and primary interpreter of revelation."[257] The problem of Christian Zionism, which a number of the above perspectives noted, is therefore a result of what George Florovksy calls, "'the sin of the Reformation,' the consequences of which," according to the Orthodox Church, "are arbitrary, subjective, and individualistic interpretations of the gospel."[258]

---

254. Georges Florovsky, *Bible, Church, Tradition: An Eastern Orthodox View* (Belmont, MA: Nordland Publishing, 1972), 20.
255. Demetrios Bathrellos, "The Eastern Orthodox Tradition for Today," 42–58 in *The Bible in Pastoral Practice: Readings in the Place and Function of Scripture in the Church*, ed. Paul Ballard and Stephen R. Holmes (Grand Rapids: Eerdmans, 2005), at 45–46.
256. Elias Oikonomou, "Scripture and Hermeneutics: An Orthodox View," *Immanuel* 26/27 (1994): 49–56, at 55.
257. Florovsky, *Bible, Church, Tradition*, 25. Daniel B. Clendenin lists four reasons why the Orthodox Church believes the Bible must be interpreted in connection with Tradition:

    1. First, both the church itself and the apostolic kerygma existed for nearly three centuries before the ecumenical councils and the establishment of the scriptural canon.

    2. Second, Orthodoxy would insist that nobody operates with a clean slate, a *tabula rasa*, and accordingly, noncanonical traditions are a practical and hermeneutical inevitability.

    3. Third, liturgical precedent also reveals the importance of non-canonical tradition.

    4. Fourth, the necessity of the extrabiblical tradition finds broad-based support in the theological methodologies of any number of early fathers.

(Clendenin, *Eastern Orthodox Christianity*, 110–13)

What, then, is the Orthodox hermeneutic of the Old Testament?[259] First, the Orthodox Church maintains the unity between the Old and New Testaments. Elias Oikonomou lists three grounds supporting this unity: theological, linguistic, and methodological.[260] Theologically, the unity of Scripture can be seen through the lens of progressive revelation, which affords both continuity and climax. Oikonomou argues:

> What is common to both is the inner or spiritual unity and continuity of the Old and New Testament. The Old Testament did not come to an end with the coming of the New; the New did not abolish the Old but its self-sufficiency, its self-supporting adequacy. The Old Testament contains the germs and the announcements of what has been realized through the New Testament.[261]

Linguistically, there is a clear dependence of the NT on the OT, and methodologically, Oikonomou contends that in the Orthodox hermeneutic tradition "there is no theological treatise, hermeneutic or polemical, that does not link the Old and New Testament and does not argue by way of cross references."[262] Thus there is a unity between the Old and New Testaments.

Second, the Orthodox hermeneutic of the Old Testament blends the principle of progressive revelation, which maintains Scripture's continuity and revelatory evolution and climax in Christ, with a theological interpretation of these events. Practically, this fusion interprets the Old Testament typologically.[263] Georges Florovsky

---

258. In Clendenin, *Eastern Orthodox Christianity*, 105.
259. The authorized Old Testament text for the Orthodox Church is not the Hebrew Bible but rather the Septuagint (LXX). It is interesting to note that "whenever this text [LXX] differs from the original Hebrew, it is believed [by the Orthodox Church] that the changes occurred under the guidance of the Holy Spirit." Bathrellos, "The Eastern Orthodox Tradition for Today," 46.
260. Oikonomou, "Scripture and Hermeneutics," 52–53.
261. Ibid., 53.
262. Ibid.
263. Florovsky compares the methods of allegory and typology as follows: "For an allegorist the 'images' he interprets are reflections of a pre-existing prototype, or even images of some eternal

clarifies that "not every event of the Old Testament has its 'correspondence' in the New. Yet there are certain basic events in the old dispensation which were the 'figures' or 'types' of the basic events in the new."[264] Among the "figures" and "types" that are scattered throughout the Old Testament and are relevant to the present discussion is that of "Israel" as a type of the "church."

Georges Florovsky argues that Israel is likened more to a church than to a nation in the Old Testament.[265] First, he says that the term "nation" is primarily used to describe the heathen and pagans in contrast to "the only nation or people that was also (and primarily) a Church of God."[266] Second, he writes that all the traditional elements that define the church are prefigured in Israel. He explains: "Israel was a divinely constituted community of believers, united by the Law of God, the true faith, sacred rites and hierarchy."[267] On this basis Florovsky concludes that Israel is a type for the church.

In view of the hermeneutical matrix of typological interpretation of the Old Testament in Florovsky's arguments, the church is not only the New Israel because of the continuity and progression of divine purposes but also the "true" Israel on the basis of the christological climax of God's covenantal purposes. Accordingly, Florovsky concludes, "The only true constitution of the old covenant was in the Church of Christ."[268] This conclusion has practical implications for an Orthodox hermeneutic of the Old Testament. First, the Old Testament is to be interpreted solely in "relation to the Church."[269] Second, and pertinent to the above reference to Christian

or abstract 'truth.' They are pointing to something that is outside of time. On the contrary, typology is oriented towards the future. The 'types' are anticipations, *pre*-figurations; their 'prototype' is still to come." Florovsky, *Bible, Church, Tradition*, 32.
264. Ibid., 31.
265. Ibid., 32–36.
266. Ibid., 32.
267. Ibid., 33.
268. Ibid.
269. Ibid., 34.

Zionism, "one has no right to isolate certain elements of the old dispensation, apart from their immediate relation to the life of the Church, and set them as a Scripture pattern for the temporal life of the nations."[270]

How, then, does the Greek Orthodox Church in Israel and Palestine interpret the Old Testament in light of the foundation of the state of Israel? As the above survey has shown, traditional Orthodox Christian hermeneutics makes it difficult to affirm that the text of the Old Testament belongs to anyone besides the Christian Church. Moreover, as church-state relations in the Greek Orthodox Church become more inclined toward its Palestinian constituency, and among other things the church begins including more Arab clergy members in its hierarchy, Palestinian national identity will clearly increase within the church and make it difficult to affirm "the reality today of the covenant God made with the Jewish people at Sinai."[271] Ultimately the Orthodox Church reads, experiences, and interprets the Bible "primarily as a liturgical celebration, other than in their private reading and study."[272] This is true of the Old Testament in particular. "The Psalms are the backbone of the daily offices, and after the Gospels, are the most familiar part of Scripture to Orthodox Christians."[273] The foundation of the state of Israel may cause a degree of tension whenever a Palestinian Arab Orthodox reads the Old Testament or recites the Psalms during liturgy. Nevertheless,

---

270. Ibid., 34.
271. Cf. Heldt, "A Brief History of Dialogue," 212; McDermott, "Shaping the Church," 53.
272. Michael Prokurat, "Orthodox Interpretation of Scripture," 59–100 in *The Bible in the Churches: How Various Christians Interpret the Scriptures*, ed. Kenneth Hagan (Milwaukee: Marquette University Press, 1994), at 60. Cf. Theodore G. Stylianopoulos, "Scripture and Tradition in the Church," 21–34 in *The Cambridge Companion to Orthodox Christian Theology*, ed. Mary Cunningham and Elizabeth Theokritoff (Cambridge: Cambridge University Press, 2008), at 26.
273. Archimandrite Ephrem Lash, "Biblical Interpretation in Worship," 35–48 in *The Cambridge Companion to Orthodox Christian Theology* (2008), at 37. Other than the Psalms, "outside of Lent the Old Testament is little used liturgically." Ibid., 40.

whenever he or she participates in the daily offices or hears the Old Testament readings during the church feasts he or she is continually reminded that the Old Testament is primarily the church's text. It belongs to the church and is read and properly interpreted within and for the church. It is in this sense that a Palestinian Christian reads and interprets the OT within the Greek Orthodox Church.

Conclusion

This is the formidable struggle for many Arab Christians who live in Israel and Palestine: "Being Christians, these people are committed to the unity of the Bible and to the Jewish antecedents of the Gospel. Being Arabs, they share with the total Arab Islamic world the tragedy that Israel constitutes for their experience. But they do so with a peculiar strain of loyalties when 'Israel' is both the Israel of say, Isaiah and that of Menachem Begin."[274] Naim Ateek and Mitri Raheb are right to claim that the foundation of the state of Israel and the ensuing Arab-Israeli conflict was a "catastrophe" not just in the physical realm but in the spiritual as well. With the exception of Naim Khoury, the vast majority of contemporary Palestinian Christians struggle to find a hermeneutic of the OT that is true to their particular tradition and identity as Palestinian Christians as well as to the various elements of PCHOT. This fact was underscored above. The questions that now need to be asked are: "To what extent has Palestinian Christian understanding of the Old Testament actually changed since the foundation of the state of Israel, and what have been the deciding factors that have influenced its development? Has the political or religious context in which Palestinian Christians have found themselves governed the manner in which they have viewed and interpreted the OT?" To answer these questions we need to look at

---

274. Cragg, *Arab Christian*, 101.

Palestinian Christianity and its understanding of the OT before and after the foundation of the state of Israel. The next section of this book (History) will survey this development. Chapter 2 will look at Palestinian Christianity before 1917, that is, during the early days of Zionism. Chapter 3 will analyze Palestinian Christianity between 1917 and 1948, that is, from the time of the signing of the Balfour Declaration and during the British Mandate. Chapter 4 will outline in greater detail Palestinian Christianity's development since 1948, from the time of the great "catastrophe" for Palestinians in the foundation of the state of Israel.

PART II

Palestinian Christians and the Old Testament: History

2

Palestinian Christianity and the Dawn of Zionism

The 1881 pogroms of southern Russia destroyed, among other things, the hope Russian Jews had for assimilation. The *Bilu* was founded as a result.[1] This group of "young Russian Jews . . . pioneered the Zionist program of resettlement of the Jewish people in the land of Israel as a solution to the Jewish question."[2] Their "Manifesto," which was written en route to Palestine, challenged their "brethren and sisters in exile" to recognize: "Hopeless is your state in the West (with the prospect of assimilation); the star of your future is gleaming in the East (with respect to a home in Zion)." And so began the first of many *aliyot*.[3]

---

1. Their name, *Bilu* (בילו) was coined by taking the opening letter of the first four words of Isa 2:5, "O house of Jacob! Come, let us walk in the light of the Lord!" (Hebrew: בית יעקב לכו ונלכה באור יהוה)
2. Paul R. Mendes-Flohr and Jehuda Reinharz, eds., *The Jew in the Modern World: A Documentary History* (Oxford: Oxford University Press, 1980), 421. Emphasis added.
3. *Aliyah* (singular) literally means "going up." It refers to Jewish immigration to Israel, or in this case, Palestine.

Despite the anticipation of a new life in Palestine, the new *yishuv* (that is, the Jewish community in Palestine before the foundation of the modern state of Israel)[4] was faced with numerous challenges, which stemmed from the political and religious complexities of nineteenth-century Palestine. Among the abundance of issues confronting this burgeoning community, the presence of a long-established Arab population in the land was one of the most serious matters demanding their attention. Yitzhak Epstein, a leader in the First Aliyah, argued in *HaShiloach*, "Among the grave questions linked with the concept of our people's renaissance on its own soil, there is one question which is more weighty than all the others combined. This is the question of our relations with the Arabs. Our own national aspirations depend upon the correct solution of this question."[5] Not all Zionists agreed with Epstein's concern, however. Many condemned his apparent sensitivity to Arab sentiment. For example, Ze'ev Smilansky, a leader of the Second Aliyah, deplored Epstein's views. "He is attracted to the wretched Arabs," Smilansky argued.[6] "We are told by Epstein that we are not entitled to redeem the land of our forefathers with money, even if we do this in a fair and peaceful manner. . . . So we have nothing to worry about except the fate of the Palestine Arabs?"[7] The comments made by both Epstein and Smilansky prove, on the one hand, that Jewish-Arab relations were a key issue for the early Jewish settlers. That the issue was fervently debated in the *yishuv* proves it was a palpable concern of the Jewish community. Smilansky's remarks, on the other hand, show that it was certainly not the only concern of the burgeoning *yishuv*.

4. The Jewish community in Palestine before the dawn of Zionism is usually termed the Old *Yishuv* while the Jews who made *Aliyah* to Palestine during the late Ottoman period and British Mandate are usually classified as the New *Yishuv*.
5. Howard M. Sachar, *A History of Israel: From the Rise of Zionism to Our Time* (New York: Knopf, 1993), 163.
6. Ibid., 164.
7. Ibid.

The same was true of Palestinian Christianity and its encounter with the dawn of Zionism before 1917. The increased Jewish presence in the land definitely concerned parts of the Arab Christian population.[8] However, it was certainly not the only issue or indeed the main subject matter that occupied their attention. At the end of the nineteenth century Palestine was home to a complicated mix of local and foreign aspirations, and indeed communities.

> Palestine was . . . a small land of profound spiritual significance for millions, remote from European capitals, but an important outpost of the imperialist ruling powers, belonging to the Ottoman Empire but partly ruled by the European consulates. The population was small, about six hundred thousand, but the divisions were many and profound. The Arabs were divided into a Muslim majority and a Christian minority, belonging to various sects. The small Druze community was set apart from them all. The Jewish minority was made up of two different societies: the "old Yishuv" community and the new one.[9]

Each of these elements, whether local or foreign, impacted the views and state of the respective communities in Palestine and not least the native Christian communities in Palestine.

In what follows I will outline some of this context, summarizing the political and religious situation of Palestinian Christianity before 1917 and then describing a few of the key Arab Christian leaders in

---

8. See Neville J. Mandel, *The Arabs and Zionism before World War I* (Berkeley: University of California Press, 1976). Mandel evaluates the growing awareness and response of the Arab population to Zionism before the First World War, showing that the local Arab population was aware of Jewish immigration (including the *Biluim*) and the Zionist movement from the beginning, though with varying degrees of consternation. He notes how the Christian editors of the journal *al-Muqtaṭaf* received a letter in the summer of 1882 about the "increased flow of Jews through Beirut on their way to Palestine." The same journal also commented shortly after the first Zionist congress in 1897 (Mandel, *Arabs and Zionism*, 32, 44, 223). For the thoughts of Néjib Azoury and Farid Kassab, two influential Arab Christians, on the matter, see Albert Hourani, *Arabic Thought in the Liberal Age: 1798–1939* (Cambridge: Cambridge University Press, 2003), 277–79; Mandel, *Arabs and Zionism*, 49–52; and Stefan Wild, "Ottomanism versus Arabism: The Case of Farid Kassab (1884–1970)," *Die Welt des Islams* 28 (1988): 607–27.
9. Yosef Gorny, *Zionism and the Arabs 1882–1948: A Study of Ideology* (Oxford: Clarendon Press, 1987), 11.

Palestine during this time, evaluating, among other things, how they viewed the Bible and interpreted the Old Testament.

The Political Context of Palestinian Christians Before 1917

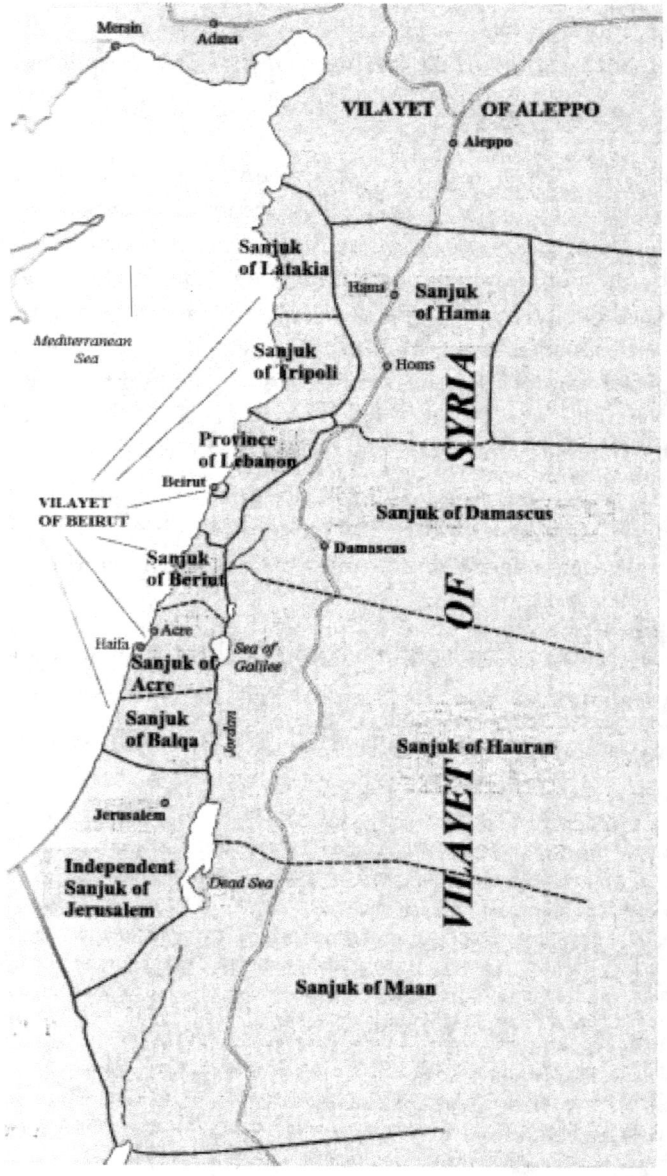

Palestine remained under Ottoman rule for four hundred years (1517–1917).[10] In the nineteenth century the land of Palestine was divided into three separate *sanjaks*, or administrative areas: Acre, Nablus, and Jerusalem.[11] The *sanjaks* of central Palestine, that is Acre and Balqa, were part of the *vilayet* of Beirut, a *vilayet* being the larger provincial unit, often made up of a number of *sanjaks*.[12] This meant, among other things, that the local inhabitants of Acre and Balqa had recourse to Constantinople only through the jurisdiction of Beirut, while the *sanjak* of Jerusalem, which was independent, answered directly to Constantinople.

Palestine was under Ottoman rule, yet its inhabitants did not all have the same rights and privileges. Minorities in the Ottoman Empire, such as Jews and Christians, were subjugated to *dhimmī* status. *Dhimmī*, or *ahl al-dhimma*, literally means "pact" or "people of the pact/protection." It was a legal term referring to an agreed-upon "pact" or "contract" between the Muslim ruler and the non-Muslim communities.[13] Under this system Jews and Christians agreed to adhere to the following conditions, as summarized by Bernard Lewis.

> The basis of the contract was the recognition by the *dhimmīs* of the supremacy of Islam and the dominance of the Muslim state, and their acceptance of a position of subordination, symbolized by certain social restrictions and by the payment of a poll tax (*jizya*) to which Muslims

---

10. General Allenby's triumphant entry into Jerusalem on December 11, 1917 is often held to mark the end of Ottoman rule in Palestine. Nevertheless, the rest of Palestine was not wrested from Ottoman hands until after the war. Official capitulation of Ottoman rule to the Allied Powers did not take place until October 30, 1918.
11. "Ottoman levant" in *Wikimedia Commons, the free media repository*, accessed March 18, 2015: http://en.wikipedia.org/wiki/Ma'an#/media/File:Ottoman_levant.png.
12. A *vilayet* was an administrative division of the Ottoman Empire. This system of administration was introduced as part of a number of the *Tanzimât* reforms during the years 1839–1876. See n. 19 below for a brief explanation of the *Tanzimât* reforms.
13. Bernard Lewis, *The Middle East: A Brief History of the Last 2,000 Years* (New York: Scribner, 2003), 210.

were not subject. In return they were granted security of life and property, protection against external enemies, freedom of worship, and a very large measure of internal autonomy in the conduct of their affairs.[14]

Although the way the Muslim majority treated Jews and Christians on a personal basis is a subject of significant debate, it is outside the parameters of the present book and will not be discussed here.[15] Politically, the Ottoman government dealt with the *dhimmī*, or non-Muslim subjects of their realm, collectively. They were organized into *millets*, which were autonomous religious and confessional communities.[16] Each *millet* was granted a certain level of independence and was able to oversee a range of activities, including matters of religion, administration, and justice. As Anthony O'Mahony explains, "Their jurisdiction embraced, in the religious sphere, clerical discipline; in the administrative sphere, the control of properties, including cemeteries, educational institutions and churches; in the judicial sphere, marriage, dowries, divorce and alimony, and ... civil rights."[17]

Initially, the Ottoman Empire recognized three principal *millets*: the Greek Orthodox, the Armenian Orthodox, and the Jews. However, in the wake of the Crimean War[18] and as a result of the *Tanzimât* reforms[19] and Western political and religious influence the

---

14. Ibid.
15. For a discussion of the treatment of *Dhimmī* under Islam, see Bat Ye'or, *The Dhimmi: Jews and Christians under Islam* (Cranbury, NJ: Associated University Presses, 1985).
16. For how the *millet* system was organized under the Ottoman Empire see Anthony O'Mahony, "Palestinian Christians: Religion, Politics and Society, c. 1800–1948," 9–55 in idem, ed., *Palestinian Christians: Religion, Politics and Society in the Holy Land* (London: Melisende, 1999), at 17–27. Cf. Roger Heacock, "International Politics and Sectarian Policy in the Late Ottoman Period," 20–31 in *Patterns of the Past, Prospects for the Future: The Christian Heritage in the Holy Land*, ed. Thomas Hummel (London: Melisende, 1999).
17. O'Mahony, "Palestinian Christians," 19.
18. The Crimean War (October 1853–February 1856) took place between the Russian Empire and the combined forces of the British, French, and Ottoman Empires. The concerned parties undoubtedly had numerous reasons for their involvement in the war, but it is often painted by historians as a conflict over the holy places in Jerusalem.

number and diversity of *millets* had increased substantially by the end of the nineteenth century. They included communities belonging to the Eastern Orthodox churches, the Oriental Orthodox churches, the Latin, Eastern, and Oriental Catholic churches, and "Protestants."[20] The increase of *millets* was no doubt facilitated by "capitulations."

The term "capitulation" comes from the Latin *capitula*, literally meaning "chapters," and was a contract or agreement between the Ottoman Empire and Western powers[21] that initially carried with it economic privileges for Western powers. It allowed citizens of Western countries to "reside and trade in the Muslim dominations without being liable to the fiscal and other disabilities imposed by these Muslim rulers on their own non-Muslim subjects."[22] In time, the Western understanding of the terms of agreement amalgamated (whether intentionally or not is open to debate) to "an almost unlimited right of interference in almost every aspect of Ottoman internal affairs."[23] Of particular importance for Western powers was the "protection" of religious minorities.[24]

Bernard Lewis is right to say that "such religious protection took many forms."[25] It included everything from education and the custody of holy sites to actual physical intervention on behalf of religious minorities. The Russians established their "protectorate"

---

19. *Tanzimât* literally means "reorganization." This reorganization or reform took place between 1839 and 1876 in an effort to secure the territorial integrity of the Ottoman Empire against nationalist movements and aggressive colonialist powers. For more information see, William L. Cleveland and Martin Bunton, *A History of the Modern Middle East* (5th ed. Boulder: Westview Press, 2013), 75–94.
20. See O'Mahony, "Palestinian Christians," 21.
21. Lewis, *Middle East*, 291.
22. Ibid.
23. Ibid., 294.
24. The extent to which the Ottoman Empire saw eye to eye with Western interpretation is debatable. On the one hand this could have been an unforeseen consequence of the disintegration of the Empire. On the other hand, with the Ottoman Empire's disintegration the rulers may not have been in a position to change the policies anyway. See Roger Heacock's "International Politics" as an entrée to the political complexities of the time.
25. Lewis, *Middle East*, 294.

over the Orthodox, the French over the Catholics, and the British, Germans, and Americans over the Protestants. The "protectorates" were not established, however, without any vested interest. In a confidential memorandum to the Foreign Office on "Christian Minorities in the Middle East" the General Secretary of the Church of England, Reverend H. M. Waddams, rightly illustrates this point with respect to France and Russia: "France used the Uniate Churches as the means of furthering their own interests, posing as the Catholic power *par excellence* and therefore claiming a right to interfere in the interests of its protégés. Russia claimed to be the defender of the Orthodox interests and incidentally did its best to weaken the traditional Greek position in the ancient Patriarchates of Antioch and Jerusalem."[26] The Western powers, therefore, "battled it out" (both literally and figuratively) for their place in the Ottoman Empire, sometimes sounding outright manipulative in their "concern" for Christian minorities and at other times appearing, and in certain cases definitely being, more altruistic. A perusal of the political correspondence in the nineteenth century confirms that Western countries were concerned that Eastern Christians were "suffering" and that the Ottoman government was either compliant or unable to do anything.[27]

Within the political complexity of religious "protection," however, an entire infrastructure was created that was of particular benefit to the Christian minorities.

> The religious and educational needs of the Ottoman Christians and Jews were met by an increasingly ramified network of missions, schools, and

---

26. In Bejtullah D. Destani, ed., *Minorities in the Middle East*. 10 vols. (Slough: Archive Editions, 2007): *Christian Minorities 1838–1967: Christian Communities in the Levant, Part III, 1861–1955 and Jeddah 1858, 1895*, 279.
27. In particular see Destani, ed, *Minorities in the Middle East: Christian Minorities 1838–1967: Christian Communities in the Levant, Part II, 1860–1861*. The latter volume deals with the events following the 1860 massacre.

other educational, cultural, and social institutions. These were mostly Christian, a few Jewish, and some designated as secular, and they attracted a growing number of Muslim as well as minority pupils. Products of Western schools in the Middle East went to universities in the West for higher education, and from the second half of the nineteenth century Western colleges were established in a number of Middle Eastern cities. Education became an important means of extending the cultural and therefore also ultimately the economic and political influence of the sponsoring power.[28]

With the education the West afforded, the local Christians, and in many cases the Muslim community as well, appropriated instruction for the benefit of their communities and, in the case of *al-Nahdah,* for the wider Arab community.

Al-Nahdah literally means "renaissance" and is commonly referred to in English as the Arabic revival or "Awakening."[29] This "Awakening" owed much of its impetus to the increase in education as well as the intentional use of the Arabic language in many of its schools.[30] George Antonius highlights in particular the role of American missionary activity in this regard:

> The educational activities of the American missionaries in that early period had, among many virtues, one outstanding merit; they gave pride of place to Arabic, and, once they had committed themselves to teaching in it, put their shoulders with vigor to the task of providing an adequate literature. In that, they were pioneers; and because of that, the intellectual effervescence which marked the first stirrings of the Arab revival owes most to their labours.[31]

---

28. Destani, *Christian Minorities 1838–1967*, 294–95.
29. See George Antonius, *Arab Awakening* (London: Hamish Hamilton, 1938). Cf. Qustandi Shomali, "Arab Cultural Revival in Palestine," 283–307 in *Patterns of the Past, Prospects for the Future*; Manuel Hassassian, "The Influence of Christian Arabs in the National Movement," 308–30 in ibid.
30. Shomali details five aspects of the Arab cultural revival in Palestine: first, education; second, the printing press; third, the establishment of literary clubs and societies; fourth, appearance of newspapers and magazines; and fifth, translation. Shomali, "Arab Cultural Revival in Palestine," 283–85.
31. Antonius, *Arab Awakening*, 43.

It is true that American missionary activity played an important part in enabling the birth of Arab nationalism.[32] Nevertheless, American missionaries do not deserve sole credit. As Abdul Tibawi illustrates in convincing fashion, educational institutions were also established under Russian, French, and British influence.[33] Each of these nations, therefore, should be acknowledged for facilitating in part the rise of Arab nationalism.

Christian communities in the Ottoman Empire were not the only ones privy to Western education. Muslim families often enrolled their children in schools established by the Orthodox, Catholic, and Protestant churches. Nevertheless, because it was easier for Christian individuals to have access to this education they became, as Antonius acknowledges, some of the leading figures of *al-Nahdah*. The Christian minority before 1917 was therefore not just a passive party in the conflict between Ottoman and Western politics. Benefiting from the educational opportunities presented to them, they were active in their role in the incipient Arab "Awakening" and subsequent rise of Arab nationalism.

It should be said, however, by way of conclusion, that Arab Christian political activity was far from straightforward. Kenneth Cragg makes a strong case that Arab Christians were pressured in three different directions, so that the Ottoman Empire was treated either with "fealty" or as a "foe," the West as a "factor" or a "foreigner," and the incipient Arab nationalism with favor or ambivalence.[34] Moreover, "each of these impinged on the reading of the other," thereby creating a "triangular field of interaction."[35]

---

32. The establishment of the American University of Beirut in 1856 by American missionaries proves this point.
33. Abdul L. Tibawi, *British Interests in Palestine, 1800–1901: A Study of Religious and Educational Enterprise* (Oxford: Oxford University Press, 1961), 170–77. As Tibawi shows, Orthodox and Catholic schools were sometimes of higher standard than their Protestant counterparts.
34. Kenneth Cragg, *The Arab Christian: A History in the Middle East* (Louisville: Westminster John Knox, 1991), 147.

Decision-making for an Arab Christian was therefore quite onerous. The first choice was whether to maintain loyalty to Ottoman rule at the expense of one's *millet* and opportunities afforded by Western contact. In addition, fidelity to the Ottoman Empire went against a growing sense of Arab identity. Next, association with Western establishments offered its own advantages for personal and community advancement but risked cementing the Arab Christian minority in their already precarious position as *dhimmī*.[36] Finally, commitment to the rapidly expanding cause of Arab nationalism risked serious repercussions from Ottoman and Western powers. What was the Arab Christian to do? Bernard Lewis sums it up well:

> During the nineteenth century, the Christian minorities in the Ottoman Empire pursued three different and ultimately irreconcilable objectives. The first of these was equal citizenship in the Ottoman state, that is to say equal rights with the Muslim majority. . . . The second objective . . . was that of independence, or at least autonomy within a national territory of their own. . . . The third aim . . . was the retention of the privileges and autonomies which the *millets* had had under the old order—the right to the maintenance and enforcement of their own religious laws, to the control of their own educational systems in their own languages, and generally to the maintenance of their own distinctive cultures. . . . In the long run, these three objectives were incompatible.[37]

Political activity was not the only field in which the local Palestinian Christian community was involved. Over the course of the nineteenth century and the first part of the twentieth, Palestinian

---

35. Ibid.
36. Bernard Lewis details the interesting relationship between the West and the Arab Christian minority. "In the Middle East, exceptionally, the agents and also the immediate beneficiaries of change, both inside and outside, were themselves outsiders. The foreigners were of course Europeans, but even inside the Muslim countries the main actors, if not actually foreigners, were members of religious minorities, regarded as marginal by the dominant majority society." Lewis, *Middle East*, 293.
37. Lewis, *Middle East*, 324–25.

Christians began to assume more and more leadership in their respective religious communities. The theological opinions of these early Palestinian Christian leaders were influenced not just by the political context of which they were a part but also largely by their religious context. It is for this reason that the next section describes in detail the religious context of the Palestinian Christian community before 1917, to provide the basis on which to properly evaluate Palestinian Christian religious opinion during this period as well as the way Palestinian Christians interpreted the Old Testament.

The Religious Context of Palestinian Christians Before 1917

The religious context of Christians in Palestine before 1917 was as varied and complex as the political milieu.[38] By the end of the nineteenth century the Ottoman authorities had recognized a whole congeries of Christian *millets* representing each of the main branches of the Christian church.[39] The increase in number and range of Christian *millets* owed much of its impetus to the swell of missionary activity and the corresponding establishment of religious institutions.[40] The sum total of this activity indelibly transformed the religious landscape of Palestine before 1917.

In this section I will summarize the basic motivations and grounds for this increase in missionary fervor and then describe some of the key missionary societies and religious institutions active in Palestine before 1917. Particular attention will be given to the opinions and activities of Protestant Christians during this time. This is not to

---

38. It is perhaps misleading to distinguish between the political and religious contexts of the Christian church in Palestine before 1917 when in fact there was no clear-cut division. As explained in the previous section, Christian minorities were divided politically into *millets* according to their religious distinctions.
39. See above section, "The Political Context of Palestinian Christians Before 1917."
40. It is true that these missionary societies and religious institutions were not always joined in the same motivation or purpose. Indeed, Orthodox, Catholic, and Protestant interests and endeavors varied not just between but also within their respective traditions.

discount the initiative and role of the Catholic and Orthodox churches. Each Christian tradition bears some responsibility for the changing religious context of Palestine. Nevertheless, Protestant missionary activity and its associated religious institutions were one of the key constitutive elements that transformed the religious context of Palestine before 1917.[41] Therefore the motivations of Protestant Christians as well as their missionary societies and institutions will be summarized. This survey will in turn provide a basis from which to understand and evaluate the views of some of the most noteworthy Protestant Palestinian Christians during the period in question.

The Basis and Motivations of Protestant Missions in Palestine

The start of the Protestant missionary movement in Palestine is rooted in the rise of political power and religious interests in Western Europe and North America.[42] Western political prominence provided the opportunity and vehicle for missionary activities, and the religious awakenings of the eighteenth and nineteenth centuries supplied its impetus.[43] As Michael Marten explains,

> The Evangelical Revival of the Protestant churches across Europe, whether in Germany, Scandinavia, or Britain, led to an unprecedented level of missionary fervour. Personal conversion and holiness were

---

41. Cf. Charlotte Van der Leest, "Conversion and Conflict in Palestine: The Missions of the Church Missionary Society and the Protestant Bishop Samuel Gobat." (Ph.D, diss., University of Leiden, 2008), 14–15. Indeed, it is impossible to understand the basis of the reestablishment of the Latin Patriarchate in 1847 and the return of the Orthodox Patriarch of Jerusalem after years of residence in Constantinople without recognizing the competition and religious and political motivations that followed the establishment of the Protestant Bishopric in 1841.
42. Michael Marten, *Attempting to Bring the Gospel Home: Scottish Missions to Palestine, 1839–1917* (London: Tauris Academic Studies, 2006), 2–4. Cf. Stephen Neill, *A History of Christian Missions* (2d ed. Harmondsworth: Penguin, 1986), 207–21; Dana Robert, *Christian Mission: How Christianity Became a World Religion* (Oxford: Wiley-Blackwell, 2009), 41–52, 56–57.
43. It should be said that political and religious interests were not always as cooperative as the above comment makes it out to seem. They were frequently muddled and blurred and often in conflict. Cf. Section 3.2; Robert, *Christian Mission*, 48; and Tibawi, *British Interests*, 122–48.

coupled with an intense sense of civic responsibility, and this manifested itself in social concern . . . and missionary zeal. The appearance of non-denominational missionary societies across Europe was a new phenomenon, and this activity led to an unprecedented expansion of missionary influence around the globe, the fast new communications systems and existing or developing colonial structures facilitating such movements and their support.[44]

While it is true that the presence of Protestant missionary societies and religious institutions in Palestine would have been unthinkable without the reality of both Western political prowess and growing religious earnestness, the aforementioned religious realities deserve particular attention, for they help explain the basic motivation of Protestant missionary interest at the time.[45]

In general, "the two poles that essentially spurred the worldwide missions effort of the 19th century were gratitude for what was experienced as a free salvation on the one hand, and on the other the dominical command to spread the word of this salvation 'to the uttermost parts of the earth' (Acts 1:8; cf. Matt 28:18-20).'"[46] This also provided the ground and motivation for much of British and German Protestant missionary work in Palestine.[47] Although it

---

44. Marten, *Attempting to Bring the Gospel Home*, 4.
45. This is not to deny Michael Marten's contention that "[m]ission history needs to be a dialectic: whilst the missionaries may have had, in their own perspective, altruistic or 'heavenly' aims, their actions were very much 'earthly' ones, intrinsically connected to the world around them: the world they came from (in the case of this study, a major imperial power) and the world they were going to (here: Palestine, an Ottoman-controlled territory)." Ibid., 2.
46. David A. Dorman, "The Artillery of Ideology: A Critique of Ussama Makdisi's *The Artillery of Heaven*. A Review Essay," *NEST Theological Review* 30:2 (November 2009): 233–34.
47. Cf. Marten, *Attempting to Bring the Gospel Home*, 4. With regard to German missionary work, Siegfried Hanselmann writes: "Like the modern missionary movement of the Protestant Church in general, the German Protestant mission in Palestine is closely related to the Revivalist movement. It is true that it was rather late in leading to practical steps in the Palestine mission. Elsewhere at that time it was possible to look back at a century of mission history. Nevertheless, it would be wrong to conclude that the Awakening had no interest in missionizing the Holy Land. On the contrary, it can be shown that the roots of the [German Protestant] mission in Palestine are to be found in Revivalist Christianity." (*Wie die neuzeitliche Mission der evangelischen Kirche allgemein, so steht auch die deutsche evangelische Palästinamission in engem Zusammenhang mit der Erweckungsbewegung. Es ist zwar erst spät zu praktischen Schritten in der*

manifested itself differently among Jews, Christians, and Muslims, the underlying principle for all Protestant missionary work was the same. Everyone in Palestine was "fair game"; everyone fell under the umbrella of Christ's commission to "make disciples of all nations" (Matt 28:18-20). Therefore some sought to evangelize the Jews, others labored to "revive" the Christians in the land, and although it was technically illegal to try to convert Muslims, missionaries also hoped that, in the renewal of Eastern Christians, Muslims might convert with greater ease.[48]

The Protestant Missionary Societies and Institutions in Palestine Before 1917

The first Protestant missionaries in Palestine were Pliny Fisk and Levi Parsons. Commissioned by the American Board of Commissioners for Foreign Missions (ABCFM)[49] in 1819, Fisk and Parsons traveled to Palestine and established a mission there in 1821. It lasted until 1844, when, due to hardships and lack of tangible results, the mission withdrew from Palestine and concentrated its efforts in Lebanon and Syria.[50] Although the efforts of the ABCFM in Palestine did

---

Palästinamission gekommen. Andernorts konnte man um die gleiche Zeit schon auf eine hundertjährige Missionsgeschichte zurückschauen. Doch wäre es falsch, daraus zu schliessen, die Erweckung habe kein Interesse an einer Mission im Heiligen Land gehabt. Im Gegenteil, es lässt sich zeigen, dass gerade im Erweckungschristentum die Wurzeln der Palästinamission liegen.) Siegfried Hanselmann. *Deutsche Evangelische Palästinamission: Handbuch ihrer Motive, Geschichte und Ergebnisse*, ET 14 (Neuendettelsau: Verlag der Evangelisch-Lutherische Mission Erlangen, 1971), 13. As for British missionary work, "The Evangelical Revival represents a sharp discontinuity in the Protestant Tradition . . . . The old polemical divinity, with its metaphysical distinctions and ecclesiastical preoccupations, faded away before the preaching of a simple gospel." David Bebbington, *Evangelicalism in Modern Britain: A History from the 1730's to the 1980's* (London: Unwin Hyman, 1989), 47.

48. Julius Richter, *A History of Protestant Missions in the Near East* (Edinburgh: Oliphant, Anderson & Ferrier, 1910), 11.
49. The ABCFM was established in 1810. For a history of the mission before 1917 see Rufus Anderson, *History of the Missions of the ABCFM to the Oriental Churches*, 2 vols. (Boston: Congregational Publishing Society, 1872).
50. Cf. Abdul L. Tibawi, *American Interests in Syria, 1800–1901: A Study of Educational, Literary, and Religious Work* (Oxford: Clarendon Press, 1966). Among the most notable achievements was

not go unnoticed, British and German-speaking missionaries would establish a more permanent presence in Palestine and be responsible for the birth of a native Palestinian Protestant community.[51] The following will survey some of their key missionary societies and institutions.

British Missions and Institutions

The Church Missionary Society (CMS) was not the only British missionary society or religious institution in Palestine before 1917.[52] The London Society for Promoting Christianity amongst the Jews (LSPCJ or LJS)[53] and the Protestant Bishopric in Jerusalem,[54] which was originally a joint venture between the Church of England and the United Evangelical Church in Prussia, were also prominent in Palestine. These organizations represented a variety of interests and "often conflicting agendas."[55] As Thomas Hummel explains,

> The London Society for Promoting Christianity amongst the Jews (LJS) was interested primarily in the spiritual welfare (conversion) and physical condition (health and income) of the Jewish population. The

---

the creation of the "Smith-Van Dyck Version," the first Arabic version of the Bible in nearly 200 years. John Alexander Thompson, *The Major Arabic Bibles: Their Origin and Nature* (New York: American Bible Society, 1956).

51. On the efforts and influence of American missionaries, Julius Richter comments, Bishop Samuel Gobat "reaped" where the Americans had "sown." Richter, *History of Protestant Missions*, 236.
52. It is true that the CMS had its origins in Great Britain. Nevertheless, it recruited many of its missionaries from Europe, most notably the Basel seminary. Tibawi notes this reality with a tinge of cynicism as he comments on the quality of British missionaries. Tibawi, *British Interests*, 18.
53. The LJS, or LSPCJ as it was originally called, was established in 1809 and sent out Lewis Way and John Nicolayson as its first missionaries to Palestine in 1822. For an overview of the history of the LJS see Kelvin Crombie, *For the Love of Zion* (London: Hodder & Stoughton, 1991); W. T. Gidney, *The History of the LSPCJ* (London: LSPCJ, 1908); and Yaron Perry, *British Mission to the Jews in Nineteenth-Century Palestine* (London: Frank Cass, 2003).
54. Cf. "Protestant Bishopric in Jerusalem," in chap. 3 below.
55. Thomas Hummel, "Between Eastern and Western Christendom: The Anglican Presence in Jerusalem," 147–70 in *The Christian Communities of Jerusalem and the Holy Land: Studies in the History, Religion and Politics*, ed. Anthony O'Mahony (Cardiff: University of Wales Press, 2003), at 147.

bishop, especially the second, Samuel Gobat, became more focused on the spiritual, intellectual and physical wellbeing of the native Christians, and with the help of the Church Missionary Society (CMS) began schools, clinics and, most controversially, native Protestant churches.[56]

In the end it was the work of the CMS and the Protestant bishopric that were largely responsible for the formation of an indigenous community of Anglicans in Palestine. They will be the focus of the following two sections.

The CMS was founded in London on April 12, 1799.[57] Its work in Palestine before 1917 developed in roughly four stages. It started in Malta in 1811(15), became a bona fide presence in Palestine in 1851, ordained its first Palestinian Protestant clergy in 1874, and helped coordinate the establishment of the Palestine Native Church Council (PNCC) in 1905. Cleardo Naudi is often cited as the individual responsible for the start of the work of the CMS in Malta. "Two English friends of the Society," as Eugene Stock describes them, happened to make the acquaintance of the Catholic doctor in their travels through Malta in 1811.[58] Disheartened by the state of the Catholic Church and by the dissolution of the *Propaganda Fide*[59] following Napoleon's occupation of Rome, Naudi found solace in the prospect of renewed missionary work in Palestine through the CMS.[60] He implored the "friends of the Society," saying: "It now,

---

56. Hummel, "Between Eastern and Western Christendom," 147.
57. For a history of the CMS see Eugene Stock, *The History of the Christian Missionary Society*, 4 vols. (London: CMS, 1899–1916).
58. Ibid., 1: 222.
59. *Sacra Congregatio de Propaganda Fide* means the Sacred Congregation for the Propagation of the Faith. It was renamed in 1982 by Pope John Paul II and is now called *Congregatio pro Gentium Evangelisatione* or The Congregation for the Evangelization of the Peoples. It is the main branch of the Catholic Church responsible for overseeing its worldwide mission work.
60. Thomas Stransky details the dire state of the Catholic Church at the time and the effects Napoleon had on Catholic missions. "Pope Clement XIV's suppression of the Jesuits in 1773, the religious paralysis caused by the French Revolution, the attempts of Napoleon to establish a French church independent of Rome, and the secularized dissolution of religious communities in most of Europe etched a most gloomy picture. When Napoleon's General Miollis occupied

therefore ... devolves upon you to enter on this labour of propagating the Christian Faith among Infidels, and of confirming it among the Ignorant."[61] As a result of these interactions and the ensuing correspondence between Naudi and the CMS, William Jowett was sent to Malta in 1815 as the CMS's first missionary in the area.

Jowett's work set the stage and tone for future CMS work.[62] Among other things, he established a printing press in Malta and published his views on "the state of religion on the shores of the Mediterranean" and the "best methods of 'propagating Christian knowledge.'"[63] According to Jowett, Christians, Jews, and Muslims were all, in varying degrees, in a degenerate state.[64] He argued that the best way of changing this situation was through the distribution of Bibles and through education. As Tibawi summarizes:

> Christian education was deemed to be the sure way to the hearts and minds of the people. But Jowett knew only too well that any education combined with Christian instruction would not be tolerated by the Turkish authorities if it were offered to Muslim children. Hence, he suggested the education of the children of Eastern Christians, for they,

---

Rome in 1808, he was ordered to seize the finances, properties, and archives of the Vatican Congregation for the Propagation of the Faith (*Propaganda Fide*). Thus, the French in effect dissolved the central organ for Catholic worldwide missions activity." Thomas Stransky, "Origins of Western Christian Missions," 137–54 in *Jerusalem in the Mind of the Western World, 1800–1948*, ed. Yehoshua Ben-Arieh and Moshe Davis; vol. 5 of *With Eyes toward Zion* (London: Praeger, 1997), at 138.

61. Stock, *CMS*, 1: 223.
62. Samuel Gobat himself worked for a period of time in Malta as a CMS missionary and, as will be seen later, resonated with many of the views propagated by Jowett.
63. Stock, *CMS*, 1: 224. Jowett's work was published in the following volumes: William Jowett, *Christian Researches in the Mediterranean, from 1815 to 1820: In Furtherance of the Objects of the Church Missionary Society* (London: Seeley, 1822); idem, *Christian Researches in Syria and the Holy Land, in 1823 and 1824: In Furtherance of the Objects of the Church Missionary Society* (London: Seeley, 1826). For a brief overview of Jowett's work see Tibawi, *British Interests*, 21–26.
64. Of particular importance is Jowett's view of Eastern Christians. He argued that there are four principal types of Christians: the superstitious, the hypocritical, the covert infidel, and the sincere inquirer. Each class of Christian carries symptoms of "degeneracy" and is in dire need of "revival." Jowett, *Christian Researches in the Mediterranean*, 3–9.

in God's time, would be so imbued with the pure form of Christianity that they would resume the duty, abandoned by their fathers for centuries, of converting the Muslims. This view may seem fanciful, but it proved in fact to be the basis on which a great deal of the future thought and practice of the C.M.S. rested. It was one of the main excuses for embarking on missionary work—and in consequence proselytism—among Eastern Christians.[65]

The end result, therefore, was that the CMS focused its efforts on the "renewal" of Eastern Christians as the primary means of influencing the non-Christian population of the region.[66]

Despite their grand aspirations and determined efforts, however, the CMS failed to see "Oriental Christendom . . . quickened into fresh life by the Christendom of the West."[67] When the English and Prussians established their joint Protestant bishopric in Jerusalem in 1841 the CMS still had "no work in Palestine,"[68] and when the *CMS* celebrated is fiftieth anniversary in 1849 its "Jubilee Statement" lamented the fact that they had not fulfilled their "first hopes and expectations" and therefore had no plans of reviving the work.[69] However, the CMS did renew its work and became a bona fide presence in Palestine when Samuel Gobat, the second Protestant bishop in Jerusalem and former CMS missionary, sent an appeal

---

65. Tibawi, *British Interests*, 23.
66. As Tibawi rightly recognizes, this was a significant change in policy from that established in the CMS's initial "resolutions." Tibawi, *British Interests*, 20.
67. Stock, *CMS*, 1: 231. Stock retails that the CMS had a possible breakthrough with two individuals: the Archbishop of Jerusalem of the Syrian Jacobite Church and the Patriarch of Constantinople. The Syrian Jacobite Archbishop sought an audience with CMS in London after a failed attempt in Rome and Paris to have scriptures translated into the vernacular (Arabic with Syrian script). There is no name mentioned, and then there is this curious statement by Stock: "The Archbishop was taken leave of at a large public meeting at Freemason's Hall. . . ." In addition, and probably more detrimental to the work of the CMS with the Eastern churches, the Patriarch of Constantinople, who had supported both Bible translation and distribution, was murdered on May 6, 1821 by a "Turkish mob" while conducting a service. Stock, *CMS*, 1: 229–31.
68. Ibid., 1: 422.
69. Stock, *CMS*, 2: 140

to the CMS for help in working with Eastern Christians and the burgeoning Palestinian Protestant community.[70]

The CMS's work in Palestine was not without controversy. Along with Samuel Gobat, the CMS was hard-pressed to defend itself against the allegation of proselytizing the established churches in the Ottoman Empire. They claimed that their motivation to work among the established churches in Palestine was neither underhanded nor intentionally divisive. They argued:

> It has *never* been the object . . . to form among these Oriental Christians congregations according to the model of the Church of England, as in heathen countries: our object has been by journeys, by press, and by education, to disseminate the knowledge of Scriptural truth throughout the country, in order, by God's grace, to raise the tone of Christian doctrine and practice.[71]

Despite the best intentions, however, Protestant congregations were still established out of former Catholic and Orthodox adherents, and in the course of time some of the Palestinian converts began to serve alongside CMS missionaries. By 1874 three Palestinian Christians had been ordained by the Church of England: Seraphim Boutaji (1871), Michael Kawar (1871), and Chalil Jamal (1874).[72] This trend continued into the twentieth century to such an extent that the Palestine Native Church Council (PNCC) was established in 1905 in order take into consideration the increased role and desired administrative autonomy and responsibility of the local Christian community and its clergy.[73]

---

70. Stock notes, "Gobat found that the distribution through so many years of the Scriptures and Christian tracts (chiefly from the old C.M.S. Press at Malta) had produced its effect, and a good many members of the Eastern Churches were seeking more light. Naturally, therefore, his heart and his energies turned also in their direction; and he appealed to his old Society to come to his help." Ibid., 2: 142.
71. Ibid., 2:144. Emphasis added.
72. Stock, *CMS*, 3: 115.

Protestant Bishopric in Jerusalem

The following section will outline the background to the establishment of the Protestant bishopric in Jerusalem and briefly detail the tenure of the following bishops:

1. Michael Solomon Alexander (1841–1845)
2. Samuel Gobat (1846–1879)
3. Joseph Barclay (1879–1881)
   Vacancy and Restructuring   (1881–1887)
4. George F. P. Blyth (1887–1914)

The principal agents behind the formation of the Protestant Bishopric in Jerusalem were the Seventh Earl of Shaftesbury (1801–1885) and King Frederick William IV of Prussia (1795–1861).[74] Shaftesbury, or Lord Anthony Ashley Cooper as he was also known, was an English MP and a prominent Anglican layman who, along with many other "evangelical Anglicans" at the time, "connected the return of the Jews to Palestine and their conversion to Christianity with the fulfillment of biblical prophecy and the second coming of Christ."[75] He was also one of the first British individuals to argue for some sort of official Anglican representation in Palestine. He wrote in 1839:

---

73. The development and workings of the PNCC will be discussed in greater detail in the next chapter.
74. As Tibawi notes, both were moved by "deep religious motives" and "took advantage of the changed political situation in Syria." Tibawi, *British Interests*, 44–45. With the end of the Syrian War of 1839–1840 and the subsequent signing of a treaty between the Ottoman Empire and Britain, Prussia, Austria, and Russia, Europe's opportunity to influence the political and religious landscape of the Ottoman Empire undoubtedly grew.
75. Lester Pittman, "The Formation of the Episcopal Diocese of Jerusalem 1841–1948: Anglican, Indigenous and Ecumenical," 85–104 in *Patterns of the Past, Prospects for the Future*, at 87. See also Anthony Ashley Cooper, "State Prospects of the Jews," *Quarterly Review* 63 (January 1839): 166–92.

It is well known that for centuries the Greek, the Romanist, the Armenian, and the Turk have had their places of worship in the city of Jerusalem, and the latitudinarianism of Ibrahim Pasha had lately accorded that privilege to the Jews. The pure doctrines of the Reformation, as embodied and professed in the Church of England, have alone been unrepresented amidst all these corruptions; and Christianity has been contemplated both by Mussulman and Jew, as a system most hateful to the creed of each, a compound of mummery and image-worship.[76]

King Frederick William IV was also interested in an official Protestant presence in Jerusalem, albeit in a more ecumenical form than envisioned by Shaftesbury, who, as we have seen, believed the "pure doctrines of the Reformation" were "embodied and professed" solely in the Church of England. Following the Syrian War of 1839–1840, King Frederick inquired of the British government, the Archbishop of Canterbury, and the Bishop of London through his personal envoy in the court of Queen Victoria, Christian Charles von Bunsen (1791–1860), how protection "should be afforded to the subjects of both powers in the Turkish dominions, without distinction of creed" and "how far the Church of England, which is already possessed of a minister's residence on Mount Zion, and has begun to build a church on the spot, would be inclined to grant the Evangelical National Church of Prussia rank, as a sister-Church, in the Holy Land."[77] As a premise, King Frederick William IV indicated his conviction that

"Protestant Christianity can entertain no hope of enjoying full and permanent recognition in the East, and especially in the Holy Land, or of reaping any blessed and lasting fruits from its labours

---

76. Edwin Hodder, *The Life and Work of the Seventh Earl of Shaftesbury*, 3 vols. (London: Cassell, 1886), 1: 240. Later that year Shaftesbury wrote in his diary, "Could we not erect a Protestant Bishopric at Jerusalem, and give him jurisdiction over all the Levant, Malta, and whatever chaplaincies there might be on the coast of Africa?" Ibid., 1: 235.
77. William Hechler, *The Jerusalem Bishopric*, 2 parts (London: Trübneck, 1883), 2: 2.

or its diffusion, unless it exhibits itself, to the utmost possible extent, as a *united body* in those countries."[78] He argued that utmost care must be taken to maintain "the *greatest unity of action* on the part of both Churches throughout the Turkish dominions, and in the Holy Land more particularly,"[79] and, in an unprecedented gesture of ecumenical spirit, promised that if "the Church of England should institute a Bishopric in Jerusalem," then "one or more of the clergy and missionaries of Prussia should connect themselves with this episcopal foundation."[80] With rather uncharacteristic speed, Britain and Prussia reached an agreement.[81] Five months after Frederick William IV made his initial inquiry in June 1841, Michael Solomon Alexander was consecrated as the first Protestant bishop of Jerusalem (November 7, 1841), and two months later, in January 1842, Alexander set sail for Jerusalem in the British steam frigate *Devastation*.[82]

Michael Solomon Alexander (1799–1845) was a Jewish convert, former missionary with the LJS and Professor of Hebrew and Jewish Studies at King's College in London.[83] Many saw his induction as

---

78. Ibid., 2: 4.
79. Ibid., 2: 16.
80. Ibid., 2: 16, 18. Frederick William IV was also quick to add that this "united body" should not repress the identity of either of the national churches and that the "independence" and "individuality of the German people" was to be protected.
81. The agreement stipulated that "the two sides would rotate nominating the bishop of Jerusalem, with the provision that the Archbishop of Canterbury would have the right to veto and the consecrated bishop would be under his jurisdiction." Rafiq Farah, "Evangelical Missions and Churches in the Middle East: Palestine and Jordan," 727–34 in *Christianity: A History in the Middle East*, ed. Habib Badr (Beirut: MECC, 2005), at 728. The plan, however, was not without controversy and was strongly resisted in both Prussia and Great Britain. Cf. Martin Lückhoff, "Prussia and Jerusalem: Political and Religious Controversies Surrounding the Foundation of the Jerusalem Bishopric," 173–82 in *Jerusalem in the Mind of the Western World, 1800–1948*, at 176; John Henry Newman, *Apologia Pro Vita Sua* (London: Routledge, 1907), 162; Tibawi, *British Interests*, 47.
82. The original ship offered to Alexander was the steam frigate *Infernal*. Alexander "objected to travelling on a vessel bearing such a name." Ironically, he seems to have boarded the *Devastation*, which was definitely "not much better," without any misgivings. Tibawi, *British Interests*, 50–51.

the first Protestant bishop in Jerusalem as a restoration of the ancient Episcopate of St. James. Shaftesbury, for one, rejoiced on the occasion of Alexander's first sermon and benediction that this was "'the first Episcopal benediction that had fallen from Hebrew lips for seventeen hundred years'—that is to say, the first since Jude, the last of the sons of Abraham mentioned in Eusebius, occupied the Episcopal See in the Holy City."[84] Moreover, the induction kindled the hopes of many that Alexander was the first fruits of a future harvest of Jewish converts to Christianity. The *Church of England Quarterly Review* pronounced: "A bishop of the Hebrew race and a Bishop of Jerusalem, cannot but excite attention among the Jews, and if it lead to nothing farther than provoking to jealousy, in the first instance, even this is preparation for another step, whether that be their gathering into the Christian Church, or reinstating them in that land which was so often promised to their fathers."[85]

Alexander's presence and work certainly drew the attention of the Jews in Palestine, although not in the way he might have hoped.[86] He established educational, industrial, and medical services, but inroads into the Jewish community were hard to make, and conversions were few.[87] Moreover,

---

83. Michael Solomon Alexander was born to an English Jewish family living in Schönlanke, Prussia on May 1, 1799. His father was a rabbi, and he later followed in his footsteps in England. While serving as a rabbi and teacher of Talmud and the German language in Norwich he converted to Christianity. Shortly after, he was ordained a deacon in the Church of England and later joined the LJS to serve as a missionary to the Jews in Danzig. After three years he returned to London and became a professor of Hebrew and Jewish Studies at King's College, Cambridge. It was from this post that he was selected to become the first Protestant bishop in Jerusalem.
84. Hodder, *Life and Work of the Seventh Earl of Shaftesbury*, 1: 379.
85. Crombie, *For the Love of Zion*, 48.
86. For an overview of Alexander's tenure as bishop and his work with the Jewish community in Palestine see Rafiq Farah, *In Troubled Waters: A History of the Anglican Church in Jerusalem, 1841–1998* (Leicester: Christians Aware, 2002), 24–31; Gidney, *History of the LSPCJ*, 232–45; and Tibawi, *British Interests*, 61–64.
87. Among other things Alexander set up the Hebrew College in 1842 and a vocational school for Jewish converts.

All members of the Jewish community were ordered to keep away from the members of Alexander's mission, to avoid at all costs using the facilities of the missionary medical service, to destroy any missionary literature that might have been received by the unheedy among them, and to accept no employment by missionaries or to supply food to them. The penalty for disobedience was total ostracism, religious, social and legal.[88]

Despite the challenges and opposition he faced, Alexander's work among the Jews was heralded as a success, not least by the thirty-one Jewish converts who lamented his passing in 1845, saying: "He was a burning and a shining light; and when he was raised to the highest dignity in the Church, he conferred the most conspicuous honour on our whole nation, but especially on the little band of Jewish believers. With him captive Judah's brightest earthly star has set, and the top stone has been taken away from the rising Hebrew Church."[89]

Samuel Gobat (1799–1879) was the next Protestant bishop of Jerusalem and, in contrast to Alexander, who "sought the spiritual and temporal benefit of the children of Israel," focused on the "spiritual benefit of the ignorant and depraved natives of all denominations."[90] The end result of these efforts was the birth of an indigenous Protestant church in Palestine. This naturally led Gobat into conflict with the Catholic and Orthodox churches in Palestine, as well as with individuals in England and Prussia who thought that he transgressed the statutes prescribed in his Letter Commendatory.[91] The Orthodox and Catholic churches often complained and sometimes even

---

88. Tibawi, *British Interests*, 64. It is interesting to note that "Jewish opposition to his work led Moses Montefiori to donate 4000 Pounds Sterling to build a Jewish hospital in Jerusalem." Farah, *Troubled Waters*, 31.
89. Gidney, *History of the LSPCJ*, 241.
90. Samuel Gobat, *Samuel Gobat, Bishop of Jerusalem: His Life and Work* (London: James Nisbet, 1884), 215–16. Samuel Gobat was born on January 26, 1799, in Crémines, Switzerland. He grew up in the Reformed Church of Switzerland and attended the famous Basel Seminary, St. Chrischona. He read Arabic in Paris and was ordained in the United Church of the Grand Duchy of Baden. In 1825 he moved to England to work with the CMS, with whom he later served as a missionary in Malta and Abyssinia.

resorted to mob violence against Gobat's work and the growing Protestant presence in Palestine.⁹² In England and Prussia, Gobat also met with a torrent of displeasure. In England, for instance, an "official" memorial was issued against him by over one thousand English priests and sent to the Eastern Churches in Palestine.⁹³ Despite all the opposition Gobat faced, he persisted in his work as bishop, facilitated the proliferation of English and German-speaking missionary societies and religious institutions in Palestine, and helped make possible a Palestinian Protestant Church.⁹⁴

91. The charge of proselytism was and still is levied against Gobat, who seems clearly to have gone against the limits prescribed by the Letter Commendatory. Tibawi, for instance (*British Interests*, 92), claims that Gobat engaged in an explicit strategy to proselytize the Eastern Churches. He says, "His tactics were simple: he first engaged from those round him what he called 'native Bible readers' and instructed them to encourage 'a spirit of enquiry among those willing to hear readings from the Holy Book; then he encouraged prospective teachers to invite their influential kinsmen to call on the Bishop asking him to open schools for their children." Hummel ("Between Eastern and Western Christendom," 154) contends: "He [Bishop Gobat], like most of the other Protestants, believed the Orthodox and Catholic churches to be in the grip of superstition, and that what was needed was the liberating effects of hearing the gospel pure and unencumbered. . . . Gobat probably believed that to encourage the reading of the Bible would elicit a reformation of the eastern churches—that he would not need to convert Christians because the eastern churches would reform themselves in the face of the self-evident nature of the biblical message." Perhaps the best way to resolve the matter is to hear Gobat's defense. In a letter to King Frederick William IV he wrote: "And now what am I to do? I have never wished to make converts from the old Churches, but only to lead to the Lord and to the knowledge of His truth as many as possible. From henceforth I shall be obliged to receive into our communion such as are excluded for Bible-truth's sake from other Churches; and I trust that in doing so, even though men should blame me for it, the Lord will grant His blessing." Gobat, *Samuel Gobat, Bishop of Jerusalem: His Life and Work*, 263–65.
92. Cf. Tibawi, *British Interests*, 95, 108; Van der Leest, *Conversion and Conflict in Palestine*, 150, 211–36.
93. 'Official' is in quotes not because the memorial was unauthentic, for over 1000 English priests, who were affiliated with the Oxford Movement or otherwise known as Tractarians, *did* sign it and *did* send it to the Eastern Churches. 'Official' is in quotes because the memorial was sent without the expressed sanction of the four Archbishops of the Church of England and Ireland at the time. The said Archbishops eventually backed Gobat and sent their own letter to the Eastern Churches saying, "The said memorial does not in any manner emanate from the said Church, or from persons authorized by that Church to pronounce decisions." Stock, *CMS*, 2:146.
94. Regarding the German missionary presence in Palestine, Mitri Raheb writes, "As long as Alexander was Bishop of Jerusalem there were scarcely any German missionaries belonging to a German missionary society. The first (which were the *Chrischona-Brüder*) didn't come to Palestine until after 1846, that is, not until after Gobat was appointed Bishop. Therefore one can justifiably say that Gobat was the '*Wegbereiter*' (or pioneer) of the German Protestant

Joseph Barclay (1831–1881) was consecrated as the third Bishop of Jerusalem two months after the death of his predecessor in 1879.[95] As Hummel points out, "It was an appointment to highlight a concern for the founding goals of the mission, which had been underemphasized during Gobat's tenure."[96] Barclay had been an LJS missionary and the head of the LJS in Jerusalem (1856–1870). He was well acquainted with life and ministry in Palestine and was returning to the welcome of many friends and acquaintances.[97] Unfortunately, Barclay encountered a number of insurmountable hurdles that were not of his making. The LJS and CMS had begun to function independently of the bishop, which naturally prevented him from providing any ecclesial oversight, direction, and reorganization. Furthermore, Protestants in Palestine were divided on "linguistic and national lines," and Barclay was left overseeing a small British expatriate and Hebrew Christian community.[98] He did recommend that the Protestant bishopric be reviewed and reorganized, and he

---

mission in Palestine. But he was more than just a '*Wegbereiter.*' It was he who requested that Fliedner send some deaconesses and who asked of the *Jerusalemsverein* whether they were ready to take over the mission station in Bethlehem. Probably Gobat was also behind Schneller's mission in Palestine. Thus all these institutions owe their origins to Bishop Gobat." ("*Solange Alexander Bischof in Jerusalem war, gab es dort fast keine deutschen Missionare, die zu einer deutschen Missionsgesellschaft gehörten. Die ersten (es waren Chrischona-Brüder) kamen erst nach 1846 nach Palästina, also nachdem Gobat zum Bischof ernannt war. Somit gilt Gobat mit Recht als der 'Wegbereiter' der deutsch-evangelischen Palästinamission. Aber er war mehr als nur ein Wegbereiter. War er es doch, der Fliedner um die Sendung einiger Diakonissen bat und der bei dem Jerusalemsverein anfragte, ob dieser bereit sei, die 'Station Bethlehem' zu übernehmen. Vermutlich stand er darüber hinaus auch hinter der Sendung Schnellers nach Palästina. Somit verdanken alle diese Anstalten ihre Enstehung Bischof Gobat.*") Mitri Raheb, *Das reformatorische Erbe unter den Palästinensern: Zur Entstehung der Evangelisch-Lutherischen Kirche in Jordanien* (Gütersloh: Gerd Mohn, 1990), 56–57. Rafiq Farah (*In Troubled Waters*, 32) underscores Gobat's role in the birth of a Palestinian Protestant Church by describing his tenure as bishop as "The Creation of Nuclei of Arab Congregations."

95. Joseph Barclay was born on August 12, 1831 in County Tyrone, Ireland. He was ordained a deacon in the Church of Ireland in 1854. In 1855 he was ordained priest and then began serving as a missionary with the LJS.
96. Hummel, "Between Eastern and Western Christendom," 156.
97. Farah notes that the Greek Orthodox Patriarch went down to Jaffa to welcome Barclay in person as "they were great friends before." Farah, *In Troubled Waters*, 47.
98. Tibawi, *British Interests*, 215.

requested that the salaries of Palestinian clergy be increased.[99] However, Barclay's proposals were not heeded, and his tenure as a bishop ended after just two years.[100]

The premature death of Joseph Barclay in 1881 afforded the relevant parties associated with the bishopric an opportunity to voice their opinions and express their dissatisfaction with the existing structure of the Protestant Bishopric. Only the members of the LJS and CMS were keen for it to continue. The High Church Party in the Church of England wanted an end to the entire project, and the German government and clergy showed little interest in continuing their relationship with the bishopric unless the following points of concern were addressed:

> The first of these two points concerns the right to veto reserved to the Archbishop of Canterbury, relative to the nomination of a bishop by the Prussian Crown, whereby His Majesty is placed in a position towards the English Archbishop which does not conform to their relative stations. The second point concerns the question whether the bishop nominated by the Prussian Government if he belongs to a German-Evangelical church besides the Episcopal consecration is to submit also to a re-ordination by the Anglican Church and to subscribe to the 39 Articles thereof.[101]

The line in the sand was drawn, and neither the Archbishop, the German Crown Prince, nor their clergy would concede. Finally, in 1886, Kaiser William I nullified the agreements with the Anglican Church and the joint Protestant Bishopric between the Anglican and Prussian churches in Jerusalem was at an end.[102]

---

99. In Farah, *In Troubled Waters*, 50.
100. Martin Lückhoff describes the episcopate of Joseph Barclay as merely an "epilogue" in comparison "to the effectiveness of Gobat, which spanned more than three decades.... Barclay was clearly unable to make his own mark." Lückhoff, *Anglikaner und Protestanten im Heiligen Land: Das gemeinsame Bistum Jerusalem, 1841–1886* (Wiesbaden: Harrassowitz, 1998), 306.
101. Quoted in Farah, *In Troubled Waters*, 61.
102. There were additional reasons the German clergy were hesitant to continue their association with the bishopric. "The German parishes, which had been increasing in numbers, were

The Anglican Church, however, reconstituted the bishopric in 1887 with the important proviso that "to make English proselytes of the members of those (i.e., Eastern) Churches . . . is not after the spirit or usage of the foundation."[103] Furthermore, the bishop would no longer be called the "Bishop *of* Jerusalem" but the "Bishop *in* Jerusalem" in order to underscore both the ecumenical spirit of the reconstituted bishopric and the fact the bishop would have "no territorial jurisdiction."[104] This was an important shift in the ethos of the bishopric. The new Anglican bishopric had "matured"[105] and carried with it a "new spirit."[106] It only remained to find someone who fit the ethos of the newly reconstituted Anglican bishopric in Jerusalem.

George Blyth (1887–1914) was "sufficiently high church in the noblest way to be trusted to reverence other churches and put his foot on proselytism . . . and sufficiently Evangelical."[107] Blyth had significant overseas experience and was sympathetic to the work of missionary societies. Nevertheless, he quickly found himself at loggerheads with both the CMS and the LJS. When Blyth claimed the right as bishop to oversee and direct the local CMS proceedings as his predecessors had done, it did not sit well with them. They categorically refused.[108] As a result, Blyth was left with no way to

gaining self-sufficiency with the help of the emerging German institutions. Above all, the nationalization of the German presence in Palestine fostered their separation and independence. This development can be seen in the visit of the Prussian crown prince in 1869 and the foundation of the German empire." Lückhoff, *Anglikaner und Protestanten im Heiligen Land*, 306.
103. In Arthur Christopher Benson, *The Life of Edward White Benson: Sometime Archbishop of Canterbury*, 2 vols. (London: MacMillan, 1899), 2: 166.
104. Ibid. Emphasis added.
105. Tibawi entitles the chapter on the new bishopric "Maturity." Tibawi, *British Interests*, 206–35.
106. Hummel, "Between Eastern and Western Christendom," 157.
107. Tibawi, *British Interests*, 222. George F. P. Blyth was born in Yorkshire on April 25, 1832. He studied at Lincoln College, Oxford, where he received a doctorate in theology. In 1856 he was ordained priest. He served as a military chaplain in India as well as in Fort William, Scotland. From 1879 to 1886 he was Archdeacon in Burma. Blyth was home in London on furlough in 1886 when Archbishop Benson approached him to consider becoming bishop of the newly reconstituted bishopric in Jerusalem.

oversee or control the work of the CMS.[109] He also wanted to bring the LJS under the umbrella of the bishop's jurisdiction. This was met initially with little resistance, but when Blyth revealed his plan to turn Christ Church into a collegiate church with a dean and canons the LJS adamantly refused.[110] As a result of his conflict with the CMS and the LJS Blyth was left with no congregations or missionary societies at his disposal, and he was forced to find his own premises to build what would become St. George's Cathedral. Blyth would not be deterred, however. He started the Jerusalem Bishopric Fund, which later became the Jerusalem and East Mission (JEM) in 1896, in order to build the cathedral and create his own ecumenical and missionary institutions. It was through the JEM that Blyth expanded the work of the Anglican bishopric in Jerusalem until his death in 1914.

German Missions and Institutions

Jakob Eisler writes that "the origin of German missionary activity in Palestine is closely associated with the work of Christian Friedrich Spittler."[111] It is true that Spittler (1782–1867) influenced a large number of missionaries and clergy in Palestine, including Samuel Gobat and Johann Ludwig Schneller. He was the secretary general of the Deutsche Christentumgesellschaft (German Christian Association, 1780) as well as the founder of the Basler Missionsgesellschaft (Basel Missionary Society, 1815) and St.

---

108. As a former CMS missionary, Gobat was obviously accommodating to the independence and work of the CMS. It was feared, however, that Bishop Blyth would show no such leeway and support.
109. It must be noted that the splintering of the Anglican work in Jerusalem was not all Blyth's fault. He was right to challenge the double standard set by the CMS in claiming its independence while many of its missionaries were ordained in the Anglican Church. According to canon law the bishop should rightfully have had oversight of some of the CMS's members.
110. Crombie, *For the Love of Zion*, 126.
111. "*Der Ausgangspunkt der deutschen Missionstätigkeit in Palästina ist eng mit dem Wirken von Christian Friedrich Spittler verbunden.*" Author's translation. Jakob Eisler and Arno G. Krauss, *Nach Jerusalem müssen wir fahren* (Birsfelden: arteMedia 2002), 10.

Chrischona (Basel, 1840), an educational institution that trained missionaries and traveling craftsmen. He also set up the Pilgermissionsgesellschaft (1833/1840), a forerunner of the Jerusalemsverein (Berlin, 1851). Nevertheless, it is better to say that it is in the work of Spittler's pupils that the basis of German missionary activity is rooted, and in particular that of Gobat and Schneller. The following will therefore outline the various agencies that came into being through their influence and detail their development up to the year 1917.

Hanselmann properly refers to Gobat as the "Pioneer (*Wegbereiter*) of the German Protestant mission in Palestine."[112] During his tenure as the Protestant bishop of Jerusalem, he was responsible not only for the activities of the CMS in Palestine but also for the introduction of numerous German missionary societies and institutions. Following a fever epidemic in Palestine in 1850, Gobat asked Theodor Fliedner to send two deaconesses to Jerusalem.[113] They arrived the following year and established a small hospital on May 4, 1851; so the work of the Kaiserwerth Diakonissen in Palestine was born.[114] At the same time the deaconesses started a small school for girls that later became known as "Talitha Kumi."[115]

As Gobat continued to serve as the Protestant bishop of Jerusalem and more and more missionaries and institutions of German-speaking origin began springing up in Palestine, interest back in Germany likewise increased. It is on this basis that the

---

112. Hanselmann, *Deutsche Evangelische Palästinamission*, 61. Indeed, without Gobat, Protestantism in Palestine would be inconceivable or "*undenkbar*," as Raheb claims. Raheb, *Das reformatorische Erbe*, 58.
113. Gobat had met Theodore Fliedner, the founder of the "Kaiserwerth Deaconesses," in London in 1845 around the time of his consecration as bishop. Raheb, *Das reformatorische Erbe*, 59.
114. Ibid., 60. The house of the deaconesses also doubled as a "Protestant hospice for German pilgrims in the Holy Land." Frank Foerster, "German Missions in the Holy Land," 183–95 in *Jerusalem in the Mind of the Western World, 1800–1948*, at 189.
115. The school was initially connected with the Gobat school until 1868, when it became independent and took on the name "Talitha Kumi." Raheb, *Das reformatorische Erbe*, 60–61.

Jerusalemsverein was established in 1852. Friedrich Adolf Strauss, who had previously written a book called *Sinai und Golgatha*, which "called for the German people to become involved in the Holy Land . . . and lamented the loneliness of the German Protestants in the Levant who lacked the care of their home church in Germany," founded the Jerusalemsverein in Berlin in order to "support the German Protestant activities in Jerusalem."[116] In 1860 the Jerusalemsverein became more than just a "support" for German Protestant activities when it was commissioned by Gobat to take over the school and missionary station in Bethlehem, which had originally been run by the CMS.[117] As Foerster points out, "Now the Jerusalemsverein assumed two tasks: to support the German Protestant institutions and parishes in the Levant, and to provide leadership to the Arab Christians who were in contact with the German Protestant mission."[118] This they did, and when their work expanded to Beit Jala in 1879 they at the same time commissioned Bishara Canaan as its first Arab Evangelist.[119]

The other key institution established in the early years of German Protestant missionary work in Palestine was the Syrische Waisenhaus. Johann Ludwig Schneller had been sent by Spittler to Jerusalem in 1854, along with six others from St. Chrischona, to establish a Brüderhaus.[120] However, for financial reasons the Brüderhaus came to

---

116. Its opening statute declared: "Under the name Jerusalemsverein a society was established in Berlin to support, to enlarge, and to multiply the German Protestant institutions and undertakings such as the hospice (or pilgrims' guest house), the Deaconesses' House in Jerusalem, etc. which were established in the Holy Land as the result of the bishopric in Jerusalem." Foerster, "German Missions in the Holy Land," 188–89. Cf. Raheb, *Das reformatorische Erbe*, 79.

117. Raheb suggests that this was done as a "Gentlemen's Agreement" so the British and German missionaries would not compete with one another but serve in separate areas. Raheb, *Das reformatorische Erbe*, 81.

118. Foerster, "German Missions in the Holy Land," 190.

119. Raheb, *Das reformatorische Erbe*, 92–95.

120. Undoubtedly influenced by the work of Nikolaus Ludwig Graf von Zinzendorf in Herrnhut, Spittler remarked of establishing a Brüderhaus in Jerusalem: "My intention is this: to establish

naught, and Schneller split from the Basel mission.[121] He nevertheless stayed in Jerusalem, and shortly after the tragic events of 1860 in Lebanon he established the Syrische Waisenhaus.[122]

After the termination of the Protestant bishopric in Jerusalem in 1881 the German missionary societies and institutions were forced to restructure their presence in Palestine. In the end Carl Reinicke's suggestions won the day.[123] He proposed:

1. The immediate start of the construction of a church, "so that the German Protestant Church outside might look within the Holy Land and find just representation."
2. The German Protestant congregation in Jerusalem should establish a local council.
3. Third, to raise the office of the pastor of Jerusalem (or Jerusalem pastorate) to that of a Superintendent or *Propst*.[124]

---

a Brüderhaus in Jerusalem, as the Brethren Church was accustomed to begin its missions a century ago, so that the poor people there might see with their own eyes a living example of how true Christians live, pray and work together, treat their surroundings with love and try to help with word and deed. The first brothers must be truly pious and practical people...." (*Meine Absicht ist die: ein Brüderhaus, wie vor hundert Jahren die Brüdergemeinde ihre Missionen anzufangen gewohnt war, in Jerusalem zu errichten, damit die armen Leute dort an einem lebendigen Beispiel mit Augen sehen, wie wahre Christen untereinander leben, beten und arbeiten, ihre Umgebung mit Liebe behandeln und mit Rat und Tat ihnen zu helfen suchen. Die ersten Brüder müssen wahrhaftig fromme und brauchbare Leute sein...*) Friederich Veiel, *Der Pilgermission von St. Chrischona, 1840–1940* (Giessen: Brunnen, 1940), 57–58.

121. It was decided that the Brüderhaus was going to be turned into a hospital. Raheb, *Das reformatorische Erbe*, 65.
122. For an overview of Schneller and the Syrische Waisenhaus see Raheb, *Das reformatorische Erbe*, 62–77.
123. Carl Reinicke was the German Protestant pastor in Jerusalem from 1876 to 1884. Raheb, *Das reformatorische Erbe*, 106.
124. 1. *Die baldige Inangriffnahme des Baues einer Kirche, "damit der deutsche Protestantismus auch nach aussen hin im heilgen Lande eine würdige Repräsentation finde."*
   2. *Eine Gemeindevertretung für die deutsch-evangelische Gemeinde in Jerusalem ins Leben zu rufen.*
   3. *Drittens: Die Pfarrstelle Jerusalems zu einer Superintendentur bzw. Propstei zu erheben.*
   Source: Raheb, *Das reformatorische Erbe*, 106.

As suggested by Reinicke, new statutes were written for the German Protestant community, the Erlöserkirche was built in 1898, and its pastor took the title of Propst.[125] The other German missionary societies and institutions did not cease to operate in Palestine, however. They continued to work in their respective regions, but besides Bishara Canaan there was little Arab representation in the leadership of those organizations.[126] This would change after 1917.

Chalil Jamal

Biographical Sketch of Chalil Jamal

Chalil Jamal was born in Nazareth just one year before the establishment of the Protestant bishopric in Jerusalem on January 18, 1840.[127] Jamal and his family had belonged to the Greek Catholic Church, but they converted to Protestantism after becoming acquainted with its teachings in 1848 through the missionary efforts of John Bowen. In Jamal's words, "[Bowen] preached to us Christ and him crucified, and explained the pure Word of God to the family circle." As a result of this encounter Jamal was sent to Nazareth's first Protestant school, and in September 1850 he was admitted to the "diocesan boys' school" in Jerusalem. After graduating, Jamal taught Arabic in Haifa and at the school in Jerusalem.

During these years as a teacher Jamal made every effort to grow in his knowledge and understanding of the Bible and of the Christian life. Taking advantage of every spare moment, he studied the Bible intensely and read, among other things, John Bunyan's *Holy War*

---

125. The Weinachtskirche was built in Bethlehem in 1889.
126. For an overview of the German Protestant work in Palestine from the end of the Protestant bishopric to 1917 see Hanselmann, *Deutsche Evangelische Palästinamission*, 107–38; Raheb, *Das reformatorische Erbe*, 99–124.
127. The following biographical sketch is based on Chalil Jamal's own autobiography, which was composed in Jerusalem and dated February 16, 1874. Chalil Jamal, "A Sketch of My Autobiography." Birmingham/UL, C M/O 36/3b.

(1682) and *Pilgrim's Progress* (1678), Benjamin Elliot Nicholls' *Help to the Reading of the Bible*,[128] Thomas Boston's *Human Nature and its Four Fold State* (1676–1732), John Gregory Pike's *Immanuel the Christian's Joy* (1784–1854), Philip Doddridge's *The Rise and Progress of Religion in the Soul* (1745), and Albert Barnes's *Notes on the New Testament* (1798–1870). Through the reading of Scripture and the aforementioned books, Jamal says, "I discovered the wickedness of my heart and that by nature I am nothing but a child of wrath." He became convinced that the only solution was that he be "born again" and "sanctified with the Spirit of Sanctification." After much "wrestling with God," Jamal testifies that he did win a "new heart" and "holy life."[129] As a result, he states, "I began to feel, and that for the first time, the duty of making him known to all my friends, and this I did with pleasure." Jamal was soon asked to preach and conduct the Arabic service.[130] As a result, his desire to become a "preacher of the Gospel" increased. He writes:

> Two or three years before I left the school, I had a desire to become a preacher of the Gospel to grown up persons, and not only to the children in the school. This desire grew more and more in me, but I kept it in my heart, leaving the matter to my God to do according to His all wise will, and when it pleased Him who does every thing well, I was appointed by the Revnd Mr. Klein in 1865 to be his assistant in Jerusalem with the full will & consent of his Lordship the Anglican Bishop of Jerusalem.

---

128. It is assumed with good reason that this is the book to which Jamal refers as "Nicolas help to the reading of the Bible." The misspelling of Nicholls's name is due either to the fact that Jamal is recalling these authors and titles from memory or that he is retranslating them back into English from Arabic. In any case, it seems clear that he is referring to Benjamin Elliot Nicholls, *Help to the Reading of the Bible* (London: SPCK, 1853).
129. Jamal admits that later he often "wrestled against sin" and felt it "reigning in me," yet he found equal comfort in reading the Bible and Romans 7 in particular.
130. Frederick Augustus Klein, the local CMS missionary stationed in Jerusalem and also the individual responsible for finding the Mesha Steele (or "Moabite Stone"), asked Jamal to preach in his periodic absence from Jerusalem. This he did with greater and greater frequency.

Jamal served in this role as "catechist" for just over nine years.¹³¹ On November 29, 1874, he was ordained deacon in the Anglican Church.¹³² Priesthood followed a few years later, on September 23, 1877, when he was ordained in Jerusalem by Bishop Samuel Gobat. He served as priest until his death on August 1, 1907.¹³³

Chalil Jamal's Thought and Practice

Chalil Jamal was an evangelist at heart.¹³⁴ That is, he desired, first and last, to communicate what he perceived to be the "good news."¹³⁵ He did this not only in the formal settings of catechism and church services but in the informal settings of a home. Hospitality was a customary practice, and he took full advantage of the opportunities

---

131. "Catechist" was the official designation for Jamal's position. In his autobiography he lists some of his responsibilities. "My work has been to hold Bible meetings, to visit the members of the Community in their own house, to attend at the Bible Depot, to make occasionally Missionary tours, to teach the Preparandi class, to speak with people in their shops, and to preach every second Sunday."
132. This date, which was also Advent Sunday, marked the opening of St. Paul's Church in Jerusalem as well. St. Paul's was a church specially designated for the growing Arabic-speaking Protestant community in Jerusalem. Cf. Stock, *CMS*, 3: 115.
133. In the last months of his life Jamal was unable to perform his duties as a priest because of ill health. In "Extracts from Minutes of the Third Meeting of the Palestine Church Council held in Jaffa, March 10th–16th, 1907" (St. Antony's College, Oxford, J&EM 21/1) the PCC notes this with sadness and proposes to support him financially in his last days.
134. Jamal's letters and reports are full of examples of his efforts to persuade his listeners of the both the truth and their need of the gospel. The following is typical of such conversations: "I spoke with Hadj Faris . . . about the origin of sin, and how our parents were sent out with disgrace from their happy abode in Paradise, and how they were looked at by God as dead in trespasses & sin. After some time speaking and explaining to him how through the sin of Adam we were made sinners before God, I asked him if he feels himself to be a sinner, to which he answered, "No. I am not a sinner, because I neither commit adultery, nor kill nor steal, nor bear false witness against my neighbor or anybody, and thank God, I never missed repeating my prayers, and I also fast the holy month of Ramadan, and I give tithes and alms according to my ability.["] After much pains I was able to convince him that all these good deeds can not justify him before God, and then I spoke to him about the atonement & how we are justified by the precious blood of Christ; then I taught him this short prayer. ["]Lord pardon my sins for the sake of the atonement of our Lord Esa (Jesus).["] "Report of a Visit to Es-Salt and Jebl-Ajloon," July–September 1876. Birmingham/UL, C M/O 36/5.
135. That this was Jamal's highest priority can be seen in his closing prayer at the end of his 46-day missionary tour. He prays in conclusion, "May the Lord of the harvest send forth labourers unto His harvest." Jamal was far from territorial in his ministry, but sought co-laborers to spread the "Gospel." "Report of a Visit to Es-Salt and Jebl-Ajloon."

afforded him in both his own home and in the homes (and tents) of others. Jamal writes that he had an "open-door" policy for Muslims and Christians alike, so that he could seize "every possible opportunity to speak with them about our holy religion."[136] To say that this was time-consuming is an understatement. It was common for neighbors to visit him from "morning till rather late in the night."[137] Jamal's only complaint was that he often lacked the means that the demands of hospitality put upon him and his family.[138]

Jamal was also rooted in the Protestant conviction that the Bible alone was the source of all things necessary for salvation and holiness. It not only informed the Gospel he endeavored to proclaim; it framed his understanding of ecclesiology. When addressed by an individual who said "In honour to our forefathers we ought not to give up or part with the traditions of the fathers, though we see ourselves in error," Jamal answered, "I won't give up the Bible, and am willing to part with any tradition that may be contrary to God's precious word."[139] For Jamal the Bible trumped tradition, and every tradition that was not rooted in the Bible should be abandoned.[140] This is not to say that individuals had to leave their respective churches, but they should at a minimum speak out and seek to reform the traditions of their churches in accordance with biblical standards.[141]

---

136. See "Letter to the Secretary of the CMS in Jerusalem," July 14, 1880. Birmingham/UL, C M/O 36/4.
137. Ibid.
138. See for example, "Letter to the Rev. F. A. Klein" July 19, 1876. Birmingham/UL, C M/O 36/3.
139. "Report of a Visit to Es-Salt and Jebl-Ajloon," July–September 1876.
140. That Jamal saw his own tradition as being rooted in the Bible can be seen in the following quotation: "Several questions were put to us from the Bible with the desire of knowing the true meaning, they mean to follow the doctrine of the Gospel, I will not say of our Church, because I know that they are the Gospel doctrines." "Report of a Visit to Es-Salt and Jebl-Ajloon" July–September 1876.
141. For example, see "Annual Letter," November 17, 1875. Birmingham/UL, C M/O 36/7.

Chalil Jamal and the Old Testament

Having detailed the fact that the Bible was Jamal's sole authority for matters of faith and practice, we should now take a closer look at the way in which he actually viewed and interpreted biblical texts.[142] This information can be gleaned from two main areas.[143] First, Jamal's views can be ascertained from the biblical passages he cites throughout his letters and reports as well as from the manner and context in which he employs these passages. Second, his opinions can be determined from one of his annual reports to the CMS, in which he actually specifies the way he interprets and expounds biblical texts. Together, these two sources will provide a window into Chalil Jamal's hermeneutic of the Bible and the Old Testament in particular.

Firstly, by looking at the biblical passages Chalil Jamal cites throughout his letters and reports, as well as at the manner and context in which he uses them, one can catch a glimpse of how he viewed the Bible and interpreted it. We have said that Jamal was an "evangelist at heart" in that he sought to communicate what he believed to be the good news to those he encountered. Sometimes this was purely evangelistic, but at other times it was pastoral. For example, Jamal describes how on one occasion he told a number of people about Elisha in Dothan and cited a number of biblical passages from the Old and New Testaments to encourage them in the truth that "God watches over his people or those that fear Him as is mentioned in Psalm 34:7. 'The Angel of the Lord encampeth round about those that fear Him.'"[144] He then "dwelt much upon the

---

142. It will be recalled that Chalil Jamal highlights a number of books that proved informative for his understanding of the Christian faith and the Bible. Of particular importance was Benjamin Nicholls's *Help to the Reading of the Bible*. See above "Biographical Sketch of Chalil Jamal." Cf. Chalil Jamal, "A Sketch of My Autobiography," Birmingham/UL, C M/O 36/3b. Some of Nicholls's work will be quoted in this section to underline and clarify some of Jamal's statements, but for the main, Jamal's views will be made plain through his own words.
143. One can conjecture about other areas of influence on Jamal's biblical hermeneutic, but the two mentioned in this text are explicit, being rooted in Jamal's own words.

words 'that fear Him.' And showed them in what does the fear of God consist."[145] Another time Jamal encouraged a woman at one of the Bible study and prayer meetings for mothers. "Once while reading to them 1 Sam 1," Jamal writes, "one of them who is very unfortunate with children, was, all the time I was reading and explaining the chapter, in tears. I requested her to make Hannah's promise, and then soothed and comforted her sorrowful heart with Eli's words. She is now expecting a child, and that very soon, and I hope that she will fulfill her promise."[146]

One can see from the above examples that Jamal took literally the words of 2 Timothy 3:16: "All scripture is inspired by God and is useful for teaching, for reproof, for correction, and for training in righteousness, so that everyone who belongs to God may be proficient, equipped for every good work." Any biblical passage, including the characters therein, is useful for teaching and encouraging others about God and the Christian faith. The Old Testament especially is a resource throughout Jamal's letters and reports. He mentions numerous Old Testament characters and frequently quotes the Psalms. He notes among other individuals Adam, Eli, Hanna, Samuel, Elijah, Elisha, David, and Isaiah. The psalms[147] he cites are read at the beginning of each day of his missionary tour.[148] They are used to evangelize,[149] to preach,[150] and to encourage people in their Christian faith.[151]

At the heart of Jamal's practice of evangelism, biblical instruction, and pastoral care was the conviction, to which the above quotation

---

144. "Report of a Visit to Es-Salt and Jebl-Ajloon," July–September 1876.
145. Ibid.
146. "Annual Letter," November 29, 1879. Birmingham/UL, C M/O 36/11.
147. Jamal's letters and reports refer to Pss 1; 34; 72; 110; 119; and 133.
148. "Report of a Visit to Es-Salt and Jebl-Ajloon," July–September 1876.
149. "Letter to the CMS Secretary in Jerusalem," July 14, 1880 (Birmingham/UL, C M/O 36/4) Jamal cites Ps 72:9 to prove that the Bedouin tribes will one day worship Jesus.
150. "Report of a Visit to Es-Salt and Jebl-Ajloon," July–September 1876.
151. Cf. n. 143 above and its reference to Ps 34:7.

from 2 Timothy 3:16 alluded, that the Bible was the divinely inspired Word of God, and it was authoritative for all matters of faith and practice. This can be seen throughout Jamal's writings, where practically every letter refers to the Bible as the "Word of God."[152] In one case he writes, "I have comforted and encouraged him by the Word of God."[153] On another occasion he closes a letter with the prayer: "May the Lord our God bless His Word spoken to them, and bring them back unto Him with his everlasting love."[154] Not only did Jamal believe the Bible was God's Word, he also encouraged those he taught to approach it similarly. It is for this reason that he always opened and closed Bible studies with prayer, so that those in attendance might adequately prepare their minds to hear the voice of God rather than just the voice of a man.

According to Jamal, the Bible was not only the inspired Word of God, it was authoritative for all matters of faith and practice. Moreover, it was, in the words of Benjamin Nicholls, "an instrument in the hand of God for imparting his grace to mankind."[155] The Bible transformed individuals, curbed the immoral excesses of societies, and even renewed Christian traditions. The problem was, however, that there was a dearth of biblical knowledge. And so Jamal, like other Bible readers, catechists, and missionaries of the CMS, encouraged the reading of the Bible, so that in the hearing of the "Word of God," or better yet, in reading it for themselves, people and institutions such as the Eastern Christian churches could be reformed. This is why Bible studies, the use of biblical citations in conversations, and Christian schools where the Bible could be taught were so important for the CMS and for Jamal himself. A large portion of one of Jamal's

---

152. Most letters refer to the Bible in some manner as the "Word of God." For a number of examples, see "Report of a Visit to Es-Salt and Jebl-Ajloon," July–September 1876.
153. Ibid.
154. In letter written to the CMS on September 7, 1869. Birmingham/UL, C M/O 36/1.
155. Nicholls, *Help to the Reading of the Bible*, 8.

annual letters was given to just this point. In this letter, for example, Jamal commends to the central committee of the CMS the biblical knowledge of his students in Salt.[156] The Bible truly was, in Jamal's opinion, an "instrument" for "imparting" God's grace and for disseminating information pertaining to matters of faith and practice.

But how did Chalil Jamal actually interpret the Bible? One does not have to look very far to find that in his annual report to the CMS in 1879, Jamal indicates on two occasions how he believes a biblical text should be interpreted. In the first case he describes for the central committee what was included in the first examinations given at the boys' school in Salt. "The lessons in which the boys were examined are Geography, History, Arithmetic, Lectures, an essay on wealth and poverty, Reading grammatically Deut 4.[,] Matt. 5.[,] & Rom. 13.[,] Hymns, Text, Catechism, and Bible history, etc."[157] Of relevance to our present discussion is that Jamal highlights that the boys are instructed to read the Bible "grammatically." Later in the report he also comments on the manner in which he conducts the Bible and prayer-meetings and says, "My way in these meetings is, to begin with a prayer, then to read the portion for the night, and to catechize those present verse by verse in a historical & homiletical way, the youngest boy, as well as the oldest man, are catechized in the same way, and they are not offended. At the end one of the brethren concludes with a prayer and I pronounce the blessing."[158] Where the first citation highlighted the importance of reading the biblical text "grammatically," this excerpt from the annual report makes plain that Jamal trained those in attendance by interpreting a biblical passage "verse by verse" as well as "historically" and "homiletically." What Jamal means by the words "grammar" and "history" is not completely

---

156. See "Annual Letter," November 29, 1879.
157. "Annual Letter," November 29, 1879.
158. Ibid.

clear, however. That the Bible should be read "grammatically" and "historically" has meant different things to different people over the years. Nevertheless, a brief look at Benjamin Nicholls's book, *Help to the Reading of the Bible*, will clarify the "grammatical" and "historical" elements of Jamal's hermeneutic of the Bible.

Nicholls's *Help to the Reading of the Bible* was published in 1853, shortly before Jamal began to research the Bible and the Christian faith with increased intensity.[159] In his chapter, "On the Interpretation of the Bible," Nicholls discusses a number of issues concerning how the Bible should be read and understood. Nicholls warns against the "danger of quoting detached passages of Scripture, without regard to their context, or to the light which other parts of God's word may throw upon their interpretation."[160] Particular attention, therefore, must be given to the "immediate context" of a given passage, namely, "what goes before or follows a particular sentence, verse, or chapter."[161] This is one of the foundational principles of biblical interpretation, and it is this way of reading the Bible to which Jamal refers when he reports to the central committee of the CMS that students were tested on their "grammatical" interpretation of Deuteronomy 4, Matthew 5, and Romans 13.[162] That Jamal was mindful of this principle is further verified by the fact that during catechism he would instruct his students from the Bible "verse by verse."[163] Special attention was given to each sentence of a given passage and to the immediate context in which it was written.

However, as one sifts through Jamal's correspondence, one realizes that he understood that a proper reading of the Bible meant more than just paying attention to a the "grammatical" limits of a text's

---

159. Benjamin Elliot Nicholls, *Help to the Reading of the Bible* (London: SPCK, 1853).
160. Ibid., 95.
161. Ibid. 95.
162. "Annual Letter," November 29, 1879.
163. Ibid.

"immediate context." Following Nicholl's lead, he argues that sometimes a biblical passage is best explained by a text outside its immediate context.[164] For example, when asked on one occasion, "I read in my Bible that all have sinned and come short of the glory of God, but have never read about Samuel or Elijah that they ever sinned," he answered, "Samuel and Elijah have sinned."[165] Samuel sinned by "not punishing his two wicked children and in not dismissing them from being judges in the land."[166] Elijah sinned as well by "distrusting the Lord God of Israel and flying from the face of wicked Jezebel."[167] That Jamal interpreted "Scripture with Scripture" is clear from the fact that sin is not an element original to the stories of Samuel and Elijah. The idea that they "sinned" has been borrowed from the New Testament and superimposed onto the characters of Samuel and Elijah. Romans 3:23, which makes the claim that "all have sinned," is therefore the lens through which Jamal interprets these Old Testament passages.

With Jamal's reading of the Old Testament passages of 1 Samuel and 1 Kings in light of the New Testament book of Romans, we get our first clue into the way he interpreted the Bible "historically." For Jamal, the entire Bible is inspired and is authoritative for matters of faith and practice. The Old Testament should not be overlooked as a result. Nevertheless, one must attend to the text's place in the history of redemption, and that which is revealed in and through the person of Jesus Christ sheds light on that which precedes it in the pages of the Old Testament. For example, Jamal maintained that the Old Testament contains various types that have their fuller meaning in the New Testament. He writes on one occasion, "Spoke with my night visitors about the Geography of Palestine and about the cities

---

164. Nicholls, *Help to the Reading of the Bible*, 95, 99.
165. "Report of a Visit to Es-Salt and Jebl-Ajloon," July–September 1876.
166. Ibid. Jamal cites 1 Sam 8:1-5.
167. Ibid. Jamal cites 1 Kgs 19:1-18.

of refuge, and their spiritual meaning. Christ is our only refuge & his death is our salvation."[168]

This, then, is the "historical" consciousness to which Chalil Jamal refers.[169] Reading the Bible "historically" did not mean inquiring into the history behind a given text or believing that a text's provenance might be at odds with the view of authorship traditionally accorded to it. Jamal, like Nicholls and the CMS with whom he served, were conservative in this regard. The "historical" questions they asked centered on how and in what manner a given Old Testament text either foreshadowed or foretold a truth more fully revealed or "fulfilled" in the New Testament.

An Appraisal of Jamal

Eugene Stock spoke for the whole CMS when he said that of the "native clergy" in Palestine, Chalil Jamal "had long been especially valued."[170] Jamal embodied the beliefs and principles of the CMS.[171] He sought above all else to "propagate the knowledge of the Gospel."[172] That is, he was an evangelist at heart. He was also kind and considerate. He cared for those over whom he had oversight and those whom he encountered daily, often citing biblical passages to encourage them. Jamal's habit of quoting Scripture highlights the importance it had in his thought and practice. The Bible was, in Jamal's estimation, the sole source for Christian faith and praxis. It not only informed the content of the gospel he preached; it outlined the rules for daily life and defined his understanding of ecclesiology. The Bible was after all, in Jamal's view, the "Word of God" and should be read and obeyed as such.

---

168. Report of a Visit to Es-Salt and Jebl-Ajloon," July–September 1876.
169. In his "Annual Letter" of November 29, 1879.
170. Stock, *CMS* 3: 529.
171. For the resolutions established by the CMS at its foundation see Stock, *CMS* 1: 68–69.
172. This was the first resolution of the CMS.

The way Jamal interpreted the Bible was seen in his statements to the central committee of the CMS as well as in a comparison with Benjamin Nicholls's *Help to the Reading of the Bible*, which in Jamal's words "helped me very much to the understanding of the Bible."[173] Jamal maintained that the Bible should not be read in connection with tradition. The Bible can be understood on its own by paying attention to its "grammar" and "history." Reading "grammatically," the reader should be mindful of each verse in succession, paying attention to sentence structure, the flow of the argument, and the text's immediate context. At the same time a text can be read in connection with the wider context of Scripture. That is, one can read a given passage in light of the "historical" developments in the Bible. In other words, there is a historical progression from the Old Testament to the New. The Old Testament prepares for the coming of Christ, and now that Christ has come he becomes the means through which to properly read and understand the Old Testament.

Before we move on to discuss the life and practice of Seraphim Boutaji and Michael Kawar, the other two Palestinian Christians ordained by the Church of England in the 1870s, a brief word should be said about the manner in which Chalil Jamal viewed Jewish people. Jamal does not discuss or even mention the present state of the Jewish people in any of his letters or reports to the CMS. The paucity of references to the Jews is understandable, however. Jews began to immigrate to Palestine en masse only toward the end of Jamal's ministry, and the location and character of Jamal's work would have prevented him from having much interaction with those Jews who were already in Palestine. Apart from his time in Jerusalem, Jamal worked in areas with little or no Jewish population. This is especially true of his tenure in Salt. Besides, the work of the CMS in

---

173. In "A Sketch of My Autobiography," February 16, 1874.

Palestine focused almost exclusively on work among Arab Muslims and Christians, and this was especially true under the bishopric of Samuel Gobat. That Jamal's own ministry resembled the ethos and work of the CMS of the time can be seen in his letters and reports. Jamal consistently mentions having conversations with Muslims and Christians but never records that he shared the good news with any Jew.[174]

Despite the difficulty of determining what Jamal believed about the Jewish people, it is still reasonable to conclude that he would have held similar views to Nicholls and others like him. Jamal's views were largely similar to other Protestant missionaries of the time, and the paucity of references on the matter probably has more to do with the time and place in which Jamal worked than with any disagreement he might have had with Nicholls and others on the issue.

What were the views of Nicholls and others on the "preservation of the Jews as a separate people?"[175] Nicholls admits that "their preservation . . . is in itself a lasting miracle."[176] This is especially true when one considers how long they have lived in a state marked by "suffering and dispersion."[177] Nicholls explains:

> Ever since that event, i. e. for more than 1700 years, their land has been "trodden down of the Gentiles"; they themselves have been driven from their country, scattered over the face of the whole earth without distinction of tribes, without a king, without a prince, without even the form of a civil government, without a temple, with no officiating priesthood, without the means of sacrifice; for where can it be offered? Yet they still exist; unbelievers in Christianity, and yet the guardians of those very prophecies which prove the unreasonableness of their unbelief; mingled among, but distinct from, those around them; the wonder and scorn of the world; "as a bush on fire, and not consumed."[178]

---

174. This is different with Seraphim Boutaji. See "Seraphim Boutaji, Michael Kawar, and the Old Testament," below.
175. Nicholls, *Help to the Reading of the Bible*, 28.
176. Ibid.
177. Ibid., 30.

Although Nicholls marvels at the "preservation" of the Jewish people, he does not lament their sad condition, nor does he see it as something to be rectified. He highlights their present state of "suffering and dispersion" as a fulfillment of prophecy.[179] It proves that the Bible is the "Word of God." The "miracle" of their preservation, in other words, underscores the veracity of Scripture and the truthfulness of Christianity.

Jamal may never have said anything like Nicholls about Jews as such, but he definitely agreed with Nicholls on the inspiration and infallibility of Scripture. He also interpreted the Bible and the Old Testament in particular in a manner akin to Nicholls. Therefore, it is reasonable to conclude that there is a strong possibility that Jamal might have resonated with Nicholls's views on "the preservation of the Jews as a separate people."[180] What remains implicit with Jamal, however, becomes more and more explicit with other Palestinian Christian clergy, not least with Seraphim Boutaji and Michael Kawar, to whom we now turn our attention.

Seraphim Boutaji and Michael Kawar

Bibliographical Sketch of Boutaji and Kawar

Seraphim Boutaji was born in Acre, and like Chalil Jamal came from a Greek Catholic family.[181] He converted to Protestantism through the work of Rev. Fleischacker and became a catechist with the CMS in 1864.[182] He was ordained deacon in 1871 and priest on September

---

178. Ibid.
179. Ibid.
180. Ibid.
181. The following biographical sketch is based largely on *Register of Missionaries (Clerical, Lay, and Female), and Native Clergy, from 1804 to 1904*. Birmingham/UL, CMS BV 2500.
182. There is no known record of Rev. Fleischaker's first name. The above *Register of Missionaries* simply notes that Seraphim Boutaji "[r]eceived his first instruction in Evangelical truth through Rev. – Fleischacker, of Acca." Ibid.

23, 1877. Michael Kawar was also ordained priest on the same day as Boutaji, making them the first two Palestinian Protestant clergymen. Kawar was born in Nazareth, and his family was Greek Catholic as well. He was employed by Bishop Gobat as a catechist from 1854 to 1862, and in 1864 he became an official catechist of the CMS. In 1871 he was ordained deacon, and as noted above, he received his orders as a priest in 1877.

Boutaji and Kawar's Thought and Practice

Like Jamal, both Boutaji and Kawar were representative of the values and principles of the CMS and the evangelical wing of the Church of England at the time. The following letter will illustrate this point. On December 27, 1877, Jamal, Boutaji, and Kawar wrote a joint letter to the Rev. C. C. Fenn, CMS general secretary 1864–1891. After acknowledging with due thankfulness their receipt of a letter of congratulations from the "Parent Committee" of the CMS for their (specifically Kawar's and Boutaji's) "promotion to the Presbytery of the Church of England" on September 23, 1877, the three wrote:[183]

> You have mentioned in your letter that "if 'our' judgment and conscience do not permit 'us' to conform to the Church of England, it will be 'our' duty to separate from 'you,' as 'you' are in all respects a Church of England Society." In answer we beg to state that before we joined the Church of England we fully examined its doctrines and Articles of Religion, and they are that which have convinced and persuaded us to be members of the Church of England. Certainly this conviction and persuasion was through the effectual work of God's Holy Spirit within us. One of us M. Kawar has been a preacher of the word of God and a member of the Church of England for 25 years; and S. Boutaji for 20 years and Ch. Jamal has been a member of this Church from his childhood, for his parents have been in connection with the Church of England since the year 1848 when the late and

---

183. Michael Kawar, Seraphim Boutaji, and Chalil Jamal, "Letter to the Rev. C. C. Fenn," December 27, 1877. Birmingham/UL, C M/O 8/117.

much lamented Bishop Bowen was a Missionary in Nazareth. And by the grace of God we are what we are. But should we have had scruples about the doctrines of the Church of England, we would most certainly have hesitated to accept our Deacon's Orders. We are most willing to labour in true and loyal obedience to the Church of England as we have hitherto been obedient. But if any of our European brethren here were doubtful of our true and loyal obedience to the Church of England, we think it to be their duty to make mention of it directly to us; but our hearing nothing of this kind from them makes us believe that they are satisfied with us.

That we are under the control of the Bishop of the Diocese, we know very well, for this is also the manner of ecclesiastical government in the eastern churches, and the *Scripture teaches this* Acts 15:2, 13, 19.

We acknowledge also that we are under the control of the European Missionaries who are themselves under the control of the "Parent Committee" to whom the character of each of them is fully known. The committee can not be expected to understand all the circumstances and the individual character of the native clergymen in their various different Missions, we therefore submit to this control, and we have publicly vowed and promised to do so by the help of the Lord, when the Bishop asked each of us separately the last question stated in "the Ordering of Priests,"—viz. Will you reverently obey your ordinary, and other chief Ministers unto whom is committed the charge and government over you." As far as we recollect we have never given any reason to our "Ordinary and Chief Ministers" to complain of our disobedience, and in your letter you testify to this by saying, "you have been enabled so to conduct yourselves that your European brethren have been able to recommend you for this promotion, and the Bishop has seen his way to comply with their recommendation. This further acknowledgment of your fidelity and to a certain extent of your competence is a fact, for which you may thank God and take courage."

We hope that by the Grace of God we shall be able to live together in full harmony and concord and to give them satisfaction as regards our subordination and obedience to them, and at the same time we pray the Lord to enable them to look upon us as brethren and fellow labourers and not as inferiors and servants, as is often the case with superiors.

May we here ask about the *extent* of our obedience to our European superiors that there be no misunderstanding on our part whatever.

With much thankfulness to you for your kindness and love to us in permitting us to be ordained as Priests.

The letter underlines the fact that Boutaji, Kawar, and Jamal were committed to both the Church of England and the CMS.[184] Not only did they acknowledge the oversight of the Bishop and the "Parent Committee" of the CMS, they were convinced of the veracity of its core beliefs. They make it abundantly clear that they do not have any "scruples" with the Church of England's central "doctrines and Articles of Religion."[185] This can be seen when one looks at the way Boutaji and Kawar viewed and interpreted the Bible.

Seraphim Boutaji, Michael Kawar, and the Old Testament

Boutaji, Kawar, and Jamal sought to allay any fears on the part of the religious establishments to which they were accountable about any putative "scruples" they might have about the "doctrines and Articles of Religion" of the Church of England. They establish at the outset of their letter to Fenn that even "before we joined the Church of England we fully examined its doctrines and Articles of Religion, and they are they which have convinced and persuaded us to be members of the Church of England."[186] A look at some of the Articles of Religion can give us a general framework for how Boutaji and Kawar

---

184. The letter also highlights the fact that there was an underlying tension between the native clergy and the "European brethren," for Boutaji, Kawar, and Jamal note that some of the "European brethren" doubted their loyalty to the Church of England. These misgivings, however, were not articulated to the native clergy themselves but were expressed to the "Parent Committee" of the CMS, which subsequently issued a letter of concern to the Palestinian clergy. That there was ill feeling between the native clergy and the "European brethren" can be seen with both Nasir Odeh and Seraphim Boutaji. Cf. Tibawi, *British Interests*, 241–48; letter "To the Church Missionary House," January 30, 1878. Birmingham/UL, C M/O 16/3.
185. "Letter to the Rev. C. C. Fenn."
186. Ibid.

viewed the Bible. The precise manner in which they interpreted the Bible will be fleshed out from some of their letters and annual reports.

The Church of England's Articles of Religion seek to walk a fine line between the Bible and tradition. Tradition is not discounted, but the Bible is given primacy in matters of faith and practice. This can be seen when one compares the sixth and twentieth articles. Article 6 states with regard to the "Sufficiency of the Holy Scripture for Salvation":

> Holy Scripture containeth all things necessary to salvation: so that whatsoever is not read therein, nor may be proved thereby, is not to be required of any man, that it should be believed as an article of the Faith, or be thought requisite or necessary to salvation. In the name of the Holy Scripture we do understand those canonical Books of the Old and New Testament, of whose authority was never any doubt in the Church.

The twentieth article reveals the Church of England's position on the "Authority of the Church."

> The Church hath power to decree Rites or Ceremonies, and authority in Controversies of Faith: and yet it is not lawful for the Church to ordain anything that is contrary to God's Word written, neither may it so expound one place of Scripture, that it be repugnant to another. Wherefore, although the Church be a witness and a keeper of Holy Writ, yet, as it ought not to decree anything against the same, so besides the same ought it not to enforce any thing to be believed for necessity of Salvation.

The Bible alone, therefore, as opposed to the traditions of the church, contains all that is necessary for salvation. The church can nevertheless institute its own "rites or ceremonies," but these must be in accordance with "Holy Writ." True to Church of England practice, Boutaji and Kawar also sought to balance the place of tradition in relation to the importance and sufficiency of "Holy Scripture."

For example, Boutaji argues for the primacy of the early creeds in that they conform fully to the "Word of God."[187] All other doctrines, such as "the Intercession of the saints, the worshipping of Images, the Supremacy of the Pope, the Purgatory, etc. were only new inventions, not mentioned in the old creed, and that they were against, and contradictory to the significance of the Word of God."[188] He takes special exception to the recent doctrinal position arrived at by the First Vatican Council of the Roman Catholic Church. He writes:

> The decision of the Council of the Vatican, concerning the infallibility of the Pope . . . has brought many of the Catholics and Greeks to think about the ancient Councils, and when I am speaking about them, how they all made mistakes and that nothing was infallible what men did, and that infallibility was only to be found in the Bible, the people believed it.[189]

The Bible alone is infallible and contains what is necessary for salvation. Creeds can be formulated and traditions instituted by the church, but they must always conform to that which is written in scripture.

Such was the position maintained by Seraphim Boutaji, and by Michael Kawar as well. Kawar records a conversation he had with a gentleman in which he "led him to leave all the traditions of the Greek Church, and to follow the way of salvation as revealed in the pure Word of God."[190] Kawar argues that the Bible is the source of

---

187. He highlights in particular the Apostles' Creed and the Athanasian Creed.
188. "Extracts from the Journal of Serafim Boutagi of Shefarmer," September 30, 1872. Birmingham/UL, C M/O 16/12.
189. In "Extracts from the Journal of Serafim Boutagi of Shefarmer" written September 30, 1872. Birmingham/UL, C M/O 16/12.
190. "Translation of the Revd. Michael Kawar's report of the quarter ending September 30th 1873," October 15, 1873. Birmingham/UL, C M/O 40/4*.

one's knowledge of salvation. However, he does not deny that the traditions of the Church of England have merit. This can be seen in his conflict with the Plymouth Brethren in Palestine. He itemizes the conflict's history in a report written in 1877.

1. Since two years the community have [sic] observed that those who call themselves Plymouth Brethren come to our Church on every Lord's day, merely for curiosity and never hold the prayer book in their hands, and never cease from wispering [sic] into each other's ears, etc.
2. That they continually speak against the rites of our church and its ministers.
3. That they have openly declared themselves to be P.B. and began to "break bread" themselves and confess that they aim at making a division in our community.[191]

Both Bible and tradition are important to Michael Kawar. Nevertheless, the Bible is still the highest authority for his thought and practice.

This can be seen in two other examples from Kawar's ministry. On one occasion he prays for the "spread of the Word of God in our native land."[192] It is significant that he does not pray that Palestine might abound with the traditions of the Church of England. In another instance he tells of a funeral at which he wept along with others at the sight of an elderly mother laying a "copy of the Holy Bible" above the head of her deceased child, saying, "My son, let the Word of God be with thee, to accompany thee even in the grave."[193]

So despite the attention given to the traditions of the Church of England, the Bible was, for both Kawar and Boutaji, of utmost

---

191. "Annual Letter," March 15, 1877. Birmingham/UL, C M/O 40/10*.
192. "Translation of the Revd. Michael Kawar's report of the quarter ending September 30th 1873."
193. Ibid.

importance. It was the "Word of God." It was the sufficient source for salvation, containing everything necessary for faith and practice. It remains only to highlight briefly the manner in which they interpreted the Bible.

Besides the letter written by Boutaji, Kawar, and Jamal, there is no explicit evidence for how Michael Kawar interpreted the Bible in practice except what has already been adduced above. This is not the case with Seraphim Boutaji. When asked by a man how to properly interpret the Bible, Boutaji responded:

> . . . those who want to understand the Word of God so far as it is necessary for their salvation must ask for the assistance of the Holy Spirit, for nobody knows divine things except the Spirit of God. Secondly they must be obedient to the Word of God, for it has no other object than the love of God. Thirdly those who read the Word of God must not approach it as the same as other books, but reverently as the book from God, lastly they must read coursorily and repeatedly for the oftener we read it, the more light we get about it.[194]

Much like Chalil Jamal, Boutaji believed that the Bible was not like any other book. It must be read as if it were the very "Word of God." Illumination is also needed, that is, special assistance from the Holy Spirit is required in order to properly awaken the mind to understand what is communicated by God in the Bible. Therefore Boutaji often prayed before preaching on or explaining a passage from the Bible.[195]

Beyond this illustration there is little evidence of exactly how Boutaji interpreted the Bible, and the Old Testament in particular. One can conclude with reasonable certainty, however, in light of the above statements, that Boutaji and Kawar interpreted the Bible in a manner akin to Jamal's. All three had committed themselves to

---

194. "Report of the Quarter ending June 30th 1866." Birmingham/UL, C M/O 16/10.
195. On one occasion he asks that God would "pour out His Holy Spirit upon them that they may become the chosen people of God who inherit His Kingdom." "Extracts from the Journal of Serafim Boutagi of Shefarmer," September 30, 1872.

the doctrines and Articles of Religion of the Church of England. Although there were tensions between Boutaji and the "European brethren" of the CMS, these were not over biblical hermeneutics but over matters of ecclesiology and the transfer of authority from expatriate missionaries to the national clergy in Palestine. Nevertheless, one small word should be said by way of conclusion on the manner in which Boutaji viewed the present state of the Jews.

It was pointed out earlier with reference to Chalil Jamal that he most likely would have agreed with Benjamin Nicholls that the present "suffering and dispersion" of the Jews confirms the truthfulness of the Bible and the Christian religion. Seraphim Boutaji would not have disagreed. He tells of a conversation he had in which he explained "how the wrath of God fell upon the Jews, because the[y] rejected Christ, and how he was giving great power to His believers (the Christian Nations) and increased their Kingdoms and civilization. . . ."[196] Not only does Boutaji maintain that the Jews are enduring a state of suffering and dispersion because of their rejection of Christ, but the "Christian Nations," like England, are prospering because of their acceptance of Jesus. The degree to which this view remained the same after 1917 will be explored in subsequent chapters.

An Appraisal of Boutaji and Kawar

The above description of the first Palestinian Anglican priests, Seraphim Boutaji and Michael Kawar, illustrated the fact that they viewed and interpreted the Bible in a manner similar to Chalil Jamal. Despite any "scruples" they may have had with regard to the policies of their church, they nevertheless adhered to its beliefs and doctrines. The Bible was the "Word of God," the sole source of all things necessary for salvation and the measure of all things allowed for

---

196. "Translation of the Report of Serafim Boutagi for the quarter ending March 31st 1873." Birmingham/UL, C M/O 16/13.

tradition. Proper interpretation necessitates that one ask the Holy Spirit's help and that one expect to hear God's voice from the pages of Scripture. Beyond this, their hermeneutic would have been similar to that of Jamal.

Conclusion

At a CMS conference in Jerusalem in 1907 it was noted in the minutes that James Orr's book, *The Problem of the Old Testament*,[197] was going to be discussed at an upcoming meeting.[198] The missionaries had no trouble with the text of the Old Testament itself, but recent biblical criticism was another matter. They would have agreed with the book's preface, which states that critical scholarship "rests on erroneous fundamental principles, is eaten through with subjectivity, and must, if carried out to its logical issues . . . prove subversive of our Christian faith, and of such belief in, and use of, the Bible as alone can meet the needs of the living Church."[199] Chalil Jamal, Seraphim Boutaji, and Michael Kawar would have assented wholeheartedly. They were different from Palestinian Christians after 1917 and 1948. They had no difficulty with the Old Testament *per se*. For them it was the Word of God. It was infallible, inerrant, and contained an anticipation of the good news of the Gospel. It was sufficient in all matters pertaining to salvation and matters of church polity. If there was a "problem" of the Old Testament, it was that it was not read by Palestine's inhabitants.

Although it was believed that the Bible could be understood on its own, Palestinian Christians did maintain that there were methods that might help one understand it. Chalil Jamal is the prime example

---

197. James Orr, *The Problem of the Old Testament* (New York: Charles Scribner's Sons, 1906).
198. "Extracts from Minutes of Palestine (C.M.S.) Missionary Conference held in Jerusalem, from April 14th to 20th, 1907." St. Antony's College, Oxford. J&EM 21/1. There is no record that the CMS ever discussed the book.
199. Orr, *Problem of the Old Testament*, xv.

of Palestinian Christian hermeneutics prior to 1917. He argued that the Bible should be read "grammatically" and "historically." One understands a text properly when one pays attention to the grammatical structure of a sentence and pericope. One also needs to pay attention to the historical situation of a given text. This is not to be confused with how modern critical scholarship would understand this statement, however. Jamal never asked about the history behind a text. He accepted the traditionally assigned authors and history of the Bible. For Jamal, reading the Bible "historically" meant being aware of the historical developments in God's plan of salvation, that is, the progression from promise in the Old Testament to fulfillment in the New Testament. This did not mean that the Old Testament was of no use for the Christian faith. The Old Testament was a storehouse of examples that might be used to encourage others in their Christian faith. Furthermore, it pointed people to Christ and as such was useful to the Christian community in Palestine in Jamal's day.

The ease with which Palestinian Christians read and understood the Old Testament in Jamal's day would soon change, however. After 1917, Palestinian Christian hermeneutics of the Old Testament would never be the same again.

3

Palestinian Christianity and the "Promise" of a Jewish Homeland

On December 9, 1917, the British army under the leadership of General Edmund Allenby defeated the Ottoman armed forces and occupied Jerusalem. In a symbolic gesture of respect for Judaism, Christianity, and Islam, Allenby entered the city through the Jaffa Gate on foot (see illus.).[1] Jerusalem, he acknowledged, is "regarded with affection by the adherents of three of the great religions of mankind and its soil has been consecrated by the prayers and pilgrimages of multitudes of devout people of these three religions for many centuries. . . ."[2] He declared to the city's inhabitants that the British administration would do its best to ensure that all persons could carry on with their daily business "without fear of

---

1. Underwood & Underwood, "Palestine – Jerusalem: General Allenby's entrance into Jerusalem," Frank and Frances Carpenter Collection, Library of Congress. Accessed March 18, 2015: http://www.loc.gov/pictures/item/93513671/.
2. Charles F. Horne, ed., *Source Records of the Great War*, 7 vols. (London: National Alumni, 1923), 5:417.

interruption."³ However noble the intentions of Allenby and the British administration might have been, the British Mandate in Palestine certainly disrupted the political and religious landscape of the land and its inhabitants. Kenneth Cragg writes that Britain had "set two ambitions on collision course, the one or the other doomed, as far as Palestine was concerned, to frustration."⁴ These "two ambitions" were of course the dreams and expectations of Arab and Jewish nationalism.

T. E. Lawrence writes that on the night after Allied Forces entered Damascus in November 1917 the muezzin, while issuing the call to prayer, "dropped his voice two tones almost to speaking level and

---

3. Ibid.
4. Kenneth Cragg, *The Arab Christian: A History in the Middle East* (Louisville: Westminster John Knox, 1991), 235.

softly added [to the liturgical words]: 'and He [God] is very good to us this day, O people of Damascus!'"⁵ The story, as Cragg admits, might well be "apocryphal," but it underlines the "hopes that attended the entry into Damascus as the symbol and climax of the Arab Revolt against the Ottoman Turks."⁶ The Arab jubilation was based on promises Britain had made in return for Arab military support during the war.⁷ Therefore, in the eyes of many Arabs in the former Ottoman Empire, independence and political sovereignty were right around the corner.

The national aspirations of numerous Jews were also given a note of confidence in November 1917. On the second of November the British government issued the Balfour Declaration. It reads as follows:⁸

Foreign Office
November 2nd, 1917
Dear Lord Rothschild,

I have much pleasure in conveying to you, on behalf of His Majesty's Government, the following declaration of sympathy with the Jewish Zionist aspirations which has been submitted to, and approved by, the Cabinet.

"His Majesty's government view with favour the establishment in Palestine of a national home for the Jewish people, and will use their best endeavours to facilitate the achievement of this object, it being clearly understood that nothing shall be done which may prejudice the civil and religious rights of existing non-Jewish communities in Palestine, or the rights and political status enjoyed by Jews in any other country."

I should be grateful if you would bring this declaration to the knowledge of the Zionist Federation.

---

5. T. E. Lawrence in Cragg, *Arab Christian*, 233.
6. Ibid.
7. See Henry McMahon, "The McMahon Letter (October 24, 1915)," 11–12 in *The Israel-Arab Reader: A Documentary History of the Middle East Conflict,* ed. Walter Laqueur and Barry Rubin; 7th rev. and enl. ed. (London: Penguin, 2008).
8. Arthur Balfour, "The Balfour Declaration (November 2, 1917)," 16 in *Israel-Arab Reader*.

Yours sincerely,
Arthur James Balfour

It is true that "The Balfour Declaration did not 'give Palestine to the Jews.'"⁹ It merely promised to help the Jews establish a home *in* Palestine and made no claim to give the whole of it to them.¹⁰ Moreover, it was the intention of the British administration that nothing might "prejudice the civil and religious rights of the existing non-Jewish communities in Palestine." Nevertheless, the Zionist party rightly rejoiced over the issuing of the declaration. Britain had pledged itself to establish some sort of "national home" in Palestine for the Jewish people.

Despite all appearances, Great Britain did not purposely "set two ambitions on collision course," as Kenneth Cragg seems to imply. Britain did intend to take into consideration both Jewish and Arab national expectations, but the facts on the ground "belied" this dream.¹¹ The following section will survey the political context in Palestine from 1917 to 1948, outlining some of the key facts confronting both Arab and Jewish nationalism. Although the clash of these national aspirations was the main issue that plagued Jews and Arabs during this time, it was not the only item of concern for Palestinian Christians. This will become evident as the political and religious contexts of Palestinian Christians between 1917 and 1948 are surveyed.

---

9. James Parkes, *Whose Land? A History of the Peoples of Palestine* (Middlesex: Penguin, 1971), 257.
10. Cf. Winston Churchill, "The Churchill White Paper (June 1922)," 25–29 in *Israel-Arab Reader*. James Parkes adds that despite the ambiguity in the correspondence from Henry McMahon to Hussein Ibn Ali, the British did not envisage giving the whole of Palestine to the Arabs as well. Parkes, *Whose Land?* 253–57.
11. James Parkes adds, "That this world was stillborn was not the fault of the Jews." Ibid., 258.

The Political Context of Palestinian Christians 1917–1948

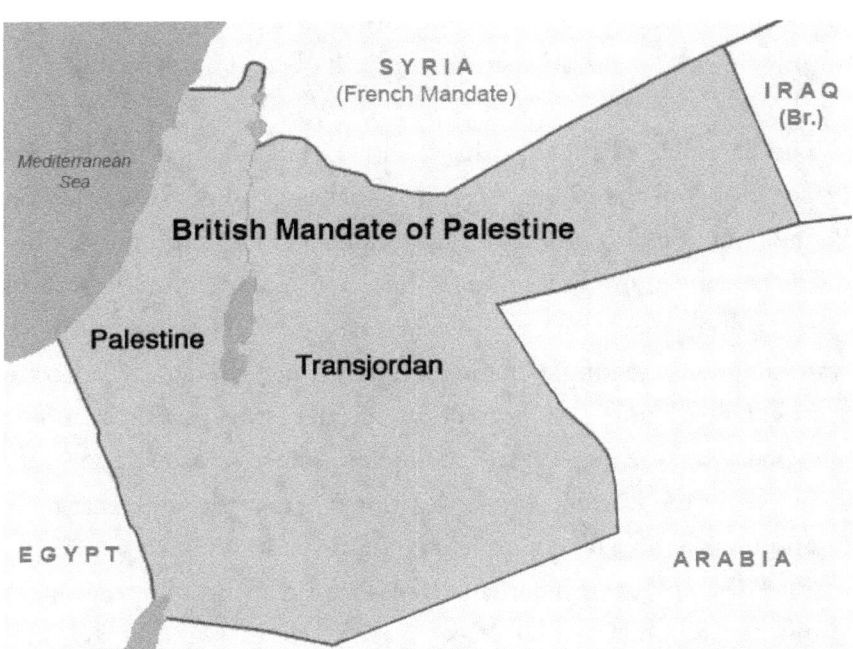

Following the end of the Great War, the Allied Powers established a number of mandates in accordance with the twenty-second article of the League of Nations, in order to manage "those colonies and territories which as a consequence of the late war have ceased to be under the sovereignty of the States which formerly governed them and which are inhabited by peoples not yet able to stand by themselves under the strenuous conditions of the modern world. …"[12] While the French Mandate extended over Syria and Lebanon, the British Mandate covered Palestine and Transjordan (see map above).[13] On the basis of Article 22 Britain was given the

---

12. Covenant of the League of Nations, Article 22.
13. "British Mandate of Palestine, 1920's," accessed March 18, 2015: http://commons.wikimedia.org/wiki/File:BritishMandatePalestine1920.png. Anthony O'Mahony rightly points out that there were different types of mandates depending on the level of a territory's development (Class A, B, and C Mandates). However, he wrongly categorizes Palestine as a

responsibility to tutor the inhabitants of the land until they were able to "stand alone."[14] The text of the British Mandate was authorized on July 24, 1922, and the mandate officially began on September 26, 1923.

The preamble of the British Mandate acknowledged the Balfour Declaration and the call to establish a "national home for the Jewish People," but it also reaffirmed its intention that "nothing should be done which might prejudice the civil and religious rights of existing non-Jewish communities in Palestine."[15] However, nothing was said about creating a "national home" for the Arabs in Palestine as well. James Parkes is right to point out, therefore, that the mandate "showed a grave underestimate of the importance of Arab opposition, or indeed of the existence of the legitimate Arab grievance that their position was almost totally undefined in the various policy statements of the British government and the Palestinian Administration."[16] Winston Churchill's White Paper was the closest thing at the time resembling an attempt to assuage the concerns of the Arab inhabitants.[17] Nevertheless, it, along with the terms of the mandate, fell short of uttering any "positive statement" that might "form the basis of cooperation with the Arab moderate opinion, or, indeed,

---

Class B Mandate. Palestine was still officially a Class A Mandate but received greater oversight on the grounds of the complexity of issues it was facing, namely, the additional call to establish a "Jewish home" in the land.

14. Covenant of the League of Nations, Article 22.
15. League of Nations, "The British Mandate (July 24, 1922)," 30–36 in *Israel-Arab Reader*, at 30.
16. Parkes, *Whose Land?* 263.
17. Churchill wrote: "Unauthorized statements have been made to the effect that the purpose in view is to create a wholly Jewish Palestine. . . . His Majesty's Government regards any such expectation as impracticable and have no such aim in view. Nor have they at any time contemplated, as appears to be feared by the Arab Delegation, the disappearance or the subordination of the Arabic population, language, or culture in Palestine. . . . In this connection it has been observed with satisfaction that at the meeting of the Zionist Congress . . . a resolution was passed expressing as the official statement of Zionist aims, 'the determination of the Jewish people to live with the Arab people on terms of unity and mutual respect, and together with them to make the common home into a flourishing community.'" Churchill, "The Churchill White Paper," 26.

bring a moderate opinion into existence by giving it a worthwhile objective consonant with the Arab sense of national dignity."[18]

Increased Jewish immigration along with a swell of land purchases only compounded the doubts and suspicions the Arabs had begun to have about British assurances.[19] Arab apprehension over the political integrity of the British Mandate and Zionism quickly led to open opposition. There were the Nebi Musa riots in Jerusalem in April 1920 as well as the Jaffa riots in May the following year. Although these skirmishes were horrific in their own right, Roland Löffler is correct in saying "the Arab national movement's resistance came to a head in the 1928/29 uprisings and, above all, in the 'Grand Palestinian Revolt' of 1936."[20]

Following the Arab riots of 1929 the Colonial Secretary, Lord Passfield, issued the Passfield White Paper, which "urged the restriction of immigration and of land sales to Jews."[21] Zionist leaders complained that the paper violated "the letter and spirit of the Mandate."[22] Prime Minister James Ramsay MacDonald was forced, as a result, to compose his own letter in order to "remove certain misconceptions and misunderstandings which have arisen as to the policy of his Majesty's Government with regard to Palestine."[23] He writes to Chaim Weizmann, "His Majesty's Government will continue to administer Palestine in accordance with the terms of the mandate as approved by the Council of the League of Nations."[24]

---

18. Parkes, *Whose Land?* 263.
19. Roland Löffler, "Aggravating Circumstances: On the Process of National and Religious Identity Within the Arab Lutheran and Anglican Congregations of Palestine During the Mandate Years," 99–124 *Christian Witness between Continuity and New Beginnings*, ed. Martin Tamcke and Michael Marten (Berlin: LIT Verlag, 2006), 100.
20. Ibid.
21. Ramsay MacDonald, "The MacDonald Letter (February 13, 1931)," 36–41 in *Israel-Arab Reader*, at 37.
22. Ibid.
23. Ibid.
24. Ibid.

He reiterated that this meant "promoting the establishment of a national home for the Jewish people" as well as doing nothing that might "prejudice the civil and religious rights of existing non-Jewish communities."[25] MacDonald insists: "This is an international obligation from which there can be no question of receding."[26]

Despite the disturbances in the early part of the British Mandate, one can see from MacDonald's letter that Britain was still firmly committed to its mandatory obligations and the prospect that the national aspirations of both the Jewish and Arab inhabitants might yet be met. By the end of the Great Arab Revolt, however, British opinion had shifted.[27] One can see the signs of this transformation in the early years of the revolt. After the first year a Royal Commission was set up and charged with the task of ascertaining the "causes of the disturbances" and the possibility of reconciling Arab and Jewish aspirations.[28] The Peel Commission, as it was called, concluded:

> An irrepressible conflict has arisen between two national communities within the narrow bounds of one small country. About 1,000,000 Arabs are in strife, open or latent, with some 400,000 Jews. There is no common ground between them. . . . National assimilation between Arabs and Jews is thus ruled out. . . . Neither Arab nor Jew has any sense of service to a single State.[29]

The British government thus began to favor partition. However, in November 1938 the prospect of partition was also rejected, forcing the British government to find "alternative means of meeting the

---

25. Ibid., 37–38.
26. Ibid., 37.
27. The Great Arab Revolt lasted from 1936 to 1939. During this period hundreds of Jews and Arabs were killed. What is not often realized is that thousands of trees were also destroyed in the conflict. Martin Gilbert records that on one occasion Arabs destroyed some 50,000 Jewish forest trees. Martin Gilbert, *The Arab-Israeli Conflict: Its History in Maps* (London: Weidenfeld and Nicolson, 1981), 26.
28. The Palestine Royal Commission (Peel Commission), "Report (July 1937)," 41–43 in *Israel-Arab Reader*, at 41.
29. Ibid., 42–43.

needs of the difficult situation described by the Royal Commission which will be consistent with their obligations to the Arabs and the Jews."[30]

On May 17, 1939, the British government issued its final White Paper with regard to Palestine, addressing the issues of self-government, immigration, and land purchase.[31] Neither Jewish nor Arab leaders were satisfied with its propositions.[32] Britain concluded, as a result, that the mandate was no longer viable, yet the onset of the Second World War prevented them from relinquishing their responsibility. On February 14, 1947, about a year and a half after the close of the war, Britain was able to "refer the Palestine problem to the United Nations,"[33] and on May 14, 1948, the British Mandate in Palestine ended. On that same day, Israel declared its independence. The next morning the surrounding Arab armies invaded the newly founded state, and the 1948 Arab-Israeli War began.[34]

The preceding survey is definitely not an exhaustive treatment of the political context of Palestine between the years 1917 and 1948.[35] It simply highlights the relevant parties in the burgeoning conflict and some of the policies by which the British Mandate in Palestine affected Jewish and Arab national aspirations. That a "national home" materialized only for the Jewish inhabitants of Palestine is an

---

30. British Government, "Policy Statement against Partition (November 1938)," 43 in *Israel-Arab Reader*.
31. With these issues in mind the White Paper was arranged under the following three headings: (1) The Constitution, (2) Immigration, and (3) Land. See British Government, "The White Paper (May 17, 1939)," 44–50 in *Israel-Arab Reader*.
32. For example, see The Jewish Agency for Palestine, "Zionist Reaction to the White Paper (1939)," 50–51 in *Israel-Arab Reader*, at 50.
33. UN Special Committee on Palestine, "Summary Report (August 31, 1947)," 65–69 in *Israel-Arab Reader*, at 65.
34. It is also known as the War of Independence.
35. For a more detailed introduction to the political complexity of life under the British Mandate in Palestine, see: Tom Segev, *One Palestine, Complete: Jews and Arabs under British Mandate* (New York: Metropolitan Books, 2000); Conor Cruise O'Brien, *The Siege: The Saga of Israel and Zionism* (London: Paladin, 1988).

unfortunate consequence of a mandate that had as its original aim to enable the inhabitants of the lands once ruled by the Ottoman Empire one day to "stand by themselves."[36] As the statements clearly show, the British *had* endeavored to establish a home for both peoples. Nevertheless, the nature of that home was unsatisfactory in the eyes of the "non-Jewish communities of Palestine" and was the cause of much of the opposition from the land's Arab inhabitants.[37]

It is not the purpose of this chapter or the objective of this section to discuss the validity of Arab grievances, the soundness of British policy, or the legitimacy of establishing a "national home" for Jews in Palestine. Rather, its aim is to sketch the political context of Palestine between 1917 and 1948 in order to help the reader understand some of the issues that challenged Palestinian Christians during this time. What remains is to give a brief overview of the religious context of Palestine and then to delineate some of the views of Palestinian Christians themselves, paying special attention to the manner in which they interpreted the Old Testament.

The Religious Context of Palestinian Christians 1917–1948

The religious context of Palestine between 1917 and 1948 is, as Roland Löffler argues, an "under-analysed topic."[38] The majority of research has focused and continues to concentrate on the political context of the British Mandate in Palestine. As a result, it has neglected some of the period's important religious questions. This is not to imply that religion and politics can be separated when writing a history of Palestinian Christianity during this period. Political

---

36. Covenant of the League of Nations, Article 22.
37. The other sources of the conflict were the continual flow of Jewish immigrants into Palestine and the regular purchase of its land.
38. Löffler says this in contrast to a statement quoted by John Bunzel earlier in his article, where the British Mandate in Palestine is referred to as an "overanalyzed topic." Löffler, "Aggravating Circumstances," 99–100.

contexts are most certainly related to religious contexts. Nevertheless, there are aspects particular to the religious context of Palestinian Christianity that must be spelled out in order to properly understand some of the actions and comments made by Palestinian Christians. This section will detail some of the most important facets of the religious context of Palestinian Christianity between 1917 and 1948. First we will offer a brief sketch of how the Great War affected the Christian communities in Palestine. The manner in which the British administration preserved and changed the status of the Christian churches during the mandate will also be explored. Particular attention will then be given to the developments that took place in the Anglican and Lutheran communities. As with the previous chapter, this is not to discount the importance of the Catholic and Orthodox churches during this time. The focus on Palestinian Protestant Christians is pragmatic and serves to establish comparisons with the previous chapter.

The Great War and Palestinian Christianity

During World War One the Turks "seized all churches and institutions belonging to the British missionary societies in Palestine."[39] Afterward the German Protestant institutions were "seized and put into English and American trust."[40] In addition, the personnel connected with those churches and institutions were either deported during the war or interned afterward, depending on their affiliation. This did little to help the strength and effectiveness of the various Christian communities during and shortly after the Great

---

39. Rafiq Farah, *In Troubled Waters: A History of the Anglican Church in Jerusalem, 1841–1998* (Leicester: Christians Aware, 2002), 82. Farah notes two exceptions. St. Luke's in Haifa and St. Paul's in Jerusalem were spared the fate of the other churches. Rev. Yacoub Khadder and Rev. Ibrahim Baz both claimed that the churches "belonged to the Native Church Council and not to a British missionary society."
40. Löffler, "Aggravating Circumstances," 104.

War.⁴¹ For example, when famine and disease wreaked havoc in Palestine during the latter part of the war the church was in a poor position to offer any assistance. The Syria and Palestine Relief Fund (SPRF) was established by the Anglican Bishop Rennie MacInnes in 1916 to aid the inhabitants of the land. However, like the majority of British religious personnel, he was unable to enter Palestine. He was forced to stay in Egypt until February 26, 1918, nearly three months after Allenby's "triumphal entry."⁴² Once the dust of the war had settled and religious personnel returned to their respective posts, a hint of "normality" was reestablished. However, things in Palestine would soon change. The British Mandate was established in 1922/3, and the status of the Christian communities was altered along with it.

The Status of Christians in Palestine between 1917 and 1948

Daphne Tsimhoni writes of the Christian community in Palestine at this time: "Having lived for hundreds of years under Ottoman rule in an inferior position, the Arab Christians expected, with the British occupation, an improvement of their situation and even some preferential treatment as co-religionists of the holders of the Mandate."⁴³ The Christians in Palestine certainly did not receive any "preferential treatment." Their status, established in the articles of the British Mandate, correlated with that of the other religious communities in Palestine. Some of the relevant articles included:⁴⁴

---

41. What is more, the inhabitants of the land were not helped by the lack of services during the war, when famine and disease plagued the area. Tens of thousands perished as a result. The Syria and Palestine Relief Fund (SPRF) was formed at this time to address these needs.
42. Rennie MacInnes, "The Bishop's Quarterly Newsletter (May 12, 1918)," 259–63 in *Bible Lands* 77, Vol. 5 (July 1918), at 259.
43. Daphne Tsimhoni, "The Status of the Arab Christians under the British Mandate in Palestine," *MES* 20 (October 1984): 166–92, at 166.
44. Cf. League of Nations, "The British Mandate (July 24, 1922)," 30–36 in *Israel-Arab Reader*.

Article 2: "The Mandatory shall be responsible . . . for safeguarding the civil and religious rights of all the inhabitants of Palestine, irrespective of race and religion."

Article 8: "The privileges and immunities of foreigners, including the benefits of consular jurisdiction and protection as formerly enjoyed by Capitulation or usage in the Ottoman Empire, shall not be applicable. . . ."

Article 9: "The Mandatory shall be responsible . . . for the personal status of the various peoples and communities and for their religious interests. . . ."

Article 13: "All responsibility in connection with the Holy Places and religious buildings or sites in Palestine, including that of preserving existing rights and of securing free access to the Holy Places, religious buildings and sites and the free exercise of worship . . . is assumed by the Mandatory. . . ."

Article 14: "A special Commission shall be appointed . . . to study, define and determine the rights and claims in connexion with the Holy Places and the rights and claims relating to the different religious communities in Palestine."

Article 15: The "free exercise of all forms of worship" shall be open to all, "subject only to the maintenance of public order and morals."

Article 16: "The Mandatory shall be responsible for exercising such supervision over religious or eleemosynary bodies of all faiths in Palestine as may be required for the maintenance of public order and good government. Subject to such supervision, no measures shall be taken in Palestine to obstruct or interfere with the enterprise of such bodies or discriminate against any representative or member of them on the ground of his religion or nationality."

Article 23: Religious holy days will be recognized.

Article 28: The rights secured by Articles 13 and 14 shall be safeguarded "in perpetuity" by the Council of the League of Nations in the event that the mandate is terminated.

These articles, which were constituted amidst statements declaring Britain's commitment to establish a "national home" for the Jews, spelled out what the Christian minority could expect from the British Mandate.[45] Civil and religious rights would be defended, autonomy in religious matters would be granted, and holy days and holy places would be recognized and respected. Given any other context, the Palestinian Christian community would have heralded these measures as an improvement in their social standing. They had been placed, after all, on equal footing with the Muslim majority.[46] Nevertheless, their status as a religious minority persisted. It is for this reason that Daphne Tsimhoni writes: "The treatment of the Christians as a religious minority by the British Mandate in Palestine represented the preservation and development of the Ottoman *millet* system."[47] This, along with the fact that the Jews were offered special privileges by the British Mandate, dampened any appreciation they might have felt toward these articles. Therefore Tsimhoni is right to conclude that the "significance attached by the British Mandate to the Christians was replaced by a growing disregard."[48] The end result was that most Arab Christians during this time found more and more affinity with the Arab Muslim majority than with the mandatory power with whom they were coreligionists.

---

45. Further provisions were made in the "Palestine Order in Council 1922," which clarified and reinforced what was stated in the mandate. Tsimhoni, "The Status of the Arab Christians," 169.
46. Anthony O'Mahony makes note of this but comments on its irony for the Muslim majority. Before the British Mandate they were not considered a "separate community" but "part of the general Islamic religious and political body which ruled the Ottoman empire." Now the Muslim community resembled an "Ottoman *millet*, which was previously the status and organisation of non-Muslim communities." Anthony O'Mahony, "Palestinian Christians: Religion, Politics and Society, *c.* 1800–1948," 9–55 in idem, ed., *Palestinian Christians: Religion, Politics and Society in the Holy Land* (London: Melisende, 1999)," at 33.
47. Tsimhoni, "The Status of the Arab Christians," 166. Cf. Chapter 3, Section "The Political Context of Palestinian Christians prior to 1917."
48. Tsimhoni, "The Status of the Arab Christians," 186.

In light of this general background of the status of Christians in Palestine between 1917 and 1948, it is now time to look at the Christian communities in Palestine more specifically.

The Anglican Church and its Agencies between 1917 and 1948

Saul Colbi argues that the "policy of the Mandatory towards the Christian communities . . . did not prevent the Protestant Churches from doing exceptionally well in the thirty years of the Mandate, both in numbers and in establishments."[49] Colbi's appraisal gives a false impression of the state of the Protestant churches during this time, as if they were devoid of conflict and almost insurmountable challenges. This is particularly true for the Anglican Church, the largest of the Protestant communities in Palestine. Here we will focus on the work of the CMS, the Anglican bishopric, and the PNCC. This will provide a better understanding of the character of the Anglican presence in Palestine during the British Mandate.

The CMS

The CMS also heralded the advent of British control in Palestine, writing:

> The fact that Jerusalem and Bethlehem . . . are now in Christian hands dominates all other events. . . . Fresh hope has been aroused that we are on the eve of a great spiritual advance. Perhaps nothing has done more to inspire this new hope than the Government's declaration in favour of the establishment in Palestine of a "national home for the Jewish people" (The Balfour Declaration).
>
> The miraculous preservation of the Jewish race, no less than prophecy, has produced a deep seated conviction that the Chosen People are destined to be one of God's chief instruments in working out his divine purpose for the human race. If these dreams are to materialise, a

---

49. Saul Colbi, *A Short History of Christianity in the Holy Land* (Tel Aviv: Am Hassefer, 1966), 51.

sustained effort must be put forward by the Christian Church to bring Israel into the fold of Christ.[50]

The CMS celebrated the fact that a "national home" would be created in Palestine for the Jews and dreamed of a mass conversion of Jews to Christianity. However, it was neither the appointed task of the CMS to see this to fruition or within its financial means to contribute to such an endeavor. Its primary aim was the evangelization of Muslims.[51] In addition, it had numerous hospitals, schools, and congregations to administer. However, the Great War had dealt a serious blow to the CMS. All its mission property had been damaged to some degree, and it no longer had the financial capability to restore its infrastructure to anything like its "pre-war scale."[52] Along with the missionary agency as a whole, the CMS mission in Palestine was forced to consider how it might cut back on its expenditure and activities. This reality met with a high degree of hostility by the CMS missionaries in Palestine. It was not until Janet MacInnes became the secretary of the CMS in Palestine in 1932 that one notes a "greater readiness to treat retrenchment not as an affront but as a challenge to new initiatives and good planning."[53] This outlook would characterize the CMS for the remainder of the Mandate.

Despite the financial difficulties that threatened the work of the CMS in Palestine, there were a number of things in which its personnel could take pride. Perhaps most significant was the growth of the church in Palestine during this period. For example, "Communicant figures for 1923 were given as 1,164 compared with

---

50. CMS, "General Review of the Year (1917–1918)," 8, in Farah, *In Troubled Waters*, 86.
51. Gordon Hewitt, *The Problems of Success. A History of the Church Missionary Society 1910–1942* (London: SCM, 1971), 361.
52. Hewitt, *Problems of Success*, 361.
53. Ibid., 369. Janet MacInnes was the wife of former CMS missionary and Anglican Bishop in Jerusalem Rennie MacInnes. The bishop died in 1931, and his wife became secretary the following year.

1,005 for 1922, and comparable figures for baptized church members were 2,620 (1923) and 2,507 (1922)."[54] Eight years later Wilson Cash, who was secretary of the CMS in Palestine before Mrs. MacInnes, could still boast to the Archbishop of Canterbury of the "Native Church" under its oversight:

> There is in being . . . a Native Church that is spiritual, evangelical and conservative. It has seven ordained clergymen, all Palestinians, 2,715 adherents and 1,220 communicants. During the last ten years . . . there have been practically no transfers from the Greek Church to the Anglican Native Church of the country. This little Church is probably the best educated church in the country. Its members are in many senior Government departments.[55]

Despite the flattery afforded the "native" Anglican Church in Palestine, there were numerous pressures challenging this small Christian minority. Among the most trying were its relations with the CMS and the Anglican bishopric in Jerusalem itself. These struggles will be outlined after a brief survey of the Anglican bishopric in Jerusalem during this time.

The Anglican Bishopric in Jerusalem

During the years of the British Mandate in Palestine the Anglican bishopric in Jerusalem was headed by Bishop Rennie MacInnes (1914–1931), Bishop George Francis Graham Brown (1932–1942), and then by Bishop Weston Henry Stewart (1943–1957). All three bishops were forced to address the mounting hostility between the Jewish and Arab communities. Each uttered statements about Zionism as well as the misappropriation of the Old Testament by members of that movement. Despite the pressures and the time required to attend to this ever-vexing conflict, the bishops were still

---

54. Hewitt, *Problems of Success*, 363.
55. Quoted in Hewitt, *Problems of Success*, 369.

able to advance the work and standing of the bishopric in Palestine and around the world.

Bishop Rennie MacInnes "firmly believed in the Old Testament prophecies and their fulfillment; but he was opposed to Zionist policies and tactics in Palestine."[56] This is evidenced by a meeting he had with Chaim Weizmann on December 13, 1919. He reports to Weizmann that he "strongly hoped for the great future of the Jewish people and that a thrill of interest went through British Christians at the idea of a return of the Jews to Palestine."[57] However, while he supported the return of Jews to Palestine he "objected to certain features of current Zionism that had led to uneasiness among Palestinian people."[58] By the end of Rennie MacInnes's bishopric his disapproval of Zionist policies overshadowed his endorsement of their ideals. In addition to his views on and contact with Zionism, Bishop MacInnes was influential in expanding the work of the Anglican bishopric in Palestine. With funding from the Jerusalem and East Mission (JEM), MacInnes appointed "experts in the four areas of the churches [sic] work: education, Judaism, eastern Christianity, and Islam."[59] Stacy Waddy was hired in 1919 and entrusted with the educational oversight of the diocese. The same year Herbert Danby, who would later become Regius Professor of Hebrew at Oxford University, was employed by MacInnes. He would serve as Residentiary Canon at St. George's from 1921 to 1936. In addition, Charles Bridgeman joined the staff to work with the eastern Christian churches. This last appointment was significant, for it marked a growing ecumenical ethos that pervaded MacInnes's

---

56. Farah, *In Troubled Waters*, 87.
57. Quoted in Farah, *In Troubled Waters*, 87.
58. Ibid.
59. Lester Pittman, "The Formation of the Episcopal Diocese of Jerusalem 1841–1948: Anglican, Indigenous and Ecumenical," 85–104 in *Patterns of the Past, Prospects for the Future: The Christian Heritage in the Holy Land*, ed. Thomas Hummel, Kevork Hintlian, and Ulf Carmesund (London: Melisende, 1999), at 99.

bishopric. Bridgeman himself was sent in cooperation with the Episcopal Church in the United States.[60]

Rennie MacInnes also desired to draw the CMJ, CMS, and PNCC under the same umbrella as the JEM, which was of course under the oversight of the bishop. This was not a terribly outlandish idea, as all four of the organizations were technically under the auspices of the Church of England; however, only the CMS welcomed the venture.[61] Both the CMJ and the PNCC refused to "surrender their autonomy by giving the bishop and the new integrated diocesan structure control over their affairs."[62] This was especially true for the PNCC, who would not sacrifice their quest to be recognized as an independent Christian community.

Like his predecessor, Bishop George Francis Graham Brown had to tackle the escalating conflict in Palestine while striving to foster the developments initiated by Rennie MacInnes. However, he differed from the former bishop in a number of areas, most notably in his view of Zionism. Whereas Rennie MacInnes favored a return of Jews to Palestine and criticized only those policies and actions of Zionists in Palestine he regarded as most iniquitous, Bishop Brown condemned its ideological foundation. He said in 1936, "Does not [Christ's] teaching of a spiritual Israel, really deny the basis of a 'National Home' in Palestine? [I]n other words, the establishment of a 'National Home' in Palestine cannot be made to depend on the prophecies of the Old Testament. . . ."[63] Similarly, Brown wrote in 1939, "The Jewish claim to Palestine on the basis of prophecy is declared throughout the New Testament to have been abrogated."[64]

---

60. The ecumenical spirit was also characteristic of Rennie MacInnes's relations with other Christian traditions in Palestine. For a number of examples see Farah, *In Troubled Waters*, 95–97.
61. The CMS saw that for the first time since Bishop Gobat (1846–1879) the Anglican Bishop in Jerusalem was sympathetic to their cause. Rennie MacInnes was, after all, a former CMS missionary.
62. Pittman, "The Formation of the Episcopal Diocese of Jerusalem," 100.
63. Quoted in Farah, *In Troubled Waters*, 111.

Despite Graham Brown's unyielding position on Zionism, he still endeavored to reconcile the Jewish and Arab inhabitants of Palestine. Rafiq Farah argues that this is illustrated especially in Graham Brown's untimely death. Bishop Brown died in a car crash with a Muslim Arab policeman and a Jewish Legionnaire. Farah comments, "Thus when the bishop died he was with members of two peoples he was trying to reconcile."[65]

When Weston Henry Stewart was consecrated as the next bishop in Jerusalem he had already been serving in Palestine for well over fifteen years.[66] As a result of his long tenure in Palestine and his service under Bishop Graham Brown there was a considerable degree of continuity between him and his predecessor. This included, among other things, his view on Zionism. Bishop Stewart was a contributor to the aforementioned memorandum "Some Christian Considerations," written in 1939. Weston Stewart himself wrote to the Anglo-American Committee in March 1946 that "there was no truth in the Zionist claims to Palestine, based on Old Testament history and prophecies. As far as the Christian understanding of the Bible is concerned, the church became the new spiritual Israel and heir to the promises, where racial and other barriers are broken down."[67] The other events and activities within Weston Stewart's bishopric will be discussed in the next chapter. Most significant were the establishment of the state of Israel in 1948 and the consecration of an Arab bishop in 1956.

---

64. Quoted in ibid., 115.
65. Ibid., 118.
66. He served as chaplain at St. George's in Jerusalem for two years, at which time he was appointed as the Archdeacon in Palestine in 1928.
67. Quoted in Farah, *In Troubled Waters*, 124.

The PNCC (Palestine Native Church Council)

As described in chapter 2, the PNCC was established in 1905 after nearly sixty years of work by the CMS in Palestine. With the formation of the council, the CMS entrusted much of the work that had once been under its authority and responsibility to the PNCC. True to its own missionary ethos, the CMS expressed its hope that the PNCC would be "self-supporting," "self-governing," and "self-extending." The PNCC succeeded in fulfilling this expectation for nearly twenty years, but the Great War caused such serious financial difficulties for the organization that it was forced to appeal to the Anglican Church for help.[68]

Financial difficulties were not the only issue the PNCC had to face between the years 1917 and 1948. It also sought to register itself with the British Government as an official and independent Christian community like "all the other Christian communities recognized officially by the Mandatory government under the Religious Community Ordinance of 1926. . . ."[69] Unfortunately, the hope of recognition for the Arab Evangelical Episcopal Community (AEEC), as they wanted to be called, would not be realized during the British Mandate.[70]

The Arab Lutheran Church in Palestine

Between the years 1917 and 1948 the Arab Lutheran Church in Palestine moved from being "*Missionsgemeinden*" (mission churches) to being "*Junge Kirche*." (the young church).[71] The first unit of this

---

68. The PNCC decided to appeal for financial assistance at their first session after World War One in March 1924. In *Palestine Church Council: Facts and Needs* (c. 1925/6). St. Antony's College, Oxford. J&EM 21/1.
69. Farah, *In Troubled Waters*, 54.
70. They would have to wait another thirty years until the first Arab bishop was consecrated and an additional twenty years until an independent diocese was established in Jerusalem in 1976.

"young church" was established in Jerusalem in 1929. A second was set up in Bethlehem four years later, in 1933.[72] The names of these congregations are significant, for they tell of the ethos and perspective of this "young: Arab Lutheran church. The Jerusalem church went by the name "*Die palästinensisch-evangelische Gemeinde Jerusalem*" (The Palestinian Lutheran Church of Jerusalem), and the church in Bethlehem was called "*Die evangelisch-arabischen Gemeinde zu Bethlehem*" (The Lutheran Arab Church of Bethlehem). The names clearly illustrate "how strong the self-awareness of Arab Christian community had become."[73] Both congregations highlight their Arab identity, and the former shows its "sympathy with the Palestinian national movement."[74] Despite the feeling one gets from the names, the "young" Arab Lutheran congregations never wanted to separate completely from the "German mother church."[75] They

---

71. Mitri Raheb, *Das reformatorische Erbe unter den Palästinensern: Zur Entstehung der Evangelisch-Lutherischen Kirche in Jordanien* (Gütersloh: Gerd Mohn, 1990), 135. This development of independent Arab Lutheran churches went hand in hand with the recognition of German individuals such as Albrecht Alt, who stated that a new situation had emerged since the end of the Great War. He wrote in 1928, "The upbuilding of independent Arab Lutheran congregations has become the focus of the Lutheran work in Palestine." (*Die Bildung selbständiger evangelisch-arabischer Gemeinden ist der Mittelpunkt der evangelisatorischen Arbeit in Palästina geworden.*) Quoted in Raheb, *Das reformatorische Erbe*, 142. However, the emergence of this "young church" did not happen without opposition, especially from the German Lutheran missionaries who wanted to grant it neither full membership in the German-speaking churches nor permission to form independent congregations. See Löffler, "Aggravating Circumstances," 99–124.
72. The establishment of independent Arab Lutheran congregations occurred nearly sixty years after that of their counterparts in the Anglican tradition. St. Paul's Church in Jerusalem held its first service for Arab Anglicans in 1874. (It was recently rededicated in March 2011.) Ben Drury, "St. Paul's, West Jerusalem, Re-Dedicated," *Bible Lands* (Summer 2011): 5.
73. (. . . *wie stark das Selbstbewusstein der arabischen Gemeinde gewachsen war*): Raheb, *Das reformatorische Erbe*, 139. It is interesting to note that the first independent Protestant Arabic-speaking church, St. Paul's, did not carry any national connotations in its name as did the later Arab Lutheran churches.
74. (*Sympathie mit der palästinensischen Nationalbewegung*): Raheb, *Das reformatorische Erbe*, 139. German distinguishes between "palästinisch" and "palästinensisch," unlike English and Arabic. Mitri Raheb explains this and tells of the history behind the congregation's name.
75. Löffler, "Aggravating Circumstances," 102. Löffler explains that the Arab members of the Lutheran Church in Palestine only wanted to form "independent congregations with independent consistories."

wanted to remain associated with their German counterparts. Mitri Raheb explains: "Through the expression '*palästinensisch-evangelische Gemeinde Jerusalem*' [Palestinian Lutheran Church of Jerusalem] the Arab Christian community also wanted to express its connection with the '*deutsch-evangelische Gemeinde Jerusalem*' [German Lutheran Church of Jerusalem]."[76] The significance of this will be borne out when Palestinian Lutheran hermeneutics of the Old Testament are discussed in the following section.

Like the First World War, the second had a devastating effect on German institutions and churches in Palestine. It was not without its blessings, though, for the Arab Lutheran Church in Palestine. As Roland Löffler explains, the war proved to be a "catalyst" for the "young church" as the "responsibility for the pastoral and school work . . . rested on the shoulders of the Arab ministers and teachers."[77] With each year that followed, the culture of "Missionsgemeinden" gave way to the growing reality and strength of the "Junge Kirche."

Palestinian Christian Hermeneutics of the Old Testament 1917–1948

During the years between 1917 and 1948, Arab national sentiment began to pervade the ranks of the Protestant Church in Palestine more and more. This has led scholars such as Roland Löffler to conclude: "The national question preoccupied the native population far more than confessional details."[78] Nevertheless, "confessional" identity was still important, however fragile it might have been.[79]

---

76. (*Durch die Wortstellung 'palästinensisch-evangelische Gemeinde Jerusalem' wollte auch die arabische Gemeinde den Zusammenhang mit der 'deutsch-evangelischen Gemeinde Jerusalem' zum Ausdruck bringen.*): Raheb, *Das reformatorische Erbe*, 139.
77. Löffler, "Aggravating Circumstances," 121.
78. Ibid.
79. Roland Löffler ("Aggravating Circumstances," 122–23) points out that Anglican identity was much stronger than Lutheran identity. This is proven by the fact that the Lutheran Church in Palestine was always battling against the departure of some of its members to the Anglican

Many Palestinian Christians clung to the religious precepts and traditions in which they had been reared as a rallying point against the changing political and religious context. For members of the PNCC it had to do with matters of ecclesiology, and for the Arab Lutheran Church, it was about interpreting the Old Testament. The following will describe these instances further, showing how Palestinian Christians viewed their political and religious context as well as how they interpreted the Old Testament between 1917 and 1948.

Arab Anglicans in Palestine: The PNCC

The opinion of the Arab Anglican Church in Palestine is well illustrated by three statements issued over the course of the British Mandate. The first was written in 1924/5 during an intensive debate between Bishop MacInnes, the CMS, and the PNCC. MacInnes had wanted to bring all the disparate mission agencies and organizations of the Church of England in Palestine under the authority of the Anglican bishopric. The CMS had agreed, but the PNCC resisted. The committee responsible for outlining the PNCC's position explained: "Up to 1924 . . . the Council had been taught to look forward to . . . independence; now they are told they must consent to an Autocracy . . . which has never existed before."[80] This, however, is a misrepresentation of the bishop's intentions. MacInnes never wanted to administer the bishopric with an iron fist. He himself was a former CMS missionary and was sympathetic to the cause and ethos of the society. In addition, he did not discount the grievances expressed by the PNCC.[81] His efforts to organize the diocese under

---

Church. He concludes: "Lutheran identity progressed, but remained open and fragile, and never reached a sharp theological or spiritual profile. Anglican identity, on the other hand, was more stable, thanks to its cultivation of a decidedly evangelical piety."
80. Hewitt, *The Problems of Success*, 365.
81. "Letter to Sir Gilbert Clayton," March 3, 1924. St. Antony's College, Oxford. J&EM 21/1.

the jurisdiction of the bishop had to do not only with his desire to structure it along proper ecclesiastical lines but also with having the Arab Anglicans in Palestine officially recognized. This is confirmed by the fact that in response to MacInnes's communication on the subject the chief political officer of the British military administration, Gilbert Clayton, wrote:

> I am directed by His Excellency the High Commissioner to inform your Lordship that, while the Government of Palestine view sympathetically the question of the recognition of the Anglican Community in Palestine, it is necessary before any further steps can be taken, or new negotiations opened, in the matter, that the Community should be regularly organized and possessed of a definite governing body under the jurisdiction of the Anglican Bishop in Jerusalem.[82]

The PNCC, however, did not welcome MacInnes's initiative.

Surprisingly, the CMS was willing to accept the measures proposed by the bishop. This leads one to inquire: "What was the real reason behind the refusal of the PNCC to submit to the bishop's authority?" Roland Löffler argues that it was the rise of Arab nationalism, which was beginning to pervade the Protestant churches in Palestine at the time.[83] This may have been the case implicitly. However, at this point in time the reasons outlined by the PNCC were more theological than political. As can be seen in the following report, they wanted:[84]

1. To remain strict evangelicals, conforming to the *present* Prayer Book and the sacraments of the church;
2. To remain independent of the bishop, apart from such legal,

---

82. "Letter to Bishop MacInnes," March 24, 1924. St. Antony's College, Oxford. J&EM 21/1.
83. Roland Löffler argues similarly. He writes: "It is historically in no way surprising that the desire for self-governing Arab Protestant congregations arose at the time of the *Arab Awakening*. . . . Nor is it surprising that this desire grew stronger at the end of the First World War when the Arab-Zionist conflict and Palestinian national consciousness were developing." "Aggravating Circumstances," 102.
84. This letter was written by the three CMS "visitors" to the PNCC in 1924. It is quoted in Hewitt, *The Problems of Success*, 363–64.

ecclesiastical and ceremonial relations as the administering of confirmation and ordination, and representing them in case of need in approaching the government and other authorities;

3. To obtain recognition by the government as a legal entity, capable of administering property, trusts, etc.;
4. To be quite independent and self-controlled with regard to the holding and free administration of all property connected with the church;
5. To be assured that no bishop has the right to call upon them to make any alterations in the form of their services; no right to impose upon them, as of necessity, any revised edition of the Prayer Book, or to demand any change in the ritual in any church, in its furniture, in the robes of the clergy, in times of services (e.g. Evening Communion) or to insist on the appointment of one of his nominees as pastor of one of their churches;
6. To be assured of the right of inter-communion and of interchange of pulpits without reference to the bishop.[85]

Here the PNCC upholds its connection to the Church of England on the one hand and, on the other hand, maintains its independence. It says it conforms to the "*present* Prayer Book and the sacraments of the Church of England," and yet it denies the church's right to change or revise any of the said matters or their form of worship. It accepts the authority of the bishop in legal, ecclesiastical, and ceremonial matters, but it delimits them according to its desire to be "self-supporting," "self-governing," and "self-extending."[86] The PNCC was, in other

---

85. Löffler observes that their statement was a "clear dig directed at the growing influence of the High Church wing in the Anglican community and especially their supporters in the British isles, like the Anglo-Catholic Pilgrimage." "Aggravating Circumstances," 111.
86. See above section, "The PNCC (The Palestine Native Church Council)." That the PNCC recognized the authority of the Anglican Bishop in Jerusalem is further underscored by their letter to MacInnes, which highlighted their continued adherence to Article 3 of the Regulations

words, simply acting according to the ethos of the CMS and the level of independence it had been granted by the "Parent Committee," from which its primary authority was derived and in which it had operated for nearly twenty years.[87] That the PNCC, in contrast to the CMS, was not willing to accept the measures proposed by the bishop underscores the strength of their desire to be recognized as a *bona fide* community. Perhaps, as Löffler maintains, an implicit sense of nationalism was also fueling their refusal for fear that their appeal for recognition would be lost. If these patriotic feelings were oblique in 1925, they became more explicit after 1936, as can be seen in their next statement.

It was in the first year of the Great Revolt that the PNCC sent a memorandum to the Archbishop of Canterbury to inform him of the situation in Palestine and to articulate some of their concerns.[88] Palestine was suffering from the effects of the riots and the general strike. There was an inordinate amount of damage to property and loss of life. The PNCC deplored this seemingly irreconcilable reality on the one hand and, on the other hand, argued that the solution to the conflict was rather straightforward. They wrote: "The source of the trouble is well known to all. The Mandate for Palestine, embodying the Balfour Declaration, and undertaking to provide for a Jewish National Home in Palestine carries within it the germs of strife and dissension, and is responsible for our trouble, past and present."[89] They suggested that the "best solution to the present impasse is the immediate cessation of immigration for at least six

---

of the Church Council. "Letter to Bishop MacInnes," 24 April, 1925. St. Antony's College, Oxford. J&EM 21/1. Cf. Church Missionary Society, "Palestine Mission: Regulations for a Church Council, Regulations for Pastorate Committees, with Appendices," published 1910. St. Antony's College, Oxford. J&EM 21/1.

87. Ibid.
88. "Memorandum of the PNCC to the Archbishop of Canterbury," June 6, 1936. St. Antony's College, Oxford. J&EM 21/3.
89. Ibid.

months which will give time for the radical reconsideration of the Balfour Declaration."⁹⁰

In making this statement the PNCC seems to show that by 1936 it had unambiguously aligned itself with the cause of Arab nationalism and the point of view of the Arab Muslim majority. This, however, was not completely the case. The PNCC was definitely committed to the cause of Arab nationalism but along with other Arab Christians in Palestine, it refused to resist British rule violently, as the Arab Muslim majority was doing.⁹¹ Furthermore, it still held out hope that Britain could reform its ways and that this could be accomplished by an appeal through the church, namely, through the Archbishop of Canterbury. The PNCC wrote in a memorandum:

> We are constantly reminded by the Moslems here of their justice and tolerance to Christians in the centuries of their conquest of, and rule in Palestine. The Palestinian Moslems, who are at the moment the majority, feel they are badly treated by a Christian nation and placed at the mercy of the Jews. After the fate of the Armenians, the Greeks of Asia Minor, the Assyrians, the Abyssinians and the Arabs of Palestine the faith of our Christians also is being shaken not only in the Christian nations, but in the value of Christianity itself, and its effects on Western nations that have been for so many centuries under its influence. We are greatly afraid that the tide of nationality, increased by a sense of injustice, will carry many off their feet into unbelief or apostasy. The spirit of disaffection and indignation is growing among the Christians in this country, who feel as keenly as the others the injustice of the present situation. Palestine has become a theatre of politics, were [sic] people have little thought for anything else. This is making the work of the Church well nigh impossible. If the present deadlock continues and the dispute remains unsettled, it may develop into open rebellion, if it has not already done so. A way out must be found. . . . We are, therefore, appealing to Your Grace for intervention and mediation. . . .⁹²

---

90. Ibid.
91. As a result, they were accused of being disloyal to the cause of Arab nationalism and spies of the British government. See "Letter to the Bishop of London" by the Bishop in Jerusalem, May 22, 1937. St. Antony's College, Oxford. J&EM 21/3.

One can observe in the above statement both the affinity of the PNCC to the cause of Arab nationalism and its distance from it. Its members abhorred the tide of Jewish immigration and disagreed with the manner of British rule, but they still submitted to British authority and hoped that through the church a "way out" could be found.[93] They were buffeted by innumerable political and religious challenges, but their commitment to their religious tradition stood firm. At least, it did at the moment.

Moreover, the manner in which the PNCC viewed and interpreted the Bible remained surprisingly unchanged. This is underscored by a third statement.[94] Shortly after the start of the British Mandate the PNCC published a pamphlet with the purpose of eliciting funds from the Church of England. The pamphlet tells of the history of the PNCC and its work in Palestine. It also enumerates among other things the importance of the Bible and the ethos of its work. It states at the outset about the Bible:

> The Bible is read to-day in hundreds of languages, and the stories of the Old and New Testament still thrill their readers. Therein are recorded the lives of patriarchs, prophets, apostles, holy men and women, as well as the perfect story of the unique life of the Redeemer of the world, Who for us men and our salvation offered His life as a sacrifice for sin, without blemish and without spot. Here alone we find the foundation of our faith and the inspiration of holy lives.[95]

With regard to its ethos, which strongly resembled that of its "Parent Committee," it says:

---

92. "Memorandum of the PNCC to the Archbishop of Canterbury," June 6, 1936.
93. By contrast, see the account of Schedid Baz Haddad in Raheb, *Das reformatorische Erbe*, 181–85.
94. In contrast to the previous chapter, in which there were ample sources by which to determine the hermeneutics of the Old Testament applied by Palestinian Christians, there is a paucity of information for the period between 1917 and 1948. This may be due to the fact that Palestinian Christians were sidetracked by other concerns, namely, their efforts for ecclesiastical independence and their burgeoning conflict with Zionism and the British Mandate.
95. *Palestine Church Council: Facts and Needs* (c. 1925/6). St. Antony's College, Oxford. J&EM 21/1.

Although the Council at present is necessarily occupied chiefly with the needs of its own members, yet from the beginning the congregations have recognized their duty toward their non-Christian neighbours, especially the Moslems. . . . The C.M.S. in establishing the Council put this duty plainly before it, hoping that the Council—her child—would soon become a missionary power in the land. At the last Council a definite step was taken towards co-operation with the Missionary Conference in this important matter.[96]

The PNCC, therefore, although confronted by various political and religious challenges between 1917 and 1948, stayed true for the most part to its religious tradition, namely, the founding ethos of the CMS. The same was true for the Arab Lutheran Church in Palestine, which highlighted its "confessional" identity and drew strength from the religious tradition in which it was reared. The following account of the life and work of Hanna Bachut will illustrate this point.

Hanna Bachut: An Arab Lutheran Pastor in Palestine

Hanna Bachut was twenty-nine years old when he was called to be the pastor of the Arab Lutheran Church in Jerusalem. Born in about 1906, he was reared in an "Arab Catholic family," but he converted to Protestantism at an early age.[97] Bachut had been a pupil of the Syrisches Waisenhaus (Syrian Orphanage) and a recipient of training from various American theological institutions.[98] He taught for a time at a school associated with the Jerusalemsverein in Beit Sahour, served as a pastor of an Anglican church in Jerusalem and

---

96. *Palestine Church Council: Facts and Needs* (c. 1925/6). St. Antony's College, Oxford. J&EM 21/1.
97. It is interesting to note that Löffler refers to Bachut's background as being "Arab Catholic" as opposed to identifying him with the precise Catholic tradition of which he was a part. Moreover, "Arab Catholic" is not the appropriate terminology. It would have been better to say he belonged to an Eastern Catholic tradition. Roland Löffler, *Protestanten in Palästina* (Stuttgart: Kohlhammer, 2008), 382.
98. It is not clear where exactly Bachut studied. Roland Löffler mentions only vaguely an "American Preacher's School" and an "American Lutheran Institution." Löffler, "Aggravating Circumstances." 117–18.

then briefly at the Weihnachtskirche in Bethlehem, where he was ordained by an American Lutheran pastor.[99] Despite the diversity of Bachut's experiences in ministry and training, he was "strongly Lutheran."[100] This will become evident as we view some of the activities in which Bachut engaged during his brief tenure as pastor of the Arab Lutheran Church in Jerusalem.[101]

One of the most explicit examples of Bachut's Lutheran identity can be seen in the events surrounding Reformation Sunday in 1937.[102] On that day Bachut had written Martin Luther's Ninety-Five Theses on a giant chalkboard and placed them before the altar. His action left such an impression on the congregation that after the service the parishioners had the Theses photographed so that they could distribute them as a "*Reformationsurkunden.*"[103]

As this example shows, Bachut's affinity for the Lutheran tradition was rooted in his appreciation of the work and theology of Martin Luther. He avidly read and translated much of Luther's work into Arabic, including Luther's *Open Letter on Translation, Large Catechism,* and *Prefaces to the Old Testament.*[104] It was this last work by Martin Luther that had a profound impact on the way Hanna Bachut interpreted the Old Testament. This is evident in at least two instances: in the "Protestant Evenings" hosted by the Arab Lutheran Church in Bethlehem and in a sermon Bachut preached on May 10, 1936.

Hanna Bachut, Schedid Baz Haddad, and others organized a number of "Protestant Evenings" to address some of the questions

---

99. Ibid.
100. "Bachuths Brief an Ulrich vom 14.2.1938," quoted in Löffler, *Protestanten in Palästina*, 383.
101. Bachut served as pastor in Jerusalem for only four years. He immigrated to the United States in 1939.
102. The following events are recorded in Löffler, *Protestanten in Palästina*, 383.
103. That is, "Reformation Document." Löffler, *Protestanten in Palästina*, 383.
104. Bachut's translation of Luther's *On Sins* was the first Lutheran pamphlet to be translated into Arabic. Löffler, *Protestanten in Palästina*, 383.

that troubled the Palestinian Christian community during this time.[105] These "Protestant Evenings" were held every second Thursday at the Arab Lutheran congregation in Bethlehem to consider some of these "contemporary issues from the standpoint of a Protestant Interpretation of Scripture and understanding of Revelation."[106] Among the topics discussed at some of the meetings were:[107]

1. "How did Jesus relate to his native land?"
2. "Christ and Nationalism."
3. "Zionism and the prophets of the Old Testament"
4. "Luther's View of Old Testament Prophecy"
5. "Luther and Judaism"

One can see from this list that Martin Luther's views were repeatedly discussed and most likely influenced the way the Palestinian Protestant community interpreted the Old Testament and regarded the Jewish religion and people. This is especially true in the case of Hanna Bachut. His sermon resembles the way Martin Luther approached Old Testament prophecy.

Mitri Raheb records how before Bachut's sermon numerous American and English missionaries had infiltrated the countryside and had heralded the influx of Jews to Palestine as a fulfillment of

---

105. Mitri Raheb writes, "The Arab Protestant Church could not remain unaffected by the incessant waves of Jewish immigration, the determination of the British Mandate to establish a Jewish 'national homeland' in Palestine, and the strengthening of the Palestinian national movement. (Indeed) new questions began to emerge in the congregations that had not been so acute before." (*Die starken Einwanderungswellen der Juden, die Entschlossenheit der britischen Mandatsregierung, in Palästina eine jüdische »Nationalheimstätte« zu errichten, und das Erstarken der palästinensischen Nationalbewegung konnten die arabisch-evangelischen Gemeinden nicht unberührt lassen. Neue Fragen tauchten in den Gemeinden auf, die bis jetzt so nie akut waren.*) Raheb, *Das reformatorische Erbe*, 179.
106. (*Gegenwartsfragen unter dem Gesichtspunkt evangelischer Schriftauslegung und Offenbarungsauffassung*)" Raheb, *Der reformatorische Erbe*, 179.
107. Ibid.

Old Testament prophecy and a sign of "one of the last stages of God's plan of salvation."[108] Bachut's sermon was delivered in this context and sought to repudiate the claims of these "*Missionsansprachen*" (missionary claims) as a "*Missbrauch*" or "abuse" of the Word of God.[109] In his sermon Bachut asserted that

> The prophecies that are contained in the [books of the] Prophets had their fulfilment before or at the latest with the appearing of Jesus and for us are a thing of the past. According to the New Testament, though, the Jews will, after their repudiation, have in different ways the prospect of a final inclusion with the other nations; but an inclusion in God's eternal kingdom; not a word is said about the "earthly" Palestine.[110]

Bachut argues that Old Testament prophecy is not applicable to the present context; it has ceased to be of any relevance. Every OT prophecy has been fulfilled in or before the coming of Jesus Christ. The New Testament confirms this as it proclaims an "eternal reign of God" that has no consideration of any future "earthly" Palestine.[111] To maintain, therefore, that Old Testament prophecy has a function in the present "economy" is thoroughly mistaken. It is "as if the intervening period (almost 3,000 years) never existed, as if Christ had not appeared, and as if the Christian churches did not have a second part in their Bible."[112]

What is most interesting about Hanna Bachut and the community in which he served is the ease with which they drew strength from

---

108. (. . . *eine der letzten Stufen des göttlichen Heilsplan*): Raheb, *Der reformatorische Erbe*, 180.
109. Ibid.
110. (*Die in den Propheten enthaltenen Weissagungen seien schon vor oder spätestens mit Jesu Erscheinen in Erfüllung gegangen und damit für uns erledigt. Im Neuen Testament dagegen werde den Juden zwar verschiedentlich nach ihrer Verstossung eine endliche Aufnahme nach all den anderen Völkern in Aussicht gestellt; aber eine Aufnahme im Gottes ewiges Reich; nicht mit einem Worte sei dabei an das irdische Palästina gedacht.*) Raheb, *Der reformatorische Erbe*, 180.
111. Ibid.
112. (. . . *als ob in der Zwischenzeit [fast 3000 Jahre] nichts geschehen wäre; als ob Christus nicht erschienen wäre und als ob die christlichen Gemeinden keinen zweiten Teil in ihrer Bibel hätten.*) Raheb, *Der reformatorische Erbe*, 180.

the Lutheran tradition. If members of the PNCC were on the brink of losing their faith in the "Christian nations" and in the "value of Christianity itself," Bachut and the Arab Lutheran Church in which he served had no such problem.[113] They had no qualms about accepting and highlighting the tradition in which they were reared. They were staunch Lutherans. This was evident in their celebration of Reformation Sunday in 1937, the "Protestant Evenings" at the *Weihnachtskirche* in Bethlehem, and the way Bachut interpreted the Old Testament. This last is especially relevant for the present discussion. Bachut approached the Old Testament, and Old Testament prophecy in particular, in a way analogous to the approach of Martin Luther. This will become readily apparent below.

As intimated above, Luther's *Prefaces to the Old Testament* strongly influenced the way Bachut interpreted the Old Testament and thereby warrant investigation.[114] At the outset the Reformer highlights the OT's enduring value. "There are some," he says, "who have little regard for the Old Testament. They think of it as a book that was given to the Jewish people only and is now out of date, containing only stories of past times. They think they have enough in the New Testament and assert only a spiritual sense is to be sought in the Old Testament."[115] Luther contends that in actuality the Old Testament should not be "despised," but "diligently read," for it provides the "ground and proof of the New Testament."[116] He asks

---

113. Cf. "Memorandum of the PNCC to the Archbishop of Canterbury," June 6, 1936.
114. Luther's *Preface to the Old Testament* was written to introduce Luther's translation of the Pentateuch (1523) and therefore deals primarily with the first five books of the Old Testament, but it was kept as the opening preface to Luther's entire Old Testament translation (1534/1545). The *Preface to the Prophets* (1532) originally introduced Luther's translation of the prophetic books and was likewise included when the whole of his translation was collated (1545). From now on each preface will be referred to individually. Martin Luther, *Prefaces to the Old Testament*, in *Luther's Works* 35, ed. Helmut T. Lehman and E. Theodore Bachmann; trans. Charles M. Jacobs (Philadelphia: Fortress Press, 1960).
115. Luther, *Preface to the Old Testament*, 235.
116. Luther cites a number of New Testament passages to corroborate his point (John 5:39; Acts 17:11; Rom 1:2; 1 Cor 15:3-4; 1 Tim 4:13). *Preface to the Old Testament*, 235–36.

rhetorically: "And what is the New Testament but a public preaching and proclamation of Christ, set forth through the sayings of the Old Testament and fulfilled through Christ?"[117]

Granted, there are differences between the Old and New Testaments. Luther writes: "[T]he chief teaching of the New Testament is really the proclamation of grace and peace through the forgiveness of sins in Christ," and "the chief teaching of the Old Testament is really the teachings of laws, the showing up of sin, and the demanding of good."[118] Nevertheless, the aim of both Testaments is the same: to point people to Christ. Therefore, when a person reads the Old Testament she or he should ask *"was Christum treibet"* (what drives Christ?)[119] This is why Luther writes his *Preface to the Old Testament*. It is, as he says, a "brief suggestion for seeking Christ and the gospel in the Old Testament."[120]

Luther's views on Old Testament prophecy follow accordingly. The aim of Old Testament prophecy is to drive people to Christ. It does so by keeping people "conscious of their own impotence through a right understanding of the law" and providing examples of those who "have Moses right and those who do not, and also of the punishments and rewards that come to both." [121] For Luther, therefore, the prophets are "nothing else than administrators and witnesses of Moses and his office, bringing everyone to Christ through the law."[122] If there is a foretelling component to Old Testament prophecy, it is that the "prophets proclaim and bear witness to the kingdom of Christ in which we now live, and in which

---

117. Ibid., 236.
118. Ibid., 237.
119. Joseph F. Burgess, "Lutheran Interpretation of Scripture," 101–28 in *The Bible in the Churches: How Various Christians Interpret the Scriptures*, ed. Kenneth Hagan (2d ed.; Milwaukee: Marquette University Press, 1994), at 116.
120. Luther, *Preface to the Old Testament*," 248.
121. Ibid., 247.
122. Ibid., 247.

all believers in Christ have heretofore lived, and will live until the end of the world."[123] The possibility of a future reconstituted Jewish political entity in Palestine on the basis of Old Testament prophecy would have been inconceivable for Luther. For him, the prophets point to Christ alone.

That Bachut interpreted the Old Testament, and Old Testament prophecy in particular, similarly to Luther is without question. He appropriated Luther's *Vorreden zum Alten Testament* [*Prefaces to the Old Testament*] wholly and unreservedly and then applied them to his own context. As Roland Löffler rightly concludes, "Luther took those prophecies in the Prophets intended for the people of Israel and interpreted them christologically. The Arab Lutherans understood this interpretation politically and applied it to the Arab-Zionist conflict and concluded that the Jews should not feel that they were heirs of the Holy Land."[124] Therefore for Bachut and the Arab Lutheran tradition in Palestine between 1917 and 1948 there was no problem with the OT itself, only its misappropriation, misinterpretation, and even "*Missbrauch*."

Conclusion

The political and religious contexts of Palestine between 1917 and 1948 certainly affected the Palestinian Christianity community.[125]

---

123. Luther, *Preface to the Prophets*, 265.
124. (*Luther setzte hier mit den prophetischen Weissagungen für das Volk Israel ein und interpretierte sie christologisch. Der arabische Lutheraner verstand diese Auslegung politisch, übertrug sie auf den arabisch-zionistischen Konflikt und folgerte daraus, dass sich die Juden nicht als Erben des Heiligen Landes fühlen sollten.*) Löffler, *Protestanten in Palästina*, 383.
125. It is also possible that the political and religious contexts outside of Palestine influenced the views of Palestinian Christians as well. This can be seen in the following letter by Bishop George Francis Graham Brown detailing his conversation with some theological students in Palestine. He writes: "I was speaking to them about the position of Christian minorities in Iraq and they fully approved of the need of securing that their rights as citizens should be maintained; when I applied the same principles to the rights of the Jewish minority in Germany at the present time they were unwilling to apply the principles accepted for the Christian minorities in Iraq and explained that their reason for this was as the Jews had betrayed the

The burgeoning national aspirations of Arabs and Jews, the corresponding hostilities between the two parties, and the subsequent breakdown of Mandatory Palestine were noted, lamented, and decried by Christians across the board, and not least by the PNCC and the Arab Lutheran Church in Palestine. As a result, Palestinian Christians sympathized more and more with the political views of the Arab Muslim majority, and they increasingly distrusted the administration of the British Mandate, with whom they were co-religionists.[126] In addition, their status as a religious minority persisted. They struggled in vain for ecclesiastical independence. Despite all these challenges, their numbers increased and their hermeneutic of the Old Testament remained unchanged. There was a growing awareness that the Old Testament was being abused or misinterpreted, yet this did not seem to alter or hinder their use or understanding of it. In some cases, as with Hanna Bachut and the Arab Lutheran Church, their connection with their religious tradition and the way they interpreted the Bible grew even stronger. However, all this would change after 1948.

Germans in the War they were now receiving their due punishment as God had said it would extend even to the third and fourth generation." "Letter to The Rev. W. W. Cash," July 26, 1933. St. Antony's College, Oxford. J&EM 21/3. Granted, not all Palestinian Christians would have believed in the "Stab in the Back Theory" that was being propagated in Germany at the time, which maintained that the reason Germany lost WWI was that the Jews had betrayed them. Nevertheless, the letter illustrates how the political and religious contexts outside of Palestine may have influenced the views of Palestinian Christians between 1917 and 1948, and in particular their views regarding Jews.

126. For instance, Schedid Baz Haddad questioned whether he could or even should pray for Britain as part of the "Fürbittengebet" or Intercessory Prayer. Cf. Mitri Raheb, *Das reformatorische Erbe*, 181–85.

4

Palestinian Christianity and the "Catastrophe" of the Modern State of Israel

The British Mandate officially ended at midnight on May 14, 1948. On the eve of its termination the members of the National Council, who were meeting in Tel Aviv, declared independence and thereby established the modern state of Israel. However, the surrounding Arab nations of Egypt, Lebanon, Syria, and Iraq attacked Israel the following day and thus started the Arab-Israeli War. The founding of the state of Israel and the subsequent war, with all its repercussions, are as hotly debated as any event that will be discussed in this section. May 14, 1948 is remembered by many in Israel as its יום העצמאות, that is, its Day of Independence. Likewise, the ensuing war between Israel and the Arab nations is known as the מלחמת העצמאות, that is, the War of Independence. However, for many Arabs in Palestine the occasion of Israel's independence and the aftermath of the Arab-Israeli War are seen as a catastrophe. It is therefore commemorated as يوم النكبة, that is, the Day of Catastrophe.

The debate will not be rehearsed here; it has been adequately recounted elsewhere.[1] The first section of this chapter will only briefly sketch the political and religious contexts of Palestinian Christians after 1948, and subsequent sections will focus on how Palestinian Christianity and its hermeneutic of the Old Testament have developed since the foundation of the state of Israel.

The Political Context of Palestinian Christians after 1948

Conor Cruise O'Brien writes, "The condition of the region, after the Armistice Agreements, was one of neither war nor peace."[2] The borders between Israel and the surrounding Arab nations were drawn in 1949, but this did not mean that hostilities had ceased. As any history of the Arab-Israeli conflict will show, the region continued to be marred by further incursions and battles between the respective parties.[3] O'Brien is right to conclude that the Armistice Agreements did not end the state of war; they merely suspended it.[4] This turbulent and unrelenting situation profoundly affected the Palestinian Christian community. The following will enumerate the main battles and political climate of the conflict, as well as noting the shift in borders between Israel and its Arab neighbors. In so doing it will paint a picture of the political context of Palestinian Christians since 1948.

---

1. See Chap. 1, where some of the issues confronting the Palestinian Christian community since 1948 are described.
2. Conor Cruise O'Brien, *The Siege* (London: Weidenfeld and Nicolson, 1986), 362.
3. It should be noted that the Western Powers played a significant role in the persistent conflict between Israel and its surrounding Arab neighbors.
4. O'Brien, *Siege*, 362.

THE "CATASTROPHE" OF THE MODERN STATE OF ISRAEL

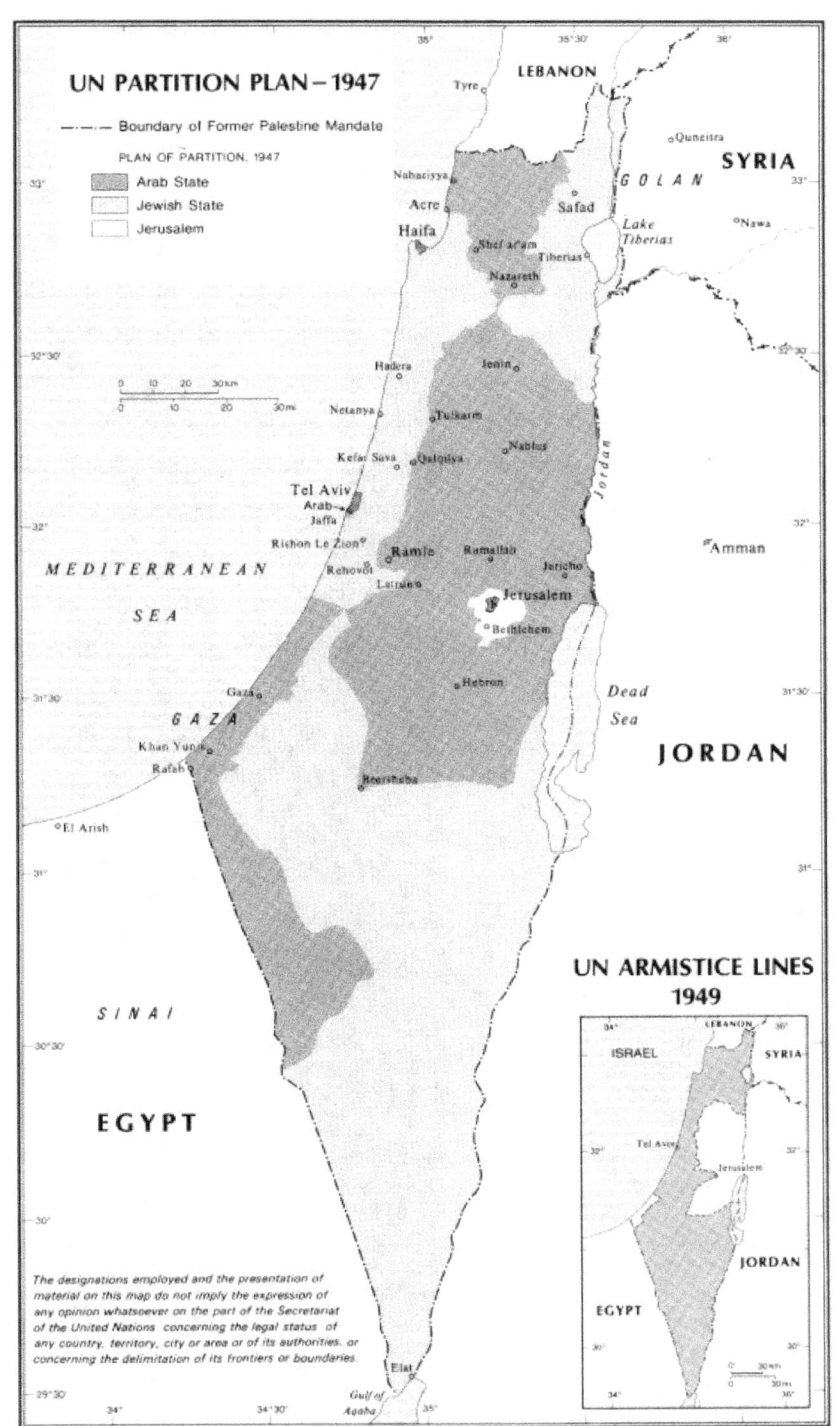

When the Armistice Demarcation Lines were drawn after the Arab-Israeli War of 1948–1949, Israel found itself within a territory significantly larger than it had anticipated in light of the United Nations partition plan of 1947 (see map at right).[5]

The Old City of Jerusalem along with the West Bank fell into the hands of Jordan, and the Gaza Strip was controlled by Egypt. Despite further altercations in the 1950s, and not least with the Suez Crisis of 1956, the borders between Israel, Jordan, and Egypt remained unchanged until 1967,[6] when the Six Day War drastically altered these boundaries.[7] The Sinai, Gaza Strip, Golan Heights, and West Bank were occupied by Israel over the course of just a few days (see map at right).

These last three pieces of land have all remained under Israeli control/occupation. The Sinai Peninsula, however, was returned to Egypt in 1979 in exchange for peace and Egypt's recognition of the state of Israel.[8] This treaty was remarkable, considering that the 1973 Yom Kippur War had taken place just a few years earlier.

The treaty between these two nations did not mark the end of the Arab-Israeli conflict. Although Israel's relations with the surrounding Arab nation states were gradually normalizing, Israel faced a growing unease and hostility from Palestinians both in the surrounding Arab countries as well as within its own borders. It was because of the former that Israel invaded Lebanon in 1982.[9] The Palestine Liberation Organization (PLO) had been active in the country's southern region

---

5. "UN Partition Plan 1947 and UN Armistice Lines 1949, Map No. 3067 Rev.1, April 1983." Used by permission, United Nations Publication Board, New York.
6. After the Suez Crisis, Israel occupied the Sinai until 1957, at which time the UN sent its UNEF to ensure the 1949 Armistice Lines would be respected by Israel and Egypt.
7. It is also known as the June War and the 1967 Arab-Israeli War.
8. There were other issues that encouraged Egypt and Israel to sign a peace treaty in 1979, not least the impact of the Camp David Accords in 1978.
9. Israel remained in southern Lebanon until its withdrawal in 2000.

following their expulsion from Jordan. In 1987, Palestinians within the Gaza Strip, East Jerusalem, and the West Bank joined forces in a nonviolent popular uprising against Israeli jurisdiction in the above territories. This First *Intifada*, as it was to be called, lasted until 1993, when the Oslo Accords were signed. It was on the heels of these accords that Israel and Jordan signed their own peace agreement in 1994.

The future between Palestinians and Israel, and the latter's relations with the surrounding Arab nations, seemed very bright in the mid 1990s. This proved to be short-lived, as the Arab-Israeli conflict had only been "suspended." The Camp David Summit in 2000 proved to be a failure, and when Ariel Sharon provocatively marched on the Temple Mount in September of that year a second Palestinian uprising was ignited. In contrast with the First *Intifada*, this Second *Intifada* was marked by excessive violence and loss of life on both sides.

Israel withdrew from the Gaza Strip in 2005 following the death of Yasser Arafat and the ensuing splintering of Palestinian political leadership.[10] This marked the end of the Second *Intifada*. However, Israel reentered the Gaza Strip in December 2008. This time it was not under the guise of occupation but under the pretext of war. The Gaza War, or Operation Cast Lead as it was otherwise known, lasted just under a month, but in the course of the operation it wreaked havoc on an already impoverished piece of land.

The prospect of peace remains uncertain. War always seems to be just "suspended." The Arab Spring, which began in Egypt in December 2010 and has spread throughout the Arab world, has aroused both hope and fear in the hearts of many in the Middle East. Similarly, so has Mahmoud Abbas's petition to the United Nations

---

10. There is a debate over when the second *Intifada* ended, for sporadic fighting persists between the two sides. Nevertheless, it is reasonable to conclude that the *Intifada* ended around 2004/5.

in September 2011 to recognize Palestine as an official political state. It remains to be seen what effect these two events will have on Israel's relations with the Palestinian people and the surrounding Arab nations. Until then, the state of affairs between Israel and its neighbors remains "one of neither war nor peace."[11]

The Religious Context of Palestinian Christians after 1948

The religious context of the Palestinian Christian community after 1948 comprises a myriad of factors. Each one has helped craft what their church and community is today. Not least among them is the impact of the political context. The continuing conflict between Israel and its Arab neighbors as well as its altercations with the Palestinian people themselves have undeniably affected the Palestinian Christian community. As a result, Palestinian Christians have often lived lives marked by displacement,[12] division,[13] and

---

11. These lines were written in 2012. The events of the last few years further corroborate the point that war always seems to be just "suspended." The cessation of hostilities may give the illusion of peace, but the speed at which things escalate into full-scale war, as during "Operation Protective Edge (2014)," proves otherwise.
12. Besides the loss of life, the chief "catastrophe" the Palestinian community had to face after the 1948–1949 Arab-Israeli War was the displacement of hundreds of thousands of their countrymen. The Six Day War multiplied this number, and for the most part the plight of these refugees remains unresolved. Cf. Bernard Sabella, "Palestinian Christians: Historical Demographic Developments, Current Politics and Attitudes Towards Church, Society and Human Rights," 39–93 in *The Sabeel Survey on Palestinian Christians in the West Bank and Israel* (Jerusalem: Sabeel, 2006). Ilan Pappé argues that the main cause of the refugee crisis was less the sad reality of war and more the tactic of the Israeli military to "ethnically cleanse" the region of its Arab inhabitants. Pappé, *The Ethnic Cleansing of Palestine* (Oxford: Oneworld Publications, 2007).
13. The 1948–1949 Arab-Israeli War also divided the Palestinian Christian community. When the Armistice Lines were finally drawn, Palestinian Christians found themselves scattered between Israel, Jordan, Lebanon, Syria, and Egypt. This had the effect of creating three different classes of Palestinians: Arab Israelis, Palestinians of the West Bank and Gaza Strip, and Palestinians in Diaspora. For a discussion of the often overlooked community of Arab Israelis or Palestinian Israelis see Ilan Pappé, *The Forgotten Palestinians: A History of the Palestinians in Israel* (London: Yale University Press, 2011). Not only were Palestinian Christians divided; many of them were also separated from their churches and institutions. This was especially true in Jerusalem where the Armistice Lines "cut right through the city separating the 'New City' and its western suburbs from the Old City and its eastern suburbs." Consequently, many of the "major holy sites of Christianity, such as the Church of the Holy Sepulchre, the Garden of Gethsemane,

disillusionment.[14] They have lived under a plurality of political authorities, and the status afforded them by these regimes has played no small part in their present condition.[15] Despite the precariousness of their situation, the religious traditions with which Palestinian Christians have been associated have matured, shown signs of growth, undergone a significant degree of indigenization and, in the case of the Anglican[16] and Lutheran[17] churches, become independent.

Palestinian Christian Hermeneutics of the Old Testament (PCHOT) since 1948

The chief characteristics of contemporary PCHOT have already been introduced above.[18] The present section will outline only the history of its development since 1948. Since the foundation of the state of

---

the Church of the Ascension, were located in the Jordanian sector" while many "newly-built and valuable properties" were situated in the "Israeli sector." The splitting up of the Palestinian Christian community inconvenienced not only the people themselves but also their clergy, as they had to find ways to cross the various borders in order to fulfill their pastoral obligations. Michael Dumper, "Faith and Statecraft: Church-State Relations in Jerusalem after 1948," 56–81 in *Palestinian Christians: Religion, Politics and Society in the Holy Land*, ed. Anthony O'Mahony (London: Melisende, 1999), at 59. It should be noted that Israel and Jordan did grant permission to clergy to pass to and from their respective countries on numerous occasions. "Christian News from Israel," (No. 2, September 1949). St. Antony's College, University of Oxford. J&EM 18/4.

14. One of the principal manifestations of this was emigration. Cf. Bernard Sabella, "The Emigration of Christian Arabs," 127–54 in *Christian Communities in the Arab Middle East: The Challenge of the Future*, ed. Andrea Pacini (Oxford: Clarendon Press, 1998).
15. For the authoritative account of Palestinian Christian life since 1948 see Daphne Tsimhoni, *Christian Communities in Jerusalem and the West Bank since 1948: An Historical, Social, and Political Study* (London: Praeger, 1993).
16. The Province of the Episcopal Church in Jerusalem and the Middle East was established in 1976, and Faik Ibrahim Haddad was consecrated as its first bishop. For an account of this development see Rafiq Farah, *In Troubled Waters: A History of the Anglican Church in Jerusalem, 1841–1998* (Leicester: Christians Aware, 2002), 56–59, 161–67. For a critical appraisal of the new Diocese/Church and its name see Kelvin Crombie, *For the Love of Zion* (London: Hodder & Stoughton, 1991), 250–55.
17. The *Evangelisch-Lutherische Kirche in Jordanien* (ELKJ) became independent in 1979, and Daoud Haddad was consecrated as its first bishop. For an account, see Mitri Raheb, *Das reformatorische Erbe unter den Palästinensern: Zur Entstehung der Evangelisch-Lutherischen Kirche in Jordanien. Die Lutherische Kirche* (Gütersloh: Gerd Mohn, 1990), 213–19, 246–48.
18. Cf. Chapter 1, "The Elements of Palestinian Christian Hermeneutics of the Old Testament."

Israel, Palestinian Christian Hermeneutics of the Old Testament has developed in roughly four stages.[19]

- *First Phase*: Before 1967
- *Second Phase*: Between 1967 and 1975
- *Third Phase*: Between 1983 and 1987
- *Fourth Phase*: After 1987

Using that timeline, the following sections will highlight individuals and statements representative of each period in order to show how Palestinian Christian hermeneutics of the Old Testament has changed and evolved to the present day.

PCHOT between 1948 and 1967

Immediately after the foundation of the modern state of Israel one notices the added difficulty Palestinian Christians had with reading the Old Testament. Whereas the previous struggle was over the "*Missbrauch des Wortes Gottes*," or "abuse of the Word of God,"[20] the present problem was more elemental. It had to do with the text of the Old Testament itself, and in particular with any reference to Israel in biblical and liturgical texts. The issue was widely noted and came to a head during the second meeting of the WCC in Evanston, Indiana, in 1954.

The Second Assembly of the WCC had as its theme "Christ—The Hope of the World."[21] As part of the "Discussion of the Statement

---

19. Cf. Uwe Gräbe, *Kontextuelle palästinensische Theologie* (Neuendettelsau: Erlanger Verlag, 1999), 18–21. There is an obvious gap between the second and third phases. Gräbe explains that this is on account of the shift in focus that occurred in connection with the start of the Lebanese Civil War in 1975. When Israel invaded Lebanon in 1982 the "*palästinensische Frage*" (Palestinian Question) returned to the forefront of the discussion. Gräbe, *Kontextuelle palästinensische Theologie*, 77–78.
20. See Chapter 3, "Hanna Bachut."

on the Report of the Advisory Commission on the Theme of the Assembly," a number of delegates moved that references to Israel be deleted.[22] On the first day of deliberation Weston Stewart, the Anglican Bishop in Jerusalem, "moved modification of references to Israel. He said that he lived where every statement about Israel was apt to become bitterly controversial and emphasized that many hopes other than that of Israel were fulfilled by Christ's coming."[23] On the third day of discussion, concerns were raised by other representatives from the Middle East. Farid Audeh, who was a delegate on behalf of the Evangelical Synod of Syria and Lebanon, was critical of the fact that specific reference was being made to the Jews. As Visser't Hooft summarizes, "He asked whether Christ was less the hope of all peoples than of one and said he did not believe the Assembly wished to make the task of churches in the Near East more difficult. He read a telegram from Dr. Charles Mallik disclaiming any suggestion that political events at present befalling the Jews were associated with the fulfillment of Christian hope."[24] Aziz Sorial Atiya from the Coptic Orthodox Church in Egypt added that "it would be a disservice to the cause of the World Council in the Near East to mention Israel. Nor would mention of Israel be historically expedient at the present time."[25] Despite the defense put forward by Hendrikus Berkhof of the Netherlands Reformed Church, the motion in favor of eliminating references to Israel was "adopted by 195 votes to 150."[26]

---

21. W. A. Visser't Hooft, ed., *The Evanston Report: The Second Assembly of the World Council of Churches 1954* (London: SCM, 1955).
22. Ibid., 72–79.
23. Ibid., 74.
24. Ibid., 78.
25. Ibid.
26. Ibid. A statement was later published by those delegates who wished to express the "conviction that the Christian hope included the hope for the conversion of Israel." Ibid., 79. See "Statement on the Hope of Israel," in ibid., 327–28. These delegates clarified: "Our concern in this issue is wholly biblical and is not to be confused with any political attitude toward the State of Israel." Ibid., 327.

This development was confirmed two years later in Beirut at a conference meeting to discuss some of the issues confronting Palestinians at the time.[27] Two of the participants noted the difficulty many Arab Christians were having with certain biblical and liturgical texts. One wrote:

> Quietly and tactfully, voices were raised at the Beirut conference to try to persuade the Arab Christians and American missionaries working in that area that they are doing violence to Christianity in going to such extremes as to root out all references to Israel from the Psalms and liturgy of the Church. Every word of admonition is bitterly resisted and resented and I am sorry to confess that little progress has been made.[28]

The other responded:

> Incidentally, your mention of the "neo-Marcionism" of the present-day Arab Christianity reminds me of a problem which arose when I preached last winter at St. George's Cathedral in Jordan. . . . We could not use the first lesson from Genesis assigned by the lectionary because in it the Lord is quoted as promising to Abraham "and his seed forever" this good land! We didn't want half the congregation to walk out before the sermon was reached; so we used something innocuous from the apocryphal book of Ecclesiasticus.[29]

The above two comments, along with the account of the Second Assembly of the WCC in Evanston, show that the "principal problem for Palestinian Christians was to find a suitable approach to the Old

---

27. The conference was put on by the Near East Christian Council (NECC), International Missionary Council (IMC), and World Council of Churches (WCC). Larry Ekin, *Enduring Witness: The Churches and the Palestinians* (Geneva: Oikoumene, 1985), 6–16. Ekin also notes (p. 16) the irony that, in a conference talking about refugees, the delegates refused to discuss the issue of Jewish refugees from Arab lands.
28. "Letter from Franklin Clark Fry to James A. Pike," October 15, 1956. In Gräbe, *Kontextuelle palästinensische Theologie*, 50. Franklin Fry was president of the United Lutheran Church in America at the time. James Pike was an American Episcopal bishop who was active in the American civil rights movement.
29. "Letter from James A. Pike to Franklin Clark Fry," October 24, 1956. In Gräbe, *Kontextuelle palästinensische Theologie*, 50.

Testament that could sustain itself even in a situation of conflict with the young state of Israel."[30] Moreover, they underscore at what an early date Palestinian Christians had difficulty with the Old Testament. It is not something peculiar to contemporary Palestinian Christians; it has been a problem since the foundation of the state of Israel. What is most striking about Palestinian Christian hermeneutics of the Old Testament between 1948 and 1967, however, is the lack of method. It is not that they had no system by which to interpret the Bible; they simply opted to remove those texts with which they had problems instead of seeking to understand and explain them in light of their new surroundings. This practice would change as Palestinian Christian hermeneutics became more nuanced, but the earlier practice does show how cataclysmic the foundation of the state of Israel was for the faith of Palestinian Christians in the years immediately following 1948.

PCHOT between 1967 and 1975

There were two distinct realities that shaped the development of Palestinian Christian hermeneutics of the Old Testament between 1967 and 1975.[31] One was a proliferation of localized ecumenical activity in the Middle East and the other, following on from the first, was the variety of official statements on biblical interpretation that were issued and framed in response to the situation. The following section will briefly enumerate these two realities and show how PCHOT developed during this period.

At the start of 1967 the main center of ecumenical activity was in Geneva with the WCC. In the years following the Six Day War,

---

30. ([D]*as grundsätzliche Problem palästinensischer Christen, einen angemessenen Zugang zum Alten Testament zu finden, der sich auch in einer Situation des Konfliktes mit dem jungen Staat Israel bewährt.*) Gräbe, *Kontextuelle palästinensische Theologie*, 50–51.
31. For an overview of this period see Gräbe, *Kontextuelle palästinensische Theologie*, 51–97.

however, a number of statements were made by the WCC that encouraged localized ecumenical activity in the Middle East.[32] The most significant of these was that issued in Nicosia, Cyprus in 1969.[33] Of particular importance is the opening paragraph of its suggested guidelines to the churches, which says:

> There is a growing awareness of the reality of a Palestinian community, and manifestation of a Palestinian identity as shown, for example, in the Palestine Liberation Movement. Awareness of this Palestinian identity may be a first step towards the redress of the injustices done to the Palestinians. This means specifically that all of our work, both in the humanitarian fields and in preparation of educational and informational material, must be done not only *for* Palestinians but *with* them.[34]

That last point in particular provided the basis on which local ecumenical efforts could flourish. Especially relevant for the present discussion is the influence of the statement on biblical interpretation. The consultation in Nicosia affirmed the suggestion made in Canterbury that the "subject of biblical interpretation be studied in order to avoid the misuse of the Bible in support of partisan political views. . . ."[35] It also went one step farther and determined, in light of the aforementioned guideline, that a chief priority would be a "major interpretation programme to Churches outside of the Middle

---

32. The various documents and statements published by the WCC during this period are printed in Michael Christopher King, *The Palestinians and the Churches, Vol. 1, 1948–1956* (Geneva: World Council of Churches, 1981), 127–37.
33. This is not to discount the statement issued by the WCC in Canterbury in August 1969, which not only welcomed the plans for the upcoming conference in Nicosia but also provided the basis for much of the discussion that was to take place at Nicosia and suggested in particular that, at the meeting, "the subject of biblical interpretation be studied in order to avoid the misuse of the Bible in support of partisan political views and to clarify the bearing of faith upon critical political questions." WCC Central Committee, "Statement on the Middle East (Canterbury, August 1969)," in King, *The Palestinians and the Churches*, 129–30.
34. WCC in the Middle East, "Consultation on the Palestine Refugee Problem (Nicosia, September–October 1969)," in King, *The Palestinians and the Churches*, 130.
35. WCC Central Committee, "Statement on the Middle East (Canterbury, August 1969)," 130. Cf. WCC in the Middle East, "Consultation on the Palestine Refugee Problem (Nicosia, September–October 1969)," 131.

East shaped and led by the Churches and people within the Middle East. . . ."³⁶ The end result of this new ecumenical ethos, which placed a priority on listening to Christians in the Middle East, was a proliferation of "local" conferences and organizations and their statements on biblical interpretation.³⁷ It is on these statements that the discussion will now focus.

Just a few days after the Six Day War a group of "Middle Eastern theologians" issued a "Memorandum" on the "Palestine problem"³⁸ The document was intended to help Christians "make a clear judgment" on three questions:³⁹

1. The facts leading to the present situation.
2. What is revealed in the Bible concerning the confusion between the ideals of Judaism and Zionism.
3. Some ideas on a just solution to the Palestinian problem.

Of particular importance is the Memorandum's second section, which provides a picture of Palestinian Christian hermeneutics of the Old Testament as well as the manner in which Palestinian Christians viewed topics such as election, the promise of land and posterity made to Abraham, and the nature and vocation of the Jewish people.

Uwe Gräbe points out with reference to the Memorandum's approach to the Old Testament: "Where it was possible to mention

---

36. Ekin, *Enduring Witness*, 54.
37. This growth of "local" ecumenical activity in the Middle East was also fueled by a "revival" in the Greek Orthodox Church in the Middle East and subsequent involvement in the aforementioned ecumenical activity. Cf. Ekin, *Enduring Witness*, 43–44.
38. Jean Corbon, George Khodr, Maître Albert Lahham, and Samir Kafity, "A Memorandum by a Group of Middle Eastern Theologians (June 18, 1967)," 130–35 in Ekin, *Enduring Witness*. Of particular importance is Samir Kafity, who later became the second Palestinian Anglican Bishop in Jerusalem (1984–1998). Ekin (p. 38) rightly points out that the document is highly significant, for it not only "served as a basis for later discussions" but also "provides an understanding of the thinking of men who would emerge as figures of major importance to the ecumenical movement in the region."
39. Corbon et al., "Memorandum," 130.

the name 'Israel,' they showed that they were taking the first steps toward overcoming 'Neo-Marcionitism' to some extent."[40] Whereas before 1967 there was a tendency simply to avoid or remove references to Israel in the Old Testament and the liturgy, here one sees an effort to avoid the accusation of being ignoring or depreciating the Old Testament in the manner of Marcion. Although this was clearly an improvement on earlier approaches to the Old Testament, one also notices in the Memorandum the authors' continuing difficulty with the text. Of the fourteen biblical citations in the Memorandum, only five are from the Old Testament, and whereas the New Testament references are always indicated and quoted word for word, the Old Testament references are "paraphrased, allusive, and practically hidden [*umschreibend, anspielend und fast versteckt*]."[41] For example, where one might expect a reference to Genesis 17 in the Memorandum's discussion of election and the promise of land, the Old Testament reference is conspicuously absent.[42] All this underscores the persistent difficulty Christians in the Middle East were having with the OT.

In addition to seeing how Palestinian Christians approached the Old Testament, the Memorandum also provides a picture of how they viewed a number of theological topics. With regard to election the Memorandum states:

> The Jewish people have been called to live out in their own history, the history of the whole of humanity. A history in which God saves man. It is because of this that they are not people with temporal or political destiny. They were chosen to reveal that humanity as a whole is not intended to succeed in "this world" but in the "world that is to come," the kingdom of heaven.[43]

---

40. (*Wo es möglich wird, den Namen "Israel" auszusprechen, dort zeigen sich bereits erste Schritte zu einer ansatzweisen Überwindung des "Neo-marcionitismus."*) Gräbe, *Kontextuelle palästinensische Theologie*, 57.
41. Ibid., 57–58.
42. Ibid., 58.

Regarding the promise of land and posterity made to Abraham, the Memorandum argues that the promise finds its "fulfillment in Christ."[44] The authors contend, therefore, that "to understand the promise made to Abraham in the material sense is to pervert God's plan."[45] They also comment on the nature of the Jewish people, saying that the Jews are a "consecrated people, a nation which is consecrated, a nation of priests. It belongs only to God and not the earthly kingdom."[46] As to their vocation, the Jewish people are called to be "prophetic."[47] They are to serve as a foil for God's work "among the nations."[48] In other words, the Jewish people is "chosen to serve the Salvation of Humanity and not establish itself in any particular religious or racial way."[49] Therefore, "from the Christian point of view it is clear . . . that the creation of an exclusively Jewish State of Israel goes directly against God's plan for the Jewish people and the World."[50] These views and the aforementioned approach to the Old Testament would be taken up and developed by subsequent conferences and statements.

As intimated above, numerous local conferences in and statements from the Middle East followed in the wake of the Six Day War and the subsequent resolutions of the WCC.[51] There were consultations in connection with the World Student Christian Federation (WSCF),[52] the World Conference of Christians for Palestine

---

43. Corbon et al., "Memorandum," §12, 132–33.
44. Ibid., §13, 133.
45. Ibid.
46. Ibid., §14, 133.
47. Ibid., §15, 133.
48. Ibid. They write, "By its election, it reveals that all men are beloved by God with a love that is elective. By its infidelity it reveals that humanity is 'locked in sin.' Because God's love is stronger than its sin, it reveals that all humanity finds salvation through pure mercy."
49. Ibid., §16, 133.
50. Ibid., §17, 133.
51. The culmination of this process was the establishment of the Middle East Council of Churches (MECC) in 1974.
52. Gräbe, *Kontextuelle palästinensische Theologie*, 59–62.

(WCCP),[53] and the Near East Ecumenical Bureau for Information and Interpretation (NEEBII).[54] These conferences and their statements show the increasing importance of the Middle Eastern context for matters of interpretation, the growing disregard for Western models of biblical interpretation, the corresponding influence of Orthodox Christian interpretation on other Christian communities, and in turn the nature and state of Palestinian Christian hermeneutics between 1967 and 1975. For example, in the opening meeting of the WCCP, which was held in Beirut in May 1970 and had some four hundred representatives from thirty-seven countries, there quickly arose a sharp disagreement between the Western and Middle Eastern participants over the question of the significance of the Jews for theology and faith.[55] For instance, Hugh Harcourt[56] and William Holladay[57] argued that one can distinguish between the abiding "link between the Church and Israel [*Verbindung von Kirche und Israel*]" on the one hand and the "*Realpolitik* and exclusivism [Realpolitik *und Exklusivismus*]" of Zionism on the other.[58] George Khodr disagreed. He argued that "God's plan concerns the whole world and all people; therefore the fulfilment of the promises 'in the flesh' through a specific people and in a particular land is not possible; their aim is solely a 'spiritual' fulfilment."[59] For Khodr the

---

53. Ibid., 62–67.
54. Ibid., 67–72. Cf. Ekin, *Enduring Witness*, 61–67.
55. A second conference was held in Canterbury in September 1972. Gräbe, *Kontextuelle palästinensische Theologie*, 63.
56. From the American University of Beirut.
57. From the Near East School of Theology.
58. Gräbe, *Kontextuelle palästinensische Theologie*, 64. Gräbe writes "While Holladay denounced Neo-Marcionite interpretations of the Old Testament and Harcourt even spoke of an 'enduring election of the Jews,' the consequence, they said, was that the concept of 'Zionism' represents an eclectic (and thus Neo-Marcionite-like) interpretation of the Bible [and stands for] temporal triumphs, brutal *Realpolitik*, and exclusivism." (*Während Holladay neomarcionitische Interpretationen des Alten Testamentes anprangert und Harcourt gar von einer 'bleibenden Erwählung der Juden' spricht, steht der Begriff des 'Zionismus' ihnen zu folge für eine eklektische (und damit dem Neomarcionitismus ähnliche) Bibelauslegung, für temporäre Triumphe, brutale Realpolitik und Exklusivismus.*)

promises of land and posterity in the Old Testament were to be understood not just as spiritual promises fulfilled in Christ and applied to all people, but solely as such.[60] This is evident not just in the above statement but also in Khodr's comments to the NEEBII, where he, as an Orthodox Christian, questioned the appropriateness of the concept of salvation history as a means of understanding Scripture, and proposed instead that Scripture be read "typologically," or "im Geiste," that is, spiritually.[61] Khodr claimed accordingly that "'Land' refers to the promise of heaven and 'Jerusalem' is a type of the spiritual event between God and humankind, which for Christians takes place in the Eucharist."[62]

One can see from the above that in this period there was not only an increase in localized ecumenical activity but also a growing and concerted effort to tackle issues of biblical interpretation. A greater number of Orthodox Christians, such as George Khodr, joined the fray and offered their own hermeneutic as a way forward. Nevertheless, the struggle with the Old Testament persisted, and by the end of 1975 one notices that, for reasons that will appear, there was a significant shift away from trying to solve the dilemma of reading the Old Testament in the "shadow" of Israel.

---

59. Ibid. (*Gottes Plan betreffe die ganze Welt und alle Menschen, daher sei eine Erfüllung von Verheissungen "im Fleische" durch ein einziges Volk im einem bestimmentem Land gar nicht möglich; sie zielten allein auf eine Erfüllung "im Geiste" ab.*)
60. This view is underscored by the conference's closing statement, the "Call from Beirut," which states: "Affirming that the Gospel reveals a Messiah whose kingdom is not of this world while it is being manifested in this world, we reject the manipulation of Biblical texts for the purposes of political powers. Being contrary to the spirit of Christianity, the Zionist political interpretation seems to us as unacceptable for Christians as it is for Jews faithful to the spiritual message of the Old Testament. It leads in effect to scriptural legitimization of the grave injustices which the Palestinian people and other Arab people have undergone, in the face of which the human conscience must protest. Thus the Zionist state, like any political-religious system, whether based on a living faith or not, is opposed to the dignity and liberty of man." Gräbe, *Kontextuelle palästinensische Theologie*, 64.
61. Ibid., 70–71.
62. Ibid., 71. (*"Land" wird hier zum verheissenen Himmelreich, "Jerusalem" zum Typos eines spirituellen Geschehens zwischen Gott und Mensch, welches sich für Christen in der Eucharistie ereignet.*)

PCHOT between 1975 and 1982

There were three main reasons for the change in PCHOT between 1975 and 1982.[63] The first was geographical. Between 1975 and 1982 all eyes shifted northward to Lebanon and its civil war.[64] In addition, interest in matters of biblical interpretation receded during this period. "Context" was becoming more important than "text." As Gräbe points out, "The question about biblical interpretation and hermeneutics in the Middle East conflict was no longer the focal point, but rather the existential situation of the local community."[65] Furthermore, the change also had to do with the fact that "[b]y 1979 the justice of the Palestinian cause was sufficiently acknowledged by most of the churches and church agencies in the ecumenical family that no call for a new program of information and interpretation was necessary."[66]

PCHOT between 1982 and 1987

This period is characterized by a number of new initiatives and a consolidation of some old ones. In May 1983, participants at the joint MECC and WCC "Consultation on the Christian Presence and Witness in the Middle East" lamented that "we cannot afford to await another eight years before we hold a similar consultation."[67] With this statement two of the three proposed principles of Palestinian Christian hermeneutics between 1975 and 1982 had been overturned. There was a renewed focus on the "Palestine Problem" in the wake

---

63. Ibid., 77–78.
64. The war itself lasted from 1975 to 1990, but when Israel invaded southern Lebanon in 1982 attention returned to Israel and the corresponding "Palestine Problem."
65. (*Nicht mehr die Frage nach Bibelauslegung und Hermeneutik im Nahostkonflikt steht hier offenbar im Mittelpunkt, sondern vielmehr die existentielle Situation der Gemeinde vor Ort.*) Gräbe, *Kontextuelle palästinensische Theologie*, 77.
66. Ibid., 78.
67. Ibid., 99.

of Israel's invasion of southern Lebanon in 1982. In addition, there was an implicit recognition that some new initiative or program was needed. The conclusions reached at the conference and reinforced by subsequent conferences involving the MECC and the EMOK (*Evangelische Mittelostkommission*) would have a lasting impact on Palestinian Christian hermeneutics of the Old Testament. Here we will sketch some of the conference resolutions as they have to do with the state of Palestinian Christian hermeneutics during this period.[68]

In May 1983 the MECC and the WCC met in Geneva as part of a "Consultation on the Christian Presence and Witness in the Middle East."[69] Uwe Gräbe summarizes its decisions insofar as they have to do with the present topic as follows:

> Beginning with the existential question of "Christian Presence," constituted henceforth a break with the approach of previous consultations. This [new] program no longer claimed that one could contribute to a solution to the problems in the Near East through "exegetical compromise" ("Biblical Understanding and its Bearing . . .") or avoiding a "misuse" of the Bible. Exegetical reflections play hardly any role in the documentation of the consultation; rather, Near Eastern Christians express their own concerns [namely]: What (theological) meaning can our minority existence have in the Near East? And what is the content of our witness, our Christian message within this context? Central to this discussion, for example, was the call for interreligious dialogue for peace and justice.[70]

---

68. For an overview see ibid., 97–120.
69. Gräbe, *Kontextuelle palästinensische Theologie*, 354.
70. Ibid., 93–100. (*Mit dem Ansatz bei der existentiellen Frage christlicher Präsenz findet nunmehr ein Bruch mit dem Ansatz der früheren Konsultationen statt. Dieses Programm erhebt nicht mehr den Anspruch, als könne durch eine exegetische Verständigung ("Biblical Interpretation and its Bearing…") oder durch die Ausräumung eines "Missbrauchs" der Bibel ein Beitrag zur Lösung der Probleme im Nahen Osten geleistet werden. Exegetische Überlegungen spielen in den Dokumenten der Konsultation fast keine Rolle, vielmehr bringen nahöstliche Christen ihr eigenes Anliegen zum Ausdruck: Welche Bedeutung kann unsere Minderheitenexistenz im Nahen Osten (theologisch) haben? Und was ist der Inhalt unseres Zeugnisses, unserer christlichen Botschaft, innerhalb dieses Kontextes? Zentral sind dabei beispielsweise der Aufruf zu einem interreligiösen Dialog für Frieden und Gerechtigkeit.*)

Perhaps the most significant point in the statement was the intent to abandon biblical interpretation in favor of asking questions of contemporary identity, presence, and witness.[71] This was the key development of PCHOT between 1982 and 1987. Whereas before 1982 the Middle Eastern "context" was only *becoming* more important than the biblical "text," after 1982 that context had actually *become* more important. As Gräbe points out, "The direction was no longer from Scripture to situation, but rather the other way around, from situation to Scripture."[72] The goal was to establish a "localized exegesis" of the biblical text.[73] It did not matter whether Middle Eastern Christians differed in how they interpreted the biblical text *per se*. As long as it was faithful to the Middle Eastern (Palestinian) context it was seen as a "contribution toward a common Christian witness of the 'local churches' in the Near East and an expression of their common 'eschatological' hope."[74] And only the churches in the Middle East and Israel/Palestine could "determine the nature and form of their witness."[75] All other churches were duty-bound "to strengthen their presence and support their ministry. . . ."[76] This was the nature and context of PCHOT between 1982 and 1987 and beyond.

---

71. This period saw the publication of numerous statements and books by Christians in the Middle East that illustrate this shift in emphasis. Cf. Elias Chacour, *Blood Brothers* (Grand Rapids: Chosen Books, 1984).
72. (*Der Weg führt nicht mehr von der Schrift zur Situation, sondern umgekehrt von der Situation in die Schrift hinein.*) Gräbe, *Kontextuelle palästinensische Theologie*, 119. Subsequent conferences between the MECC and EMOK illustrate this shift. Cf. Ibid., 100–5.
73. Ibid., 104.
74. (*Beitrag zum gemeinsamen christlichen Zeugnis der 'lokalen Kirchen' im Nahen Osten und Ausdruck ihrer gemeinsamen eschatologichen Hoffnung*) Ibid., 105.
75. Ibid., 100.
76. Ibid.

PCHOT since 1987

The elements of contemporary PCHOT have already been described.[77] Nevertheless, a few words should be said about the factors that gave rise to the development of PCHOT after 1987, of which there are three. The first *Intifada* provided its context and impetus, the induction of Michel Sabbah as the Latin Patriarch of Jerusalem gave it authority, and the profusion of statements, conferences, and organizations in the wake of the *Intifada* afforded it the content, structure, and personnel who would influence its future direction.[78] PCHOT today is largely indebted to these three factors.

Conclusion

Before the foundation of the state of Israel, Palestinian Christians had no difficulty with the Old Testament. The only problem they had with the Bible was convincing Eastern Christians to read it and take it as their sole authority for matters of life and doctrine. Before 1917, Palestinian Christians adopted the hermeneutic of the Protestant missionaries without exception. Between 1917 and 1948 there was a growing sense that the Old Testament was being "abused" and "misinterpreted," but Palestinian Christians themselves were quite comfortable reading and interpreting the Old Testament according to their respective traditions. The foundation of the state of Israel, however, drastically disrupted the way Palestinian Christians used and interpreted the Old Testament. Numerous liturgical and

---

77. Cf. chap. 1 above.
78. This is not to discount the establishment of independent Episcopal and Lutheran churches in Israel/Palestine in 1976 and 1979 and the related induction of these churches' first Palestinian bishops. As Gräbe points out, however, "Now that for the first time one of the 'big' churches in the Holy Land was being led by an indigenous representative, the Arab Church leadership as a whole was a factor whose importance had to be taken into consideration." (*Indem nun zum ersten Mal auch eine der "grossen" Kirchen im Heiligen Land über einen einheimischen obersten Repräsentanten verfügt, stellen die arabischen Kirchenleitungen insgesamt einen Faktor dar, der als solcher ins Gewicht fällt.*) Gräbe, *Kontextuelle palästinensische Theologie*, 122.

Old Testament texts were avoided or simply abandoned. After 1967 one begins to notice a positive change in the way Palestinian Christians approached the Old Testament. With Western encouragement there was a massive increase in localized ecumenical activity, including a proliferation of conferences and statements on how the Bible should be interpreted. During this time the views of the Orthodox Church also challenged the traditionally accepted Western models of biblical interpretation. The years between 1967 and 1975 set the stage for a gradual minimizing of the importance of biblical interpretation. Between 1975 and 1982 there was a brief hiatus as attention shifted northward to Lebanon, but after the Israeli invasion of southern Lebanon discussions of the "Palestine Problem" and matters of biblical interpretation resumed once again. The years between 1982 and 1987 really paved the way for Palestinian Christian hermeneutics. Western models of biblical interpretation were abandoned in favor of establishing the nature of Middle Eastern (Palestinian) Christian identity, presence, and witness, and a "localized exegesis" of a biblical text that would be faithful to the context. The Arab (Palestinian) context became more authoritative for matters of hermeneutics than the biblical text. PCHOT after 1987 were largely similar to those of the previous period, with a few important exceptions. The first *Intifada* fueled Palestinian Christian hermeneutics with political expediency. The induction of Michel Sabbah gave it authority, and the proliferation of conferences and organizations gave way to an increase and diversity of statements and personnel, of which the second chapter provided a glimpse.

How, then, might a Palestinian Christian read the Old Testament today? The question implies that some of the ways Palestinian Christians have read and continue to read the Old Testament are unsatisfactory. It also suggests that some are asking hermeneutical questions again and are having difficulty arriving at a satisfactory solution. In addition, it insinuates that this writer has an answer, which is presumably presumptuous in light of the 1983 statement of the WCC and the MECC: "While only the churches of the Middle East can determine the nature and forms of their witness, it behooves all churches to strengthen their presence and support their ministry."[79] The following proposal will not discount this admonition. It is offered in humility, but still with confidence. The remaining chapters will set forth an effort toward outlining a way forward for Palestinian Christians to read the Old Testament. It will take the conclusions of the preceding chapters into consideration as well as considering some of the suggestions made by other Western scholars in recent years. The proposal will be made in light of what has been said and what has been found wanting. It is to this offer of a Palestinian Christian hermeneutic of the Old Testament that this book now turns.

---

79. Ibid., 100.

PART III

Palestinian Christians and the Old Testament: Ideology

5

Perspectives on Palestinian Christian Hermeneutics of the Old Testament

An ideology is a set of ideas, beliefs and attitudes, consciously or unconsciously held, which reflects or shapes understandings or misconceptions of the social and political world. It serves to recommend, justify or endorse collective action aimed at preserving or changing political practices and institutions. The concept of ideology is split almost irreconcilably between two major senses. The first is pejorative, denoting particular, historically distorted (political) thought which reinforces certain relationships of domination and in respect of which ideology functions as a critical unmasking concept. The second is a non-pejorative assertion about the different families of cultural symbols and ideas human beings employ in perceiving, comprehending and evaluating social and political realities in general, often within a systemic framework. Those families perform significant mapping and integrating functions.[1]

---

1. Michael Freeden, "Ideology," 381–82 in *Concise Routledge Encyclopedia of Philosophy* (London: Routledge, 2000).

Any perspective that sets itself up as the grounds of a course of action is ideological. This does not necessarily mean, however, that all ideas and points of view are insidious "distortions" of the facts and covert attempts to "dominate" others. Many beliefs are honest attempts to make sense of the world and are put forward as suggestions for "preserving" or "changing" social, political, or even religious ideas and institutions. The move from a "non-pejorative" ideology to a "pejorative" one happens when someone persists in his or her belief and course of action after being confronted by certain facts that warrant a change in perspective and practice. In other words, all perspectives are ideological, but not all are necessarily bad. It is this distinction that must be kept in mind as various suggestions on how Palestinian Christians might read the Old Testament are enumerated.

This chapter will highlight the work of Michael Prior, Charles Miller, and Gershon Nerel. Each of these scholars approaches the subject of Palestinian Christians and the Old Testament from a different perspective. Prior argues that Palestinian Christians should read the OT with the "Eyes of the Canaanite," Miller with the "Eyes of Tradition," and Nerel with the "Eyes of Jewish-Christian *fraternité*." Each of their proposals will be spelled out and critiqued. This evaluation will then serve as a basis for framing my own hermeneutic, which will be detailed in Chapter 6.

Michael Prior (1942-2004): Reading with the Eyes of the Canaanite

Background

The development of Michael Prior's hermeneutic is linked to his experiences in Israel and Palestine.[2] He writes: "My studying the

---

2. "Vincentian priest, Scripture scholar, teacher, musician, linguist, poet, liberation theologian, peace activist and advocate of Palestinian rights: Michael Prior was all of these." Thus Duncan

Bible in the Land of the Bible provoked perspectives that scarcely would have arisen elsewhere."³ In 1972 he visited Israel and Palestine for the first time and described his first impressions as follows:

> Albeit one inquiring virtually exclusively into the archaeological remains of ancient civilisations, the visit offered the first challenge to my favourable predispositions towards Israel. I was disturbed immediately by the ubiquitous signs of the oppression of the Arabs, whom later I learnt to call Palestinians. I was witnessing some kind of "institutionalised oppression"—I cannot recall whether "apartheid" was part of my vocabulary at the time.⁴

Subsequent visits reinforced Prior's growing disillusionment with the state of Israel and his increasing support for Palestinians. In 1981 he was "shocked" by the "reality of land expropriation and the on-going Jewish settlement in the West Bank."⁵ In 1984, when he heard that members of the *Gush Emunim* Underground were caught in an effort to blow up the Dome of the Rock and the Al-Aqsa Mosque, he started to detect the "religious dimension of the conflict" and the "abuse" of the biblical land traditions for various terrorist activities.⁶ Later that year he went on record at Tantur, noting his "displeasure . . . that the land traditions of the Bible appeared to mandate the genocide of the indigenes of 'Canaan.'"⁷ He challenged Marc Ellis, who was just starting to develop a Jewish Theology of Liberation, saying, "It would be no more difficult to construct a Theology of

---

Macpherson eulogized Prior following his untimely death in 2004. In Michael Prior, *A Living Stone: Selected Essays and Addresses*, ed. Duncan Macpherson (London: Melisende, 2006), 5.

3. Michael Prior, "Studying the Bible in the Holy Land," 104–27 in *They Came and They Saw: Western Christian Experiences of the Holy Land* (ed. Michael Prior; London: Melisende, 2000), at 104.
4. Michael Prior, "A Moral Reading of the Bible in Jerusalem," 16–45 in *Jerusalem in Ancient History and Tradition*, ed. Thomas L. Thompson (Sheffield: Sheffield Academic Press, 2003), at 24–25.
5. Ibid., 25.
6. Ibid., 25–26.
7. Ibid., 26.

Oppression on the basis of other biblical traditions, especially those dealing with Israelite origins that demanded the destruction of other peoples."[8] From that point onward, as academic and publishing commitments allowed, Prior focused his attention on critiquing the "land traditions of the Bible."[9]

Michael Prior's Hermeneutic

Michael Prior's hermeneutic is rooted in his perception that there is a "moral problem" with the land traditions of the Bible. He writes: "What struck me most about the biblical narrative was that the divine promise of land was integrally linked with the mandate to exterminate the indigenous peoples, and I had to wrestle with my perception that those traditions were inherently oppressive and morally reprehensible."[10] It is not just the fact that these texts are often co-opted and misused. The problem is not, in other words, only in reception history and involving the "predispositions of the biblical interpreter."[11] Prior argues that "several traditions within the Bible lend themselves to oppressive interpretations and applications precisely because of their inherently oppressive nature."[12] He takes up the issue of how one solves this "moral problem" of the biblical land traditions in his *The Bible and Colonialism: A Moral Critique* (*BC*).

In the opening chapter of *BC*, Prior enumerates the land traditions in the OT, itemizing each occurrence as it appears in the Torah, Prophets, and Writings. He then writes in response:

> Were it not for their religious provenance, such biblical sentiments would be regarded as incitements to racial hatred. *Prima facie*, judged by

---

8. Ibid.
9. Ibid., 27. For a full list of Prior's published works see Prior, *Living Stone*, 301–9.
10. Prior, "A Moral Reading," 27.
11. Michael Prior, *The Bible and Colonialism: A Moral Critique* (Sheffield: Sheffield Academic Press, 1997), 45.
12. Ibid., 46.

standards of ethics and human rights to which our society has become accustomed, the first six books of the Hebrew Bible reflect some ethnocentric, racist and xenophobic sentiments that appear to receive the highest possible legitimacy in the form of divine approval. On moral grounds, one is forced to question whether the *Torah* continues to provide divine legitimacy for the occupation of other people's land and the virtual annihilation of the indigenes.[13]

In part two of *BC*, Prior follows the "moral" imperative set forth in the first part of his book and investigates the appropriation of the land traditions to justify the colonial ventures that took place in Latin America, South Africa, and Palestine. A summary chapter follows, offering a comparative analysis of those colonial traditions. Prior concludes with regards to the Zionist enterprise in Palestine:

> Fundamentally, the Jewish claim to return rests with the Bible, since there is no other convincing moral ground supporting it. What most distinguishes the wholesale foundational plunder which Zionism perpetrated on the indigenous Palestinians is the fact that it is generally regarded favourably in the West, and in most theological and religious circles is viewed as being no more than what the Jewish people deserve in virtue of the promises of God outlined in the Bible. The Bible is a *sine qua non* for the provision of alleged moral legitimacy, and without it Zionism is a discourse in the conquest mode, as against a moral one. The Bible read at face value provides not only a moral framework which transposes Jewish claims into a divinely sanctioned legitimacy, but postulates the taking possession of the Promised Land and the forcible expulsion of the indigenous population as the fulfilment of a *mitzvah*. One could scarcely imagine that the Messianic Age would open with colonial plunder.[14]

In light of the fact that the biblical land traditions have been used in numerous colonial enterprises to justify and encourage the colonialists' efforts, Prior states at the beginning of the sixth chapter

---

13. Ibid., 34.
14. Ibid., 212–13.

that it is therefore "appropriate to re-examine these narratives."[15] Following the lead of Philip R. Davies, Keith Whitelam, Thomas L. Thompson, and Niels Lemche, Prior scrutinizes the Pentateuchal and Conquest-Settlement narratives in turn.[16] He concludes that these narratives are not "simple history" but the work of authors "whose reconstruction of the past reflected their own religious and political ideologies."[17] Therefore, he writes,

> ... a major epistemological question arises. Do texts which belong to the genre of folkloric epic or legend, rather than of a history which describes what actually happened, confer legitimacy on the "Israelite" possession of the land and on subsequent forms of colonialism which looked to the biblical paradigm, understood as factual history, for legitimization later? Does a judgment which is based on the premise that the genre of the justifying text is history in that sense not dissolve when it is realized that the text belongs to the genre of *myths of origin*, which, as we have seen, were deployed in the service of particular ideologies?[18]

Prior answers in the affirmative, and therefore sets forth in his final chapter an outline of his hermeneutic: "Rehabilitating the Bible: Towards a Moral Reading of the Bible."[19] He begins this final chapter of his book by critiquing the paucity of academic interest in the land theme. He notes Gerhard von Rad's 1943 foundational essay, "The Promised Land and Yahweh's Land in the Hexateuch,"[20] but only to reinforce his claim that so little has been written on the subject. He acknowledges the fact that the land theme has been taken up in significant measure by both W. D. Davies[21] and Walter

---

15. Ibid., 216.
16. Ibid.
17. Ibid., 247
18. Ibid., 252.
19. Ibid., 253–86.
20. Gerhard von Rad, "The Promised Land and Yahweh's Land in the Hexateuch," 79–93 in idem, *The Problem of the Hexateuch and Other Essays* (Edinburgh: Oliver & Boyd, 1966).
21. W. D. Davies, *The Gospel and the Land: Early Christianity and Jewish Territorial Doctrine* (Berkeley: University of California Press, 1974); idem, *The Territorial Dimension of Judaism*

Brueggemann,[22] but he critiques their work for not being sensitive to the "moral questions involved in one people dispossessing others."[23] For Prior it is clear there is a definite moral problem with the land traditions of the Bible. The only solution is to "allow for a moral critique which respects the discourse of human rights and international law to which our generation is accustomed," hence the designation of his hermeneutic as "A Moral Reading of the Bible."[24]

Prior argues that the first step in practicing a "moral reading of the Bible" is to acknowledge that the biblical land traditions are morally problematic. Not only is the reception history of these biblical texts questionable; there is a problem with the texts themselves. With regard to the former, Prior says, "It is undeniable that injustices have been committed through processes of colonialism, and, as we have seen, biblical and theological discourse has been a vivifying component in propelling them."[25] Concerning the latter he asserts: "There exists within the Bible a degree of violence and praise of violence that is surpassed by no other ancient book.... The existence of such texts within Sacred Scripture is an affront to moral sensitivities."[26] In addition, one must realize that these land traditions are situated not just in any literature but are found within the canon

---

(Berkeley: University of California Press, 1982); idem, *The Territorial Dimensions of Judaism: With a Symposium and Further Reflections* (Minneapolis: Fortress Press, 1991).
22. Walter Brueggemann, *The Land: Place as Gift, Promise, and Challenge in Biblical Faith* (Philadelphia: Fortress Press, 1977).
23. Prior, *Bible and Colonialism*, 258. In the preface to the second edition of Brueggemann's book, *The Land*, he acknowledges the significance of Prior's work and accepts his critique. He writes: "Michael Prior has most fully and explicitly considered these matters. Among other things, he has rightly chastened me (along with a number of other interpreters) for being inattentive to the ideological dimension of the land promise." Walter Brueggemann, *The Land*, 2nd ed. (Minneapolis: Fortress Press, 2002), xiv–xv.
24. Prior, *Bible and Colonialism*, 260.
25. Ibid., 261.
26. Prior, *Bible and Colonialism*, 261. He adds (p. 263): "A major problem with some of the traditions of the Old Testament . . . is its portrayal of God as what many modern people would regard as a racist, militaristic xenophobe, whose views would not be tolerated in any modern democracy."

of Jewish and Christian scripture. This fact has critical consequences for the way the text is approached and read; therefore they must be addressed. Prior explains:

> Failure to appreciate the critical difference between an ordinary reader's disposition before a literary text and a Jew's or Christian's disposition in the face of the biblical text leads to a fundamental misunderstanding of what is in fact taking place. One is not dealing merely with the pre-understanding (*Vorverständnis*) of a biblical text, but with the much more pervasive *through-understanding* of the text, that is, the consolidation of one's understanding of the text due to the ongoing encounter with it. One must acknowledge the after-effects of the encounter with the biblical text—what I suggest we call the *after-understanding*.[27]

It is precisely because of this "*after-understanding*," which stems from the fact that the biblical text is not just any text in the mind of the reader but one to which higher (i.e., canonical) authority is conceded, that the reader is faced with a unique set of challenges in explaining (away) some of the appalling contents of these texts.

Prior says that traditionally the Christian Church has handled the moral problem of the Bible in three ways. One, Christians have traditionally read these texts through the lens of the New Testament, that is, "in the light of the Christian faith."[28] Certain problem texts are therefore read "in a spiritual sense," as witnessed by the Church Fathers' use of the allegorical method. In addition, Prior writes, "Another mode of dealing with the unacceptable elements in the biblical tradition is to assert that 'the Bible reflects a considerable moral development, which finds its completion in the New Testament.'"[29] Last, Prior shows that the church has traditionally exercised a certain degree of "ascesis" or "censoring" in its liturgical traditions, and even in liberation theologians' use of the Exodus

---

27. Ibid., 265.
28. Ibid., 272.
29. Ibid., 272.

metaphor.³⁰ Prior seems to applaud the aforementioned efforts customarily employed by the Christian Church. According to him it has done right to censor the land traditions in that it "reads the Old Testament in light of the death and resurrection of Jesus Christ. ... A christological and messianic interpretation of the Old Testament allows these books to show forth their full meaning in the New Testament (*Dei Verbum*, pars. 15-16)."³¹

Prior's harshest words are for the academics who devote much time to researching the "land theme" in the Bible but "characteristically stop before they get to the hard part, contemporary issues of land in the Holy Land."³² They must "set [their] own house in order by articulating ethical criteria by which dispositions unworthy of a civilized person may not be accorded a privileged place as part of a sacred text."³³ Again, he says, "biblical scholars cannot continue to seek refuge by expending virtually all their intellectual energies on an unrecoverable past, thereby releasing themselves from the obligation of engaging in contemporary discourse. Nor are they justified in maintaining an academic detachment from significant engagement in real, contemporary issues."³⁴ The task of the biblical scholar is without question to practice a "moral reading of the Bible." According to Prior's vision that hermeneutic will draw the scholar away from the primitive, ideological, immoral, and unhistorical narratives of the ancient text and into the factual world of today, with its discourse framed by modern moral sensitivities.

A few years after writing *BC*, Michael Prior refined his hermeneutic of reading the biblical text in accordance with contemporary standards of morality by specifying one way in which

---

30. Ibid., 273–84.
31. Ibid., 284.
32. Ibid., 294, referring particularly to Walter Brueggemann.
33. Ibid., 295.
34. Ibid., 295–96.

this should take place. He maintained that one should read the Bible, and the OT in particular, with "the eyes of a Canaanite." He explains the evolution in his hermeneutic:

> [Discovery of the way the OT was being used to justify apartheid in South Africa and had been used to support colonialism in Latin America led to a] development in my perceptions [that] suggested the necessity of considering the perspective of the victims of various colonial enterprises, an endeavor analogous to reading the biblical text "with the eyes of the Canaanites"; that is, with a sensitivity to the moral question of the impact which colonizing enterprises and the Zionist conquest and settlement in Palestine in particular, have had on the indigenous populations.[35]

That this was a new development in Prior's hermeneutic, both in its understanding and nomenclature, is validated by the title of one of his final papers. At a three-day conference in Amman, Jordan, in April 2004, he presented a paper entitled, "Reading the Bible with the Eyes of the Canaanite: In Homage to Edward H. Said."[36] He said:

> I was well into my own study of the relationship between the biblical traditions on land with colonialism when I came across the phrase, reading the biblical narratives "with the eyes of the Canaanites." The first person I read of to use the phrase was the North American Indian, Robert Allen Warrior. It was in Said's collection, *Blaming the Victim* . . . as far as I recall, that I first encountered Warrior's sentiment.[37]

If it had not been for Prior's untimely death, he no doubt would have continued to apply and advance Warrior's hermeneutic in the Palestinian context, advocating that the OT be read with the "eyes of the Canaanite."

---

35. Prior, "A Moral Reading of the Bible," 39.
36. Michael Prior, "Reading the Bible with the Eyes of the Canaanite: In Homage to Edward H. Said," 273–96 in Prior, *Living Stone*.
37. Ibid., 277.

Critique of Michael Prior's Hermeneutic

Prior's hermeneutic, "Reading with the Eyes of the Canaanite" is undoubtedly unique and has evoked a mixed response from the scholarly community.[38] Prior does raise a number of good points, but some of his conclusions are off the mark. There are three things in particular that need to be addressed. First, Prior is right to highlight with horror how the land traditions of the OT have been coopted to justify a number of colonial enterprises. However, that a given text might appear morally repugnant and lend itself to being "abused" at a later date does not mean that the text itself is inherently "immoral."[39] It needs to be read and understood in its own context before it is prematurely abandoned.[40] Second, Prior is right that the OT is replete with examples of violence, but he is wrong to say that the OT is any *more* violent than other Ancient Near Eastern literature.[41] Finally, Prior is correct in saying that the land traditions do not convey "simple history"; they in fact reflect the "religious and political ideologies" of a later time.[42] However, he is wrong to cite the works of Philip R. Davies, Whitelam, Thompson, and Lemche as if their views had won the day. The jury is still out on the possibility of

---

38. On one end of the spectrum Prior's views are treated with the utmost respect. See the articles in the commemorative issue of *Holy Land Studies*: vol. 3, No. 2 (November 2004): 129–43. On the other end Prior's comments are likened to "blasphemy." Cf. Paul Richard Wilkinson, *For Zion's Sake: Christian Zionism and the Role of John Nelson Darby* (Milton Keynes: Paternoster, 2007), 57. It is unfortunate that Wilkinson seems to draw a connection between Prior's apparent "blasphemy" and his untimely death. That type of language is both inappropriate and insensitive; it will no doubt hinder the reception of Wilkinson's work in the future. For someone with similar views but much more tact see Paul Merkley, *Christian Attitudes Towards the State of Israel* (London: McGill-Queen's University Press, 2001).
39. See chap. 6 below.
40. See chap. 6 below. This is my major critique of Prior's hermeneutic.
41. Cf. Sa-Moon Kang, *Divine War in the Old Testament and in the Ancient Near East* (Berlin: de Gruyter, 1989); Norbert Lohfink, "The Strata of the Pentateuch and the Question of War," 173–226 in *Theology of the Pentateuch: Themes of the Priestly Narrative and Deuteronomy*, trans. Linda M. Maloney (Minneapolis: Fortress Press, 1994), at 181.
42. Prior, *Bible and Colonialism*, 247

writing a history of "ancient Israel."[43] Therefore the OT land traditions should not be discarded without further investigation.[44]

Charles H. Miller (b. 1933): Reading with the Eyes of Tradition

Background

Charles H. Miller is a Marianist priest, a graduate of Sant' Anselmo in Rome with a S.Th.D. (*Doctor of Sacred Theology*), and former Professor of Theology at St. Mary's University in Texas. Over the years Miller has written a number of works on the interpretive tradition of the Catholic Church, and in 2006 he published an article, "Hermeneutical Problems for a Palestinian Catholic Reading the Old Testament and Current Pastoral Responses," with an eye to the Catholic Church in Israel and Palestine[45] This article is of particular importance for the present discussion.

Miller acknowledges at the beginning of his article the difficulty countless Palestinian Christians have had in "reading and praying the Old Testament" over the last sixty years.[46] He recognizes that this has become a serious "spiritual problem" and "something of a contentious element in their Heritage. . . ."[47] In an effort to help the Catholic

---

43. Cf. James Barr, *History and Ideology in the Old Testament: Biblical Studies at the End of the Millennium* (Oxford: Oxford University Press, 2000), 59–101; Lester L. Grabbe, ed., *Can a 'History of Israel' be Written?* (Sheffield: Sheffield Academic Press, 1997). This point is especially important, for Prior has influenced a number of Western scholars and Palestinian Christians who believe his statements represent a foregone conclusion. Cf. Nur Masalha, *The Bible and Zionism: Invented Traditions, Archaeology and Post-Colonialism in Palestine-Israel* (London: Zed, 2007).
44. See chap. 6 below.
45. Charles H. Miller, *"As it is Written": The Use of Old Testament References in the Documents of Vatican II* (St. Louis: Marianist Communications Center, 1973); idem, "Translation Errors in the Pontifical Biblical Commission's *The Jewish People and Their Sacred Scriptures in the Christian Bible*," *Biblical Theology Bulletin* 35 (2005): 34; idem, "Hermeneutical Problems for a Palestinian Catholic Reading the Old Testament and Current Pastoral Responses," in *ARAM* 18–19 (2006–2007): 307–24.
46. Miller, "Hermeneutical Problems," 307.
47. Ibid.

community in Israel and Palestine to reestablish the importance and place of the Old Testament in its life and liturgy, Miller proposes a course of action.

> This paper will try to show that a more consciously *critical reading* of the Old Testament according to *Catholic standards* can assist in reducing the painful confusion between the political and spiritual experiences of Christians both in Israel and in Occupied Palestine, and hopefully restore to them the Old Testament as a valuable resource for their spiritual lives, while leaving intact the loyalty that they owe to their respective civic communities. If the critical method can help to establish more clearly the distinctions between the biblical Israelites/promises/election and the current situation, it could free Palestinian Christians to be able to re-read and use the biblical narratives of liberation as paradigmatic for their own hopes, at once saving the Old Testament for their Christian heritage and simultaneously drawing from it hope instead of despair.[48]

In short, Miller argues that the best way to resolve the dilemma of a Palestinian Christian's reading of the Old Testament is to follow a hermeneutic that reads the Bible "critically" according to "Catholic standards." What these "standards" are and what role they play in Miller's hermeneutic is important to make plain. They hold the key to discerning the nature of his method of interpretation and how his unique hermeneutic, which will be labeled in the present study "Reading with the Eyes of Tradition," differs from that of Michael Prior and others.

Charles Miller cites four Catholic documents that are of particular importance for the Palestinian Christian community. They are the Pontifical Biblical Commission's 1993 publication, *The Interpretation of the Bible in the Church*,[49] Michel Sabbah's Pastoral Letter *Reading*

---

48. Miller, "Hermeneutical Problems," 309–10. Emphasis added.
49. Pontifical Biblical Commission, *The Interpretation of the Bible in the Church* (Boston: Pauline Books, 1993).

the *Bible Today in the Land of the Bible*,⁵⁰ the statement of the 2000 Diocesan Synod of the Catholic Churches in Bethlehem, *The General Pastoral Plan*, and the Pontifical Biblical Commission's 2001 document, *The Jewish People and Their Sacred Scriptures in the Christian Bible*.⁵¹ The second and third documents were issued by and under the auspices of the Latin Patriarchate, while the first and fourth were produced by the Pontifical Biblical Commission for the universal Catholic Church. As evident from the list of documents, Miller juxtaposes the local and worldwide contexts in order to see the "efforts" of the Latin Patriarchate in "their proper worldwide context."⁵² The significance of this will be seen more fully later. For now, a quick overview of these four documents is necessary before we proceed to evaluate the way Miller appropriates them.

The Sources of Miller's Hermeneutic

The Interpretation of the Bible in the Church

The first of the Catholic standards Miller highlights is the Pontifical Biblical Commission's 1993 document, *The Interpretation of the Bible in the Church (IBC)*.⁵³ This document follows in a tradition of earlier encyclicals, discussions, and statements in which the Roman Catholic Church has sought to wrestle with the emergence and proper appropriation of modern critical methods for the interpretation of the Bible.⁵⁴ The first of these encyclicals, *Providentissimus Deus*, was issued

---

50. Sabbah, "Reading the Bible Today in the Land of the Bible," 23–60.
51. Pontifical Biblical Commission, *The Jewish People and Their Sacred Scriptures in the Christian Bible* (Boston: Pauline Books, 2002). The normative text of the document is in French: *Le peuple juif et ses Saintes Écritures dans la Bible chrétienne* (Città del Vaticano: Libreria Editrice Vaticana, 2001).
52. Miller, "Hermeneutical Problems," 311.
53. Cf. Joseph A. Fitzmyer, *The Biblical Commission's Document "The Interpretation of the Bible in the Church": Text and Commentary* (Rome: Pontifical Biblical Institute, 1995); and J. L. Houlden, ed., *The Interpretation of the Bible in the Church* (London: SCM, 1995).

by Pope Leo XIII in 1893. The second, *Divino Afflante Spiritu*, was laid out by Pope Pius XII in 1943.[55] The 1993 publication of *IBC* was "an attempt to take the bearings of Catholic exegesis in the present situation," on the centennial and semi-centennial anniversaries of *Providentissimus Deus* and *Divino Afflante Spiritu*.[56]

Charles Miller is right to conclude that Catholic interpretation has certainly advanced over the past sixty-plus years.[57] He heralds the decision by Pope Pius XII to "embrace the exegetical principles of the historical-critical method" as one of the key factors in helping the Catholic Church abandon its "pre-critical mindset" and begin to interpret the Bible "critically."[58] The culmination of this development, in Miller's opinion, can be seen in *IBC*. He therefore, takes time to articulate the views put forth in the document.

IBC enunciates as its purpose "to indicate the paths most appropriate for arriving at an interpretation of the Bible as faithful as possible to its character both human and divine" and to help the Bible "become more and more the spiritual nourishment of the members of the people of God, a source for them of a life of faith, of hope and of love—and indeed a light for all humanity."[59] With this aim in mind, *IBC* evaluates the whole spectrum of contemporary methods

---

54. *IBC* states in its introduction, "For a long period the Church in her pastoral prudence showed herself very reticent in responding to this question, for often the methods, despite their positive elements, have shown themselves to be wedded to positions hostile to the Christian faith. But a more positive attitude has also evolved, signaled by a whole series of pontifical documents." Houlden, *Interpretation*, 8.
55. Miller writes that the 1943 Papal encyclical *Divino Afflante Spiritu* was the turning point in biblical interpretation in Catholic tradition. Miller, "Hermeneutical Problems," 312.
56. *IBC* also notes the significance of the 1964 PBC declaration, *Sancta Mater Ecclesia*, and the 1965 *Dei Verbum* of Vatican Council II. Houlden, *Interpretation*, 8.
57. As noted above, Miller writes that the 1943 papal encyclical *Divino Afflante Spiritu* was the turning point for Catholic exegesis. Nevertheless, it should not be overlooked that there is both discontinuity *and* continuity in the development of the Catholic Church's position. Cf. Joseph Cardinal Ratzinger, preface to *IBC* in Houlden, *Interpretation*, 3–4.
58. Miller, "Hermeneutical Problems," 312.
59. Houlden, *Interpretation*, 10.

and approaches available for interpreting the Bible.[60] It concludes: "Catholic exegesis freely makes use of the scientific methods and approaches which allow a better grasp of the meaning of texts in their linguistic, literary, socio-cultural, religious and historical contexts, while explaining them as well through studying their sources and attending to the personality of each author (cf. *Divino Afflante Spiritu: Ench. Bibl.* 557)."[61] What distinguishes Catholic exegesis, however, is that it "deliberately places itself within *the living tradition of the church*."[62] Hence there is an inherent dialectic within Catholic interpretation between "modern scientific culture" and the "religious tradition emanating from Israel and from the early Christian community" with which the Catholic Church sees itself in direct continuity.[63] The latter dynamic has always been characteristic of Catholic interpretation. What is new is the former.

Reading the Bible Today in the Land of the Bible

The second "standard" Charles Miller cites is Michel Sabbah's 1993 Pastoral Letter, *Reading the Bible Today in the Land of the Bible*. Miller provides both a detailed summary and a critical analysis of the letter. As an overview of *Reading the Bible Today in the Land of the Bible* has already been given, however, the details of Michel Sabbah's letter will not be repeated here.[64] Miller's evaluation of the letter will be

---

60. Charles H. Miller's summary is sharp and succinct. "The Commission itself evaluates the diachronic historical-method (How did the text originate and develop into its final form? What were the meanings over that period of development?) and synchronic methods of rhetorical, narrative, and semiotic analyses (How did and does the text function after the close of the canon? What meanings can it carry today?). It distinguishes these 'methods' from what it calls 'approaches,' including canonical criticism, Jewish traditions of interpretation, *Wirkungsgeschichte* (What meanings and impacts did the text carry through later centuries?), the borrowing from human sciences (sociology, cultural anthropology, psychology), and contextual (liberationist, feminist) approaches.... Only a Fundamentalist approach is explicitly and categorically rejected." Miller, "Hermeneutical Problems," 313.
61. Houlden, *Interpretation*, 58.
62. Houlden, *Interpretation*, 58. Emphasis added.
63. Houlden, *Interpretation*, 58.

recorded below after a brief sketch of the remaining two Catholic standards.

The General Pastoral Plan

Miller writes that *The General Pastoral Plan* "does not directly address the hermeneutical problem of the Old Testament, even while alluding to it, other than to urge more and deeper research."[65] Thus it does not play a significant role in Miller's hermeneutic, except that he points to its recommendation to study the biblical themes that are most problematic for Palestinian Christians, namely, "election" and the "promise of the land."[66]

The Jewish People and Their Sacred Scripture in the Christian Bible

The final standard Miller cites is the 2001 document by the Pontifical Biblical Commission, *The Jewish People and Their Sacred Scripture in the Christian Bible.*[67] In the wake of the Vatican's establishment of political ties with the state of Israel in 1993 and the request of Pope John Paul II in 1997, the Pontifical Biblical Commission was given the task of producing a document that would help contribute toward the Catholic Church's efforts to "reassess their relations with the Jewish people."[68] Focusing its efforts on a critical analysis of both the

---

64. For an overview of Sabbah's *Reading the Bible Today in the Land of the Bible* see chap. 1 above.
65. Miller, "Hermeneutical Problems," 311.
66. Ibid., 308.
67. The normative edition of the 2001 PBC document is in French; it was published in English in 2002. For a summary of its background and key points see Henry Wansbrough, "The Jewish People and its Holy Scripture in the Christian Bible," *ITQ* 67 (2002): 265–75.
68. Pontifical Biblical Commission, *The Jewish People and Their Sacred Scripture in the Christian Bible*, §1. The document is available at: http://www.vatican.va/roman_curia/congregations/cfaith/pcb_documents/rc_con_cfaith_doc_20020212_popolo-ebraico_en.html. In addition to the establishment of diplomatic ties between the Vatican and the state of Israel, the atrocities of the *Shoah* and the Second Vatican Council's *Nostra Aetate* no doubt had a substantial influence on the commissioning of the new PBC document.

Old and New Testaments, the PBC statement seeks to examine what kind of relationship the Christian Bible establishes between Jews and Christians.[69]

The PBC argues that a cursory look at the Christian Bible demonstrates that an "intimate relationship" between Jews and Christians is "undeniable."[70] "A closer examination, however, reveals that this is not a straightforward relationship, but a very complex one that ranges from perfect accord on some points to one of great tension on others."[71]

The significance of *The Jewish People and Their Sacred Scripture in the Christian Bible* lies in the way it analyzes the Old and New Testaments and reassesses the traditional concepts of continuity, discontinuity, progression, and fulfillment. For example, the document makes great strides toward curbing the customary emphasis on discontinuity between Christians and Jews by stressing the elements of continuity between the two communities. When speaking of the elements of discontinuity it asserts: "It cannot be denied that the passage from one Testament to the other also involves ruptures. *These do not submerge continuity. They presuppose it in essentials.*"[72] In addition, the document argues that those elements in the New Testament that apparently break with the teachings of the Old Testament are in actual fact hinted at the in Old Testament itself. It contends: "It is also clear that the radical replacement in the New Testament was already adumbrated in the Old Testament and so constitutes a potentially legitimate reading."[73]

The PBC document does not deny elements of progression, fulfillment, and discontinuity. It remains faithful to Catholic

---

69. *The Jewish People and Their Sacred Scripture in the Christian Bible*, §1.
70. Ibid.
71. Ibid.
72. *The Jewish People and Their Sacred Scripture in the Christian Bible*, §64. Emphasis added.
73. Ibid.

teaching, but it gives an account of its beliefs in a manner that highlights continuity. It says, "Inevitably, fulfillment brings discontinuity on certain points, because without it there can be no progress. This discontinuity is a source of disagreements between Christians and Jews, no purpose is served by hiding the fact. But it was wrong, in times past, to unilaterally insist on it to the extent of taking no account of the fundamental continuity."[74]

In light of its conclusions regarding Jewish-Christian relations, the PBC suggests to the Catholic Church the following way to read the Bible.

> *On the part of Christians, the main condition for progress along these lines lies in avoiding a one-sided reading of biblical texts, both from the Old Testament and the New Testament, and making instead a better effort to appreciate the whole dynamism that animates them, which is precisely a dynamism of love. In the Old Testament, the plan of God is a union of love with his people, a paternal love, a spousal love and, notwithstanding Israel's infidelities, God will never renounce it, but affirms it in perpetuity (Is 54:8; Jr 31:3). In the New Testament, God's love overcomes the worst obstacles; even if they do not believe in his Son whom he sent as their Messiah Saviour, Israelites are still "loved" (Rm 11:29). Whoever wishes to be united to God, must also love them.*[75]

The way forward for a Catholic reading of the OT, then, according to the 2001 PBC declaration, is to acknowledge the constitution of ancient Israel as a people of God's own choosing and as recipients and stewards of God's revelation. From this community, two communities of faith have emerged. Both are mysteriously legitimate offspring and have equally valid ways of reading the OT.

---

74. Ibid., §84.
75. *The Jewish People and Their Sacred Scripture in the Christian Bible*, §86. Emphasis added.

Charles Miller's Hermeneutic

In Miller's view the way forward for a Palestinian Catholic hermeneutic of the Old Testament is to read it according to "Catholic standards." In addition to highlighting the Pontifical Biblical Commission's 1993 document, *The Interpretation of the Bible in the Church,* Miller also references Michel Sabbah's *Reading the Bible Today in the Land of the Bible,* the 2000 Diocesan Synod's *The General Pastoral Plan,* and the PBC's 2001 document, *The Jewish People and Their Sacred Scripture in the Christian Bible*. These four provide for Miller the framework for a Palestinian Catholic reading of the Old Testament. In his opinion the views of the Catholic Church as expressed in certain documents and encyclicals have an active and prescriptive role in the way the Old Testament should be read. That is, the Old Testament should be read "with the eyes of tradition."[76]

The way Charles Miller appropriates the aforementioned "standards" is most interesting. All the above Catholic documents inform how Miller reads the Old Testament, but not all the statements and their conclusions are of equal value to him. Miller sets up the 1993 PBC document, *IBC,* and the use of the historical-critical method in particular, as the lens through which other Catholic statements should be properly understood. For example, in his analysis of *The Jewish People and Their Sacred Scripture in the Christian Bible* he says: "In the long run, the insights gained" (that is, from the use of the historical-critical method as justified by *IBC*) "can be expected to help clarify worldwide Catholic theological understanding of the historical facts (1) of the ancient Israelites as the first recipients of God's self-revelation in antiquity; (2) of the survival

---

76. My designation of Miller's hermeneutic as "Reading with the Eyes of Tradition" is influenced by *IBC,* which states: "What characterizes Catholic exegesis is that it deliberately places itself within the living tradition of the church." Houlden, *Interpretation,* 58.

of their Jewish descendants as a distinct people until today; and (3) of Christians' identity as spiritual successors of ancient Israel."[77]

In addition, Miller assesses Michel Sabbah's pastoral letter in view of the PBC's *IBC* and, as stated, in view of the historical-critical method as well. He writes, "Sabbah's principles[78] are generally in harmony with the Commission's document[79] and with popular Catholic understanding.[80] But the second principle, the Bible as a 'History of Salvation . . . through the covenants' may be seen to raise some historical-critical problems, problems for the universal Church as well. . . ."[81] Of particular difficulty for Miller is the way Sabbah portrays the covenants made with Noah, Abraham, Moses, and David as "historical" as opposed to "heuristic images of 'covenant' and 'promise of the land,' i.e. *analogies* for the relationship between God and ancient Israel."[82] Miller argues that "such a pre-critical reading could appear to remain effectively on the same grounds as Fundamentalist Christian/religious Zionist/Qur'anic literalist interpretations."[83]

How, then, should a Palestinian Catholic read the Old Testament? In Miller's view, to read the OT "with the eyes of tradition" is not to belittle the importance of modern critical methods for the interpretation of the Bible. Indeed, the Catholic Church has begun to both incorporate and endorse their use.[84] Miller himself highlights

---

77. Miller, "Hermeneutical Problems," 323.
78. Cf. Sabbah, *Reading the Bible Today in the Land of the Bible*, 28–39. See also chap. 1 above.
79. That is, the 1993 PBC's *IBC*.
80. Compare with the description (above) of *The Jewish People and Their Sacred Scripture in the Christian Bible*.
81. Miller, "Hermeneutical Problems," 316.
82. Ibid., 318. Italics in original.
83. Ibid.
84. For example, Cardinal Joseph Ratzinger writes in the preface to *The Interpretation of the Bible in the Church*, "Everything that helps us better to understand the truth and to appropriate its representations is helpful and worthwhile for theology. It is in this sense that we must seek how to use this method in theological research." In Houlden, *Interpretation*, 3.

the use of *IBC* as the measure against which other Catholic standards should be weighed and understood. Moreover, he raises the historical-critical method as a standard by which Palestinian Christians can read the OT again for their own spiritual benefit. He concludes:

> While in some cultures the perceived barrenness of the historical-critical method has itself raised problems for the faithful, some of its findings might, in this time and place, assist in developing pastoral responses to Palestinian spiritual difficulties, freeing people to understand the riches of the Old Testament in a more spiritual way; as John Paul II put it, the goal of Catholic exegesis "is to put believers into a personal relationship with God."[85]

To claim that Miller advocates an approach that reads the Old Testament "with the eyes of tradition" is to say that "the living tradition of the church," that is, the Roman Catholic Church, authorizes and governs the interpretation of the biblical text. He highlights the historical-critical method as a way forward for Palestinian Catholics to read their Bible. Nevertheless, he justifies his proposal in light of recent statements made by the church and by the 1993 *IBC* in particular. Miller therefore reads the Bible "with the eyes of tradition."

Critique of Charles Miller's Hermeneutic

Robert P. Carroll vehemently criticizes *IBC*, writing:

> The clothes may be the clothes of historical-critical methodology, but the voice is still that of crafty scheming Jacob seeking to acquire all the power for himself. The magisterium may dress up in modernist clothes, but the old authoritarian voice remains its own. It is still pronouncing on which new methods are acceptable and which are not because they do not agree with the old conciliar dogmatic belief system.[86]

---

85. Miller, "Hermeneutical Problems," 323.

To the contrary, *IBC* is an authentic attempt to reconcile the use of modern critical methods with ecclesial tradition. Carroll is unreasonable to expect that the Catholic Church should undermine itself in an official document. The Catholic Church is free to prescribe what methods and approaches it thinks are appropriate for interpreting the Bible. Still, it should be noted that *IBC* did commend nearly all critical methods and approaches to some degree or other.[87] This fact shows that the Catholic Church is willing to dialogue with "modern scientific culture" as it pertains to matters of biblical interpretation.[88] Miller's hermeneutic and his advocacy of the historical-critical method in particular is one proof among many that show the seriousness of Catholic biblical scholars in following the PBC's admonition.

In light of Miller's opening promise to study the documents from the universal Catholic Church and from the Latin Patriarchate in an attempt to "see the efforts of the latter in their proper worldwide context," he is seen to have clearly and successfully set up *IBC* as a standard by which to evaluate the documents from the Latin Patriarchate.[89] He even criticizes the PBC's *The Jewish People and Their Sacred Scripture in the Christian Bible* and recommends the use of the historical-critical method as a lens through which to properly read and understand the document.

It is this writer's opinion that the way in which Miller advocates the use of the historical-critical method while at the same time wrestling with the tradition with which he is associated is appropriate. As a result, his hermeneutic will be adopted to a great extent below. However, there is one point of weakness that must be pointed out

---

86. Robert P. Carroll, "Cracks in the Soul of Theology," 142–55 in Houlden, *Interpretation*, at 143.
87. Cf. "The Interpretation of the Bible in the Church," above.
88. Houlden, *Interpretation*, 58.
89. Miller, "Hermeneutical Problems," 311.

and addressed. Contrary to Miller's stated mode of evaluation, in which he promises to measure the "efforts" of the Latin Patriarchate in relation to the standards issued from the universal Catholic Church, the PBC's *The Jewish People* is scarcely used as a means to shed light on statements published by the Latin Patriarchate. When Miller does mention *The Jewish People*, his comments occur mostly in footnotes, and he often seems to find difficulty in saying much, if anything, at all positive about the document.[90]

One is led to conclude that Miller either believes that *The General Pastoral Plan* and Michel Sabbah's *Reading the Bible in the Land of the Bible* are totally in agreement with *The Jewish People* and only scant attention to the document is therefore needed or that he feels *The Jewish People* is in itself a substandard document with little to say to the local Catholic context in Israel and Palestine. Neither conclusion suffices. Miller would not have set up *The Jewish People* as a standard by which to assess the "efforts" of the Latin Patriarchate if the document was not in itself of any consequence and had nothing to say that might inform the Latin Patriarchate. The answer appears to lie near the close of his article. Miller makes a passing comment at the end of a footnote, saying that *The Jewish People* "will be the subject of another article."[91] It is unclear what will be the full nature of this article. Perhaps Miller will elaborate on how *The Jewish People* might inform a Palestinian Catholic reading of the Old Testament. It is true, as Miller says, that *The Jewish People* does not "have the

---

90. Miller criticizes *The Jewish People* for its awkward style and its scant references to secondary literature. He bemoans the fact that there is no substantial commentary on the document to date and that it is "not in complete consistency with the 1993 Commission document." In addition, he notes that the document does not have the "Palestinian Christian crisis specifically in mind." Miller, "Hermeneutical Problems," 311–12. It should be noted that Miller does reference *The Jewish People* positively toward the end of his article (p. 321), when he notes the document's contribution toward recognizing that "the *herem* genocides attributed to Joshua" should be seen as "retrojection of wishful thinking."
91. Ibid., 322 n. 69.

Palestinian Christian crisis in mind."[92] But then, neither does *IBC* have Palestinian Christian hermeneutics at the forefront of its deliberations, and yet it appropriately informs Miller's hermeneutic. Therefore *The Jewish People* can and should still be used as a "standard" by which to construct a Palestinian Christian hermeneutic of the Old Testament. Great strides have been made in Jewish-Christian relations because of the efforts of the Catholic Church toward *rapprochement* with the Jewish people, and this document is one such attempt. In light of the paucity of attention given to *The Jewish People* in Miller's hermeneutic, "Reading with the Eyes of Tradition," something needs to be said about a growing trend toward reading the Old Testament "with the eyes of Jewish-Christian *fraternité*."

Gershon Nerel: Reading with the Eyes of Jewish-Christian *fraternité*

Background

The twentieth century saw a marked shift in Jewish-Christian relations. The now legendary conversation between Theodor Herzl and Pope Pius X in 1904 illustrates the view of many Christians toward Jews at the start of the century. Seeking the Vatican's support for the Zionist cause in Palestine, Herzl met with the Pope, and he records the following remarks by the Pope in his diary.[93]

> THE POPE: We cannot encourage this movement. We cannot prevent the Jews from going to Jerusalem—but we could never sanction it. The ground of Jerusalem, even if it were not always sacred, has been sanctified by the life of Jesus Christ. As the head of the Church, I cannot

---

92. Ibid., 311.
93. Quoted in Sergio I. Minerbi, *The Vatican and Zionism: Conflict in the Holy Land, 1895–1925* (Oxford: Oxford University Press, 1990), 100–101.

tell you otherwise. The Jews have not recognized our Lord, therefore we cannot recognize the Jewish people. . . .[94]

Pope Pius X concluded: "And so, if you come to Palestine and settle your people there, we will be ready with churches and priests to baptize all of you."[95]

Nearly ninety years later, on December 30, 1993, the Vatican and the state of Israel signed *The Fundamental Agreement between the Holy See and the State of Israel*, thereby marking not just the establishment of diplomatic relations but also a definite change in the attitude of the Roman Catholic Church to the Jewish people. The recognition of the state of Israel and the preceding change of opinion toward the Jewish people, however, did not occur in a vacuum. The aftermath of the Second World War, along with people's growing awareness of the horrors of the Holocaust, had a profound effect on Christian attitudes toward Jews. One of the first public statements issued after the war reflecting this change of opinion is "The Ten Points of Seelisberg,"[96] published in Switzerland in 1947. The signatories, who would later be known as the International Council of Christians and Jews (ICCJ), acknowledged their sadness over the "outburst of anti-Semitism which has led to the persecution and extermination of millions of Jews" and called on Christian churches to be aware of and to "avoid any presentation and conception of the Christian message which would support antisemitism under whatever form."[97]

---

94. Ibid., 100.
95. Ibid., 101.
96. "The Ten Points of Seelisberg" is argued by many as the "first milestone" on the path to *rapprochement* between Jews and Christians. Petra Heldt, "For Brothers to Dwell Together: Rethinking Christianity in Israel," 30–48 in *The Mountain of the Lord: Israel and the Churches* (London: Council of Jews and Christians, 1996), at 32.
97. International Conference of Christians and Jews, "An Address to the Churches (The Ten Points of Seelisberg)," accessed 13 Jan 2011: http://www.ccjr.us/dialogika-resources/documents-and-statements/ecumenical-christian/567-seelisberg. The "Ten Points" were written in Seelisberg, Switzerland on August 5, 1947.

With this goal in mind, the Christians and Jews at Seelisberg stated the following ten points:[98]

1. Remember that One God speaks to us all through the Old and the New Testaments.
2. Remember that Jesus was born of a Jewish mother of the seed of David and the people of Israel, and that His everlasting love and forgiveness embraces His own people and the whole world.
3. Remember that the first disciples, the apostles and the first martyrs were Jews.
4. Remember that the fundamental commandment of Christianity, to love God and one's neighbour, proclaimed already in the Old Testament and confirmed by Jesus, is binding upon both Christians and Jews in all human relationships, without any exception.
5. Avoid distorting or misrepresenting biblical or post-biblical Judaism with the object of extolling Christianity.
6. Avoid using the word Jews in the exclusive sense of the enemies of Jesus, and the words "the enemies of Jesus" to designate the whole Jewish people.
7. Avoid presenting the Passion in such a way as to bring the odium of the killing of Jesus upon all Jews or upon Jews alone. It was only a section of the Jews in Jerusalem who demanded the death of Jesus, and the Christian message has always been that it was the sins of mankind which were exemplified by those Jews and the sins in which all men share that brought Christ to the Cross.
8. Avoid referring to the scriptural curses, or the cry of a raging mob: "His blood be upon us and our children," without remembering that this cry should not count against the infinitely

---

98. Ibid.

more weighty words of our Lord: "Father forgive them for they know not what they do."
9. Avoid promoting the superstitious notion that the Jewish people are reprobate, accursed, reserved for a destiny of suffering.
10. Avoid speaking of the Jews as if the first members of the Church had not been Jews.

A year later, in 1948, the Synod of the Evangelical Lutheran Church of Saxony published its *Declaration of Guilt Towards the Jewish People*,[99] and the First Assembly of the World Council of Churches (WCC) issued its *Report on the Christian Approach to the Jews*.[100] These documents, along with others in subsequent years, were positive steps toward Jewish-Christian *fraternité* but, as Edward Kessler rightly notes, they "insisted that Christians were still obligated to include Jews in their evangelistic work, since Israel's election had passed to the Church."[101] Therefore, despite the consternation of many,[102] a full-fledged theological revision of Christian beliefs regarding the Jews did not take place, and the views promulgated by the Ten Points of Seeligsberg stayed a "minority position."[103]

Still, there was progress. As Francesco Rossi de Gasperis writes, the "re-engagement with the Jewish people" sparked by an initial movement of guilt and remorse over the Holocaust "stimulated a secondary, and much more fundamental movement, leading to the

---

99. Cf. Synod of the Evangelical Lutheran Church of Saxony, "Declaration of Guilt Towards the Jewish People," accessed 13 Jan 2011: http://www.ccjr.us/dialogika-resources/documents-and-statements/protestant-churches/eur/754-elcsaxony1948.
100. Cf. First Assembly of the WCC, "The Christian Approach to the Jews," accessed 13 Jan 2011: http://www.ccjr.us/dialogika-resources/documents-and-statements/ecumenical-christian/737-wcc1948.
101. Edward Kessler, *An Introduction to Jewish-Christian Relations* (Cambridge: Cambridge University Press, 2010), 8.
102. See Henrikus Berkhof, "Israel as a Theological Problem for the Christian Church," *Journal of Ecumenical Studies* 6 (1969): 329–47.
103. Kessler says: "Deep-seated theological transformation began two to three decades after the Holocaust." Kessler, *Introduction to Jewish-Christian Relations*, 8.

rediscovery of the essentially Jewish roots of the Christian Faith."[104] Theological reflection continued slowly but steadily throughout the 1950s and 1960s and culminated in the landmark declaration of the Second Vatican Council, *Nostra Aetate*,[105] the "Declaration on the Relationship of the Church to Non-Christian Religions." *Nostra Aetate* was issued council on October 28, 1965. Its views on the Jewish people are stated in the fourth point of the document.[106]

> As the sacred synod searches into the mystery of the Church, it remembers the bond that spiritually ties the people of the New Covenant to Abraham's stock.
>
> Thus the Church of Christ acknowledges that, according to God's saving design, the beginnings of her faith and her election are found already among the Patriarchs, Moses and the prophets. . . . The Church, therefore, cannot forget that she received the revelation of the Old Testament through the people with whom God in His inexpressible mercy concluded the Ancient Covenant. Nor can she forget that she draws sustenance from the root of that well-cultivated olive tree onto which have been grafted the wild shoots, the Gentiles. Indeed, the Church believes that by His cross Christ, Our Peace, reconciled Jews and Gentiles, making both one in Himself.
>
> . . .

---

104. Francesco Rossi de Gasperis, "Interreligious Dialogue in Jerusalem," accessed 12 March 2012: http://www.etrfi.org/uploads/1/0/7/9/10798906/interreligious_dialogue_in_jerusalem.pdf.
105. That this is viewed by both Jews and Christians as a landmark in Jewish-Christian relations can be seen from recent statements by Pope Benedict XVI and Rabbi David Rosen, former Chief Rabbi of Ireland and current International Director of Interreligious Affairs of the American Jewish Committee (AJC). Rabbi Rosen stated in his speech to the Special Vatican Synod on the Middle East on October 13, 2010, "The relationship today between Christianity and the Jewish people is a blessed transformation in our times—arguably without historic parallel. In his words in the great synagogue here in Rome last January, H. H. Pope Benedict XVI referred to the teaching of the Second Vatican Ecumenical Council as 'a clear landmark to which constant reference is made in our attitude and our relations with the Jewish people, marking a new and significant stage.'" See David Rosen, "The Jewish-Christian Relationship and the Middle East," accessed 13 Jan 2011: http://rabbidavidrosen.net/Articles/Christian-Jewish Relations/The_Jewish-Christian_relationship_and_the_Middle_East_October_2010.pdf.
106. *Nostra Aetate* may be accessed at: http://www.vatican.va/archive/hist_councils/ii_vatican_council/documents/vat-ii_decl_19651028_nostra-aetate_en.html.

> Since the spiritual patrimony common to Christians and Jews is thus so great, this sacred synod wants to foster and recommend that mutual understanding and respect which is the fruit, above all, of biblical and theological studies as well as of *fraternal dialogues.*
>
> True, the Jewish authorities and those who followed their lead pressed for the death of Christ; still, what happened in His passion cannot be charged against all the Jews, without distinction, then alive, nor against the Jews of today. Although the Church is the new people of God, the Jews should not be presented as rejected or accursed by God, as if this followed from the Holy Scriptures. All should see to it, then, that in catechetical work or in the preaching of the word of God they do not teach anything that does not conform to the truth of the Gospel and the spirit of Christ.
>
> Furthermore, in her rejection of every persecution against any man, the Church, mindful of the patrimony she shares with the Jews and moved not by political reasons but by the Gospel's spiritual love, decries hatred, persecutions, displays of anti-Semitism, directed against Jews at any time and by anyone....[107]

The document unambiguously affirms the church's indebtedness to its Jewish roots, highlights the continuity between the Old Testament covenants and the church today, and decries all forms of anti-Semitism. The significance of this should not go unnoticed.[108] Edward Flannery comments that *Nostra Aetate* "terminated in a stroke a millennial teaching of contempt of Jews and Judaism and unequivocally asserted the Church's debt to its Jewish heritage."[109] Perhaps more important still is the point made in the middle of the

---

107. Emphasis supplied.
108. Eugene Fischer highlights the fact that "*Nostra Aetate* is distinctive among the Conciliar documents in not referring to a single previous ecumenical council or Father of the Church." The reason for this is that the statements issued by earlier councils and popes regarding the Jews were largely "disciplinary" and/or could be described as *Adversus Iudaeos* literature. The Second Vatican Council had to "go directly to the biblical text itself and begin afresh to form Catholic tradition concerning the mystery of Israel." Eugene Fischer, "The Influence of Christian-Jewish Dialogue on Catholic Biblical Studies," *SCJR* 3, Issue 1, Article 20 (2008): 2.
109. Edward Flannery, "Seminaries, Classrooms, Pulpits, Streets: Where We have to Go," 128–48 in *Unanswered Questions: Theological Views of Jewish-Catholic Relations*, ed. Roger Brooks (Notre

fourth paragraph that "although the Church is the new people of God, the Jews should not be presented as rejected or accursed by God, as if this followed from the Holy Scriptures." In these few short words the Catholic Church adjusted its long-established view of supersessionism and affirmed in no uncertain terms that the Jews have *not* been replaced by the church; they (the Jews) still remain a "people of God." Pope Pius X's remarks to Theodor Herzl were consequently overturned.

Not only did the Second Vatican Council reject supersessionism, it also laid down a challenge to the Catholic Church, and indeed to the Christian church worldwide, to redefine its relationship with the Jewish people from one of mission and supersession to one of "fraternity" and mutual affirmation.[110] Subsequent documents from both Catholic and Protestant traditions have been issued largely on the basis of this understanding.[111] In addition, biblical interpretation has also been affected. Eugene Fischer notes five ways in which biblical studies have been "enriched by the 'dialogical hermeneutics' implicitly called for by *Nostra Aetate*'s appeal for a dialogue of 'mutual esteem' between Catholics and Jews."[112] He notes first of all the

---

Dame, IN: University of Notre Dame Press, 1988), at 128–29, quoted in Kessler, *Introduction to Jewish-Christian Relations*, 141.

110. For a discussion of the significance of *Nostra Aetate* for the Protestant community see Petra Heldt, "Protestant Perspectives after 40 Years: A Critical Assessment of *Nostra Aetate*," 163–74 in *Nostra Aetate: Origins, Promulgation, Impact on Jewish-Catholic Relations*, ed. Neville Lamdan and Alberto Melloni (Berlin: LIT Verlag, 2007).

111. Among the most important of these within the Roman Catholic tradition have been the documents of the Pontifical Commission for Religious Relations with the Jews, *Guidelines and Suggestion for Implementing the Conciliar Declaration* Nostra Aetate (1975); *Notes on the Correct Way to Present the Jews and Judaism in Preaching and Catechesis* (1985); *We Remember: A Reflection on the Shoah* (1999); and the Pontifical Biblical Commission's *The Jewish People and Their Sacred Scriptures in the Christian Bible* (2001). Within the Protestant tradition see the document of the WCC's Commission on Faith and Order, *The Church and the Jewish People* (1967); the Leuenberg Church Fellowship's *Church and Israel: A Contribution from the Reformation Churches in Europe to the Relationship between Christians and Jews* (2001), and the International Council of Christians and Jews' *Revision of the 10 Points of Seelisberg* (2009).

112. Fischer, "The Influence of Christian-Jewish Dialogue on Catholic Biblical Studies," 2.

advancement of biblical criticism. Additionally, Catholic, Protestant, and Jewish scholars have become more "collaborative" in their research and ethos. The issues of anti-Semitism in the Bible as well as the notion of "discontinuity" between the Old and New Testament have also been attended to by both Jewish and Christian scholars.[113] Referencing the 1985 document of the Pontifical Commission for Religious Relations with the Jews, *Notes on the Correct Way to Present Jews and Judaism in Catholic Preaching and Teaching*, Fischer says in conclusion that the "model of discontinuity and triumphalism" has been replaced by a model of "common hope for the Kingdom of God and the great heritage of the Prophets."[114]

How should one read the Bible, and the Old Testament in particular, in light of the recent advances in Jewish-Christian relations? Using Gershon Nerel as a case in point, it will be argued here that those who read the Bible with the "eyes of Jewish-Christian *fraternité*" are at the very least open to reflecting and adopting to a certain degree the change of views and sentiments that has characterized Jewish-Christian dialogue since the middle of the last century.

Gershon Nerel's Hermeneutic

Gershon Nerel currently resides with his family on the outskirts of Jerusalem in Yad Hashmona, a kibbutz-like community of Christians from around the world.[115] Nerel graduated from Hebrew University in 1997 with a PhD in Comparative Religion. Published in Hebrew, his dissertation was submitted under the title, *Messianic Jews in Eretz-Israel (1917–1967): Trends and Changes in Shaping Self-Identity*.[116] His

---

113. Fischer highlights here the significance of the 2001 Pontifical Biblical Commission's *The Jewish People*. Ibid., 5.
114. Ibid.
115. See, for an overview of the community's activities and history, "Yad Hashoma: Biblical Village in the Judean Hills," accessed 10 Feb 2011: http://www.yad8.com.

research interests were undoubtedly born out of his active participation and leadership in the Messianic Jewish community. He has served as the Israel Secretary of the International Messianic Jewish Alliance and has been a leading member of the Messianic Jewish Alliance of Israel.[117] In addition to publishing a number of articles dealing with issues regarding the Messianic Jewish community, Nerel is responsible, along with his wife Sara, for revising Franz Delitzsch's translation of the Hebrew New Testament in 2003.[118] In the same year he was invited to speak at a conference at the Hebrew University organized by the Vidal Sassoon International Center for the Study of Antisemitism (SICSA). At this conference he gave a paper entitled "Anti-Zionism in the 'Electronic Church' of Palestinian Christianity."[119] Gershon Nerel's views as articulated in the above paper will form the basis of our discussion.

Nerel's article is based on the premise that the "internet is a revolutionary tool shaping the Christian Church today."[120] Its presence in contemporary society and within religious communities carries with it both positive and negative consequences. Nerel himself highlights some of its more sinister uses, especially in connection with the dissemination of ill-informed and subversive propaganda.

---

116. For a summary of Nerel's Hebrew dissertation see Gershon Nerel, "'Messianic Jews' in *Eretz Israel (1917–1967),*" *Mishkan* 27 (1997): 11–25. See also the bibliographical note in Gershon Nerel, "'Post-mission' and 'Messianic Judaism'—Semantics and Reality (A Response to Dr. Mark Kinzer's *Postmissionary Messianic Judaism Three Years Later: Reflections on a Conversation Just Begun*)," accessed 10 Feb 2011: http://www.narkis.org/Archives/Lindsey Lectures/G.Nerel (Response to Kinzer) 2008.pdf.
117. See the bibliographical note in Louis Goldberg, ed., *How Jewish is Christianity? Two Views on the Messianic Movement* (Grand Rapids: Zondervan, 2003).
118. For the history and motives behind this new translation see Gershon Nerel, "The Flagship of Hebrew New Testaments: A Recent Revision by Israeli Messianic Jews," *Mishkan* 41 (2004): 49–56.
119. Gershon Nerel, "Anti-Zionism in the 'Electronic Church' of Palestinian Christianity," *ACTA* 27 (2006). A video of Nerel's lecture can also be seen on YouTube. Gershon Nerel, "Between Palestinians and Israelis: The Church and the Media," accessed 11 Feb 2011: http://www.youtube.com/watch?v=Mdxtm3me9Fg.
120. Nerel, "Anti-Zionism," 4.

Utilizing Jacques Ellul's research on the use and effects of propaganda, Nerel affirms that "disinformation is most effective when it reaches an individual 'alone in the masses,' cut off from group participation."[121] Consequently, the internet becomes a "powerful tool of inducement" influencing "thousands of *isolated individuals* who benefit from 'freedom of press,' but lack a sense of proportion that would come from being exposed to *other* points of view."[122] Nerel argues that the Palestinian Christian churches and their clergy are guilty of this. They coopt the Internet to propagate their own "religious, social, and political agenda," thereby "isolating" their constituency from the recent advances in Jewish-Christian dialogue and, more importantly, from Jewish-Christian *fraternité*.[123] He contends that "because Palestinian Christians fully identify with the nationalist aspirations of Arab/Muslim Palestinian society, anti-Zionism and anti-Israelism are major components in their propaganda."[124]

Nerel opens his article on anti-Zionism by claiming that "historic anti-Jewish theology" and "anti-Israel attitudes" are still very "attractive and influential" within the churches.[125] He writes: "This is especially true of Arab churches within the Palestinian Authority which still adopt, revive and revise the anti-Israel heritage of Christianity."[126] The presence of Christianity's "anti-Israel heritage" within numerous Palestinian Christian churches, however, is not just an inescapable retrogression on their part. In Nerel's estimation it is an "attack," a "battle," a "spiritual *intifada*" against both Israel and its Christian supporters.[127]

---

121. Ibid.
122. Ibid., 4–5.
123. Ibid., 4.
124. Ibid., 6.
125. Ibid., 3.
126. Ibid.

This "spiritual *intifada*" is spearheaded by the mainline Palestinian Christian churches. Nerel cites "the *Palestinian* Latin Church," "the *Palestinian* Anglican Church," "the *Palestinian* Lutheran Church," and a number of "other *Palestinian* churches," including those affiliated with Baptist and Evangelical denominations.[128] According to Nerel all of these churches broadcast their anti-Zionist and anti-Israeli propaganda through their respective media outlets. It is the leadership groups of these traditions, however, that are at the vanguard of this "attack." They provide for their constituency an "arsenal" of statements, sermons, and articles. What is more, this "arsenal" is accorded a high degree of credibility by virtue of the religious leaders' status within their traditions.[129] Nerel therefore takes time to describe some of the statements and sermons by these key Palestinian Christian leaders.

After highlighting a number of examples,[130] Nerel makes an effort to critique what he calls the "De-Judaization of the Bible: Marketing

---

127. Gerson Nerel, "Spiritual *Intifada* of Palestinian Christians and Messianic Jews," 205–19 in *Israel: His People, His Land, His Story*, ed. Fred Wright (Eastbourne: Thankful Books, 2005), at 205–6. See also idem, "Anti-Zionism," 4.
128. Nerel, "Anti-Zionism," 6–9. Emphasis added. Nerel no doubt knows the proper nomenclature for the respective churches. He redefines the churches in order to highlight their *Palestinian* identity and ethos. His choice of terminology should therefore not go unnoticed.
129. Gershon Nerel says ("Anti-Zionism," 6): "It is particularly within the hierarchical Episcopalian churches—Catholic, Anglican, and Lutheran—that the figure of the Palestinian *bishop* functions as *the* visible (or incognito) historiographer of 'Palestinian Ecclesiastical History.'" Nerel is incorrect in his statement here. It was only during the joint Protestant Bishopric in Jerusalem between the Church of England and the Evangelical Church of Prussia (1842–1886) that one could possibly classify Lutherans as Episcopalians. Even then, despite being ordained as Anglican priests, the Lutheran ministers retained much of their traditional understanding and practice. Moreover, Nerel's statement overlooks the ecclesiological differences between the Catholic and Protestant churches. Only with the 2009 Apostolic Constitution, *Anglicanorum Coetibus*, can one speak of some sort of symbiosis between the Catholic and the Anglican churches. Nevertheless, this provision was for Anglicans deciding to leave their respective tradition and come into full communion with the Catholic Church. See Pope Benedict XVI, "Apostolic Constitution *Anglicanorum Coetibus*: Providing for Personal Ordinariates for Anglicans Entering into Full Communion with the Catholic Church," accessed 18 March 2015: http://w2.vatican.va/content/benedict-xvi/en/apost_constitutions/documents/hf_ben-xvi_apc_20091104_anglicanorum-coetibus.html. Yes, all three churches have bishops, but their ecclesiastical structures are different.

the Palestinian Cause."[131] He argues that this process of "de-Judaization" is seen in the historiography and hermeneutics of the Palestinian Christian leaders. Regarding historiography, Nerel states that on a number of occasions Palestinian Christians have been guilty of historical revisionism. For example, geographical terminology in the Bible is altered so that the "Land of Israel" is reclassified as the "Land of Palestine." Nerel contends that this is a subversive attempt to "erase the Jewishness of various biblical passages."[132] Nerel also references a number of places where Palestinian Christians refer to Jesus, Mary, and the apostles as "Palestinians." In these cases the Jewish identity of Jesus, Mary, and the apostles is simply expunged. Nerel insists: "Ignoring historical facts, the creation of a 'Palestinian' Jesus, of a 'Palestinian' Mary and 'Palestinian' Apostles is pure nationalism and serving a political cause."[133] Finally, Nerel states that Palestinian Christians are guilty of construing some rather dubious historical connections between present-day Palestinians and first-century Palestinians. Quoting Naim Ateek as an example, Nerel criticizes those who similarly "create the false impression that contemporary Palestinians are identical with first-century 'Palestinians.'"[134] In summary, the revision of geographical terminology in the Bible and of the Jewish identity of key biblical figures along with drawing questionable connections between first-century and contemporary Palestinians are all seen as evidence of a

---

130. Nerel cites the views of Munib Younan on martyrdom, Naim Ateek on suicide bombing, and some of the more "sensational" statements and sermons by Riah Abu El-Assal and the current Lutheran pastor in Bethlehem, Mitri Raheb. Nerel, "Anti-Zionism," 10–24.
131. Ibid., 24.
132. Ibid.
133. Ibid., 25.
134. Ibid., 24. Nerel quotes Naim Ateek as saying: "Jesus Christ's resurrection took place in Jerusalem. Therefore, the first witnesses to the resurrection were Palestinians. The Church was born in Palestine as the early disciples and followers of Jesus were Palestinians." Cf. Ateek, *Justice and Only Justice*, 113.

process of "de-Judaization" of the Bible marketed under the guise of sound historiography to promote the Palestinian cause.

According to Nerel the "de-Judaization" of the Bible can also be seen in Palestinian Christian hermeneutics. He says: "Scriptural exegesis among Palestinian Christians has shaped a new Arab theology which denies any continuum between biblical Israel, the Land of Israel, and the Jewish people of today."[135] Furthermore, "the clergy question the full authority of the Hebraic Old Testament."[136] To illustrate his point he draws attention to the work of Naim Ateek and Mitri Raheb. Regarding the authority of the OT for the Christian faith, Nerel quotes Ateek: "As a Christian, I cannot begin my study of the Bible from Genesis. . . . What God did for the world in Christ far exceeded the best the prophets predicted and anticipated."[137] With reference to the continuity between biblical Israel, the land of Israel, and the Jewish people of today he cites Mitri Raheb's view on election in *I am a Palestinian Christian*: "Israel failed because it laid claim to election as law, according to Paul. But Christ has put an end to all law (Rom. 10:4). In him, the law has achieved its real purpose and election its original meaning."[138] Nerel assesses these statements rightly and concludes: "For Raheb and Ateek, then, Israel's election and God's covenant with Israel in the OT, which includes divine promises related to land, are null and void after the coming of Christ and Israel's rejection of Christ."[139]

How, then, should a Palestinian Christian read the Old Testament? Nerel does not offer many suggestions to advance Palestinian Christian hermeneutics. His article is more a critical appraisal of Palestinian Christianity than a constructive proposal for Palestinian

---

135. Nerel, "Anti-Zionism," 25.
136. Ibid.
137. Ibid.
138. Ibid.
139. Ibid.

Christian interpretation. He lambastes the Palestinian Christian churches and their leaders for taking advantage of the "public's general ignorance of the text," and indeed its history of interpretation, and disseminating through the Internet a "sophisticated distortion of canonical scripture" for their own political ends.[140] Nevertheless, when one compares Nerel's opening and closing statements it is clear that he believes the Bible should be read with the "eyes of Jewish-Christian *fraternité*." Nerel says at the beginning of his article: "The establishment of the State of Israel on May 14, 1948, was a severe shock to historical Christian theology, undermining the concept of supersession or replacement, which led the Church to define itself as 'Verus Israel,'"[141] and in conclusion he writes:

> Although Western and Palestinian Christians share the same biblical heritage, they do not regard Israel's unique position in the same manner. There is a growing dichotomy between Palestinian and Western believers in the Old and New Testaments. Palestinian Christians fervently adopt the traditional Church antagonism towards Judaism, dressing it in a new oriental garb. This parting of the ways reflects an unfinished battle over theological influence and territorial inheritance.[142]

From all this it can be concluded that Nerel would argue for an increase in dialogue between Palestinian and Western Christianity, especially as it concerns the positive advancement of Jewish-Christian relations since the Second World War. He believes that the international Christian community and its official representatives should speak out against the anti-Zionist and anti-Israel propaganda of Palestinian Christians,[143] and although Arab Christians were not

---

140. Nerel says, "Within 'liberation theology,' neo-Marcionism has been particularly influential with the help of highly manipulative propaganda." Ibid., 28.
141. Ibid., 4.
142. Ibid., 38.

directly involved in the atrocities associated with the Holocaust, they should still at a minimum be bound to entertain the notion that the Old Testament should be read "with the eyes of Jewish-Christian *fraternité*."

Critique of Gershon Nerel's Hermeneutic

Francesco Rossi de Gasperis is correct in his estimation that the development of Jewish-Christian relations in the West over the last sixty-plus years has not been "understood, or shared, by the Churches of the Middle East. In these Churches it is regarded as the expression of a guilt complex formed in the western Churches as a result of the Holocaust, but by no means affecting eastern Christians."[144] Similarly, Nerel concludes in consternation that only a small portion of the Palestinian Christian community read the biblical text with eyes of Jewish-Christian *fraternité*. It is true that most of the Palestinian Christians he cites, and indeed most of the ones described in the second chapter, do not read the Old Testament with what has been defined as "Jewish-Christian *fraternité*."[145] Nerel is right to commend a change in attitude in this regard. However, he does not offer any suggestions about how Palestinian Christians might do this. Instead, he derides the Palestinian Christian churches and their leaders as being "anti-Zionist," "anti-Israel," and even "anti-Jewish." A minimal understanding and/or articulation of Palestinian Christianity's

---

143. Nerel laments (ibid., 32–33): "There is not a single Church document—Roman Catholic or mainline Protestant—that denounces or even criticizes Palestinian Christianity's anti-Zionism."
144. Francesco Rossi de Gasperis, "Interreligious Dialogue in Jerusalem," accessed 12 March 2012: http://www.etrfi.org/uploads/1/0/7/9/10798906/interreligious_dialogue_in_jerusalem.pdf.
145. Nerel is also right that Palestinian Christians in general never opened their arms to the influx of Jewish immigrants. He references the 1921 CMJ report that details the Arab riots in Jaffa in 1921. Rev. A. C. Martin, an English missionary, describes the situation as follows: "A large number of the Jews are terror-stricken. . . . Unfortunately for the work, Arabs, who call themselves Christians, united with the Moslems in their endeavours to shed Jewish blood, so we have the unpleasant task of explaining and apologising for the falseness of this un-Christlike Christianity." Quoted in Nerel, "Anti-Zionism," 31.

historic conditions would temper Nerel's observations. Furthermore, the very fact that these Palestinian Christians wrestle with how to read the Old Testament in light of the foundation of the state of Israel, and for them the associated *Nakba*, should be seen as a positive sign.[146] Therefore they should not be called "anti-Zionist," "anti-Israel," and "anti-Jewish." They should rather be lauded for their attempt to reappropriate the use of the OT in a predominantly Arab and Muslim context and in light of the aforementioned "catastrophe of faith." We may hope that, in the course of time, Palestinian Christians will begin to move more toward Jewish-Christian *fraternité* in their reading of the OT. Nerel, however, does not offer any steps for them to take to get there.

Conclusion

Prior's "Reading with the Eyes of the Canaanite," Miller's "Reading with the Eyes of Tradition," and Nerel's "Reading with the Eyes of Jewish-Christian *fraternité*" all demand that Palestinian Christians should read the OT in a certain way, and are thus ideologically driven. This is a given. The question that must be asked, however, is whether any of them, in their insistence on reading the OT in a certain way, are ideological in the "pejorative" sense. This is difficult to say, for they all make some valid points that need to be taken into consideration. Prior reminds the reader of the atrocities certain biblical texts have engendered. Miller is wise to present the benefits of reading the OT in line with tradition, especially as it has to do with

---

146. A lesson from history underscores this point. See Rolf Rendtorff's article detailing the way Wilhem Vischer and Gerhard von Rad rescued the OT for many German Christians in the wake of Hitler's rise to power in 1933, the corresponding establishment of the Deutsche Evangelische Kirche, and the "de-Judaization" of the OT when parts that were deemed "un-German" and too "Jewish" were removed. Rolf Rendtorff, "Christological Interpretation as a Way of 'Salvaging' the Old Testament? Wilhelm Vischer and Gerhard von Rad," 76–91 in *Canon and Theology: Overtures to an Old Testament Theology* (Minneapolis: Fortress Press, 1993).

the Roman Catholic Church's encouragement to use the historical-critical method. Nerel points out the laudable advances in Jewish-Christian relations in the last sixty-plus years. Nevertheless, it can be said that the flaw in each perspective is its starting point and these scholars' insistence that that be the basis for determining how the OT should be read, when in fact one ought to start with hermeneutics and the proper understanding of a given OT text.[147] Only then should the aforementioned perspectives be brought into play. In the following chapter I will present my own suggested hermeneutic.

---

147. Charles Miller is closest to the present writer in his suggestion that the historical-critical method be used as the basis for a Palestinian Christian reading of the OT.

6

A Prescription for a Palestinian Christian Hermeneutic of the Old Testament

How *should* a Palestinian Christian read the Old Testament? Inherent in the very structure of this book is the clue to the proposed hermeneutic. In other words, the "how," or prescription, of PCHOT is specified in the order of this work's constituent parts. Hermeneutics and the proper understanding of a given Old Testament text are foundational for PCHOT. The way forward for Palestinian Christians, therefore, is not to *start* one's reading of the OT by reading with the eyes of the "Canaanite," "Tradition," or "Jewish-Christian *fraternité*," or from *any* extraneous perspective, vantage point, or ideology. PCHOT must start with understanding the nature of hermeneutics and a given text in its own particular context.

The *Hermeneutics* of a PCHOT

As defined above, hermeneutics refers to the "art of understanding." The problem, as Friedrich Schleiermacher rightfully contends, is that "non-understanding" is normative.[1] There are two schools of thought in hermeneutics. The first, argues Schleiermacher, is "the more lax practice in the art" and "assumes that understanding results as a matter of course and expresses the aim negatively: *misunderstanding should be avoided*."[2] The second school "assumes that misunderstanding results as a matter of course and that understanding must be desired and sought at every point."[3] He calls this "the more strict practice."[4] Understanding is, therefore, slow and sometimes tedious, but nevertheless possible. Problems materialize when, through haste or prejudice, the road to understanding is short-circuited. Schleiermacher writes: "Misunderstanding is either a consequence of hastiness or of prejudice. The former is an isolated moment. The latter is a mistake which lies deeper. It is the one-sided preference for what is close to the individual's circle of ideas and the rejection of what lies outside it. In this way one explains in or explains out what is not present in the author."[5]

It has been argued that Palestinian Christians do not have the luxury of time, which the "art of understanding" requires.[6] This may be excused if, as Schleiermacher points out, it is only an "isolated moment." However, to continually use the emergency situation to

---

1. Friedrich Schleiermacher, *Hermeneutics and Criticism: And Other Writings*, trans. and ed. Andrew Bowie (Cambridge: Cambridge University Press, 1998), 227.
2. Ibid., 21. Emphasis in original.
3. Ibid., 22.
4. Ibid.
5. Ibid., 23.
6. In a discussion with a Palestinian Christian in 2007 the present author was asked: "Do you ask the inhabitants of a house that is on fire to sit down and discuss the nature of the fire whilst the house is burning around them? No, you get them out of the house and put out the fire." The question was posed in the context of discussing the issues of justice and reconciliation. Conversation/ Interview: Anonymous, "Justice and Reconciliation," (Jerusalem, July 23, 2007).

justify one's negligence in properly "understanding" a text borders on "prejudice." Hermeneutics is fundamental to all human discourse. It is the natural mediation between one person's utterance and the communication of someone else's words to a third person. To persistently misunderstand and thereby misrepresent what someone says would be sharply and rapidly condemned in any oral or written conversation today. The fact that authors from antiquity are not in a position to respond to the misinterpretation and misrepresentation of their work should not excuse anyone from failing to take the time and make the effort to try and correctly understand what was said in the past.

Moreover, it has been pointed out that the particular "strain of loyalties" with which Palestinian Christians are confronted traps some in a cycle of interpretation that leaves little room for dialogue. Najla Kassab writes: "The war situation in the Middle East has created a world of extremes which silence and hinder any attempt at a dialogue between our religious thoughts and the prevailing political situation."[7] Kassab's statement seems to imply as a consequence that Palestinian Christians are excused for any "prejudice" that, in the words of Schleiermacher, "explains in or explains out what is not present in the author." They are not to be blamed, therefore, for "misunderstanding" the speech or text of an "Other."

It is beyond the scope of this book to discuss at any length or depth the notion of ethical hermeneutics. Without belittling the grievances of all parties involved, however, a quick word should nevertheless

---

7. Najla Kassab, "A Middle Eastern Christian Approach to the Old Testament," *Theological Review* 13, no. 1 (April 1, 1992): 35–48, at 35–36. She continues: "Some have banished the O.T. from their church life so that they will not risk making a political statement by using the O.T. Others have kept the O.T., but avoided using critical passages or terms." She also (p. 36) enumerates a third extreme, fundamentalist Christians, who "naïvely point to the fulfillment of the prophecies of the O.T. and preach the 'end of days' whose signs are made clear in the establishment of the State of Israel, and thus they await the rebuilding of the temple, disregarding the daily pain and injustices caused by such ideas."

be said about the "obligation one owes to the representation of the other."[8] Rooted largely in the thought of Emmanuel Levinas, ethical hermeneutics emerged out of his understanding of the "face."[9] For Levinas the human face is *the* ethical space. When asked about this "phenomenology of the face," he responded:

> I do not know if one can speak of a "phenomenology" of the face, since phenomenology describes what appears. So, too, I wonder if one can speak of a look turned toward the face, for the look is knowledge, perception. I think rather that access to the face is straightaway ethical. You turn yourself toward the Other as toward an object when you see a nose, eyes, a forehead, a chin, and you can describe them. The best way of encountering the Other is not even to notice the color of his eyes! When one observes the color of the eyes one is not in social relationship with the Other. The relationship with the face can surely be dominated by perception, but what is specifically the face is what cannot be reduced to that.[10]

For Levinas, therefore, the "Other" is not an "object" simply to be observed. The "Other" is a person who demands a "relationship." Levinas challenges the traditional philosophical notion that the subject is a self-enclosed entity. Much as in Martin Buber's *I and Thou*,[11] the subject for Levinas is defined in its exposure to the "Other."

---

8. Ben Faber, "Ethical Hermeneutics and the Theater: Shakespeare's Merchant of Venice," 211–24 in *Hermeneutics at the Crossroads*, ed. Kevin Vanhoozer (Bloomington: Indiana University Press, 2006), at 213.
9. See Emmanuel Levinas, "The Face" 85–92 in *Ethics and Infinity: Conversations with Philippe Nemo* (Pittsburgh: Duquesne University Press, 1985). Despite the tradition of ethical hermeneutics that has emerged on the basis of Levinas's work, he himself stated: "My task does not consist in constructing ethics; I only try to find its meaning. In fact I do not believe that all philosophy should be programmatic. It is Husserl above all who brought up the idea of a program of philosophy. One can without doubt construct an ethics in function of what I have just said, but this is not my own theme." Ibid., 90.
10. Ibid., 85–86.
11. Martin Buber, *I and Thou* (Edinburgh: T & T Clark, 1947).

What does this have to do with hermeneutics? It means that the presence of the Other demands a relationship, and indeed "discourse." Levinas writes:

> Face and discourse are tied. The face speaks. It speaks, it is in this that it renders possible and begins all discourse. I have just refused the notion of vision to describe the authentic relationship with the Other; it is discourse and, more exactly, response or responsibility which is the authentic relationship.[12]

Relationship with the Other is connected to discourse or conversation. The "Other" speaks and demands a "response." "Response," however, necessitates listening and in turn "understanding." Understanding, therefore, is the necessary arbitrator between speech and response. Ethical hermeneutics calls for understanding the speech of the "Other."

How does this play out when there is a third party or, in the case of Palestinian Christians, a "strain of loyalties?" Levinas writes:

> Everything that takes place here "between us" concerns everyone. … [T]he presence of the face does not invite complicity with the preferred being, the self-sufficient "I-Thou" forgetful of the universe; in its frankness it refuses the clandestinity of love. . . . The third party looks at me in the eyes of the Other."[13]

In the same way that the "Other" demanded a "response" above, so the third party in this instance commands both attention and an answer. The balancing act is required if there is to be "justice." Levinas explains:

> In a spirituality which I define by this responsibility for the other . . . I must henceforth compare; I must compare incomparables, uniquenesses. No returning to the "for-oneself of each": it is necessary to judge others.

---

12. Levinas, "The Face," 87–88.
13. Emmanuel Levinas, *Totality and Infinity* (Dordrecht: Kluwer Academic Publishers, 1991), 212–13.

In the meeting with the face, it was not one's place to judge: the other, being unique, does not undergo judgment; he takes precedence over me from the start; I am under allegiance to him. Judgment and justice are required from the moment the third party appears. In the very name of the absolute obligations towards one's fellow man a certain abandonment of the absolute allegiance he calls for is necessary.[14]

The challenge, therefore, for Palestinian Christians, and indeed for all the parties involved, is to relinquish any "absolute allegiance[s]" that may be held. Even-handedness is required in one's "response" to all the faces or "eyes" one encounters in the debate.

Perhaps the most ignored voice in the whole discussion of PCHOT is the Old Testament text itself.[15] Even the proposals articulated in the last chapter stressed that the OT should be read primarily from a perspective external to the text.[16] This is not to say that those contexts are unimportant. Indeed, as Levinas argued, all the contexts demand attention. Nevertheless, the forgotten voice in most of the above perspectives has been the voice of the text.[17]

What does this mean with regard to a Palestinian Christian reading of the Old Testament? The following hermeneutic will take for granted that the message of the Old Testament, within the confines of its own context, must first be heard and understood by itself, without the imposition of meaning from outside. Only afterward may the text be responded to and read in light of relevant secondary contexts, that is, with the eyes of the "Canaanite," "Tradition," or "Jewish-Christian *fraternité*." PCHOT, therefore, must start with understanding the text of the Old Testament itself.[18]

---

14. Emmanuel Levinas, *Entre Nous: On Thinking of the Other* (New York: Columbia University Press, 1998), 202–3.
15. Cf. Chapter 4, "PCHOT between 1982 and 1987" and "PCHOT since 1987."
16. Cf. Chapter 5.
17. This is true of all the proposed hermeneutics except the one by Charles Miller. His hermeneutic, with its advocacy of the historical-critical method, came closest to letting the voice of the Old Testament speak for itself.

The *Text* of a PCHOT

It is this author's conviction that a PCHOT must address those texts that jar Palestinian Christians the most, as opposed to those that easily beget sympathy.[19] Therefore the rest of this chapter will focus on analyzing the text of Deuteronomy 7, one of the most problematic in the OT. Deuteronomy 7 is a chapter that could easily be read by Palestinian Christians as being "against" them. The subjects of God, people, and land could be understood in the negative, so that Palestinian Christians see themselves as people who are not loved/ not elected, living in a land promised to another, and with nothing to expect but the prospect of dispossession and genocide. This is a challenge a PCHOT must address. As intimated above, the text demands a listening ear. Therefore I will analyze Deuteronomy 7 on its own terms and according to its proper context. In order to do this properly, I must first say a few words about the book of Deuteronomy as a whole. This will provide the necessary framework for listening well and comprehending what Deuteronomy 7 is actually saying. The final chapter of the book will then bring these conclusions into dialogue with the views of the Palestinian Christians already heard from and the proposals by Prior, Miller, and Nerel. In the end a PCHOT will be proposed that is faithful both to the voice of the text and to the various contexts that inform Palestinian Christians in Israel and Palestine.

---

18. This is not to negate the fact that there are other forces that bear upon a person's interpretation of the text of the Old Testament, not least those that have assigned to them "classic" or "canonical" status. See Francis Watson, "The Scope of Hermeneutics," 65–80 in *The Cambridge Companion to Christian Doctrine*, at 71. I will argue, contra Watson, that with regard to hermeneutics in general and hermeneutics of the Old Testament in particular the starting point still can and must be a venture at understanding the meaning of the text itself.
19. This is in contrast to Naim Ateek, who, in his PLT chooses "prophetic" traditions over against "torah-oriented" and "nationalist" traditions. Thus he highlights Jonah as an Old Testament example of a Palestinian liberation theologian *par excellence*. Naim Ateek, *Justice, and only Justice: A Palestinian Theology of Liberation* (Maryknoll, NY: Orbis Books, 2002), 92–100. Cf. idem, *A Palestinian Christian Cry for Reconciliation* (Maryknoll, NY: Orbis Books, 2008), 77.

Deuteronomy

Title and Outline of Contents

The Hebrew title, *Devarim*, originates from the opening words of the text, אלה הדברים, "these are the words." The English title, Deuteronomy, which is obviously different, is based on the Greek and Latin versions of the text. The Septuagint, or LXX, mistranslated Deuteronomy 17:18, משנה התורה הזאת, "a copy of this law," as τό δευτερονόμιον τοῦτο, "this second or repeated law," and labeled the book accordingly. The Latin Vulgate assumed this title and entitled the fifth book of the Pentateuch *Deuteronomium*. The Greek translation and Latin appropriation, however, are not wholly inappropriate, for in its literary context Deuteronomy "reiterates, in a somewhat revised form, laws which Moses had given earlier to Israel at Mount Horeb (= Sinai; Exod 19–24)."[20]

As the above titles suggest, Deuteronomy consists of a series of speeches or words given by Moses on the plains of Moab in which he sets forth in unique fashion the laws the people of Israel are to obey once they have entered the land of Canaan.[21] These discourses are bracketed by four superscriptions, or introductory formulas, which frame the book of Deuteronomy and its contents as follows:[22]

---

20. Ronald E. Clements, *Deuteronomy* (Sheffield: JSOT, 1989), 13.
21. That Moses is credited as the one who gave these speeches does not necessarily mean that they were actually uttered or written by him.
22. Scholars agree with the number and location of these superscriptions, but they disagree over the precise number and scope of the addresses the introductory formularies supposedly demarcate. Clements says: "These four headings lend an overall structure to the book and have clearly been intended to do so. Even if we accept, as some scholars have done, that they derive from different times and stages in the book's composition, it would seem clear that they are now set as indicators of the different sections and units which belong to it as a whole. They do in fact mark out major sections of the book." Clements, *Deuteronomy*, 14. In contrast, A. D. H. Mayes says there are only three addresses spanning Deut 1:1–30:20, with an appendix that includes the remaining material in Deut 31:1–34:12. A. D. H. Mayes, *Deuteronomy* (London: Oliphants, 1979), 5. Cf. Samuel R. Driver, *Deuteronomy* (3d ed. Edinburgh: T & T Clark, 1969), i–ii; Ernest W. Nicholson, *Deuteronomy and Tradition* (Oxford: Basil Blackwell, 1967), 18–19;

Outline of Deuteronomy's Contents

Deut 1:1–4:43	*Moses' First Address*: "These are the words that Moses spoke ..."
Deut 1:1-5	First superscription (first introduction)
Deut 1:6–3:20	Historical account: journey from Horeb to the plains of Moab
Deut 4:1-40	Sermon
Deut 4:41-43	Enumeration of the three cities of refuge in Transjordan
Deut 4:44–28:68	*Moses' Second Address*: "This is the law that Moses set before the Israelites ..."
Deut 4:44-49	Second superscription (second introduction)
Deut 5:1–11:32	Decalogue, paraenesis, and historical narration
Deut 12:1–26:15	Deuteronomic code
Deut 26:16–27:26	Prescriptions for a cultic ceremony upon entering the Land
Deuteronomy 28	Blessings and curses for obedience/disobedience
Deut 29:1–32:52	*Moses' Third Address*: "These are the words of the covenant ..."
Deuteronomy 29–30	Account of covenant renewal ceremony on the plains of Moab
Deuteronomy 31	Commissioning of Joshua
Deut 32:1-47	The Song of Moses and its epilogue
Deut 32:48-52	God's command to Moses to ascend Mount Nebo
Deut 33:1–34:12	*Moses' Final Address*: "This is the blessing with which Moses ... blessed the Israelites ..."
Deuteronomy 33	Final blessing of Moses
Deuteronomy 34	Account of Moses' death

George Adam Smith, *Deuteronomy* (Cambridge: Cambridge University Press, 1918), xi–xii; G. Ernest Wright, *Deuteronomy*, IB 2 (Nashville: Abingdon, 1953), 314–15. Patrick Miller extends the third discourse through to Deut 32:47, with the fourth and final part comprising Deut 32:48–34:12. Patrick D. Miller, *Deuteronomy* (Louisville: John Knox, 1990), ix–xii. Duane L. Christensen recognizes three discourses (Deut 1:1–4:43; 4:44–26:19; 27:1–31:30) followed by three short appendices (Deuteronomy 32, 33, and 34). Duane L. Christensen, *Deuteronomy 1–11*, WBC 6A (1st ed. Dallas: Word Books, 1991), xl–xli.

"In spite of its apparent formal unity," which the table's superscriptions implies, the actual content of Deuteronomy suggests that "the book is not a homogenous piece of work."[23] Not least among the aspects that betray the composite nature of Deuteronomy is its multiple introductions (to Deut 1:1–4:40; 4:44–11:32), additions to the central law book (Deuteronomy 29–30), and a collection of appended material (Deuteronomy 31–34) that seems to belong "less to the book of Deuteronomy proper than to the Pentateuch as a whole" and/or to the "work of the Deuteronomistic Historian."[24] In light of this, most scholars agree that the heart of Deuteronomy is in the second of Moses' addresses (Deut 4:44–28:68). These chapters constitute for them what is arguably the original book of Deuteronomy, or *Urdeuteronomium*.[25] It consists of an introduction (Deuteronomy 5–11) and a central law book or code (Deuteronomy 12–26, 28). As Samuel R. Driver points out, "the *first* part (c. 5–11) consists of a hortatory introduction, inculcating the *general* theocratic principles by which Israel, as a nation, is to be governed. The *second* part (c. 12–26, 28) includes the code of *special* laws, which it is the object of the legislator to 'expound' (15). . . ."[26]

---

23. Moshe Weinfeld, *Deuteronomy 1–11*, AB 5A (New York: Doubleday, 2006), 9. For a good overview of the problems in ascertaining the original book of Deuteronomy, or *Urdeuteronomium*, and the variety of scholarly opinion on the matter see Nicholson, *Deuteronomy and Tradition*, 18–36.
24. Nicholson, *Deuteronomy and Tradition*, 19–22.
25. Weinfeld is right to say that these chapters are "not homogenous either." Weinfeld, *Deuteronomy 1–11*, 10. Nevertheless, the bulk of them (Deuteronomy 5–26, 28) can be said to be original.
26. Driver, *Deuteronomy*, 81–82. Clements makes an important remark on the relation between the central law book and its framework, and in particular between the Deuteronomic code (Deuteronomy 12–26) and the Decalogue (Deuteronomy 5). He writes: "The relationship between the commandments and the law code of 12:1–26:19 is an important one, since, in spite of appearances, they do not represent two different collections, or classes, of law. The commandments provide the broad headings and principles of conduct, and the laws fill out these principles by showing how they must be applied in society." Ronald E. Clements, *The Book of Deuteronomy* (Peterborough: Epworth Press, 2001), 19. One could also say that the series of sermons or paraenetic material that follows the Decalogue in chaps. 6 to 11 also seeks to expound on the principles established in the Ten Commandments.

This account of Deuteronomy's contents will have a significant influence on the interpretation of the book's seventh chapter. Nevertheless, Gerhard von Rad raises an important point that also warrants exploring. He writes: "We may distinguish any number of different strata and accretions by literary criteria, but in the matter of form the various constituents form an indivisible unity. The question is thus inescapably raised of the origin and purpose of the form of *Deuteronomy* as we now have it."[27] The following two sections will therefore look at the literary form(s) of Deuteronomy and their origin and purpose.

Literary Form(s) of Deuteronomy

Questions of form usually imply an investigation of a given book's literary types or genres in order to ascertain the nature of its oral pre-history.[28] As the title of this section suggests, however, there was no oral stage in the development of Deuteronomy. Parts of Deuteronomy may have had oral antecedents, but Deuteronomy as a whole is a literary creation.[29] It is not without reason, therefore, that a number of reputable scholars refer to the "literary form(s)" of Deuteronomy and not to the "form(s)" of Deuteronomy.[30] The following will detail some of these "literary form(s)" and explore whether any of them resembles one or more forms found elsewhere in the Ancient Near East (ANE).

---

27. Gerhard von Rad, "The Form-Critical Problem of the Hexateuch," in idem, *The Problem of the Hexateuch* (London: SCM, 1984), 27.
28. This is based on the common understanding of the nature of form criticism. "Form criticism is a method of analyzing and interpreting the literature of the Old Testament through a study of its literary types or genres. In particular, form criticism is a means of identifying genres of that literature, their structure, intentions and settings in order to understand the oral stage of their development." Gene M. Tucker, *Form Criticism of the Old Testament* (Philadelphia: Fortress Press, 1971), 1.
29. An investigation of a potential "oral stage" in the development of Deuteronomy will be limited to the book's seventh chapter.
30. See, for example, Clements, *Deuteronomy*, 18; Weinfeld, *Deuteronomy 1–11*, 4.

Based on the above outline of Deuteronomy's contents, one can easily agree with Gerhard von Rad when he says that "Deuteronomy presents itself to us almost as a mosaic of innumerable, extremely varied pieces of traditional material."[31] The book seems beyond classification. However, within the pages of Deuteronomy three main types of literature can easily be detected: history, legislation, and paraenesis.[32] Driver goes so far to say that paraenesis is the most basic and characteristic element in Deuteronomy. He writes:

> Of these the parenetic element is both the most characteristic and the most important; it is directed to the inculcation of certain fundamental religious and moral principles upon which the Writer lays great stress: the historical element is all but entirely subservient to it (the references to the history, as said before, having nearly always a didactic aim): the legislative element, though naturally, as the condition of national well-being, possessing an independent value of its own, is *here* viewed primarily by the Writer as a vehicle for exemplifying the principles which it is the main object of his book to enforce.[33]

It is difficult to say definitively whether Driver is right or wrong in his estimation. Paraenesis undoubtedly colors the whole of Deuteronomy, and especially the historical and legal elements in the book.[34] Nevertheless, a number of factors need to be considered before one can reach a conclusion with any degree of certainty. Not least among these is the compositional history of Deuteronomy.[35]

---

31. Gerhard von Rad, *Deuteronomy* (London: SCM, 1966), 12-13.
32. Driver, *Deuteronomy*, xix.
33. Ibid.
34. Von Rad is not too far removed from Driver when he describes Deuteronomy as "preached law." Deuteronomy, he writes, "is not divine law in codified form, but preaching about the commandments—at least, the commandments appear in a form where they are very much interspersed with parenesis." Gerhard von Rad, *Studies in Deuteronomy*, trans. David Stalker; SBT 9 (London: SCM, 1953), 15.
35. For example, in Driver's estimation Deuteronomy 1-3, and possibly Deuteronomy 4 as well, were composed by the same hand that wrote Deuteronomy 5-26. Driver, *Deuteronomy*, lxxii. For other scholars, such as A. D. H. Mayes, this was not the case. Deuteronomy 1-3 was not composed by the author of Deuteronomy 5-26 but belongs rather to a subsequent redaction that incorporated the original version of Deuteronomy into the DH. This view leads Mayes to

In addition, one needs to evaluate how this material is presented in Deuteronomy and investigate whether there is any correspondence between the literary form(s) of Deuteronomy and the wider ANE.

The previous section pointed out that Deuteronomy is formulated as an address given by Moses on the plains of Moab shortly before his death. As Weinfeld contends, it is in the form of a final "testament" or "valedictory speech."[36] These orations, as Weinfeld shows, are "literary programmatic creations and do not convey the actual content of speeches once delivered in concrete circumstances."[37] They are "orations of an idealizing character . . . uttering the thoughts and mood of their authors. These authors put into the mouths of such national leaders as Moses, Joshua, Samuel, David, Solomon, in addition to priestly (Deut. 20) and prophetic personages (in Kings and Jeremiah), that which conformed with their own ideology."[38]

The significance of this literary practice should not go unnoticed, for it has significant bearing on what one believes to be the overall rhetorical purpose of Deuteronomy.[39] It also undermines the arguments of those like von Rad who contend that there is an oral precedent to the literary composition of Deuteronomy. Although von Rad acknowledges that "Deuteronomy in its present form is

---

claim that "in Deuteronomy large sections of the historical material, though presently joined with the parenetic, stand quite apart from the latter as history recounted not perhaps simply for its own sake, but certainly not with the object of inducing a feeling of gratitude in Israel for favours shown her by Yahweh in the past. So, for example, there is a clear distinction between the historical section in chs. 1–3 and the historical references which appear in ch. 8." Mayes, *Deuteronomy*, 35

36. Weinfeld, *Deuteronomy 1–11*, 4. See also idem, *Deuteronomy and the Deuteronomic School* (Oxford: Clarendon Press, 1972), 10–14.
37. Ibid., 51.
38. Ibid., 52. Weinfeld points out that this literary practice is rooted in Egyptian and Assyrian tradition and can also be found in Greek historiography. He cites in particular Egyptian wisdom tradition, neo-Assyrian ceremonies of succession attested in the vassal treaties of Esarhaddon (VTE), and the Greek histories of Herodotus and Thucydides. Weinfeld, *Deuteronomy 1–11*, 4–5.
39. See below for an evaluation of the differences among the views of Weinfeld, Driver, and Levinson on the matter and this writer's concluding thoughts on the overall rhetorical purpose behind Deuteronomy.

undoubtedly a literary production," he qualifies this statement by saying that the book "still bears the stamp of a cultic form that has exercised an extraordinary influence on its style."[40] For von Rad, the book of Deuteronomy "falls structurally in four sections:"[41]

1. Historical presentation of the events of Sinai, and paraenetic material connected with these events (Deuteronomy 1–11)
2. The reading of the law (Deuteronomy 12:1–26:15)
3. The sealing of the covenant (Deuteronomy 26:16–19)
4. Blessings and curses (Deuteronomy 27ff.)

On the basis of this structure, which von Rad says follows that of Exodus 19–24, he claims that Deuteronomy is based on the form of a covenant renewal ceremony that took place under the auspices of the Levites in the cultic tradition of the old Shechem amphictyony. Von Rad explains: "The remarkable way in which parenesis, laws, binding by covenant, blessing and cursing follow upon one another points . . . to the course of a great cultic celebration, namely, the old festival of the renewal of the Covenant at Shechem."[42] Despite the longstanding acceptance of von Rad's theory, his arguments are unfounded, as shown not only by the comments of Weinfeld above but also because of the work of those who have shown a connection between the form of Deuteronomy and that of the forms of the ANE.

George E. Mendenhall[43] was the first to establish a connection between Deuteronomy and ANE treaties, in particular those of the Hittites.[44] The debate continued a few years later with R. Frankena,

---

40. Von Rad, *Studies in Deuteronomy*, 14–15.
41. Von Rad, "The Form-Critical Problem of the Hexateuch," 27.
42. Von Rad, *Studies in Deuteronomy*, 14.
43. George E. Mendenhall, "Covenant Forms in Israelite Traditions," *BA* 17 (1959): 49–76. See also Dennis J. McCarthy, *Treaty and Covenant: A Study in Form in the Ancient Oriental Documents and in the Old Testament*. AnBib 21a (Rome: Biblical Institute Press, 1978), and M. G. Kline, *Treaty of the Great King: The Covenant Structure of Deuteronomy* (Grand Rapids: Eerdmans, 1963).

who suggested that Deuteronomy is more akin to eighth-seventh century BCE Assyrian treaty forms than to the earlier Hittite forms.[45] The vast majority of critical scholarship has now come to the conclusion that there are definite similarities between ANE treaty forms and Deuteronomy. Nevertheless, there is still scholarly debate over the precise relationship between the two.

Origins of Deuteronomy

That the final form of Deuteronomy was penned by the hand of Moses has long been a point of scholarly reservation. It was W. M. L. de Wette, however, who first provided an alternative *raison d'etre* for the origin and purpose of Deuteronomy. Writing in 1805, de Wette proposed that Deuteronomy reflects less the covenant between God and Israel on the plains of Moab than the great reforms initiated by Josiah in the seventh century BCE.[46] His argument was based on the fact that Deuteronomy 12 and the whole of the book more broadly suggest a strong impetus for a centralization of the cult. That this appeal must stem from the time of Josiah, or at the very earliest Hezekiah, is proved by the fact that beforehand "sanctuaries and high places were not only existent and tolerated but were even considered indispensable for the religious life of Israel."[47]

There have undoubtedly been modifications to and indeed sharp disagreements with de Wette's thesis over the years.[48] This will

---

44. The treaties of Esarhaddon had just been published a year previously in 1958. See D. J. Wiseman, "The Vassal Treaties of Esarhaddon," *Iraq* 20 (1958): 1–99.
45. See R. Frankena. "The Vassal Treaties of Esarhaddon and the Dating of Deuteronomy," *OTS* 14 (1965): 122–54.
46. W. M. L. de Wette, *Dissertatio critico-exegetica qua a prioribus Deuteronomium Pentateuchi libris diversum alius cuiusdam recentioris auctoris opus esse monstratur* (Jena: Etzdorf, 1805).
47. Moshe Weinfeld, "Deuteronomy—The Present State of Inquiry," *JBL* 86, no. 3 (September 1967): 249–62, at 249.
48. De Wette's theory was largely uncontested for over a hundred years, and despite the criticisms of Theodor Oestreicher's *Das deuteronomische Grundgesetz* (Gütersloh: Bertelsman, 1923) and Adam Welch's *The Code of Deuteronomy* (London: J. Clarke, 1924) and *Deuteronomy, The*

become evident in the following section, which will highlight the thoughts of four scholars on the question of Deuteronomy's origin and purpose. Despite the diversity of opinion, de Wette's theory rightly continues to be as close a veritable starting point as any for the critical research of Deuteronomy and for introducing the present discussion on the origin and purpose of Deuteronomy.

Duane Christensen

Duane Christensen[49] is one of the few contemporary scholars to deviate from the widely-held view that Deuteronomy reflects to a large degree the literary form of ANE treaties. Christensen highlights Deuteronomy's artistic nature and claims that the most accurate description of its literary genre is to be found neither in an ANE covenant treaty (cf. Weinfeld) nor in levitical preaching in the context of cult liturgy (cf. von Rad) but rather in the field of music and poetry. On the basis of a system of "rhythmic analysis," and stressing the strength of the Masoretic tradition, which he says rightfully preserved the "musical tradition" of the text's oral antecedent, Christensen concludes: "In short, Deuteronomy is best explained as a didactic poem, composed to be recited publicly to music in ancient Israel within a liturgical setting."[50] Christensen

---

Framework to the Code (Oxford: Oxford University Press, 1932), which argued that Deuteronomy does not argue that the cult be centralized, as well as Gustav Hölscher's "Komposition und Ursprung des Deuteronomiums," *ZAW* 40 (1922): 161–255, which rejected the idea that the cult was even centralized during the time of Josiah, de Wette's theory persevered. Weinfeld highlights by way of demonstration the articles by Julius A. Bewer ("The Case for the Early Date of Deuteronomy," *JBL* 47, nos. 3-4 [1928]: 305–21, Lewis B. Paton ("The Case for the Post-Exilic Origin of Deuteronomy," ibid., 322–57), and George Dahl ("The Case for the Currently-Accepted Date of Deuteronomy," ibid., 358–79) that were published in 1928 in a symposium in *JBL* ("The Problem of Deuteronomy") in order to settle the issue. Weinfeld, "Deuteronomy—The Present State of Inquiry," 249.

49. Duane Christensen, "Form and Structure in Deuteronomy 1–11," *BETL* 68 (1985): 135–44; idem, *Deuteronomy 1–11*; idem, *Deuteronomy 1:1–21:9* (2d ed. WBC 6a (Dallas: Word Books, 2001).

50. Christensen, *Deuteronomy 1–11*, lx.

maintains that this has major implications for the "traditional question of Mosaic authorship."[51] For Christensen, Deuteronomy was written by Moses. In addition, the book is verbally inspired and even bears the signs of God's handiwork in its composition. He writes: "The Bible as we have it is not a collection of independent books, which certain scribes in antiquity gathered together in a library. It is a single book, by a single author—if we are to give credence to the common affirmation in public worship that it is the Word of God."[52]

J. Gordon McConville

Although J. Gordon McConville[53] argues for an early date for Deuteronomy's origin and purpose and is indeed "critical of the consensus opinion," he distances himself from the notion of Mosaic authorship.[54] He maintains instead that Deuteronomy best fits within the world of the late second millennium BCE. On the basis of the conclusions of a number of conservative scholars,[55] McConville claims that Deuteronomy resembles more the thought and literary framework of the Hittite treaty than that of later Assyrian treaty forms of the eighth-seventh centuries BCE.[56] McConville's analysis resembles most closely that of Gerhard von Rad, who highlighted the hortatory nature of Deuteronomy and situated its text within the pre-monarchic cultic setting of northern Israel.[57] He argues for

---

51. Ibid. See also idem and Marcel Narucki, "The Mosaic Authorship of the Pentateuch," *JETS* 32 (1989): 465–71.
52. Christensen, *Deuteronomy 1–11*, lxi.
53. See J. Gordon McConville, *Deuteronomy* (Nottingham: Apollos, 2002), and idem, "A Dialogue with Gordon McConville on Deuteronomy III: A Response from Gordon McConville," *SJT* 56 (2003): 525–31.
54. McConville, *Deuteronomy*, 39.
55. McConville himself highlights the work of M. G. Kline, K. A. Kitchen, Eugene Merrill, Alan Millard, Peter Craigie, and Gordon Wenham and labels them "conservative." Ibid.
56. Ibid.
57. McConville himself states that his view is "not far removed" from that of Gerhard von Rad. Ibid., 38.

Deuteronomy's orality, but in contradistinction from Christensen, who, as noted above, argued for an oral antecedent to the text of Deuteronomy, McConville contends that Deuteronomy was "oral" but "only in the sense that it was intended for spoken delivery, as its hortatory form makes clear."[58] He concludes, "There was no time at which Deuteronomy was not a book. That is, the history of its composition is not a transition from oral to written."[59] As to where best to situate the composition of Deuteronomy, McConville cites Deuteronomy 31:9-39 and states that Deuteronomy is to be understood as "the document of the constitution" of Israel, composed within the context of "the assembly of Israel."[60] It is this context, he says, that does "best justice to Deuteronomy's character as both written document and spoken word."[61]

Moshe Weinfeld

Following the lead of Mendenhall and Frankena, Weinfeld acknowledges that there are many parallels between Deuteronomy and ANE treaty forms.[62] Deuteronomy, Weinfeld maintains, was influenced by both Hittite and Assyrian forms. He explains:

> Deuteronomy is actually dependent on two models of covenant: the Hittite and the Assyrian one. The Hittite model is old and seems to underlie the old biblical covenantal tradition. Deuteronomy shows connections with both sets of loyalty oaths: one of the second millennium and the other of the first millennium. The Hittite model pervaded the old biblical tradition, which Deuteronomy used and reworked in accordance with the prevalent covenantal pattern reflected in the *VTE*.[63]

58. Ibid.
59. Ibid, 38.
60. Ibid, 38.
61. Ibid.
62. See his discussion, "Treaty Form and Phraseology: Affinities with Ancient Near-Eastern Treaty Formulae," in, *Deuteronomy and the Deuteronomic School*, 59–178; see also "The Covenant on the Plains of Moab," in idem, *Deuteronomy 1–11*, 6–9.

In Weinfeld's opinion the basic composition of Deuteronomy was informed by the earlier Hittite treaties but was adapted in accordance with "the pattern of political treaties" that were current during the time of its composition, namely the later Assyrian treaty forms of the ninth to seventh centuries BCE.[64]

Although Weinfeld acknowledges the correspondence between Deuteronomy and ANE treaty forms, he stresses that this connection should not be unduly emphasized. The relationship is much more complex.[65] Weinfeld points out: "The most important deviation of Deuteronomy from the treaty form is that its central part is dedicated to civil, cultic, and criminal law."[66] He claims that Deuteronomy "combined two patterns which originally had nothing to do with each other. The law-code demands the observance of manifold precepts concerned with every area of life, while the treaty simply commands loyalty to the great sovereign."[67] How the authors of Deuteronomy understood and fused these traditions is one of the keys to rightly understanding the book of Deuteronomy.

Weinfeld shows that the author of Deuteronomy follows and continues an established pattern of appropriating, adapting and mixing separate traditions.[68] Discussing the amalgamation of the "covenant of law" and the "covenant of vassalship," he concludes:

> Like his predecessors . . . he continued to develop the covenant tradition. He enriched the covenant theme by introducing all the elements of the vassal treaty, while he blurred the covenantal pattern by putting it

---

63. Weinfeld, *Deuteronomy 1–11*, 9.
64. Weinfeld, *Deuteronomy and the Deuteronomic School*, 60.
65. Weinfeld states that the first clue to the complexity of the relationship between Deuteronomy and ANE treaties can be seen in the fact that Deuteronomy does not present the elements of ANE treaty forms in a "fixed order as befits a legal document." Ibid., 146.
66. Ibid., 148.
67. Ibid., 151.
68. Weinfeld highlights the Decalogue as an early example of the fusion of traditions. He reasons the first three commandments are "of the vassal type" while the final commandments are "of the legislative type." Ibid., 157.

into a homiletic setting. Unlike the treaty, Deuteronomy is not a legal document but an oration. The structure of the speech follows the legal pattern, but is that of a sermon. The author of Deuteronomy had in mind the covenantal pattern in the form in which it had been lying before him in the tradition and in the manner in which it was generally formulated in his time. Nevertheless he presented the materials in a style that is free from rigid adherence to formality.[69]

Such a rich and multifaceted account of Deuteronomy's composition demands that Weinfeld find an appropriate setting that can explain Deuteronomy's origin and the manner in which early forms and traditions were fashioned together in order to produce the text at hand. He writes: "The authors of Deuteronomy . . . must be sought for . . . among circles which held public office, among persons who had at their command a vast reservoir of literary material, who had developed and were capable of developing a literary technique of their own, those experienced in literary composition, and skilled with the pen and book."[70] In contrast to von Rad, Weinfeld argues that Deuteronomy did not "*originate*" with the Levitical priests.[71] It was another group of individuals who collated, adapted, and indeed composed the book of Deuteronomy.[72] Weinfeld claims that a school of scribes was responsible for its composition. These חכמים סופרים (wise men/scribes), as he terms them, had become active during the reigns of Hezekiah and Josiah and were responsible for writing Deuteronomy.

Ronald E. Clements misconstrues how Weinfeld identifies חכמים סופרים when he classifies them as "wisdom writers."[73]

---

69. Ibid., 156–57.
70. Ibid., 177–78.
71. Weinfeld contends (ibid., 53) that it was "entrusted" to the Levites later. Emphasis in original.
72. In addition to what has already been discussed with regard to the parallels between Deuteronomy and ANE covenant treaties and law codes, see Weinfeld's analysis of orations in deuteronomic literature: the valedictory address and the prophetic, liturgical and military orations. Ibid., 10–58.
73. Clements, *Deuteronomy*, 79.

Grammatically, the term can be translated as such, but, according to Weinfeld חכמים סופרים were much more than scribes who wrote wisdom literature. Weinfeld argues that the scribal activity of the חכמים סופרים was not "confined only to wisdom composition . . . but also invaded the sphere of religious literary composition."[74] Their activity indeed permeated four different social arenas: "clerical, political, didactic, and religious."[75] This school of scribes known as חכמים סופרים, who began their work with increasing prominence during the reigns of Hezekiah and Josiah, were responsible for Deuteronomy's composition.

Ronald Clements

Ronald Clements acknowledges that the Deuteronomic movement began during the tumultuous period of the eighth and seventh centuries BCE. However, he maintains in contrast to the aforementioned scholars that the "impetus for reform and revitalization of the Israelite tradition" did not reach its "zenith" until the middle of the sixth century BCE.[76] More specifically, it was in light of the "catastrophe" of 587 BCE. and the ensuing exile that large portions of Deuteronomy, and indeed the book as a whole, reached its final form. That the final form of Deuteronomy is post-exilic is without question. Indeed, this view is characteristic not just of Clements. What is unique, however, is Clements's insistence that it is precisely the post-exilic context that "offers a valuable insight into its nature and purpose."[77]

---

74. Weinfeld, *Deuteronomy and the Deuteronomic School*, 162. He references Jeremiah 8:8 and shows that the wise men of the time were also responsible for the composition of the "Torah of Yahweh."
75. Ibid.
76. Ronald E. Clements, "The Deuteronomic Law of Centralisation and the Catastrophe of 587 B.C.E," 5–26 in *After the Exile: Essays in Honour of Rex Mason* (Macon, GA: Mercer University Press, 1996), at 5.

Clements exhibits three examples from the book of Deuteronomy to defend his point: the centralization of the cult, the introduction of a "revised pattern of legal and social justice," and the views concerning the monarchy.[78] Regarding the centralization of the cult, he argues: "It was, in effect, a major and ultimately successful bid to ensure that the destruction of the sacred building by the armies of Babylon . . . was not allowed to result in the abandonment of the holy site or the transfer to another holy place (Mizpah, Bethel, Shechem or Samaria?) of the unique position that Jerusalem had enjoyed."[79] With regard to the legal innovation characteristic of Deuteronomy, Clements claims that it was precisely the collapse of the civil, royal, and religious institutions in 587 BCE that led the author(s) of Deuteronomy to set up a new "social and juridical order" in the wake of the fall into "political wilderness."[80] He writes: "It offers a kind of interim administration, calling for an attitude of self-discipline and education, produced at a time when the primary institutions of national life had collapsed."[81] Clements's perspective on "legal innovation" relates as well to his final point about the Deuteronomic attitude toward the monarchy. He argues that it is the paucity of legal material germane to the monarchy that underscores the point of its post-exilic composition. Moreover, Clements contends that the "law of the king" in Deuteronomy 17:14-20 itself supports this conclusion. The text subverts any notion of the institution's survival and/or relevance. "In its place," Clements adds, "Deuteronomy sets a *torah*-focused charter for a new Israel, with Moses as its ancestral hero

---

77. Ronald E. Clements, "The Origins of Deuteronomy: What are the Clues?" in "A Dialogue with Gordon McConville on Deuteronomy," *SJT* 56 (2003): 508–16, at 509.
78. Ibid., 511.
79. Clements, "The Deuteronomic Law of Centralisation," 8.
80. Clements, "The Origins of Deuteronomy," 514–15.
81. Ibid., 515.

and to which even the king, if a monarchy should one day be restored to Jerusalem, would have to submit."[82]

An Analysis of Deuteronomy's Origins

The following section will briefly appraise the views of Christensen, McConville, Weinfeld, and Clements on the topic of Deuteronomy's origin. All four scholars differ on when Deuteronomy was written. Christensen proposes that Moses wrote Deuteronomy. McConville argues for a late-second-millennium BCE setting for the origin of the book. Weinfeld suggests that Deuteronomy was composed during the reigns of Hezekiah and Josiah, and Clements maintains that the book was written sometime after the destruction of the temple in 586 BCE. It is this author's opinion that the most appropriate context for Deuteronomy's composition was sometime during the reigns of Hezekiah and Josiah.

Despite the best efforts by Christensen and others to recapture the role Moses might have played in Deuteronomy's composition, critical scholarship has proved that those claims are unfounded.[83] McConville's proposal is not much better than Christensen's. Although he makes a point of denying Mosaic authorship, his arguments seem to insinuate that Christensen's view of Deuteronomy's origin is not far from the truth.[84] As Bernard Levinson has shown:

> McConville maintained, with refrainlike repetition, that "the laws are consistently compatible with Deuteronomy's self-presentation as

---

82. Ibid., 516.
83. Driver compares both the historical and legal sections of Deuteronomy with Exodus–Numbers and clearly establishes that Deuteronomy could not have been written by the same author as the previous three books of the Pentateuch, and indeed not by Moses. He assumes that JE and P were composed by Moses only for the sake of disproving the Mosaic authorship of Deuteronomy. He quickly adds afterward that JE and P, and indeed the first four books of the Old Testament, were not written by Moses. Driver, *Deuteronomy*, xxxiv–lxxvii.
84. McConville, *Deuteronomy*, 39.

speeches on the verge of the promised land." With Israel still in Moab, yet to enter Canaan, the narrative time of the text has become the historical date of Deuteronomy's composition. The next step followed logically, as the narrator of the text, in its literary world, was transformed into its author, Mosaic in all but name: "it seems best to think of a single author as having been responsible for all the laws in their entirety."[85]

The problem lies in the fact that McConville suggests on the hand that Deuteronomy "fit[s] the world of the second millennium" and, on the other hand, says he does not want to "try to date the book exactly."[86] The reader is made to guess what McConville actually thinks about Deuteronomy's origin. All he says is that "the book of Deuteronomy originated in its use in the assembly of Israel as the document of the constitution, not in deuteronomistic idealism," that this "assembly" was pre-monarchic, and that the book was most likely written by a single author.[87] Levinson, then, is not wrong to assume that McConville really believes in the Mosaic authorship of Deuteronomy and therefore rightly criticizes him for it.

In contrast to the views of Christensen and McConville, Clements contends that Deuteronomy was written sometime after 586 BCE. Although Clements makes a stronger case than the aforementioned scholars, there are still a number of problems with his proposal. First of all, he misconstrues the time frame of the cult's centralization. He discounts the arguments of Norbert Lohfink[88] and says that the accounts of Hezekiah's and Josiah's efforts to centralize the cult (2 Kgs

---

85. Bernard Levinson, "The Hermeneutics of Tradition in Deuteronomy: A Reply to J. G. McConville," *JBL* 119 (2000): 269–86, at 273. Cf. idem, "McConville's 'Law and Theology in Deuteronomy,'" *JQR* 80 (1990): 396–404.
86. McConville, *Deuteronomy*, 39–40. Part of the problem is also the fact that his interests in Deuteronomy are largely theological and not historical. McConville, *Deuteronomy*, 39. This propensity is noted and criticized by Levinson, "Hermeneutics of Tradition," 270.
87. McConville, *Deuteronomy*, 38–39.
88. Norbert Lohfink, "Recent Discussions on 2 Kings 22-23: the State of the Question," 36–61 in *A Song of Power and the Power of Song: Essays on the Book of Deuteronomy*, ed. Duane L. Christensen (Winona Lake: Eisenbrauns, 1993); idem, "The Cult Reform of Josiah and Judah: 2 Kings 22-23 as a Source for the History of Israelite Religion," 459–76 in *Ancient Israelite*

18:4, 22; 21:3; 22-23) are historically tendentious. Instead, he argues from silence and says that the Deuteronomic command to worship at a single shrine stems from an exilic community that wanted to make sure the Jerusalem temple did not lose its "unique position."[89] All this presupposes, however, that Jerusalem and its temple actually had a position of prominence and uniqueness before 586 BCE. As E. W. Nicholson puts it, "The view that the centralisation of the cult is but the impracticable ideal of exiled priests can hardly be accepted if only for the simple reason that in the post-exilic period and as late as New Testament times the law of one sanctuary was accepted without question."[90] In addition, the fact that after the destruction of the Jerusalem temple "people from Shechem, Šiloh, and Samaria made pilgrimages to the temple site (Jer 41:5)" underscores its prominence and the historical credibility that there was some sort of centralization of the cult prior to the fall of Jerusalem.[91]

Clements also argues that it was the collapse of the civil, royal, and religious institutions in 586 BCE that led the author(s) of Deuteronomy to set up a new "social and juridical order" in the wake of its fall into "political wilderness."[92] It is true that there is historical precedent for "legal innovation" in the wake of political, social, and religious catastrophe.[93] Nevertheless, it follows that if there actually was a movement to center the cult in Jerusalem *before* 586 BCE, this historic reality would form the basis of and reason for establishing a

---

Religion: Essays in Honour of Frank Moore Cross, ed. Patrick D. Miller, Paul D. Hanson, and S. Dean McBride (Philadelphia: Fortress Press, 1987).
89. Clements, "The Deuteronomic Law of Centralisation," 8.
90. Ernest Nicholson, "The Centralisation of the Cult in Deuteronomy," *VT* 13 (1963): 380–89, at 381–82.
91. Weinfeld, *Deuteronomy 1–11*, 50.
92. Clements, "The Origins of Deuteronomy," 514–15.
93. It is true that one can give credence to Clements's position when comparing it with historical situations of the later Jewish community. For example, the religious and legal impetus for the composition of the Mishnah stems directly from the destruction of the Temple in Jerusalem in 70 CE. Still, one cannot ignore the legal framework of the laws in Deuteronomy.

new "social and juridical order" both pragmatically and on the "level of the text."[94] The exilic and post-exilic communities undoubtedly benefited from this new legal corpus, but the origin of the new legal material is certainly pre-exilic.

The basis of Clements's final claim is perhaps the strongest. He highlights the "mismatch between the recorded events of the reform with its high, pro-monarchic, pro-Davidic ideology" and what one finds in Deuteronomy's "law of the king" (Deut 17:14-20).[95] However, he mistakenly deduces from this that Deuteronomy was composed after 586 BCE. As Bernard Levinson shows, this does not necessarily have to be the case.

> Possibly, Deuteronomy stemmed from the hands of court scribes under Manasseh who were committed to the ideals of Hezekiah's initial cultic reform and centralization. Disillusioned by the situation under Manasseh, they drafted a utopian legal program for cultural renewal. They drew partly on the model of Neo-Assyrian state treaties, while also defying that model by installing Yahweh as the suzerain to whom exclusive loyalty (Deut. xiii 2-19) and tribute (xiv 22-28) are owed, and to whom the loyalty oath (*adê*), with its sanctions, must be sworn. The seventh century presented many opportunities for Judaean court scribes to become familiar with such Neo-Assyrian treaties, whether directly or in Aramaic translation (as at Sefire). Indeed, Manasseh's name appears in lists of vassal kings in contemporary documents from both Esarhaddon and Ashurbanipal. The mistrust of royal power, on account of Manasseh's pragmatic foreign policies, might well account for the

---

94. Bernard M. Levinson, *Deuteronomy and the Hermeneutics of Legal Innovation* (Oxford: Oxford University Press, 1997), 117.
95. Clements, "The Origins of Deuteronomy," 515. This is recognized even by scholars who disagree with Clements on when Deuteronomy was composed. For example, Levinson writes: "Deuteronomy submits a utopian manifesto for a constitutional monarchy that sharply delimits the power of the king. The Deuteronomic Torah establishes itself as sole sovereign authority, and thus in effect usurps the traditional authority of the monarch. This utopian delimitation of royal power never passed from constitutional vision into historical implementation. ..." Bernard M. Levinson, "The Reconceptualization of Kingship in Deuteronomy and the Deuteronomistic History's Transformation of Torah," *VT* 51 (2001): 511-34, at 511-12. For a good social-scientific analysis of the issue see Patricia Dutcher-Walls, "The Circumscription of the King: Deuteronomy 17:16-17 in its Ancient Social Context," *JBL* 121, no. 4 (2002): 601-16.

sharp delimitation of royal authority by the authors of Deuteronomy, as they downplay the role of the monarch while making Yahweh exclusive Sovereign and transfer to the nation the idea of divine election (Deut. xiv 1-2 . . .). Subsequently, the accession of Josiah could have provided an occasion for renewed optimism, with the monarch again viewed as an agent of cultural renewal. For that reason, the editor of the first edition of the Deuteronomistic History might well have taken over the cultic norms of Deuteronomy, elevating them to a historiographic standard of evaluation, while nonetheless departing from Deuteronomic norms by restoring to the monarch his traditional authority to intervene in the cultus.[96]

In light of these problems with Clements's proposal for a post-586 BCE date for the origin of Deuteronomy, one is left to conclude with Weinfeld that Deuteronomy's origin rests somewhere with the institutions, events, and historic context of the eighth-seventh centuries BCE.[97]

Rhetorical Purpose

What, then, is the rhetorical purpose of Deuteronomy? The answer to this question is undoubtedly influenced by the points made in the above sections on Deuteronomy's contents, literary form(s), and origin—in other words, by the questions "What is *in* the book?" "What *is* the book?" and "*When* was it written?" To answer these questions in reverse order, the core of Deuteronomy was written sometime during the reigns of Hezekiah and Josiah, which, as Weinfeld points out, was a time of national and religious "renascence."[98] A school of scribes was responsible for its

---

96. Levinson, "The Reconceptualization of Kingship in Deuteronomy," 527–28.
97. This is not to deny that there is evidence of a "change of tone, from one of national hope and bold expectation to one of tension, fear and solemn warning, that strongly points us to conclude that many parts of the book of Deuteronomy, especially in the Introduction and Epilogue, are sensitive to Judah's misfortunes at the hands of the Babylonians." Clements, *Deuteronomy*, 75. These "reflections" of post-586 BCE influence on Deuteronomy do exist. The problem is that they are only that, "reflections," and not the cause of the book's composition.

composition, and they "revised" and in some cases "innovated" older narratives and legal traditions.[99] They were, on the whole, interested in composing an "educational manual" that would be for all the people, including monarchs, priests, and parents.[100] In their writing of Deuteronomy these scribes incorporated various ANE forms, but among the most obvious is the form of a "valedictory speech," in which Moses is presented as the one delivering all of the "words" of Deuteronomy. All of the book's contents are presented under the auspices of this form.

An Interpretation of Deuteronomy 7

Text and Translation of Deuteronomy 7

1 When[101] YHWH your God brings[102] you into the land that you are entering to take possession of it,[103] and he clears away[104] many nations from you, the Hittites,[105] the Girgashites, the Amorites, the Canaanites, the Perizzites, the Hivites, and the Jebusites, seven

---

98. Weinfeld, *Deuteronomy 1–11*, 50–53, 65–84.
99. Ibid., 55. See Bernard Levinson on the topic of "legal innovation": *Deuteronomy and the Hermeneutics of Legal Innovation*, 3–22, 144–57.
100. Weinfeld, *Deuteronomy 1–11*, 55–57; idem, *Deuteronomy and the Deuteronomic School*, 298–306.
101. The LXX translates כִּי ("when") as ἐὰν δὲ. Wevers claims the latter can "hardly mean 'and if,' but must intend 'when.'" John William Wevers, *Notes on the Greek Text of Deuteronomy* (Atlanta: Scholars Press, 1995), 127. Wevers is wrong on this point. Later Greek versions would not have made it a point, as he himself shows, to remedy the ambiguity that the LXX creates with its translation. כִּי can also mean "if," as in 7:17, but when referring to time it often means "when." See BDB, 473.
102. Cf. Deuteronomy 6:10.
103. ירשׁ can mean inherit, take possession of, or dispossess. The latter two senses carry with them the idea of taking possession of and/or dispossessing someone of something "by force." BDB, 439.
104. נשׁל can carry both a transitive and intransitive meaning: slip or drop off. It can also refer to the clearing away of nations, as in this verse. Cf. 7:22; 2 Kgs 16:6. George Adam Smith writes that the aforementioned verses are the "only applications of this verb to the extirpation of human beings." George Adam Smith, *Deuteronomy* (Cambridge: Cambridge University Press, 1918), 105. The latter text refers to King Rezin of Aram (Edom) and King Pekah of Israel (Northern Kingdom) dislodging or clearing away the Judeans from Elath.
105. The Masorah parva provides a mnemonic device in the margin for the correct order of the seven nations that are cited in this verse (Cf. תגמכפוס). Carmel McCarthy, "Notes on

nations[106] more numerous and mightier than you, 2 and YHWH your God gives them to you and you defeat[107] them, you shall devote them to destruction.[108] Do not establish a covenant with them or show them mercy.[109] 3 Do not[110] intermarry[111] with them; do not give your daughter to his son or take his daughter for your son. 4 For he will turn away your son from me,[112] and they[113] will serve other/foreign gods. And then the anger of YHWH will be kindled against you[114] and

the Masorah Parva," in *Biblia Hebraica Quinta, Fascicle 3: Deuteronomy* (Stuttgart: Deutsche Bibelgesellschaft, 2007), 27.

106. For a description of the above nations, along with their use and order in the Old Testament, see Driver, *Deuteronomy*, 96–98.

107. נכה hiphil has a variety of meanings: 1. Smite, as to strike with a single, non-fatal blow; 2. Smite, as to strike fatally; 3. Smite, as to attack and destroy a company or capture a village; or 4. smite, with reference to God sending a plague, disease, etc. BDB, 645–46. The present verse carries the third meaning.

108. "You shall devote them to destruction" signals the start of the apodosis, that is, the main clause in the conditional sentence. The LXX renders the phrase as ἀφανισμῷ ἀφανιεῖς, meaning "to utterly destroy" or "to render unseen." Wevers, *Notes*, 128. See the notes on 7:26 below for other renderings of חרם as a noun. See the following selection of relevant articles on the meaning of חֵרֶם, חָרַם: BDB, 355–56; Norbert Lohfink, "חָרַם, ḥāram," *TDOT* 5:180–99; Richard D. Nelson, "Ḥerem and the Deuteronomic Social Conscience," 39–54 in *Deuteronomy and Deuteronomic Literature*, ed. Marc Vervenne (Leuven: Peeters, 1987). See also Gerhard von Rad, *Holy War in Ancient Israel* (Grand Rapids: Eerdmans, 1991).

109. Weinfeld points out that some rabbinic scholars took the basic root of חנם to mean encamp and thus "understood the verse as a prohibition against allowing the Canaanites to own property in the land (*b. >Abod. Zar.* 20b)." He thus concludes that the old English idiom "to give quarter," which means to "grant clemency," is not too far off the proper meaning of the verse. Weinfeld, *Deuteronomy 1–11*, 359.

110. Several medieval Mss read לא instead of ולא. The latter is to be preferred, as the former seems to have been harmonized with the two other negative particles in the verse, both of which are written without a waw conjunction.

111. תתחתן is a denominative of the noun חתן, "son in law." Literally 7:3a reads, "Do not make yourself a son in law with them." The context suggests intermarriage. Weinfeld, *Deuteronomy 1–11*, 359.

112. It has been proposed that the letter י is an abbreviation for YHWH. Weinfeld argues that "this is unnecessary," for Moses often speaks on God's behalf (Cf. 11:14; 17:3; 28:20; 29:4-5). Weinfeld, *Deuteronomy 1–11*, 359, 366. Cf. McConville, *Deuteronomy*, 149; Mayes, *Deuteronomy*, 168, 183–84.

113. The switch to plural in this verse is confusing. The Samaritan Pentateuch, LXX, and Vulgate therefore shift the person number of the verb back to singular.

114. Note the shift to second person plural form of address and then back again to second person singular in verse 7:4b. ". . . And then the anger of YHWH will be kindled against you (pl), and he will exterminate you (sg)." As will be discussed in more detail later, this change to plural in vv. 7:4b-5 has led Mayes and others to argue for the initial independence of these verses from 7:1-3,

he will exterminate you quickly. **5** But rather you shall do thus to them: their altars you shall tear down, their pillars you shall shatter to pieces, their *Asherim* you shall cut down, and their images you shall burn with fire. **6** For you[115] are a holy people[116] belonging to YHWH your God. YHWH your God has chosen[117] you[118] to become[119] for him a treasured people[120] from all of the peoples that are upon the earth.

---

6. Mayes, *Deuteronomy*, 181. Weinfeld argues that this does not prove the literary independence of these texts, simply different literary traditions. Weinfeld, *Deuteronomy 1–11*, 366.

115. Verse 7:6 returns to second person singular.

116. עם סגלה occurs three times in Deuteronomy (Deut 7:6; 14:2, 22). Similarly, גוי קדוש in Exod 19:6. See also the noun form קדש in Exod 22:30, where the people are described as אנשי־קדש. For a discussion of the different uses of these terms in Deuteronomy and Exodus and their significance, see Weinfeld, *Deuteronomy and the Deuteronomic School*, 227–28.

117. בחר means "to choose." It often occurs with the preposition ב for the election of people. BDB, 243.

118. A few Mss such as the SmP, LXX, Syriac version, and a number of Mss from the Cairo Geniza read ובך. This was probably done to assimilate Deut 7:6 with Deut 14:2, which read ובך instead of בך.

119. היה + ל can mean "to be or to become." The latter seems more plausible. Cf. היה II, BDB, 226. Weinfeld explains that היה + ל "means to gain a certain status in relation to somebody. Thus, for example, to be a woman to somebody . . . means to become his wife; cf. Gen 12:19; 16:13, etc." Weinfeld, *Deuteronomy 1–11*, 359. In this context the people of Israel have obtained a "certain status" in relation to God. This "status" is obviously rooted in YHWH's choice of Israel. Note the use of בחר earlier in the verse. Weinfeld explains that to become a people who belong to YHWH means Israel has gained "the status of vassalship." Weinfeld, *Deuteronomy 1–11*, 360. See below the discussion of the term סגלה and its connection with the establishment of treaties.

120. עם סגלה occurs three times in Deuteronomy (Deut 7:6; 14:2; 26:18). סגלה generally means "possession, property." In reference to YHWH's choice it means "valued property, peculiar treasure." Cf. Exod 19:5; BDB, 688. Weinfeld writes that סגלה seems to "belong to the treaty and covenant terminology and . . . they are employed to distinguish a special relationship of the sovereign to one of his vassals." Weinfeld, *Deuteronomy and the Deuteronomic School*, 226 n. 2. Dennis McCarthy writes: "In Ugaritic the cognate *sglth* describes the subject of the Hittite king in connection with his duties as a vassal: acknowledging his lord, performing the prescribed visits to the sovereign's court." McCarthy, *Treaty and Covenant* (Rome: Biblical Institute Press, 1978), 162 n. 10. Not all references found in the ANE refer to a vassal with its suzerain, however. Some speak of a wife's relationship with her husband and others tell of a king's relationship to a goddess. McCarthy concludes: "All these are special relationships and chosen. Perhaps they are not covenant as usually conceived but they fit into its language field as we define it: elected, not natural (e.g., blood ties) relationship. Israel itself used the word in association with covenant before Dt: cf . . . Ex 19,5." Ibid., 162. See also Moshe Greenberg, "Hebrew *segulla*: Akkadian *sikiltu*," *JAOS* 71 (1951): 172–74.

7 YHWH did not desire you[121] or choose you because you are more numerous than all other people, for you are (actually) the fewest[122] of all other people. 8 Because YHWH loves[123] you and keeps the promise which he swore to your fathers, YHWH brought you out with a mighty hand and redeemed[124] you from the house of slavery, from the hand of Pharaoh, king of Egypt. 9 Know,[125] therefore, that YHWH your God, he is God, the faithful[126] God (who) keeps the gracious covenant[127] for those who love him and his commandment,[128] to the

---

121. חשק means "to be attached to, love, or desire." The latter definition occurs only in later Hebrew and is rare. The verb often occurs with the preposition ב. BDB, 365–66. Weinfeld says the verb literally means to "lust after" or "hang on." He references Gen 34:8, Deut 21:11, and Ps 91:14. Weinfeld, *Deuteronomy 1–11*, 360. חשק occurs three times in Deuteronomy (Deut 7:7; 10:15; and 21:11). YHWH is the subject of the first two occurrences, and the last reference appears in the context of a discussion about female captives, where a man might "desire," or in Weinfeld's definition "lust after" one of the beautiful woman captives. Cf. Wallis "חָשַׁק, *ḥāšaq*," *TDOT* 5:261–62.

122. The article on המעט gives the "force of a superlative." Driver, *Deuteronomy*, 100.

123. אהב generally means "love." It most often refers to loving another human being or God and less frequently to the love of an object such as food, drink, or husbandry. It is also used on numerous occasions to speak of divine love for individuals (cf. Deut 4:37; 2 Sam 12:24; Prov 3:12; 15:9), Israel (cf. Deut 7:8, 13; 23:6; Hos 3:1; 9:15; 11:1; 14:5; 1 Kgs 10:9; Jer 31:3; Mal 1:2, etc.), and virtues such as righteousness (cf. Pss 11:7; 33:5; 37:28, etc.). BDB, 12–13. For an important discussion of the concept of love and its relationship to the political life of the ANE see William Moran, "The Ancient Near Eastern Background of Love of God in Deuteronomy," *CBQ* 25 (1963): 77–87. Cf. Weinfeld, *Deuteronomy and the Deuteronomic School*, 81.

124. פדה can also mean "to ransom" for an "assessed price" (cf. Exod 13:13, 15), "from violence and death" (cf. 1 Sam 14:45), or, when YHWH is subject, "from Egypt or exile." BDB, 804.

125. Note: Deut 7:9 returns to using second person singular.

126. אמן niphal participle ms. Weinfeld translates it "steadfast" as it "implies both strength and validity." Weinfeld, *Deuteronomy 1–11*, 360. For "faithful" as a translation see Christensen, *Deuteronomy 1–11*, 156; Peter C. Craigie, *The Book of Deuteronomy*, NICNT 5 (2d ed. Grand Rapids: Eerdmans, 1995), 176; Driver, *Deuteronomy*, 101. McConville translates אמן as "trustworthy." McConville, *Deuteronomy*, 148.

127. "Gracious covenant" is a hendiadys and literally reads "the covenant and the goodness/kindness/ steadfast love." For a discussion of the terms חסד and ברית, see Zobel "חֶסֶד, *ḥesed*," *TDOT* 5:44–64; and Moshe Weinfeld, בְּרִית, *berîth*," *TDOT* 2:252–79. Driver (*Deuteronomy*, 102) says, "חסד is a quality exercised mutually amongst equals; it is the kindliness of feeling, consideration, and courtesy, which adds a grace and softness to the relations subsisting between members of the same society." Driver's observation is imperfect. He misses the fact that "kindness" is often demonstrated by the superior party in a covenant relationship. Cf. Weinfeld, *Deuteronomy 1–11*, 272.

128. The Kethib writes "his commandment," while Qere reads "his commandments." Multiple mss., including the Samaritan Pentateuch, correspond with Qere and have "his commandments" as well.

thousandth generation, **10** but he repays (them)[129] who hate him[130] to[131] their face to destroy him;[132] he does not tarry for him who hates him,[133] to their face he repays him. **11** Therefore, observe the commandment, the laws, and the judgments that I command you to do today.

12 And it shall come to pass, because[134] you obey these judgments and observe and do them, YHWH your God will keep for you the gracious covenant[135] which he swore to your fathers. **13** He will love you and bless you and multiply you. He will bless the fruit of your womb and the fruit of your land, your grain,[136] fresh wine, fresh oil, the increase or your cattle[137] and the young[138] of your flock, in the

---

129. "Them" is implied by the insertion of ל to the following word, BDB, 1022.
130. The suffix is plural and has led Hempel to suggest that the text should be amended with a singular suffix. This proposal should be rejected as the context is clear in the MT and the plural suffix is used in 7:9b as well.
131. Samaritan Pentateuch uses על instead of אל when it appears in 7:10 (two times).
132. Suffix is singular but the context seems to suggest is should be plural. Weinfeld argues that it is "to be explained as distinctive: every one of them." Weinfeld, *Deuteronomy 1–11*, 360.
133. Multiple mss. and versions such as the Samaritan Pentateuch, LXX, Syriac, and the Targums have a plural suffix instead of a singular suffix in order to harmonize the phrase with 7:10a.
134. Cf. Deuteronomy 8:20. עקב marks the start of a new paragraph and weekly Torah portion (cf. Deut 7:12–11:25) Most scholars, except for Christensen, do not make a great deal of this, as the whole of Deuteronomy 7 shows remarkable signs of coherence (see below). עקב can refer to the heel of a man (cf. Gen 25:26), the mark of a heel or footprint (cf. Song 1:8), or the "hinderpart" or rear "of a troop of men (cf. Gen 49:19). BDB, 784. It can also have a figurative meaning such as "in consequence of" or "because." Christensen, *Deuteronomy 1:1–21:9*, 158; Driver, *Deuteronomy*, 103; Mayes, *Deuteronomy*, 186; Weinfeld, *Deuteronomy 1–11*, 360. Christensen suggests that it might be a pun on the name of Jacob.
135. Cf. n. 127.
136. Cf. Deuteronomy 11:14; 12:17; 14:23; 18:4; 28:51 for the products of "grain, wine, and oil" together in Deuteronomy. These are "the three chief products of the soil of Palestine" and are here referred to in their "unmanufactured state." Driver, *Deuteronomy*, 103. Therefore, דגן (grain, corn) corresponds with לחם (bread); תירוש (fresh wine, new wine) with יין (wine); and יצהר (fresh oil) with שמן (oil). In addition, Tigay points out that יצהר, תירוש, דגן, שגר, and עשתרות are all names of Semitic deities. "The use of the same word to refer to a deity and a phenomenon which that deity was thought to personify" was a common practice in the ANE. Jeffrey H. Tigay, *Deuteronomy*, JPS Torah Commentary (Philadelphia: Jewish Publication Society, 1996), 89. Cf. Weinfeld, *Deuteronomy 1–11*, 373.
137. Literally it can read "the offspring of your thousands." שגר refers to "offspring" or "young of beasts." BDB, 993. אלף can mean thousand, but in this case it refers to cattle in the plural (cf. Prov 14:4; Isa 30:24) and of their increase (cf. Deut 7:13; 28:4, 18, 51). BDB, 48.

land which he swore to your fathers to give to you. **14** You will be blessed more than all other peoples. There will not be among you and your livestock a barren male or barren female.[139] **15** YHWH will take away from you all sickness.[140] And all the evil diseases[141] of Egypt that you have known, he will not place them upon[142] you but he will put them upon all who hate you. **16** You shall devour[143] all the peoples whom YHWH your God gives to you. Your eye shall not look upon them with compassion.[144] You shall not serve their gods, for that would be a snare[145] to you.

17 If you say in your heart, "These nations are more numerous than I. How[146] can I dispossess them?" **18** Do not fear them. Remember what YHWH your God did to Pharaoh and all the Egyptians, **19** the great trials that your eyes have seen, and the signs and wonders and the mighty hand and the outstretched arm by which YHWH your God brought you out, thus will YHWH your God do to all the peoples of whom you are afraid. **20** YHWH your God will also send hornets among them until those who are left behind or are hidden are

---

138. עשתרות can refer to the name of a town or, as noted above, the goddess Astarte. However, in the present context it refers to either "ewes" or "young." BDB, 800.
139. Literally "there will not be among you a barren male or barren female and among your livestock." Both Driver and Weinfeld note the awkward syntax of this phrase. Cf. Driver, *Deuteronomy*, 103; Weinfeld, *Deuteronomy 1–11*, 360.
140. חלי means sickness or disease. BDB, 318.
141. Multiple mss. have instead the singular for מדוה in order to harmonize the verse with Deut 28:60.
142. The preposition על might be expected in this case, but the preposition ב is often used with שים when referring to disease being inflicted upon a person. BDB, 963.
143. אכל literally means "to eat," but it can often denote the concept of destruction when something or someone is devoured or consumed by drought, pestilence, sword, poverty, etc. BDB, 37. The LXX softens the severity of the text by inserting τὰ σκῦλα, rendering it "You shall eat the spoils of the nations." Wevers, *Notes*, 137.
144. חוס can mean "to pity" or "to look upon with compassion." BDB, 299.
145. מוקש literally means "bait" or "lure." It often carries a figurative meaning of "snare," especially in Proverbs. BDB, 430. It is also the noun form of the verb יקש (cf. Deut 7:25).
146. Certain Qumran mss. and the Samaritan Pentateuch read איך. The MT of Deuteronomy never uses איך but uses איכה consistently throughout (cf. Deut 1:12; 7:17; 12:30; 18:21; 32:30).

eliminated from among you. 21 Do not have any dread of them, for YHWH your God is in your midst, a great and awesome God.

22 YHWH your God will dislodge these[147] nations from you little by little. You will not be able to make an end of them quickly lest the beasts of the field multiply upon you. 23 YHWH your God will give them to you, and throw them into a great discomfiture until they are exterminated. 24 He will deliver their kings into your hand and you will obliterate their name from under the heavens. No man shall be able to stand against you, until you have destroyed them. 25 The images of their gods you shall burn with fire. You shall not covet the silver or gold upon them and keep it for yourself lest you be ensnared by it, for it is an abomination to YHWH your God. 26 Do not bring an abomination into your house, or you will be under ban like it. You shall utterly detest and abhor it, for it is under the ban.

Literary Form(s) of Deuteronomy 7

The present section will look at what type(s) of literature are evident in Deuteronomy 7,[148] the form(s) in which the chapter is presented, and the possibility of an oral stage in its compositional development. It will be recalled that Deuteronomy 7 is situated within the second of two prologues, or "hortatory introductions,"[149] to the Deuteronomic code. Within this section (4:44–11:32), the Decalogue (5:6–21) and a substantial amount of historical narrative (9:7–10:11) are also inserted. They are included, however, in a manner that does not betray the section's overall hortatory nature,[150] for the whole of the introduction

---

147. The MT reads האל (cf. Deut 4:42). A number of manuscripts and the SmP read האלה. Craigie (*Deuteronomy*, 182) suggests that the absence of the *mater lectionis*, or ה in this case, is probably due to an accidental omission during the course of the grammatical revision of the text.. Weinfeld (*Deuteronomy 1–11*, 361) notes that the Qumran mss. often omit the ה.
148. See above "Literary Form(s) of Deuteronomy," for an explanation of the title.
149. Driver, *Deuteronomy*, 81.
150. Ibid., xix.

is structured as if it were a speech, or series of speeches, delivered by Moses, reminding the people of Israel of YHWH's faithfulness and exhorting them to obedience. This introduction, then, is clearly paraenetic, as it is in the form of an address or "valedictory speech," and at its "heart" is Deuteronomy 7. It is, as Robert O'Connell points out, the rhetorical "center" of Deuteronomy 4:44–11:32, from which the surrounding chapters "take their departure."[151]

The question, first of all, is whether Deuteronomy 7 ever had a prior oral history. The significance of this should not be overlooked, for a proper understanding of the chapter's form, whether oral or literary, provides the necessary clues for determining its message. The work of August Klostermann, Gerhard von Rad, and Moshe Weinfeld will be analyzed in this regard.

August Klostermann wrote at the turn of the last century that Deuteronomy 5–11 should be understood as a "homiletic allocution introducing and accompanying the recitation of the Law in a public gathering of the congregation."[152] The homily would have "preceded" and "followed" the reading of the Law, acting as "either the exordium or the peroration."[153] Therefore Klostermann suggests that Deuteronomy 7 was originally divided between 7:1-11 and 7:12-15, and in between those verses the Law would have been read.[154]

---

151. Robert O'Connell, "Deuteronomy VII: 1-26: Asymmetrical Concentricity and the Rhetoric of Conquest," *VT* 42 (April 1992): 248–65, at 262–63. O'Connell explains (p. 262): "None of the exhortations or admonitions enjoined in the framework of Deut iv-xi . . . which require Israel's presence in the land . . . would carry any relevance were Israel to fail in their primary commission to take possession of the land."
152. Quoted in von Rad, "The Form-Critical Problem of the Hexateuch," 30. In addition, the "law book" itself reveals its oral ancestry. He quotes Klostermann as maintaining that Deuteronomy 12ff. is not a "book of the Law," but "a collection of materials for the public proclamation of the Law." Deuteronomy as a whole is the "fully developed end-product of the actual custom of a public proclamation of the Law."
153. Ibid.
154. Ibid.

Similarly, Gerhard von Rad argues that Deuteronomy 7 is paraenetic and would originally have been read in connection with the cult and the recitation of the law. He also divides the chapter between 7:1-11 and 7:12-15.[155] The latter set of verses ends the sermon that begins at verse 1 and acts as a "promise of blessing, the wording of which is clearly seen to be modelled on cultic formulae."[156] Deuteronomy 7:17-26 begins another sermon and "shows all the characteristics of the series," that is, the distinctive features of the form of a sermon.[157] What is unique to von Rad, in contrast to Klostermann, is that he sees these sermons as not simply homilies designed to arouse interest and obedience to the Law. They are "war: sermons, that is, they revive the idea of "holy war."

Von Rad argues that the original setting of these holy war sermons would have been during the period of the "old Israelite Amphictyony, that is, the period of the Judges."[158] The institution of the holy war, however, ended with the "formation of the state."[159] At this point "the wars were no longer waged under a charismatic leader but, in Judah, under an hereditary king, and they were fought by him at the head of an army which became more and more mercenary in character. . . ."[160] Despite the cessation of the institution of holy war, von Rad contends that "[t]his does not mean . . . that odd elements of

---

155. Von Rad's commentary leads the reader to the conclusion that he believes the sermon ends at 7:16 as opposed to 7:15. Von Rad, *Deuteronomy*, 68. However, in *Holy War in Ancient Israel* he maintains that the sermon ends at 7:15. Von Rad, *Holy War in Ancient Israel*, trans. Marva J. Dawn (Grand Rapids: Eerdmans, 1991), 121.
156. Von Rad, *Deuteronomy*, 68.
157. Von Rad says (*Deuteronomy*, 68–69) that the sermon "begins an outline of the psychological condition of those being addressed. . . . In opposition to this the preacher recalls Yahweh's earlier demonstrations of power against the Egyptians. . . . At v. 21 the sermon . . . reaches the main exhortation. Israel must not be afraid, for Yahweh is waging war. . . ." Cf. idem, *Holy War*, 121.
158. Von Rad, *Studies in Deuteronomy*, 46. In addition, these battle homilies would have been uttered by levitical priests. Ibid., 60.
159. Ibid., 46.
160. Ibid.

this old institution did not persist. . . ."¹⁶¹ This is evidenced by the fact that the idea of the "holy war" was revitalized after 701 BCE, when "the old militia which had passed into oblivion had to be recalled to life."¹⁶²

Contrary to Klostermann and von Rad, who explore the possibility of Deuteronomy's oral antecedents and investigate the form of Deuteronomy 7 as such, Weinfeld argues that the text of Deuteronomy does not have a prior oral history. He contends that the "orations" found in Deuteronomy are "literary programmatic creations and do not convey the actual speech once delivered in concrete circumstances. On the contrary, the early speech forms arising from some specific reality have been converted by this school into orations of an idealizing character."¹⁶³ The orations of Deuteronomy, therefore, are "the product of speculative thought and do not derive from cultic reality."¹⁶⁴ Deuteronomy is in fact a "literary imitation" of the "political treaties prevalent in the surrounding area."¹⁶⁵ The individuals responsible for the composition of the book of Deuteronomy, and of Deuteronomy 7 in particular, were a school of scribes writing sometime between the reigns of Hezekiah and Josiah.¹⁶⁶

It is this writer's opinion that, of the aforementioned scholars, Weinfeld presents the soundest hypothesis. Klostermann was right to make a connection between Deuteronomy 7 and the Law. This relationship has been recognized by a number of scholars, in connection with both the Decalogue and the Deuteronomic Code.

---

161. Ibid.
162. Ibid., 61.
163. Weinfeld, *Deuteronomy and the Deuteronomic School*, 51. Emphasis added. It is not insignificant that in his commentary on the book of Deuteronomy he investigates the "literary form of Deuteronomy" as opposed to its oral form: Weinfeld, *Deuteronomy*, 4.
164. Weinfeld, *Deuteronomy and the Deuteronomic School*, 53.
165. Ibid., 57.
166. Ibid., 158–78. Cf. idem, *Deuteronomy 1–11*, 55–57.

Driver, for instance, argues that Deuteronomy 5–11, including chapter 7, "consists essentially of a development of the first Commandment of the Decalogue. With warm and persuasive eloquence, the legislator sets before Israel its primary duty of loyalty to Jehovah, urging upon it the motives to obedience by which it ought to be impelled, and warning it against the manifold temptations to neglectfulness by which it might be assailed."[167] With regard to the Code, McConville has shown the correlation that exists between Deuteronomy 7 and 12.[168] In addition, there is undoubtedly a connection between chapters 7 and 20. Nevertheless, as Weinfeld has demonstrated, this does not mean that there are oral antecedents for connections between Deuteronomy 7 and the law. The links are literary.

Von Rad was right as well to point out the combative elements in Deuteronomy 7 and their association with the institution of the holy war. Nevertheless, as Weinfeld shows, these correlations are literary. This does not preclude the influence of earlier traditions on the composition of Deuteronomy and its seventh chapter, only the possibility of oral antecedents. Therefore in the analysis below, the message and meaning of Deuteronomy 7 will be restricted to the *Sitz im Leben* of its "literary form."

The Literary Structure of Deuteronomy 7

The following structural analysis of Deuteronomy 7 will take a brief look at the strengths and weaknesses of the work of three scholars (Duane Christensen, Norbert Lohfink, and Robert O'Connell) and

---

167. Driver, *Deuteronomy*, 82. Cf. Tigay, *Deuteronomy*, 84. Tigay writes that chaps. 7 and 8 "serve as further explications of the first two commandments of the Decalogue."
168. J. Gordon McConville, "Time, Place, and the Deuteronomic Altar Law," in idem and J. G. Millar, *Time and Place in Deuteronomy*, JSOTSup 179 (Sheffield: Sheffield Academic Press, 1994), 89–137.

then propose the best framework by which to structure the seventh chapter of Deuteronomy.

The Literary Structure of Deuteronomy 7 according to Duane Christensen

In the second edition of his commentary on Deuteronomy, Duane Christensen admits that he was previously "overly impressed" with the book's "concentric design" and saw only a "five-part or 'pentateuchal' structural design."[169] He formerly outlined the book as follows:[170]

Deuteronomy 1–3	A – The Outer Frame: Part 1: A Look Backward
Deuteronomy 4–11	B – The Inner Frame: Part 1: The Great Peroration
Deuteronomy 12–26	C – The Central Core: Covenant Stipulations
Deuteronomy 27–30	B' – The Inner Frame: Part 2: The Covenant Ceremony
Deuteronomy 31–34	A' – The Outer Frame: Part 2: A Look Forward

True to his former predilection for concentric design, Christensen structured the first of the two "inner frames" as follows:[171]

---

169. Christensen, *Deuteronomy 1:1–21:9*, xciii.
170. Christensen, *Deuteronomy 1–11*, 6.
171. Ibid., 69.

Deut 4:1-40	A – "And now, O Israel, obey YHWH's commandments."
Deut 4:41-43	B – Moses set apart three (Levitical) cities of refuge.
Deut 4:44–6:3	C – "This is the Torah": the Ten Words.
Deut 6:4–7:11	D – "Hear, O Israel, YHWH is our God, YHWH alone."
Deut 7:12-26	E – When you obey you will be blessed.
Deut 8:1-20	E' – When you disobey you will be destroyed.
Deut 9:1-29	D' – "Hear, O Israel, you are about to cross the Jordan."
Deut 10:1-7	C' – "At that time YHWH spoke the Ten Words."
Deut 10:8-11	B' – "At that time YHWH set apart the tribe of Levi."
Deut 10:12–11:25	A' – "And now, O Israel, what does YHWH ask of you?"

What is patently obvious in the above outline is that Christensen splits the seventh chapter into two parts. Deuteronomy 7:1-11 is simply the continuation of verses 6:4-25, and although Deuteronomy 7:12-26 is a self-contained unit, it is more closely related to 8:1-20 than to 7:1-11.[172] The weaknesses of this structure will soon become apparent, but first a few words should be said about the recent developments in Christensen's work.[173]

Christensen writes in the recent edition of his commentary that previously he was "not aware of the value of paying careful attention to the traditional lectionary divisions of the text as primary markers in terms of literary structure."[174] His new commentary therefore modifies his previous outlines in accordance with the traditional liturgical tradition of Palestinian Judaism.[175] In this system, eleven weeks are assigned to reading of the book of Deuteronomy, with

---

172. In a previous outline Christensen did not differentiate between Deut 7:12-26 and 8:1-20 and put them into a single unit. Christensen, "Form and Structure in Deuteronomy 1–11," 140.
173. Despite the weaknesses of the above structure, it should be noted that Mayes does echo Christensen's conclusions with regard to Deut 4:1-40 and 10:12–11:25.
174. Christensen, *Deuteronomy 1:1–21:9*, xciii.
175. For his excursus, "The Triennial Cycle of Torah Readings in Palestinian Judaism," see ibid., xcii-xcix.

the book divided into eleven corresponding portions.[176] In this arrangement Deuteronomy 7 is again divided into two parts. Deuteronomy 7:1-11 are the final verses of 3:23–7:11 (ואתחן) and Deuteronomy 7:12-26 are the opening verses of 7:12–11:25 (עקב).[177] Despite the convincing efforts of Norbert Lohfink and others,[178] Christensen maintains the separation between 7:1-11 and 7:12-26 and outlines the pericopes as follows:

Deuteronomy 7:1-11 – "They practice holiness in the land by keeping the Torah"[179]

Deut 7:1-3   A – When you enter the land, destroy the "seven nations."

Deut 7:4   B – The pagan peoples will turn your children from following me.

Deut 7:5   C – Remove their implements of worship.

Deut 7:6   X – You are a holy people to YHWH your God.

Deut 7:7-8   C' – YHWH redeemed you from Egypt because he loved you.

Deut 7:9-10   B' – YHWH is faithful to his covenant commitment.

Deut 7:11   A' – Summary: Keep God's commandments.

---

176. These divisions are easily recognized in the MT. They are as follows: 1:1–3:22; 3:23–7:11; 7:12–11:25; 11:26–16:17; 16:18–21:9; 21:10–25:19; 26:1–29:8; 29:9–30:20; 31:1-30; 32:1-52; 33:1–34:12. Each is named after one of the opening words of the first verse of each section (most often the first word).
177. It is important to point out that although vv. 1-11 and 12-26 are recognized as self-contained units, they are nonetheless relegated to the margins of their respective Torah portions. This stands in marked contrast with Robert O'Connell's view; he sees Deuteronomy 7 and 8 as the rhetorical "heart" of Deut 4:44–11:32.
178. See discussion below.
179. Christensen, *Deuteronomy 1:1–21:9*, 155.

Deuteronomy 7:12-26 – "You will be blessed above all the peoples if you obey."[180]

Deut 7:12-13   A – When you obey, God will bless you in the land.

Deut 7:14-16   B – You will be blessed above all peoples.

Deut 7:17-20   X – Do not be afraid; God will fight for you as in times past.

Deut 7:21-24   B' – God will dislodge these nations before you.

Deut 7:25-26   A' – Do not be ensnared with graven images of false gods.

The strengths and weaknesses of the above outlines will become apparent as we compare them with the structures put forward by Lohfink and O'Connell. Nevertheless, it should be said at this juncture that Christensen does himself a great disservice by separating these two texts (7:1-11 and 7:12-26), which would be better read together.

The Literary Structure of Deuteronomy 7 according to Norbert Lohfink

Contrary to Christensen, Norbert Lohfink argues that Deuteronomy 7 should be read as a single unit.[181] He claims that the structure of the chapter underscores his point. He makes a case that verses 6-14 are concentric. In addition, verses 2-3, 5 and 25-26 provide a literary and conceptual framework for the chapter and are themselves concentric as well. He outlines these sections of Deuteronomy 7 as follows:

---

180. Ibid., 162.
181. Robert O'Connell writes: "Norbert Lohfink, in his doctoral dissertation of 1963, was probably the first to recognize the concentric structure of Deut. vii." O'Connell, "Deuteronomy VII 1-26," 248. Lohfink's dissertation was published under the title *Das Hauptgebot: Eine Untersuchung literarischer Einleitungsfragen zu Dtn 5–11*, AnBib 20 (Rome: Pontifical Biblical Institute, 1963).

Norbert Lohfink – Deuteronomy 7:6-14[182]

Deut 7:6 (7)	A – מכל־העמים – "out of all the peoples"
Deut 7:6	B – על־פני האדמה – "on the face of the earth"
Deut 7:7	C – מרבכם – "you were more numerous"
Deut 7:8	D – מאהבת – "because of [YHWH's] love"
Deut 7:8	E – אשר נשבע לאבתיכם – "that he swore to your fathers"
Deut 7:9	F – שמר הברית והחסד – "keeps covenant and *ḥesed*"
Deut 7:11	G – ושמרת – "and you [sg] will keep"
Deut 7:11	H – ואת־המשפטים – "the judgments"
Deut 7:12	H' – ואת המשפטים – "the judgments"
Deut 7:12	G' – ושמרתם – "and you [pl] will keep"
Deut 7:12	F' – ושמר את־הברית ואת־החסד – "keeps covenant and *ḥesed*"
Deut 7:12 (13)	E' – אשר נשבע לאבתיכם – "that he swore to your"
Deut 7:13	D' – ואהבך – "and [YHWH] will love you"
Deut 7:13	C' – והרבך – "and he will multiply you"
Deut 7:13	B' – על האדמה – "upon the ground"
Deut 7:14	A' – מכל־העמים – "above all peoples"

Norbert Lohfink – Deuteronomy 7:2-3, 5; 7:25-26[183]

Deut 7:2	A – החרם תחרים אתם – "you shall utterly destroy them"
Deut 7:3	B – לא־תקח לבנך – "do not take for your son"
Deut 7:5	C – ופסיליהם תשרפון באש – "their images you shall burn with fire"
Deut 7:25	C' – פסילי אלהיהם . . . באש – "the images of their gods . . . fire"
Deut 7:25	B' – לא . . . ולקחת לך – "and you shall not take (it) for yourself"
Deut 7:26	A' – חרם . . . חרם – "*ḥerem* . . . *ḥerem*"

---

182. Ibid., 182. Cf. Christensen, *Deuteronomy 1:1–21:9*, 162–63.
183. Lohfink, *Das Hauptgebot*, 183.

A number of verses are noticeably absent from the above outlines (Deut 7:1, 4, 10, 15, 16, and 17-24). The reason is that, in Lohfink's estimation, not every verse in Deuteronomy 7 fits into the concentric structure. For example, he argues that Deuteronomy 7:16 is a "structurally independent command" and that no concentric structure is to be "found within the so-called 'conquest paraenesis' of vv. 17-24."[184] This does not prevent Deuteronomy 7 from being a coherent chapter, however: in other words, the lack of a concentric structure does not equal incoherence.[185] Still, the presence of a concentric structure in verses 6-14 and between 2-3, 5 and 25-26 does leave room to question the coherence of Christensen's conclusion.

The Literary Structure of Deuteronomy 7 according to Robert O'Connell

While Lohfink provided the initial ground for seeing parts of the seventh chapter of Deuteronomy as having a clear concentric structure, Robert O'Connell has shown that this concentricity extends throughout the entire chapter. He argues that where Lohfink fell short was in his "penchant for seeing only symmetrically matched tiers."[186] In contrast to Lohfink, O'Connell maintains that the literary coherence of the chapter rests in its "asymmetrical concentricity."[187] He outlines the chapter into a "thirteen-tiered asymmetrical palistrophe which incorporates vv. 17-24, with its sevenfold repetition of YHWH >lhyk, as an inset into the chapter's closing chiastic gesture."[188] The following outline is a replication of

---

184. O'Connell, "Deuteronomy VII 1-26," 249.
185. The conceptual coherence of Deuteronomy 7 will be evaluated below when the literary traditions of chap. 7 are investigated.
186. O'Connell. "Deuteronomy VII 1-26," 248.
187. Note the full title of O'Connell's article, "Deuteronomy VII 1-26: Asymmetrical Concentricity and the Rhetoric of Conquest."
188. O'Connell, "Deuteronomy VII 1-26," 250.

O'Connell's structure of Deuteronomy 7. Afterward, an abbreviated and adapted representation of his structure will be provided in order to help explain and critique O'Connell's work.

Robert O'Connell – Asymmetrical Concentricity in Deuteronomy 7:[189]
Outline 1

1–2bα	**A – Command (Total Eradication)**
1a	a – **Protasis:** When YHWH your god brings you in to the land
1bα'	b – and drive out many nations before you
1bα"-δ	Apposition (enumeration of seven foreign nations)
1bα"-β	**Axis:** Hittites, Girgashites, Amorites, Canaanites, Perizzites, Hivites, Jebusites
1bγδ	b' – Seven nations greater and mightier than you
2a	a' – **Resumption of Protasis:** When YHWH . . . gives them over to you and you defeat them
2bα	c – **Apodosis:** you must dedicate them to destruction
2bβ–4	**B – Prohibitions (Against Foreign Relations)**
2bβ–3	**Prohibitions Proper**
2bβ'	You shall make no covenant with them
2bβ"	a – and show them no mercy
3a	you shall not intermarry with them
3bα	do not give your daughter to his son
3bβ	and do not take his daughter for your son
4aα	**Negative Motive:** otherwise she would turn your son away
4aβ	b – **Intermediate Result:** so they would serve other gods
4b	Final result: then YHWH's anger would destroy you

---

189. O'Connell, "Deuteronomy VII 1–26," 250–54. Key tiers have been put in boldface by the present author.

5		C – Commands (Destroy Cult Sites)
6		Motive/Indication (Election by YHWH your God)
6abα-γ		D – YHWH your God has chosen you . . . from all the peoples
6bδ		E – on the earth
7–8aβ		Reason for Election (YHWH's covenant loyalty)
7aα'		F – Not because you were more numerous
7aα"-b		D' – . . . did YHWH choose you, for you were the least of all peoples
8aα		G – but because YHWH loves you
8aβ		H – and was keeping the oath he swore to your fathers
8aγb		I – Indication: YHWH brought you out with a strong hand . . .
9–10		Purpose of Redemption
9abαβ		J – that you might know that YHWH your god is God, the faithful god who keeps covenant loyalty
9bγ		G' – with those who love him and keep his commandments
10		K – but who destroys those who hate him
11		Exhortation
11α'		L – So keep the commandments, statutes
11α"β		M – and judgments I am commanding you

[Virtual Axis]

12a		Protasis (obedience)
12aαβ		M' – If you obey these judgments
12aγ		L' – and are careful to perform them
12b		Apodosis (Covenant Continuance)
12bαβ		J' – then YHWH will keep . . . covenant loyalty

12bγ		H' – which he swore to your fathers
13-15		**Indications: Development of Apodosis (Covenant Blessings)**
13aαβ'		G" – Thus he will love you and bless you
13aβ"-bβ		F' – and make you increase by blessing . . .
13bγ		E' – in the land
13bδ		H" – YHWH swore to your fathers to give to you
14a		D" – You will be more blessed than any [other] people
14b		F" – There will never be a childless male or female among you
15abαβ		I' – Then YHWH will remove . . . sickness and not inflict on you . . .
15bγ		K' – but will set them on all who hate you
16aαβ		**A' – Command (Total Eradication)**
16aα		c' – Only you must annihilate all the peoples
16aβ		a" – whom YHWH your god gives over to you
16aγb		**B' – Prohibitions (Against foreign relations)**
16aγ		a' – Your eye shall not regard them with pity
16bα		b' – nor shall you serve their gods
16bβ		c – for that would be a snare to you
17-24		**Inset (Conquest Paraenesis)**
17		Protasis – "If you say these nations are too many . . ."
18-24		Apodosis
18a		aa – Admonition (not to fear foreign nations)
18b		bb – Exhortation (to remember YHWH your god versus Pharaoh and Egypt)
19a		cc – Apposition (YHWH your God's plagues and exodus)
19ab		dd – Indication (YHWH your God versus feared peoples)

	[Double Axis]
20	ee – **Axis1** – Indication (YHWH your god will totally eradicate)
21a	aa' – **Axis2** – Admonition (not to fear foreign nations)
21b	dd' – Motive (YHWH your God is fearsome)
22	cc' – Indication (YHWH your God will aid in conquest)
23-24aα	bb' – Indication (YHWH your God versus Canaanite kings)
24aβγb	ee' – Purpose/Indication (total eradication)
25a	**C' – Command (Destroy cult sites)**
25b	**B" – Prohibition (Against the gilding of idols)**
25bα	You shall not desire the silver or gold on them so as to take [it] for yourself
25bβ	c' – lest you become ensnared by it
25bγ	for it is an abomination to YHWH your god
26	**Double Order (Against Exceptions to Total Eradication)**
26aα **1/A**	d – Prohibition (so do not bring an abomination into your house)
26aβ	c" – Negative Motive (otherwise you will be dedicated to destruction)
26b' **A"**	d' – Command (You shall utterly detest and abhor it)
26b"	cc''' – Reason (for it is dedicated to destruction)

Robert O'Connell – Asymmetrical Concentricity in Deuteronomy 7:[190]
Outline 2

Deut 7:1-2a	A – Command (total eradication)	
Deut 7:2b-4	B – Prohibitions (against foreign relations)	
Deut 7:5	C – Commands (destroy cult sites)	
Deut 7:6a	D – Election – the motive to carry out the commands	
Deut 7:6b	E – "on the earth"	
Deut 7:7a	F – "not because you were more numerous"	
Deut 7:7b	D' – Election – its reasons	

"Virtual Axis" – Deuteronomy 7:11-12

Deut 7:13a	F' – "and make you increase"
Deut 7:13b	E' – "in the land"
Deut 7:14a	D" – Election – its blessings – "more than any other people"
Deut 7:14b	F" – "There will never be a childless male or female . . ."
Deut 7:16a	A' – Command (total eradication)
Deut 7:16b	B' – Prohibitions (against foreign relations)

"Structural Inset" – Deuteronomy 7:17-24

Deut 7:25a	C' – Command (destroy cult sites)
Deut 7:25b	B" – Prohibition (against the gilding of idols)
Deut 7:26a	1/A – Prohibition (against bringing an abomination into one's house)
Deut 7:26b	A" – Command ('you shall utterly detest and abhor it')

There are a few features of O'Connell's structure that require clarification. One can see from the above outline that O'Connell agrees with Lohfink that the "virtual axis" of the chapter falls between

---

[190]. The following outline is the present author's explanatory adaptation of O'Connell's.

verses 11 and 12. However, they part company with each other over how verses 1-11 and 12-26 relate. O'Connell maintains: "[W]hile the concentric architecture of Deut. vii shows that repetitions of keywords balance one another about a virtual axis located between vv. 11 and 12, the pattern of repetitions lacks bilateral symmetry. Certain tiers of the main concentric structure are repeated twice, not just once, after their first statement and occur in what appears to be no prescribed order."[191] While tier "E," for example, occurs just once on each side of the virtual axis, tiers "D" and "F" show no such symmetry. Tier "D" appears twice before the virtual axis and only once after verse 12. In a similar but inverted fashion, tier "F" occurs once before the axis and twice afterward. Therefore tiers "D" and "F" are still balanced across the axis between verses 11 and 12, but not in bilateral fashion. Each tier is arranged in a "triadic frame," which is a pattern "made up of two tiers, structurally juxtaposed, which are counterbalanced against a third which lies across a major structural barrier."[192] The balancing of two or more of these frames creates what O'Connell calls a "compound inverse frame."[193] The end result of this process is that tiers "D" and "F" are balanced out thus: D, F, D'—*virtual axis*—F', D", F".

Another aspect of O'Connell's structure of Deuteronomy 7 that merits discussion is the way he incorporates verses 17-24 into the overall concentric structure of the chapter by means of "double closure."[194] As outlined above, "tiers A–B (vv. 1-4) are complemented by the combination of tiers A'–B' (v. 16a, b) and B"–1/A–A" (vv. 25b-26)"[195] and verses 17-24 are inserted as a "structural inset" within

---

191. O'Connell, "Deuteronomy VII 1-26," 254. He explains that with tiers "H–L" there is "sequential displacement," which is most likely due to "aesthetic license." Ibid., 256–57.
192. Ibid., 254.
193. Ibid.
194. Ibid., 257.
195. Ibid.

the final two "B" tiers."[196] Contrary to Lohfink, who did not see any concentric structure in the "conquest paraenesis," O'Connell claims that, in a way similar to the wider structure of the chapter, the inset also shows signs of asymmetrical concentricity. He writes: "In the concentric inset (vv. 17-24) structural cohesion is enhanced by a framing device in which two 'simple frames' interlock at the axis and thus form a two-phased axis."[197] This is accomplished in the following manner:

Robert O'Connell – Structure of Deuteronomy 7:17-24[198]

18a   aa – Admonition – "Do not fear them"

20   ee – axis1 – Total Eradication

21a   aa' – axis2 – Admonition – "Do not be afraid of them"

24aβγb   ee' – Total Eradication

In addition to the structural similarities between the inset and the wider asymmetrical concentric structure of the rest of the chapter, there are also correspondences in vocabulary and theme.[199] On this basis O'Connell concludes that the inset is "both uniform with and integral to the literary structure and rhetorical purpose of the chapter."[200]

The significance of O'Connell's asymmetrical concentric structure of Deuteronomy 7 should not go unnoticed.[201] Although his outline

---

196. Ibid.
197. Ibid.
198. Ibid. O'Connell demonstrates (p. 258) that the internal tiers (bb-bb' [18b, 23-24a]; cc-cc' [19a, 22]; and dd-dd' [19b, 21b]) fall into a concentric pattern within the above framework.
199. Ibid., 258–59. For example, there is a sevenfold repetition of "YHWH your God" in both the inset and the main concentric structure.
200. Ibid., 259–60. Because of this, O'Connell believed that the presence of this inset should not "imply that it is the product of a later redactor of this chapter." Ibid., 257.
201. Unfortunately, there are no scholars of whom this writer is aware who have interacted with O'Connell's conclusions with any degree of detail. Nelson gives a three-sentence summary in his commentary (Richard D. Nelson, *Deuteronomy*, OTL [Louisville: Westminster John Knox, 2002], 98 n. 2). McConville (*Deuteronomy*, 151, 167) cites him twice. Christensen (*Deuteronomy*

is incredibly detailed and difficult to decipher, he makes one of the strongest arguments for the structural unity and coherence of the chapter. What these three authors (Christensen, Lohfink, and O'Connell) have not done in their analysis of the seventh chapter of Deuteronomy, however, is to look at the literary traditions on which the chapter is based and the way they are incorporated into the chapter.

The Traditions of Deuteronomy 7

On the basis of his structural analysis of Deuteronomy 7–8, O'Connell concludes:

> It is difficult to imagine that these chapters came into their present form and into juxtaposition with each other apart from the design and intention of a single author or compiler. I am aware that there is evidence of redactional processes in the development of the present form of Deuteronomy, but are such processes likely to have given rise to chapters so architecturally analogous and, at the same time, so mutually integrated with their context? In particular, the plethora of redaction-critical studies on Deut. iv–xi, which have been founded on the shift between second person singular and second person plural, seem not only to give inadequate consideration to the overall form of these texts but also to show little sensitivity to possible aesthetic motivations for such shifts of person.[202]

O'Connell may be right to suggest that the final form of Deuteronomy 7 is the "design and intention of a single author or compiler," but that does not excuse one from the responsibility to investigate the potential "redactional processes" of a given chapter.

1:1–21:9, 153) cites him in his bibliography but does not mention him in the main body of his commentary.

202. O'Connell, "Deuteronomy VII 1-26," 264. Cf. idem, "Deuteronomy VIII 1-20: Asymmetrical Concentricity and the Rhetoric of Providence," *VT* 40 (1990): 437–52. The first sentences in the above quotation are contradictory. Either there is "evidence of redactional processes" or the book of Deuteronomy was composed by a "single author or compiler."

As he does not provide any evidence for or against the possibility of "redactional processes" in his article, the reader is left to wonder if he is really correct in his estimation. This section will therefore investigate the possibility of redactional activity in Deuteronomy 7. It will critically analyze the proposals put forward by George Adam Smith, Adam Welch, A. D. H. Mayes, Norbert Lohfink, and Moshe Weinfeld. In the end it will be seen whether O'Connell's conclusion still stands and how exactly Deuteronomy 7 incorporated the traditions on which it is based.

George Adam Smith

George Adam Smith, writing as early as 1918, detected "redactional" activity in Deuteronomy 7.[203] He defended the basic "integrity of the chapter" but admitted that there are "certain editorial additions."[204] These additions, he claimed, are found in verses 5, 7-8a, and 12a.[205] Whereas the rest of the chapter is written in a singular address, these verses shift unexpectedly to the plural. The reason for this change from the single to the plural form of address varies, according to Smith. With regard to verse 5 he wrote: "The change to the Pl.,

---

203. Smith himself did not refer to this process as redaction but as "editorial" activity. He referred to the individuals responsible for the final form of Deuteronomy as "compilers, adapters, and annotators." Smith, *Deuteronomy*, lxxxviii–xci.
204. Ibid., 105. Smith was not the first to recognize "editorial" activity on the basis of the frequent shift from singular to plural in the book of Deuteronomy. As he acknowledges, a number of scholars analyzed the book on the basis of this phenomenon before he wrote his own commentary (ibid., lxxiii–lxxv). The most significant of these were Willy Staerk and Carl Steuernagel. Cf. Willy Staerk, *Das Deuteronomium: Sein Inhalt und seine literarische Form: Eine kritische Studie* (Leipzig: Hinrich, 1894); Carl Steuernagel, *Der Rahmen des Deuteronomium* (Halle: J. Krause, 1894); idem, *Die Entstehung des deuteronomischen Gesetzes* (Halle: J. Krause, 1896); idem, *Deuteronomium und Josua*, HKAT 1:3 (Göttingen: Vandenhoeck & Ruprecht, 1900).
205. Smith, *Deuteronomy*, 105. Smith also acknowledges that v. 25a is in the plural form of address, but he does not believe that it is secondary to the chapter. He claims that "the isolated Pl. may be due to a scribe whose eye or ear was impressed with v. 5." Ibid., 116. This does not make sense however, for if v. 5 is a later insertion, as Smith himself states, then the original author of Deuteronomy 7 could never have been impressed with the verse. Verses 5 and 25a are either both original or are both secondary to the chapter.

together with the fact that the v[erse] does not direct the destruction of the persons of the heathen (which would have been relevant to the preceding), but only of their altars, etc., marks this verse as a quotation or later insertion."[206] Smith also believed verses 7-8a are secondary additions on the grounds that "the choice of Israel by Jehovah is not mentioned in other Pl. passages, and also because these verses are not necessary" to establish a "connection" between verses 6 and 8b.[207] In addition, he found verse 12a to be "superfluous," for verse 12b, which resumes the singular form of address, follows on "suitably" from verse 11.[208]

Adam Welch

Adam Welch also maintains that the "original form" of Deuteronomy 7 is found in the singular form of address and that the "plural additions" are secondary.[209] Therefore the primary text of Deuteronomy 7 is found in verses 1-4a, 6, 8b-11, and 12b-24, and the secondary insertions are seen in verses 4b-5, 7-8a, and 12a.[210] Welch claims that verses 25-26, which begin in the plural (v. 25a) and return to the singular form of address (vv. 25b-26), start by quoting the final three words of verse 5 and should therefore be seen as a "marginal note" on the verse.[211]

Welch differs from Smith primarily on one account. He takes a firmer stance than Smith in maintaining that verse 4b is a secondary insertion. Smith acknowledges the sudden shift to the plural in 4b (בכם), but he insists, "It is impossible to say whether this is original or an editorial addition."[212] Smith is right in this regard, for Welch

---

206. Ibid., 107.
207. Ibid., 110–11.
208. Ibid., 113.
209. Adam Welch, *Deuteronomy: the Framework to the Code* (Oxford: Oxford University Press, 1932), 70.
210. Ibid., 70–73.
211. Ibid., 73.

seems to overlook the complexity of this verse, which starts in the singular, moves to plural, and returns to singular in the span of just a few words. Welch naïvely considers verse 4b to be secondary solely on the basis of בכם. However, verse 4 as a whole makes more sense if בכם is seen to be original.

A. D. H. Mayes

Mayes acknowledges that one of the reasons why it is difficult to ascertain the "origin and growth" of Deuteronomy is the "remarkable interchange of second person singular and plural forms of address."[213] He insists, however, that this "can by no means be used on its own as the key to the solution to all Deuteronomy's difficulties," not only because this happens to be a common literary feature in many "extra biblical documents" but also because there are numerous passages in Deuteronomy "where the application of this criterion for the purpose of source division succeeds only in doing unacceptable violence."[214] This leads Mayes to conclude that paying attention to the *Numeruswechsel* [change of number] is not the best way to determine the origin and growth of Deuteronomy. Rather, this should be done by looking at the redactional activity of the Deuteronomists.[215]

In Mayes's opinion the deuteronomistic editing of Deuteronomy occurred in roughly two stages. The first redaction of Deuteronomy had history as its primary concern. It prefixed the first three chapters

---

212. Smith, *Deuteronomy*, 107.
213. Mayes, *Deuteronomy*, 34–35.
214. Ibid., 35–36. He references Klaus Baltzer, *The Covenant Formulary* (Oxford: Oxford University Press, 1971), and cites Deut 4:1-40 as a text in which "the change [in person] is a stylistic feature of the work of a single author, and cannot be used for source division purposes." Cf. A. D. H. Mayes, "Deuteronomy 4 and the Literary Criticism of Deuteronomy," *JBL* 100 (1981): 23–51.
215. Mayes, *Deuteronomy*, 41–55. For a recent discussion of deuteronomistic activity see Linda Shearing and Steven McKenzie, eds., *Those Elusive Deuteronomists: The Phenomenon of Pan-Deuteronomism* (Sheffield: Sheffield Academic Press, 1999).

to the book not as "an introduction to the deuteronomic law, but rather the beginning of a much more extensive historical work" that extended through 2 Kings.[216] Deuteronomy 5:1–6:3 and parts of 9:1–10:11 were also inserted out of "historical concern."[217] The second redaction of Deuteronomy had as its primary motive the desire to inculcate a sense of devotion and obedience to YHWH. Mayes writes: "The history of Israel does not feature in his writing; rather it is Israel standing before the divine demand, with a promise of blessing for obedience."[218] The work of this second redaction is seen primarily in Deuteronomy 4:1-40; 6:10-18; 7:4-5, 7-16, 25-26; 8:1-6, 11b, 15-16, 18b-20; 10:12–11:32.[219] In light of the above two redactions, Mayes concludes that the "original book of Deuteronomy" was composed of the following verses: Deuteronomy 4:45; 6:4-9, 20-24; 7:1-3, 6, 17-24; 8:7-11a, 12-14, 17-18a; 9:1-7a, 13-14, 26-29; 10:10-11; 12:13-15, 17-19 (20-28), 29-31; 13:1-18; 14:2ff., 21; and nearly all of 14:22–25:16.[220] He writes: "No reference was made in the book to the Sinai revelation or the giving of law then or to a covenant concluded then. This book was simply a collection

---

216. Mayes, *Deuteronomy*, 41. Cf. Martin Noth, *Überlieferungsgeschichtliche Studien 1: Die sammelnden und bearbeitenden Geschichtswerke im Alten Testament* (3d ed. Tübingen: Max Niemeyer, 1967); idem, *The Deuteronomistc History* (Sheffield: JSOT Press, 1981). Mayes elaborates (*Deuteronomy*, 41) by saying: "The chapters have no essential contact with the law beyond bringing the reader up to the historical point in time at which the law was proclaimed. Their focus is rather on the history of the people of Israel, a history which indeed stands under and is judged by the law proclaimed at its beginning. However, while the history thus stands in some connection to the law, the important point in the present context is that the history is seen in the first instance as a whole." In addition to these opening chapters, he says, parts of chaps. 31 and 34 were also inserted into Deuteronomy in order to provide a historical framework to the book and a logical transition to the book of Joshua.
217. Mayes, *Deuteronomy*, 42.
218. Ibid., 44.
219. Ibid., 45–46. Mayes explains further: "Here the aim was more fully to integrate the decalogue than had already been done. It had originally been introduced within the context of a narrative of an event of Israel's history. The later deuteronomist, however, has emphasized its actual demand for the exclusive worship of Yahweh, so continuing the theme already established in 4:1-40, and so has modified the original general exhortation of these chapters into a specific demand."
220. Ibid., 48.

of law given by Moses to Israel."[221] The purpose of the paraenesis was to "encourage obedience to the law" and to "encourage the view that Israel is Yahweh's own possession, to whom he has given the land."[222] It is this context, namely, the nature, scope, and purpose of the original book of Deuteronomy and its two redactions, that forms the background to Mayes's understanding of the seventh chapter of Deuteronomy.

As intimated above, Mayes believes that Deuteronomy 7:1-3, 6, 17-24 are the original verses of the chapter, and verses 4-5, 7-15, 25-26 were inserted during the book's second redaction. The former set of verses commands Israel to destroy the land's original inhabitants and bases its injunction on the "affirmation that Israel is Yahweh's special possession (v. 6)."[223] Deuteronomy 7:17-24 revisits this theme and seeks to assuage Israel's fears about the aforementioned nations on the basis of the promise of God's presence in their midst (7:20). The latter set of verses treats entirely different subject matter. In these verses Israel is charged to avoid the worship of foreign gods and demands the destruction of their religious paraphernalia.[224]

Deuteronomy 7:16 is the one verse that is noticeably absent from the above discussion, but it is not overlooked in Mayes's commentary on the seventh chapter. He highlights the verse as a proof of the above two sets of verses' original independence and of the redactional activity that brought them together.[225] Verse 7:16a "commands the destruction of the peoples," while 7:16b "prohibits the worship of

---

221. Ibid.
222. Ibid., 49.
223. Ibid., 181.
224. Ibid. Mayes writes that only these verses have "any reference to the law . . . [and] graven images." This leads him to establish a connection with Deut 4:1-40 and thus the second redaction of the book.
225. Ibid.

their gods."[226] One cannot help but notice with Mayes that the verse "sets the two subjects side by side."[227]

The degree to which this is significant and may prove Mayes's hypothesis of the redactional activity in Deuteronomy and in its seventh chapter to be correct remains to be seen. McConville argues: "There is no evidence, *pace* Mayes . . . that these two themes were originally developed independently, or that this chapter can be divided into separate layers according to each."[228] Unfortunately, McConville does not substantiate his claim with any sound evidence. He references Lohfink and Weinfeld but mistakenly overlooks the fact that the former acknowledged redactional activity in the seventh chapter of Deuteronomy.[229] The jury therefore is still out on the matter of Mayes's claims and the exact role of redactional activity in Deuteronomy 7. The opinion of Norbert Lohfink will now be consulted in order to see if it sheds any light on the present subject.

Norbert Lohfink

Norbert Lohfink is similar to Mayes in that he denies the importance of the *Numeruswechsel* as a tool for ascertaining redactional activity in Deuteronomy. "Every change of number" for Lohfink "is a new form of address, a new assault on the listener."[230] The shifting from second person singular to second person plural, then, is a stylistic feature of the author and does not signal the presence of redactional activity. Lohfink differs from Mayes, however, in his view of the literary growth of Deuteronomy 7. Whereas Mayes believed the original text

---

226. Ibid., 187.
227. Mayes, *Deuteronomy*, 181.
228. McConville, *Deuteronomy*, 150.
229. Ibid. McConville's strongest point against Mayes is made when he cites Joshua 4–6 and 1 Samuel 4 and shows that there is an "intrinsic connection between the destruction of the other nations and worship." This, however, does not in itself eliminate the possibility of redactional activity in the chapter.
230. Lohfink, *Das Hauptgebot*, 36.

of Deuteronomy 7 was found in verses 1-3, 6, and 17-24, Lohfink argues that verses 1-5, 13-16, 20-24 constitute the chapter's primary text.[231] These verses are a "Gilgal covenant text," and as such they are "concerned with the destruction of foreign cults."[232] The chapter's later insertions sought to bring in the "decalogue material" and include verses 6-12, 17-19, and 25-26.[233]

As is evident from Lohfink's proposed literary structure of Deuteronomy 7,[234] the fusion of these two traditions is not the "result of a slow, haphazard process, but shows evidence of a conscious shaping of material."[235] Whereas Mayes claimed that the redaction of Deuteronomy 7 took place over a number of generations, Lohfink argues that it occurred over a much shorter span of time, indeed, just enough time to incorporate the aforementioned traditions in a manner that showed literary and conceptual unity.

The accuracy of Lohfink's appraisal in contrast to that of Mayes will soon be evaluated. However, the work of Moshe Weinfeld still needs to be discussed; he builds on the arguments put forward by Lohfink and in many ways views the chapter's literary growth in the same manner.

Moshe Weinfeld

Moshe Weinfeld argues that Deuteronomy 7 is a "coherent chapter."[236] He acknowledges the phenomenon of the *Numeruswechsel* but contends that "although in some cases the interchange of singular and plural address may indicate the existence of different layers, in general the interchange reflects stylistic

---

231. Ibid., 184.
232. Ibid.
233. Ibid., 184–85. This is the one point upon which Mayes and Lohfink are in agreement.
234. See above, "The Literary Structure of Deuteronomy 7 according to Norbert Lohfink."
235. In McConville, *Deuteronomy*, 151.
236. Weinfeld, *Deuteronomy 1–11*, 380.

variations introduced by the same author."²³⁷ In other words, they are not secondary insertions but rather literary features original to the chapter's composition.²³⁸ Weinfeld explains the instances of plural address as follows:

Verse 5 is in the plural because the author is dependent on an earlier tradition, namely Exodus 34:13, which was also in the plural.²³⁹ Verses 7-8a are not treated by Weinfeld. He notes the switch back to the singular form of address in verse 8b and says that it is due to the "fact that it constitutes a (liturgical) frozen formula styled conventionally in the singular," but he fails to explain why verses 7-8a are in the second person plural.²⁴⁰ The reason for this is uncertain, but on the basis of his other statements one might suggest that Weinfeld assumed that these verses were in the plural simply as a "stylistic variation" used by the author of the chapter.²⁴¹ Verses 11-12a have been discussed above.²⁴² Verse 25a is in the plural as a result of the "author's reference to a standard, fixed formula—actually a quotation—as found in v. 6b [sic: 5b]."²⁴³ In summary, Weinfeld gives two reasons why the plural form of address is used: it is either a stylistic feature employed by the author of Deuteronomy or it is based on the traditions the author incorporates into the text.

The view that the seventh chapter of Deuteronomy is influenced by a series of traditions is not original to Weinfeld (cf. Mayes and Lohfink). Nevertheless, Weinfeld's assessment of the number and

---

237. Ibid., 16.
238. The only verses in the chapter that Weinfeld admits were of later redaction are Deuteronomy vv. 11-12a. He argues that these were "inserted by late editors who divided the Deuteronomic material for the liturgical recital, irrespective of the inner structure of the material. Thus chaps. 6–8 were divided into two: 6.1–7.11 . . . and 7.12–8.20." He adds, "This division ignores the literary integrity of chap. 7." Ibid., 372.
239. Ibid., 366.
240. Ibid., 369.
241. Ibid., 16.
242. See n. 238 above.
243. The verse Weinfeld is actually referring to is Deut 7:5b. Weinfeld, *Deuteronomy 1–11*, 376.

type of these traditions along with the manner in which he says they are crafted together to form the chapter at hand is unique. The following table summarizes and outlines his basic thought on the literary traditions of Deuteronomy 7.

The Literary Traditions of Deuteronomy 7 according to Moshe Weinfeld

Tradition	*Gilgal Tradition*	*Shechemite Tradition*	*Deuteronomic*	
References I	Exod 23:20-33	Exod 34:11-17		
References II	Deut 7:1-2, 5, 12-16, 20-26	Deut 7:3-4	Deut 7:6-11, 17-19	
Sub-traditions			Decalogue	Military Oration
References III			Deut 7:6-11	Deut 7:17-19

According to Weinfeld, Deuteronomy 7 is rooted in three basic traditions: Gilgal, Shechemite, and Deuteronomic. The bulk of the chapter draws on the Gilgal tradition. The Shechemite tradition informs a small but not insignificant segment of the chapter, forbidding the Israelites to intermarry with the land's native inhabitants. The verses not represented by the above two traditions are unique to Deuteronomy. These include verses 6-11, which Weinfeld says were "triggered" by verses 4-5 and amount to a "commentary on the Decalogue," and verses 17-19, which are a "military oration."[244]

Despite the plurality of texts that inform Deuteronomy 7, Weinfeld maintains that the chapter is nevertheless "coherent." The author(s) of Deuteronomy 7 have incorporated the aforementioned traditions, built upon them, and transformed them into a text that

---

244. Ibid., 382.

accords with their own intentions and ideology. In other words, they have made the three traditions speak their own message, one that is in some cases quite distinct from the original purposes of these texts. In the following analysis this process of "innovation"[245] will be especially significant for ascertaining the message and meaning of Deuteronomy 7. But before that discussion can begin, some concluding remarks should be made to bring the present section to a close.

Robert O'Connell was critiqued at the outset of this section for neglecting to evaluate some of the literary and conceptual complexities of the text that may have been due to redactional activity. The above survey of scholars and their views on the literary traditions of Deuteronomy 7 has substantiated O'Connell's claim that some scholars pay too much attention to the shift between second person singular and second person plural in this chapter. Mayes, Lohfink, and Weinfeld have all shown that the position held by Smith and Welch regarding the *Numeruswechsel* is errant and that by itself it does not show evidence of redactional activity. Although O'Connell is vindicated on this point, he is still wrong to neglect to inquire into the possibility of redactional activity on other grounds.

Mayes, Lohfink, and Weinfeld have all demonstrated some of the literary and conceptual complexities behind Deuteronomy 7. Mayes is correct in his understanding of the redactional activity in Deuteronomy and the way it was incorporated into the wider Deuteronomistic History (DtrH). However, he overextends the application of this theory by applying it to the seventh chapter. As Lohfink and Weinfeld have made evident, Deuteronomy 7 shows itself to be a fusion of traditions that was most likely accomplished by a single author or company of authors over a short span of time and

---

245. Levinson, *Deuteronomy and the Hermeneutics of Legal Innovation*.

not, as Mayes argued, over the span of a number of generations.[246] Although Lohfink and Weinfeld both believe that Deuteronomy 7 is informed by the Gilgal tradition, they differ on the extent to which its verses represent that tradition. The verses in question are 25-26. Lohfink maintains that these texts hearken back to the Decalogue as opposed to the Gilgal tradition. As Weinfeld shows, however, verses 25-26 recall verse 5 and therefore should be understood as belonging to the Gilgal tradition.[247]

In light of the above survey and summary, I find Weinfeld's appraisal of the literary traditions that inform Deuteronomy 7 the most convincing. Therefore I will follow him more often than the other scholars in my concluding discussion of the chapter's message and meaning.

Conclusion: The Message and Meaning of Deuteronomy 7

In this first section of this chapter I will treat the rhetorical message of Deuteronomy 7; in the second I will take the conclusions reached on the text's rhetorical message and evaluate it in view of the background material provided on Deuteronomy as a whole, namely, its contents, literary form(s), and origin.

The Message of Deuteronomy 7

It is interesting to note the various titles scholars have given to Deuteronomy 7. They range from the mundane to the insightful, and they intimate the struggle many researchers have waged to say in succinct fashion what they think is the rhetorical message of

---

246. This does not mean that one has to date the text as early as Christensen or McConville do. See the earlier discussion in "An Analysis of Deuteronomy's Origins," above.
247. Weinfeld also shows that Deut 7:17-19 is a military oration and not "decalogue material" as Lohfink asserts.

Deuteronomy 7. One scholar even refrained from labeling the chapter altogether.[248]

Titles of Deuteronomy 7	
Braulik[249]	"Israel and the Peoples of the Land"
Brueggemann[250]	"The wonder and rigor of being chosen"
Christensen[251]	"They practice holiness in the land by keeping the Torah" and "You will be blessed above all peoples if you obey"
Clements[252]	"When you live in the land"
Craigie[253]	"Israel's Policy of War"
Driver[254]	"Crusade against heathenism"
García Lopéz[255]	"A Dedicated (Consecrated) People"
Mayes[256]	"The nations of the land and their cults must be destroyed"
McConville[257]	"The election of Israel and the rejection of other nations"
Merrill[258]	"Dispossession of Nonvassals"
Nelson[259]	"Israel as a Countercultural Society"
Smith[260]	—
Tigay[261]	"Exhortations concerning the conquest of the promised land"
Weinfeld[262]	"The conquest of the land; the struggle with the Canaanites and their culture"
Welch[263]	"Separation of the Church and the World"

248. George Adam Smith, *Deuteronomy* (Cambridge: Cambridge University Press, 1918).
249. *Israel und die Völker des Landes*. Georg Braulik, *Deuteronomium*, vol. 1. Neue Echter Bibel 15 (Würzburg: Echter Verlag, 1986), 17, 62.
250. Walter Brueggemann, *Deuteronomy*, Abingdon OT Commentaries (Nashville: Abingdon Press, 2001), 93.
251. Christensen, *Deuteronomy 1:1–21:9*, 152, 159.
252. Clements, *The Book of Deuteronomy*, 35.
253. Craigie, *Deuteronomy*, 175.
254. Driver, *Deuteronomy*, 82.
255. *Un Peuple Consacré*. Félix García Lopéz, "Un Peuple Consacré: Analyse critique de Deutéronome 7," *VT* 32 (October 1982): 438–63, at 438.
256. Mayes, *Deuteronomy*, 181.
257. McConville, *Deuteronomy*, 162.
258. Eugene H. Merrill, *Deuteronomy*, NAC 4 (Nashville: Broadman & Holman, 1994), 176.

Perhaps no title can encapsulate all that lies within Deuteronomy 7. However, on the basis of an evaluation of the basic structure of the chapter one can highlight those points that help convey its chief message. This has been done effectively by Lohfink and O'Connell.[264]

Although Lohfink and O'Connell differ in a number of respects, they are united on two key points. The opening and closing verses of Deuteronomy 7 bracket the chapter and provide a literary and conceptual framework for it by focusing on the idea of *ḥerem* (Deut 7:1-5, 25-26). In addition to this there is a concentric structure that turns on a "virtual axis" or "*Hauptachse*" in the middle of the chapter (Deut 7:11-12).[265] The former verse is an "*allgemeine Ermahnung*" or general admonition, to keep the commandment[s], the laws, and the judgments (Deut 7:11).[266] This admonition is, as O'Connell says, the "central human condition on which the continued benefits of the conquest depend," for the prospect of YHWH's "keeping" his end of the bargain, that is, his covenant and promised blessing to the people of Israel, is predicated on the condition that the people of Israel "keep" the aforementioned law (Deut 7:11, 12-15).[267] Deuteronomy

---

259. Nelson, *Deuteronomy*, 94.
260. Smith, *Deuteronomy*, 105.
261. Tigay, *Deuteronomy*, 84.
262. Weinfeld, *Deuteronomy*, 357.
263. Welch, *Deuteronomy: The Framework to the Code*, 69.
264. See above, "The Literary Structure of Deuteronomy 7 according to Norbert Lohfink," and "The Literary Structure of Deuteronomy 7 according to Robert O'Connell."
265. O'Connell, "Deuteronomy VII 1-26," 251; Lohfink, *Hauptgebot*, 182. Deuteronomy 7:11 may have been inserted as a "practical conclusion," as Weinfeld says, by "late editors who divided the Deuteronomic material for the liturgical recital, irrespective of the inner structure of the material." Weinfeld, *Deuteronomy 1–11*, 372. Nevertheless, there is a parity between verses 11 and 12 that might suggest the latter was original. Lohfink, for instance, points out the "*Wortentsprechungen*" (word correspondences) between the verses as well their logical correspondence. Lohfink, *Hauptgebot*, 170.
266. Ibid.
267. O'Connell, "Deuteronomy VII 1-26," 261. Lohfink remarks on the conditionality of Deuteronomy 7:12, "This is the rule in the 'blessing texts' of the covenant formula. Corresponding to the 'parity style,' of ancient treaties a verbal correspondence is created, matching the expected actions of the two covenant parties is created: If the people keeps (*šmr*)

7, therefore, hangs on two keys ideas: law and *ḥerem*. Israel is admonished to keep the law and more specifically adhere to YHWH's command to put the nations under the 'ban,' or *ḥerem*.

The reason why the people of Israel are required to place the nations under the "ban," to avoid establishing any political or marital relations with them, to destroy their religious paraphernalia and not to bring any of it into their homes lest they be subjugated to the same treatment as those peoples, that is, *ḥerem*, is treated in Deuteronomy 7:6-10. Verse 6 says that they are a holy people,

עַם־קָדוֹשׁ, or rather, a people wholly belonging to God.[268] The following verses build on this statement and explain that "love" is at the root of this relationship. The people of Israel are called to "love" YHWH just as he has "loved" them (vv. 7-10). In return, YHWH will "love" them and continue to keep this "gracious covenant" (vv. 12-13). "Love," then, is the tie that binds Israel and YHWH together and the force that beckons Israel to obey his commands (law) and destroy the land's inhabitants (*ḥerem*).

That "love" demands such actions warrants an explanation.[269] As William L. Moran points out, "love" in Deuteronomy is different

---

these commandments (*mišpāṭîm*), then YHWH will also keep (*šmr*) the covenant fidelity based on what he swore to the ancestors." (*Das ist die Regel in den Segenstexten des Bundesformulars. Entsprechend dem "Paritätsstil" der alten Staatsverträge ist zwischen den Leistungen der beiden Bundespartner auch eine wortmässige Entsprechung hergestellt; wenn das Volk 'diese* mišpāṭîm' *beobachtet* (šmr), *hält* (šmr) *auch Jahwe die im Väterschwur gründende Bundestreue.*) Lohfink, *Hauptgebot*, 170–71. McConville (*Deuteronomy*, 139) rightly warns against having an "over-exclusive model of law and grace, in which either one or the other must have absolute priority." He explains, "The structure of v. 12 mirrors that of vv. 9-11; there, the exhortation to obey God's commands is plainly a consequence of the covenant of faithful love, which is presented as established. Here, in strict grammar, the law-keeping is a condition of God's keeping his covenant of faithful love."

268. Tigay rightly clarifies: "Kadosh, usually translated 'holy,' here has a sense of its cognate in talmudic Hebrew, *mekudeshet*, 'betrothed,' which expresses the idea that when a man betroths a woman she becomes 'forbidden to others like something consecrated' (*Kid.* 2b)." He adds by way of explanation that this meaning is different from that in the book of Leviticus. Tigay, *Deuteronomy*, 86. The different sense of קדוש in this context as opposed to Leviticus is also underscored by Weinfeld, who points out that Deut 7:6-11 is "expressly Deuteronomic." Weinfeld, *Deuteronomy 1–11*, 382.

from "love" in other places in the OT, and most notably in Hosea.[270] He therefore searched outside the OT for any parallels he might find with the concept of "love" in Deuteronomy, and found them in the "political life of the ancient Near East."[271] Moshe Weinfeld explains this politically nuanced concept of "love" as follows:

> Political loyalty was generally expressed by the term "love." Thus, the king, demanding loyalty of his subjects: enjoins: "Love me as you love yourselves." Political loyalty tolerates no compromise. Hence the suzerain demands the vassal's love of heart and soul or whole-hearted love. Loving the king with one's entire heart signified the severance of all contact with other political powers: we find in the state treaties that the suzerain frequently warns the vassal not to transfer his allegiance to other kings nor to serve their wishes. This expression, then, which served a political need in the ancient Near East, came to serve a religious need in Israel.[272]

One can see this notion of "love" being fleshed out in Deuteronomy 7, where Israel is admonished to keep the law and sever any connection with the nations of the land and even put them under the "ban." Israel belongs "wholly" to YHWH, and its people are to love him by keeping his commandments. What is particularly striking and unexpected in Deuteronomy 7, however, is that in this chapter YHWH is said to "love" the people of Israel (Deut 7:7).[273] This "love" is both

---

269. See above, "Text and Translation of Deuteronomy 7," for a brief explanation of אהב in this context.
270. This point is made by William L. Moran when he draws a distinction between the concept of "love" in the book of Hosea and that in Deuteronomy. In contrast to Hosea, he says, "Love in Deuteronomy is a love that can be commanded. It is also a love intimately related to fear and reverence.Above all, it is a love which must be expressed in loyalty, in service, and in unqualified obedience to the demands of the Law.For to love God is, in answer to a unique claim (6,4), to be loyal to him (11,1.22; 30,20),to walk in his ways (10,12; 11,22; 19,9; 30,16), to keep his commandments (10,12; 11,1.22; 19,9), to do them (11,22; 19,9), to heed them or his voice (11,13; 30,16), to serve him (10,12; 11,1.13). It is, in brief, a love defined by and pledged in the covenant—a covenantal love." Moran, "The Ancient Near Eastern Background of Love of God in Deuteronomy," 78.
271. Weinfeld, *Deuteronomy and the Deuteronomic School*, 81.
272. Ibid.

affectionate and loyal.[274] In the matter of affection, Deuteronomy 7 reflects Hittite treaty forms over against Assyrian ones. Weinfeld explains: "In Hittite treaties and in the Israelite covenant, along with the demand for love and loyalty on the part of the vassal come expressions of affection from the side of the sovereign. The Assyrians, however, demand scrupulous love and loyalty from their vassals . . . but no sign of affection from their side is indicated anywhere."[275] In contrast to Hittite treaty forms, which speak only of the sovereign's love, Deuteronomy 7 also speaks of YHWH's loyalty. YHWH's "love" in the present is based on promises made beforehand, and his "love" in the future is conditioned on the prospect of Israel's obedience in the present (Deut 7:8, 12-13).

In light of all of this, what is one to make of the rhetorical message of Deuteronomy 7? *Ḥerem*, law, and love are central themes of the chapter. The main topic is how Israel is to place the nations in the "promised land" under the "ban," that is, *ḥerem*. This command is rooted in a more general requirement that Israel keep the Law, which in itself is a primary expression of loving YHWH. Love also binds YHWH into a relationship with Israel, thereby committing him to "keep" his promises and gracious covenant. Taking all this into consideration and returning to the opening discussion of entitling Deuteronomy 7, one might offer as a title for the chapter: "Israel and the Nations: *Ḥerem*, Law, and Love."

---

273. This is also underscored by the use of חשׁק in Deuteronomy 7:7. See above, "Text and Translation of Deuteronomy 7."
274. This goes against Weinfeld when he says: "The love of God towards Israel in Deuteronomy is certainly not loyalty, and although no connotation of conjugal love can be ascribed to it, it has without doubt the meaning of affectionate love." *Deuteronomy and the Deuteronomic School*, 368.
275. Ibid., 69. In light of this, Jacqueline Lapsley was right to point out that the idea of affection remains part of the Deuteronomic conception of love. Jacqueline E. Lapsley, "Feeling our Way: Love for God in Deuteronomy," *CBQ* 65 (2003): 350–69.

The Meaning of Deuteronomy 7 in Context

Deuteronomy 7 is one of the most disturbing chapters in all of the Old Testament. Particularly troubling is the notion of *ḥerem*. Concerted effort and patience are required in order to tease out what the author of Deuteronomy 7 was actually trying to communicate when he mentioned *ḥerem*. The following section will evaluate the meaning of *ḥerem* in its context, with special attention to the literary and historical backgrounds.

We have already affirmed, on the basis of scholars' findings, that Deuteronomy 7 builds on earlier material. Exodus 23:20-33; 34:11-16 form the basis for the composition of Deuteronomy 7.[276] In particular, there are numerous verbal and structural parallels between Exodus 23 and Deuteronomy 7.[277] Some of the verbal correspondences between the two texts can be seen here:[278]

Exod 23:20, 23	Deut 7:1
Exod 23:22	Deut 7:2
Exod 23:24	Deut 7:5
Exod 23:25	Deut 7:12-13, 15
Exod 23:26	Deut 7:14
Exod 23:27	Deut 7:23
Exod 23:28	Deut 7:20
Exod 23:29-30	Deut 7:22
Exod 23:33	Deut 7:26

---

276. See above, "The Traditions of Deuteronomy 7."
277. In particular see Lohfink, *Hauptgebot*, 172–76; Weinfeld, *Deuteronomy 1–11*, 380–82.
278. Cf. Michael Fishbane, *Biblical Interpretation in Ancient Israel* (Oxford: Clarendon Press, 1985), 201.

However, what is even more striking than the similarity between the two passages is their differences,[279] and the concept of *ḥerem* in Deuteronomy is perhaps the most arresting of them all.[280] Whereas in Exodus the command is "merely" to expel the Canaanites, in Deuteronomy Israel is told to place them under the "ban," that is, to destroy them utterly (Exod 23:20-33; 34:11-16; Deut 7:2; 20:16-17). As Weinfeld points out, "[T]he *ḥerem* of the Canaanites in Deuteronomy is an *a priori* decree, not dependent on any vow or oath. . . ."[281] In addition, the command extends to the "inhabitants of a whole land, whether engaged in war or not."[282]

One immediately notices that there is an increased rigidity in the command.[283] Also, Deuteronomy 7 is more severe than Deuteronomy 20, which allows *connubium* or intermarriage.[284] What is one to make of this? Weinfeld argues: "The farther we move away from the historical situation the more rigid a picture appears, which shows the laws gradually became idealized and unrealistic."[285] The command, Weinfeld contends, is actually a utopian ideal.[286]

It should be noted that Weinfeld's theory is not the only one. The *ḥerem* command is seen by some scholars as a "metaphor for religious fidelity,"[287] "sabre-rattling,"[288] an aspect of a "cultic drama,"[289]

---

279. Ibid., 201.
280. Another key difference has to do with the "matter of intermediaries." Fishbane, *Biblical Interpretation*, 202; Weinfeld, *Deuteronomy 1–11*, 383.
281. Ibid., 365.
282. Weinfeld, *Deuteronomy and the Deuteronomic School*, 167.
283. Moshe Weinfeld, "The Ban on the Canaanites in the Biblical Codes," 142–60 in *History and Traditions of Early Israel: Studies Presented to Eduard Nielsen*, ed. André Lemaire and Benedikt Otzen (Leiden: Brill, 1993), at 159.
284. Welch, *Deuteronomy: The Framework to the Code*, 75. The reason for this difference could be, as Welch writes, that "the one is religious theory: the other is practical legislation." Ibid., 77.
285. Weinfeld, "The Ban on the Canaanites," 159.
286. Ibid., 160.
287. W. L. Moberly, "Toward an Interpretation of the Shema," 124–44 in *Theological Exegesis: Essays in Honor of Brevard S. Childs*, eds. Christopher Seitz and Kathryn Greene-McCreight (Grand Rapids: Eerdmans, 1999), at 135. Cf. Nathan McDonald, *Deuteronomy and the Meaning of Monotheism*, FAT 2/1 (Tübingen: Mohr Siebeck, 2003), 109.

"anachronistic,"[290] and even a "culture map."[291] In light of the plethora of opinions, how should one understand the ḥerem command in Deuteronomy 7? The best way to read it is in light of its historical context and, as previously discussed, the most convincing timeframe for the origin of Deuteronomy's composition was sometime during the period encompassing the reigns of Hezekiah and Josiah.[292]

In light of this context, we may say that the ḥerem command in Deuteronomy 7 was never intended to be obeyed literally. It was a "utopian" ideal, or better yet, a "kind of moral armament and strengthening of the population of Judah, who had grown timid and aimless after a century of Assyrian domination."[293] There was historic precedent for such rhetoric.[294] As Norbert Lohfink points out, "We know that Assyrian propaganda of that period worked deliberately and massively to instill in the people a sense of fear and anxiety in face of the military power of Assyria and its god. The conquest stories in DtrL act as a counter-propaganda. The even more dreadful terror of the God of the entire world, who is on Israel's side, is narratively described."[295]

Despite the suitability of the above setting, Deuteronomy 7 should not *just* be read as "counter-propaganda" or a "utopian" ideal. More

---

288. Norbert Lohfink, "The Strata of the Pentateuch and the Question of War," 173–226 in idem, *Theology of the Pentateuch: Themes of the Priestly Narrative and Deuteronomy*, trans. Linda M. Maloney (Minneapolis: Fortress Press, 1994), at 193.
289. Christensen, *Deuteronomy 1:1–21:9*, cx–cxii, 157, 166.
290. Richard D. Nelson says that the "text is not really about a long-past conquest but the situation of its contemporary (7th c. BCE) readers. The conquest is a distant memory. The real issue is a contemporary alien presence and ideology that threatens Israel's orthodoxy." Nelson, "Divine Warrior Theology in Deuteronomy," 241–60 in *A God So Near: Essays on Old Testament Theology in Honor of Patrick D. Miller*, ed. Brent A Strawn and Nancy R. Bowen (Winona Lake: Eisenbrauns, 2003), at 243.
291. Richard D. Nelson, "Ḥerem and the Deuteronomic Social Conscience."
292. Cf. "An Analysis of Deuteronomy's Origins," above.
293. Lohfink, "The Strata of the Pentateuch and the Question of War," 194.
294. Cf. The Mesha inscription, or Moabite Stone, which also used the term ḥerem to refer to some of the military campaigns of King Mesha.
295. Lohfink, "The Strata of the Pentateuch and the Question of War," 194.

should be made of the political and religious climate between the reigns of Hezekiah and Josiah. It was, after all, a period of political and religious "renascence."[296] One of the chief causes of this "revival," besides the speedy decline of the Assyrian Empire, was the influx of people from the Northern Kingdom into Judah in the wake of the fall of Samaria in 722 BCE.[297] As Weinfeld points out, the period was one of "great expansion"; efforts were being made to "draw the northern population toward Jerusalem," and it seems to have been a time of political and religious reconciliation as the "hatred between Judah and Israel vanished, and some kind of symbiosis between the sister nations was established."[298] This climate undoubtedly informed the religious literature of the time.

Much is often made of the fact that the "nationalistic and patriotic atmosphere prevailing in Deuteronomy and Deuteronomic literature" stems from this period.[299] More, however, should be made of the unprecedented reconciliation of traditions that took place during this time. Even Clements, who favors a post-586 BCE origin for Deuteronomy, writes:

> It would, then, be more likely that Deuteronomy was a literary product of a movement which set great store by this notion of Israel's unity. It is this passionate concern with the nation's oneness as the people of God that stands out in the book's teaching more than any demonstrable indication that it was distinctively favourable to Ephraimite traditions.[300]

It is this last point that has not been kept in mind by scholars when they have examined Deuteronomy 7. If Deuteronomy was composed sometime during the reigns of Hezekiah and Josiah it is reasonable

---

296. Weinfeld, *Deuteronomy 1–11*, 50.
297. Weinfeld also refers to this period as a time of "national revival" in "The Ban on the Canaanites," 159.
298. Weinfeld, *Deuteronomy 1–11*, 50–51.
299. Ibid., 51.
300. Clements, *Deuteronomy*, 83.

to assume that it not only contains "nationalistic" and "patriotic" themes but also "reconciliatory" ones as well. Read in this light, Deuteronomy 7 and its themes of ḥerem, law, and love could also be seen as a call for political and religious unity.[301] Even ḥerem, the most violent theme of all, could be read as a command to put past political and religious identity behind and unite together as one עם־קדוש (Deut 7:6).

If ḥerem is understood in this way it is possible to read Deuteronomy 7 in a positive light, for it had a role in bringing two disparate communities together with the purpose of uniting them politically and religiously (Deut 7:6; 12:1). It provided them with "moral armament" and a "utopian ideal," and the context made it clear that ḥerem was not to be carried out as prescribed. It is true, however, that if Deuteronomy 7 was composed sometime during the reigns of Hezekiah and Josiah it may have provided grounds for military action.[302] After all, there is literary and archaeological evidence of military activity and territorial expansion during the reign of Josiah.[303] This will undoubtedly trouble Palestinian Christians, but as Lohfink seeks to reassure, "since everything is written in such a way that it can no longer be seen as giving directions for present action, these present-day Israelites need not be afraid that circumstances will arise in which they will be called upon to perform such slaughters and bloodbaths."[304]

---

301. Proof of this can be seen in the variety of traditions incorporated into Deuteronomy 7. As noted above, both northern (Gilgal and Shechem) and Deuteronomic traditions make up the chapter.
302. Lohfink, "The Strata of the Pentateuch and the Question of War," 192–93.
303. Weinfeld, *Deuteronomy 1–11*, 65–69.
304. Lohfink, "The Strata of the Pentateuch and the Question of War," 194. By painting ḥerem in a positive light this author is not trying to "defend the indefensible." The words of R. W. L. Moberly are very appropriate in this regard: "something may cease to be 'literally' practiced [or, as in the present case, never have been practiced at all] and yet may retain, or even freshly acquire, considerable significance as a metaphor for religious thought and behavior.... Although to the unsympathetic this may seem simply like an attempt to defend the indefensible and a refusal to admit error and break with it (and this may, of course, sometimes be the case), it is at heart a confidence in the intrinsic wealth of resource within the existing tradition that

If Deuteronomy 7 had the message and meaning we have described in the foregoing context, it quickly changed with subsequent scribal activity.[305] As illustrated in the chart below, the composition of the book of Deuteronomy went through at least three stages.[306]

The Message and Meaning of Deuteronomy 7 in Context[307]

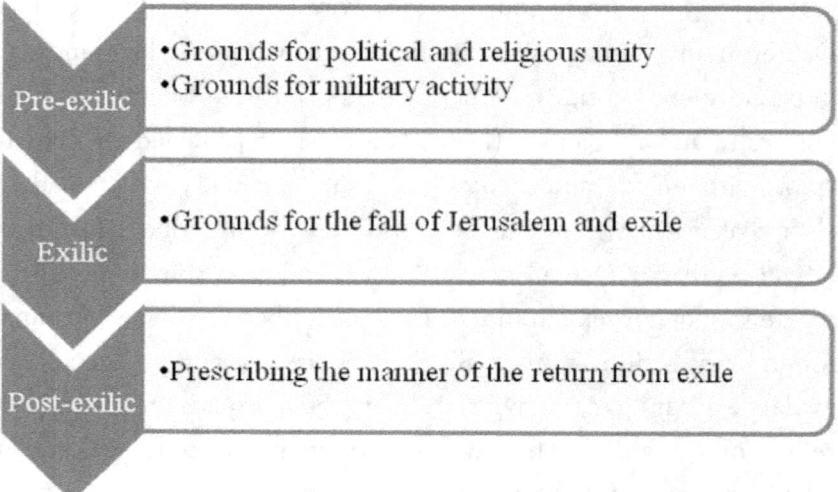

As Deuteronomy was "revised" and "expanded" with each stage, the message and meaning of Deuteronomy 7 were correspondingly altered. This can be shown by comparing the pre-exilic meaning of

---

enables renewed vitality through fresh reconfiguration and reappropriation of elements already present. The validity of any such enterprise can hardly be appraised in isolation from the actual practices in life that it encourages and enables." Moberly, "Toward an Interpretation of the Shema," 136.

305. Cf. Karel van der Toorn, *Scribal Culture and the Making of the Hebrew Bible* (Cambridge, MA: Harvard University Press, 2007).

306. This is in contrast to van der Toorn, who argues that Deuteronomy is the "end product of more than 200 years of scribal activity" in which there is evidence of four "successive editions." He calls these editions the Covenant Edition, the Torah Edition, the History Edition, and the Wisdom Edition. Ibid., 143–72.

307. This chart is this author's own rendition of the scribal activity in Deuteronomy and its significance for the meaning of Deuteronomy 7.

Deuteronomy 7 with what was communicated in the exilic and post-exilic editions of Deuteronomy.

It was Martin Noth who proposed the theory that the books Deuteronomy, Joshua, Judges, 1 and 2 Samuel, and 1 and 2 Kings "comprise a single literary unit alongside the other two great historical works in the Hebrew Bible—the Tetrateuch (Genesis through Numbers) and the Chronicles complex (1–2 Chronicles and Ezra-Nehemiah)."[308] Although originally independent, Deuteronomy was incorporated along with other traditions in order to form a single "historical narrative" stretching from Deuteronomy through Kings.[309] This was done by an anonymous individual living in Palestine in the middle of the sixth century BCE.[310] Noth refers to this person as the "Deuteronomistic" author/editor because "his language and way of thinking closely resemble those found in the Deuteronomic Law and in the admonitory speeches which precede and follow the Law."[311]

What is especially significant for the present discussion is the purpose for which Deuteronomy was included in this narrative and the bearing it has on the message and meaning of Deuteronomy 7. Noth argued that the form of Deuteronomy that Dtr. incorporated into his history was Deuteronomy 4:44–30:20.[312] Therefore Deuteronomy 1–3(4) does not introduce the Deuteronomic law but the beginning of the Deuteronomistic History (DtrH). By setting the Deuteronomic law at the outset of DtrH the author of DtrH

---

308. Steven L. McKenzie, "Deuteronomistic History," *ABD* 2:160.
309. For the way Noth believed this traditional material was incorporated into the narrative see his *The Deuteronomistic History*, 84–88.
310. Noth argues that the story of Jehoiachin's release from prison in 2 Kgs 25:27-30 in the year 562 BCE provides a "definite *terminus a quo* for the date of Dtr.'s work." He maintains: "We have no reason to put Dtr. much later than this *terminus a quo*." Noth, *The Deuteronomistic History*, 12. For who Noth thought this author was and from where he wrote, see ibid., 99.
311. Noth, *The Deuteronomistic History*, 4.
312. Ibid., 16.

(Dtr.)³¹³ intended to "show them [his contemporaries in Babylonian exile] that their sufferings were the fully deserved consequences of centuries of decline in Israel's loyalty to Yahweh. This loyalty was measured in terms of Israel's obedience to the Deuteronomic law."³¹⁴ As Noth puts it, Dtr. "constructed his history" in such a way as to show that these "early events committed the people to unbroken loyalty to God as manifested in observance of the law. . . ."³¹⁵ The end result was to "teach the true meaning of the history of Israel from the occupation to the destruction of the old order," namely, that "God was recognisably at work in this history, continuously meeting the accelerating moral decline with warnings and punishments and, finally, when these proved fruitless, with total annihilation."³¹⁶ Israel was, therefore, responsible for its own demise.³¹⁷

The meaning of Deuteronomy 7, therefore, changes when read in light of its placement in DtrH. Instead of understanding the chapter as a means of encouraging political and religious unity and the possibility of "arming" the people with courage and grounds for military activity, Deuteronomy 7 is used in the exilic context as a means of illustrating the reason for the fall of Jerusalem, the

---

313. This is Noth's preferred abbreviation for the author of DtrH. Ibid., 4, 100–1.
314. McKenzie, "Deuteronomistic History," 2:161.
315. Noth, *The Deuteronomistic History*, 91.
316. Ibid., 89.
317. This author agrees with Hans Walter Wolff's critique of Noth that the purpose of DtrH is not completely negative and written without offering any hope to those in Babylonian exile. Wolff argues that in DtrH, and especially in Judges, one notices a "pattern of apostasy, punishment, repentance, and deliverance. . . ." The intention was to "show the exiles that they were in the second stage of that cycle and therefore needed to cry out to Yahweh in repentance." McKenzie, "Deuteronomistic History," 2:161. In Wolff's words, "To cry to Yahweh—this caused the reversal which followed upon both accomplished apostasy and the burning anger of Yahweh—who had, before, carried out his judgment by handing the people over to their enemies." Hans Walter Wolff, "The Kerygma of the Deuteronomic Historical Work," 83–100 in *The Vitality of OT Traditions*, ed. Walter Brueggemann and Hans Walter Wolff (2d ed. Atlanta: John Knox Press, 1982), at 87. Noth contends that the negativity and finality conveyed in DtrH is because of the time in which Dtr. wrote, namely, the early part of the exile when there was little to no hope of return imagined or expected. Noth, *The Deuteronomistic History*, 98.

destruction of the Temple, and the subsequent exile of its populace in 586 BCE. According to DtrH the reason why Israel is now in Babylonian exile is that, among other things, it failed to put the nations to *ḥerem* and worship YHWH alone (Deut 7:1-5, 25-26). In this context *ḥerem* is not a command to be obeyed but an illustration of failure in a historical narrative.

The meaning of Deuteronomy 7 is also different in the final edition of Deuteronomy. Noth argued that the basic core of Deuteronomy, or *UrDeuteronomium*, was Deuteronomy 4:44–30:20. It was these chapters that Dtr. incorporated into DtrH. However, there is good reason to suggest that Deuteronomy 4 and the opening verses of Deuteronomy 30 are not pre-exilic, but are of late exilic or post-exilic origin.[318] The significance of this should not go unnoticed, for, as Georg Braulik demonstrates, Deuteronomy 30 noticeably alters the meaning of Deuteronomy 7. When Deuteronomy 30 is compared with Deuteronomy 7 some important differences emerge, as can be seen in the following chart:[319]

---

318. Cf. Van der Toorn, *Scribal Culture*, 162–64; Wolff, "The Kerygma of the Deuteronomic Historical Work," 93–97; Weinfeld, *Deuteronomy 1–11*, 214–17. For an overview of recent views on the authorship and redaction of DtrH see McKenzie, "Deuteronomic History," 160–67.
319. Georg Braulik, "Die Völkervernichtung und die Rückkehr Israels ins Verheissungsland: Hermeneutische Bemerkungen zum Buch Deuteronomium," 3–38 in *Deuteronomy and Deuteronomic Literature: Festschrift C. H. W. Brekelmans*, ed. Marc Vervenne and Johan Lust (Leuven: Leuven University Press, 1997), at 35. For an abbreviated translation of this article see Georg Braulik, "The Destruction of the Nations and the Promise of Return: Hermeneutical Observations on the Book of Deuteronomy," *Verbum et Ecclesia* 25 (2004): 46–67.

Deuteronomy 30:5	Deuteronomy 7:1
a וֶהֱבִיאֲךָ יְהוָה אֱלֹהֶיךָ אֶל־הָאָרֶץ	a כִּי יְבִיאֲךָ יְהוָה אֱלֹהֶיךָ אֶל־הָאָרֶץ
אֲשֶׁר־יָרְשׁוּ אֲבֹתֶיךָ	אֲשֶׁר־אַתָּה בָא־שָׁמָּה
וִירִשְׁתָּהּ	לְרִשְׁתָּהּ
b וְהֵיטִבְךָ	
וְהִרְבְּךָ מֵאֲבֹתֶיךָ	b וְנָשַׁל גּוֹיִם־רַבִּים מִפָּנֶיךָ...

Through what Braulik calls the "technique of zero-statement" the author of Deuteronomy 30 clarifies how Deuteronomy 7 should be interpreted and prescribes the manner in which the return from exile should take place.[320] In Deuteronomy 30, a chapter written in the context of returning home from exile, there is no mention of *ḥerem*. There is no call to destroy the inhabitants of the land. As Braulik illustrates in point "a," ירשׁ (qal) is used in Deuteronomy 30:5 in a "non-military way" that he says "can be compared to the redistribution of the land in a fallow year."[321] What is more, there is not any mention of the nations enumerated in the opening verses of Deuteronomy 7. This can be seen in point "b," where Deuteronomy 7:1 speaks of driving out nations "more numerous than you" while Deuteronomy 30:5 speaks of God making the people returning from exile "more numerous than your fathers."[322]

The significance of this for the meaning of Deuteronomy 7 is clear. The author(s) of Deuteronomy 30 clarify and emphasize in their final post-exilic edition of Deuteronomy that the return from exile is not to follow the prescriptions made in Deuteronomy 7. As Braulik concludes, "The resettling of Israel's fatherland will take place without any violent actions. Under no circumstances will the [*ḥerem*] command against the non-Israelites living in that land be valid any

---

320. Ibid., 59.
321. Ibid., 63.
322. Ibid.

more on return from the Babylonian exile, and neither does it apply to a new settlement at any later stage."[323]

In conclusion, we note a definite change in the meaning of Deuteronomy 7 with each stage in Deuteronomy's composition. In the pre-exilic edition of Deuteronomy, chapter 7 hoped to procure political and religious unity and in a measured manner justify military activity, albeit not in the way literally prescribed in the chapter. In the exilic edition of Deuteronomy, which was incorporated into DtrH, the *ḥerem* command provided an example of the reasons why Jerusalem fell in 586 BCE and its people were in Babylonian exile. In the final edition of Deuteronomy the scribes, who wrote either at the end of the exile or the beginning of the return, wanted to encourage the people about the possibility of returning to the land, but they clarified in their writing of Deuteronomy 30 that the return to the Land should not follow the manner prescribed for entry to it in Deuteronomy 7. As our Conclusion will summarize, this analysis of Deuteronomy 7 is of utmost significance for Palestinian Christians and their reading and understanding of the Old Testament.

---

323. Ibid., 65.

Conclusion

> A text purporting to contain knowledge about something actual . . . is not easily dismissed. Expertise is attributed to it. The authority of academics, institutions, and governments can accrue to it, surrounding it with still greater prestige than its practical successes warrant. Most important, such texts can *create* not only knowledge but also the very reality they appear to describe. In time such knowledge and reality produce a tradition, or what Michel Foucault calls a discourse, whose material presence or weight, not the originality of a given author, is really responsible for the texts produced out of it.[1]

Keith Whitelam quotes this text from Edward Said in his effort to compare the meager attention Palestinian history has received with the scholarly interest in what he calls the "invention of 'ancient Israel.'" Taking his lead from Philip Davies,[2] who argues that "ancient Israel" never really existed but is a politically motivated "literary construct" that only wears the garb of history, Whitelam writes: "We are faced with the paradox of the invention of 'ancient Israel' . . . an entity that has been *given substance* and *power* as a scholarly construct, while Palestinian history *lacks substance* or even existence in terms of our academic institutions."[3] As a result, Whitelam concludes,

---

1. Edward Said, *Orientalism* (London: Penguin, 2003), 94, in Keith Whitelam, *The Invention of Ancient Israel: The Silencing of Palestinian History* (London: Routledge, 1996), 3-4.
2. Philip Davies, *In Search of Ancient Israel* (London: Sheffield Academic Press, 1992).
3. Whitelam, *Invention of Ancient Israel*, 4. Emphasis added.

"Attempts to challenge this powerful narrative are likely to be dismissed as politically or ideologically motivated and therefore unreasonable."[4]

Eighteen years later, the tide has certainly turned. Scholarly interests and sensitivities have shifted. Palestinian voices are being heard, their texts are being read, and their message has created a tradition of definite "material presence and weight." Melanie May's latest book, *Jerusalem Testament: Palestinian Christians Speak, 1988–2008*, substantiates this point.[5] It is a collection of statements by the Jerusalem Heads of Churches over the last twenty years that "bear a common witness to their faith and to their hope: an end to occupation and a just peace."[6] The impression given by the title, however, is that this is not *just* a collection of statements. May writes of why she has called her book "Jerusalem Testament":

> I have named this body of texts "Jerusalem Testament" because first and foremost these statements by the Jerusalem Heads of Churches bear witness. . . . This body of texts is also a testament because it calls . . . all Christians in all places . . . to a new covenant with sisters and brothers in the Holy City, Jerusalem, who live under the more and more dangerously deteriorated conditions of Israeli occupation and dispossession."[7]

The canon-like authority allotted to the Palestinian Christian message is hard to miss. May's title unquestionably gives an added "weight" and "material presence" to the collection. It is the Jerusalem "Testament" and, as Keith Whitelam wrote, "attempts to challenge this powerful narrative are likely to be dismissed as politically or ideologically motivated and therefore unreasonable."[8]

---

4. Ibid.
5. Melanie May, *Jerusalem Testament: Palestinian Christians Speak, 1988–2008* (Grand Rapids: Eerdmans, 2010).
6. Ibid., 1.
7. Ibid., 2.

CONCLUSION

It is not being argued here that attention directed toward Palestinians, and Palestinian Christians in particular, is unmerited. This book stands on the assumption and credible conviction that the foundation of the state of Israel in 1948 was both a physical *and* spiritual "catastrophe" for Palestinian Christians and that for many of them their view and use of the Old Testament has been "adversely affected."[9] Nevertheless, a Palestinian Christian "tradition" has emerged in recent years, so much so that the attempt of biblical, historical, and theological scholars and students to approach the text of the Old Testament impartially, or at least with a mind attentive to the whole multiplicity of communities and contexts involved, has been deemed unwarranted and in some cases devious and sinful.[10] I do not want the biblical text to be used as a "blunt instrument in the oppression of people."[11] I simply believe that any solution to the problem of Palestinian Christians and the Old Testament must consider all the manifold contexts involved. The present work makes a start at doing just that. The following sections will summarize the findings of each of the foregoing chapters, critically review the claims made in chapters 1–5 in light of my own hermeneutic in chapter 6, and then propose a way forward for Palestinian Christians and the Old Testament that is faithful to both the biblical text and the respective communities and contexts.

---

8. For the original context of Whitelam's statement *Invention of Ancient Israel*, 4.
9. Naim Ateek, *Justice, and Only Justice: A Palestinian Theology of Liberation* (Maryknoll, NY: Orbis Books, 2002), 77. Cf. Mitri Raheb, *I am a Palestinian Christian* (Minneapolis: Fortress Press, 1995), 56.
10. Cf. Michael Prior, *The Bible and Colonialism: A Moral Critique* (Sheffield: Sheffield Academic Press, 1997), 295–96.
11. Michael Prior, "The Moral Problems of the Land Traditions of the Bible," 41–81 in *Western Scholarship and the History of Palestine*, ed. idem (London: Melisende, 1998), at 80.

Summary

Palestinian Christians and the Old Testament: A Critical Review

Hermeneutics

Part I described the basic elements of contemporary Palestinian Christian hermeneutics of the Old Testament. As chapter 1 made plain, PCHOT is not just an issue of hermeneutics in general, although the "art of understanding" is foundational to its topic. Neither is it just a question of how to interpret the Old Testament, although knowledge and use of the various methods of biblical interpretation are essential. Moreover, it is not just an issue of how a Christian should interpret the Old Testament, although this topic is important enough to merit its own discussion. PCHOT is significantly modified and informed by its *Arab* modifier and *Palestinian* context. The Palestinian Christian context and interpretation of the Old Testament, however, is by no means uniform. Naim Ateek, Mitri Raheb, Naim Khoury, Yohanna Katanacho, Michel Sabbah, and Atallah Hanna all approach and read the Old Testament differently. They have interpreted the Old Testament in unique fashion according to their different self-understandings and traditions. Nevertheless, with the possible exception of Naim Khoury, they are in marked agreement about the core issues they face as Palestinian Christians, centering on the topics of people, land, and dispossession. What is more, these are all interpreted in the negative. As Mitri Raheb says: "The Bible I had heretofore considered to be 'for us' had suddenly become 'against us.'" Just so, most contemporary Palestinian Christians read the Old Testament as a people not loved/not elected, in a land promised to another, and as a people dispossessed (with the prospect of future dispossession) under divine sanction.[12]

History

Part II investigated the degree to which Palestinian Christianity and the way it reads the Old Testament have actually changed over the years. Chapter 2 looked at the years before 1917 (during the dawn of Zionism), chapter 3 at those between 1917 and 1948 (during the British Mandate), and chapter 4 at those following 1948 (in light of the so-called "catastrophe" of the foundation of the modern state of Israel). In chapter 2 the thoughts of Chalil Jamal, Seraphim Boutaji, and Michael Kawar were discussed. These three individuals adopted the methods and beliefs of the Protestant missionaries unreservedly and had no difficulty reading the Old Testament. If there was any problem with the text it was that Eastern Christians in Palestine were neglecting the truths of its teachings. The Old Testament was taken "at its word," and there was an aversion to any suggestion that its readers should adopt the methods of critical scholarship, which were beginning to appear at the time. With regard to Judaism and the "preservation of Jews as a separate people," there is marked silence.[13] Nevertheless, enough has been recorded to conclude that Palestinian Christians accepted the tenets of their predecessors, namely, that whereas the Jews were subject to "suffering and dispersion" on account of their rejection of Jesus as their Messiah, the Christian nations, such as England and Prussia, were experiencing blessing and increase on account of their belief in Christ. There was an overwhelming tendency on the part of Palestinian Christians before 1917 to accept the views of the Old Testament and Judaism conveyed by the religious tradition(s) of which they were a part.

Although the political and religious climate changed drastically between 1917 and 1948, chapter 3 showed that the burgeoning

---

12. Raheb, *I am a Palestinian Christian*, 56.
13. See Benjamin Elliot Nicholls, *Help to the Reading of the Bible* (London: SPCK, 1853), 28.

Palestinian Protestant Christian community continued to read the Old Testament in accordance with their respective traditions as before, sometimes highlighting it as a means to buttress their Arab/Palestinian identity as well. There are hints of this in the PNCC's refusal to acknowledge the authority of the Anglican bishop in Jerusalem and the various "Protestant Evenings" coordinated by Arab Lutherans, Hanna Bachut, and Schedid Baz Haddad. It is true that many were starting to believe that the Old Testament was being "abused" and "misinterpreted." However, confidence in the Old Testament itself and the way it had been read for generations persisted in the respective Protestant traditions in Palestine for much of the British Mandate, although one notices an increasing ambivalence toward those traditions near the end of the Mandate. This is readily apparent in the PNCC's memorandum to the Archbishop of Canterbury in 1936. This mounting tension would reach a breaking point in 1948.

As chapter 4 illustrated, the foundation of the state of Israel in 1948 brought about a clear crisis or "catastrophe" for Palestinian Christians and their reading of the Old Testament. Almost immediately after 1948, Palestinian Christians began to abandon liturgical and biblical texts that mentioned Israel or the promise of land to Abraham and his descendants. It was not without reason, therefore, that many noted with apprehension that Palestinian Christians were in danger of becoming Marcionite in their use (or non-use) and reading of the Old Testament. It is not until shortly after the Six Day War that one detects a move beyond a naïve censoring of the Old Testament toward developing a nuanced hermeneutic faithful to both the text of the Old Testament and the Palestinian context. The Old Testament continued to be problematic for Palestinian Christians, but there was at least a concerted effort to fight past the impasse of not using the text at all. Unfortunately, this effort proved unsuccessful, or at least unsatisfactory, because after 1982 discussions of biblical interpretation were largely abandoned in favor of asking local existential questions of identity, presence, and witness. "The direction [or method of interpreting and applying Scripture] was no longer from Scripture to situation, but rather the other way around, from situation to Scripture."[14] This is not to say that questions of hermeneutics and biblical interpretation fell completely by the wayside, but new proposals, as Gräbe notes, were framed in such a way as to establish an "*ortsgebundene Exegese*," or "localized exegesis" of the biblical text. Although contemporary Palestinian Christians offer various suggestions for reading the Old Testament, as chapter 2 pointed out, they have seldom deviated from this governing proviso.

Ideology

It may have seemed rather presumptuous of me to include a third section in this book. It is at minimum contentious, for many would argue that the present work should stop short of being prescriptive, focus on the descriptive elements, as chapters 1–4 have done, and let Palestinian Christians get on with interpreting the Old Testament as they please. Unfortunately, this is insufficient. A number of proposals have been put forward recently for how a Palestinian Christian might read the Old Testament. They are all ideologically driven. These needed to be addressed, and not written off without critical consideration. Chapter 5 thus itemized a cross-section of these perspectives, detailing Michael Prior's "Reading with the Eyes of the Canaanite," Charles Miller's "Reading with the Eyes of Tradition," and Gershon Nerel's "Reading with the Eyes of Jewish-Christian *fraternité*." Building on the strengths and weaknesses of these

---

14. (*Der Weg führt nicht mehr von der Schrift zur Situation, sondern umgekehrt von der Situation in die Schrift hinein.*) Uwe Gräbe, *Kontextuelle palästinensische Theologie: Streitbare und umstrittene Beiträge zum ökumenischen und interreligiösen Gespräch* (Geneva: Erlanger Verlag, 1999), 119.

proposals and the development of PCHOT, chapter 6 articulated my own hermeneutic for the Palestinian Christian community and illustrated it by providing an in-depth analysis of Deuteronomy 7. What remains to be seen is how this proposal measures up against the claims of those in chapters 1–5.

Palestinian Christians and the Old Testament: A Critical Review

A Palestinian Christian hermeneutic of the Old Testament must begin with hermeneutics and an effort to understand a given text in its own words and context. It is for this reason that the previous chapter spent so much time examining Deuteronomy 7. Using the tools of the historical-critical method, I elicited insights pertinent to the future of a Palestinian Christian reading of the Old Testament. To confirm this, the following section will revisit the approaches of Palestinian Christians past and present as well as the proposals of Prior, Miller, and Nerel, critique them in light of my own hermeneutic and findings in Deuteronomy 7, and then highlight the future prospects for a Palestinian Christian reading of the Old Testament.

Palestinian Christians and the Old Testament: Past and Present

Palestinian Christians and the Old Testament: Before 1948

Before 1948, Palestinian Christians adopted the beliefs and interpretive practices of their respective religious traditions. This was particularly striking within the burgeoning Palestinian Protestant community, who assumed the Evangelical beliefs and methods of biblical interpretation from their respective traditions without reserve. They followed the basic Protestant principles, *sola scriptura* (Scripture alone) and *scriptura sui ipsius interpres* (Scripture is its own interpreter). There was no need for tradition to arbitrate the meaning of a biblical text; the meaning was contained within the pages of the Old and New Testaments. Furthermore, Scripture was seen as a unity, capable of interpreting itself. What these early Palestinian Protestant Christians and their forebears never accepted, however, was the historical conditionality of these texts and the corresponding need to adopt some of the critical methods of interpretation emerging in Europe at the time. Therefore, despite the praiseworthiness and resilience of these early Palestinian Protestant Christians, their method of interpreting the Old Testament could not be a source to help contemporary Palestinian Christians read problematic Old Testament texts such as Deuteronomy 7.

Palestinian Christians and the Old Testament: Since 1948

As indicated above, Palestinian Christian hermeneutics of the Old Testament went through roughly four stages after 1948. There was the initial crisis following the foundation of the modern state of Israel and the corresponding aversion to using liturgical and biblical texts that mentioned the name "Israel." This lasted for nearly a generation. After the Six Day War one notices an effort to address the crisis and look into matters of biblical interpretation. However, it was an unfortunate consequence of the increase in localized ecumenical activity and interpretation programs that were "shaped and led by the Churches and people within the Middle East" that Western models of biblical interpretation were too quickly disregarded.[15] Although it is understandable that this was a necessary stage in the development of Palestinian Christian identity and hermeneutics, the end result was that there was a delay in the appropriation of critical models of interpretation. This tendency has continued for the most part to the

---

15. Larry Ekin, *Enduring Witness* (Geneva: World Council of Churches, 1985), 54. It is understandable that this reaction to took place in light of the struggle being waged by Palestinian Christians for ecclesiastical independence and the indigenization of their clergy.

present day, and it is because of this that so much has been made of the historical-critical method in the present work as a way forward for reading the Old Testament, including texts such as Deuteronomy 7.

Palestinian Christians and the Old Testament: Contemporary Examples

Despite Naim Ateek's effort to reestablish the Old Testament as a resource for the Palestinian Christian community, his hermeneutic could not elicit from Deuteronomy 7 the same results as my own. Ateek's insistence on reading the Old Testament as a Palestinian Christian and finding those Old Testament texts that most closely underscore his Palestinian theology of liberation meant that texts such as Deuteronomy 7 could not find a place in his *schema*. In addition, his use of models of interpretation employed by other liberation theologians, such as "correspondence of relationships" and "correspondence of terms," would preclude Palestinian Christians from reading and gleaning any benefit from the OT text.

Of the six Palestinian Christians whose hermeneutics were discussed, Mitri Raheb resembles this author most closely in his use of the historical-critical method, but with one exception. In his chapter on election Raheb writes:

> "Election" is and will always be a statement of faith; it is solely a promise. It is a promise to those, above all, who see themselves as unworthy, weak, and powerless. . . . It is to them that God promises election. Thus it is no wonder that most of the statements about election in the Old Testament date from the time of the exile. With the exception of the Psalms, most of the statements . . . occur in Deuteronomy and Isaiah. A promise is given to the scattered, the defeated, and the banished.[16]

---

16. Raheb, *I am a Palestinian Christian*, 65.

Raheb then cites Deuteronomy 7:7 as a prime example. However, as established in the previous chapter, Deuteronomy 7 was not written in exile but rather sometime between the reigns of Hezekiah and Josiah. This undercuts Raheb's argument and challenges him to address the fact that one of the key texts that speak about election was not originally addressed to the "scattered, the defeated, and the banished."[17] While Raheb's argument fails on this account, this author's analysis of Deuteronomy 7 acknowledges this reality and appropriately provides a way for Palestinian Christians to read the text.

Although Naim Khoury can be commended for his bravery in being sympathetic to the Jewish people and the foundation of the modern state of Israel, his reading of Scripture, and of the OT in particular, is not satisfactory to the majority of Palestinian Christians. The way he reads the Old Testament and applies Old Testament prophecy without regard to its original provenance is simply alarming in the present context. His reading of Deuteronomy 7 would probably cause additional harm to the Palestinian Christian community, and it would definitely not provide a means for Palestinian Christians to dialogue with Jews on the matter.[18]

Although the Evangelical tradition continues to include a minority of the Palestinian Christian community, it is publishing a disproportionate amount of material on the topic of Palestinian Christians and the Old Testament. This is in large part because of leaders such as Salim Munayer, Munther Isaac, and Yohanna Katanacho, the last of whose writings on the OT are among the most

---

17. Ibid.
18. It should be said that Khoury is not the sole Dispensational voice in Israel/Palestine. Individuals such as Tony Maalouf, although of Lebanese origin, have made a considerable effort to reconcile some of the tenets of Dispensational theology with Arab concerns. Cf. Tony Maalouf, *Arabs in the Shadow of Israel: The Unfolding of God's Prophetic Plan for Ishmael's Line* (Grand Rapids: Kregel, 2003).

commendable among Palestinian Christians.[19] Katanacho's work is largely credible. However, because of his Evangelical heritage he has a preference for synchronic rather than diachronic readings of the Old Testament.[20] This would prevent him from sharing my conclusions on Deuteronomy 7.

Michel Sabbah's hermeneutic of the Old Testament is commendable in many ways. He rightly insists on the value of the Old Testament for Palestinian Christians and Jews alike. He contends that "God's Word in the books of the Old Testament is addressed not only to Palestinian Christians and Jews, but also to every person and to every people. . . ."[21] The problem of the Old Testament, he goes on to insist, is not with the text itself but with its manipulation.[22] In order to guard against this, he writes, "The study and correct understanding of the Bible are done in the closest bond of union with the Church, in light of Tradition and scientific research, in order to reach an understanding of the revealed truths, in an overall and unified consideration of Revelation, in its entirety, regarding the whole Scripture from a Christological point of view."[23] Tradition does provide a guardrail against erroneous and sometimes heinous interpretations, and Sabbah is right to commend tradition as such.

---

19. See especially his recent article on Psalm 87. Yohanna Katanacho, "Jerusalem is the City of God: A Palestinian Reading of Psalm 87," 181–99 in *The Land Cries Out: Theology of the Land in the Israeli-Palestinian Context*, ed. Salim J. Munayer and Lisa Loden (Eugene, OR: Cascade Books, 2012). Cf. idem, *The Land of Christ: A Palestinian Cry* (Bethlehem: Bethlehem Bible College, 2012).
20. Yohanna Katanacho, "Approaches to the Bible," Paper presented at ICCJ–Kairos Consultation, Beit Jala, October 27, 2011, 2–4. This is characteristic of the vast majority of Evangelical scholarship. However, there are some Evangelicals advocating the use of the historical-critical method. It remains to be seen how soon, and how willingly, Evangelicals will accept these principles. Cf. Kenton L. Sparks, *God's Word in Human Words: An Evangelical Appropriation of Critical Biblical Scholarship* (Grand Rapids: Baker, 2008).
21. Michel Sabbah, pastoral letter "Reading the Bible Today in the Land of the Bible," in idem, *Faithful Witness: On Reconciliation and Peace in the Holy Land* (Hyde Park, NY: New City Press, 2009), 41, §36.
22. Ibid.
23. Ibid., 58, §61.

However, although he mentions the use of "scientific research," he does not cite any examples of its use, reference any encyclical, or mention any of the documents of the Pontifical Biblical Commission that commend its practice.[24] This is one of the key weaknesses in Sabbah's letter and one of the main reasons why I believe my own hermeneutic is more appropriate than Sabbah's for dealing with OT texts such as Deuteronomy 7.[25]

The Orthodox Church was largely responsible for influencing the direction of Palestinian Christian hermeneutics of the Old Testament and the resultant abandonment of Western models of biblical interpretation in the period following the Six Day War.[26] As seen in the section discussing Atallah Hanna and the Greek Orthodox Church, they continue to advocate the traditional Orthodox model of biblical interpretation and have therefore never appropriated any critical methods for interpreting the Old Testament.[27]

Perspectives of Prior, Miller, and Nerel

Michael Prior's "Reading with the Eyes of the Canaanite," Charles Miller's "Reading with the Eyes of Tradition," and Gershon Nerel's "Reading with the Eyes of Jewish-Christian *fraternité*" all have aspects worthy of consideration. Prior rightly emphasizes the danger that certain OT texts can engender. Nerel correctly perceives the "unfinished battle" of Jewish-Christian relations in Israel and

---

24. A possible reason for this could be that the PBC's *Interpretation of the Bible in the Church* was not published until 1993, the same year that Sabbah wrote his pastoral letter. One can only conjecture whether Sabbah's letter would have been different if he had been privy to the PBC document before he wrote his pastoral letter.
25. It should perhaps be repeated that Sabbah had wanted to write a sequel to his letter and to look at texts from either Deuteronomy or Joshua from a Palestinian Christian perspective. Unfortunately, that letter was never written. Conversation/Interview: Jamal Khader, "The Church in Palestine: Crisis and Challenge" (London: Heythrop College, June 24, 2009).
26. See in chap. 4, "Palestinian Christian Hermeneutics of the Old Testament between 1967 and 1975."
27. See in chap. 1, "Atallah Hanna: A Greek Orthodox Perspective."

Palestine and the need to address it. Miller, who puts forth the strongest case of the three, suggests that tradition, if properly understood and employed, can be both a safeguard against erroneous interpretations and a way forward for Palestinian Christians to read the Old Testament. In particular, he highlights the importance of the historical-critical method as one of the most important breakthroughs in Catholic tradition.

Despite the strengths of their arguments, the perspectives of Prior, Miller, and Nerel are all flawed. The weakness of Prior's perspective is that he wrongly bases his research on Philip R. Davies, Keith Whitelam, Thomas L. Thompson, and Niels Lemche *alone* when a substantial percentage of OT scholarship is not in agreement with them. Nevertheless, Prior holds them up as authorities and maintains that these texts are all ideologically driven and "inherently oppressive and morally reprehensible."[28] A naïve reading from a vantage point of some 2,600 years later and from the perspective of a Canaanite would undoubtedly lead one to question their suitability as sacred texts, but when understood in their proper context, many are not nearly as horrific as at first sight. They are in fact liberating and empowering both for Palestinian Christians and for the future of interreligious dialogue.

Nerel's fault lies in the fact that he does not seem to recognize the critical importance the foundation of the modern state of Israel had and continues to have for a Palestinian Christian reading of the OT. What Nerel perceives as solely a "De-Judaization of the Bible" is in fact an effort, albeit somewhat misinformed, to rescue the Old Testament for the Palestinian Christian community. Furthermore, he does not offer any practical suggestions as to how Palestinian

---

28. Prior, "A Moral Reading of the Bible in Jerusalem," 16–45 in *Jerusalem in Ancient History and Tradition*, ed. Thomas L. Thompson (Sheffield: Sheffield Academic Press, 2003), 27.

Christians might overcome their supposed "De-Judaization of the Bible," let alone read texts such as Deuteronomy 7.

In contrast to Prior's and Nerel's proposals, Miller is on the one hand sensitive to the difficulties Palestinian Christians have with the OT and on the other hand aware of the progress that has been made in Jewish-Christian relations. He is right to emphasize the importance of tradition, highlight the necessity of using the historical-critical method, and draw the reader's attention to four important documents from the Roman Catholic Church. However, he leaves one wondering about the respective authority of each document and how one might reconcile them with each other.[29]

Palestinian Christians and the Old Testament: Future Prospects

How, then, might Palestinian Christians approach the texts of the Old Testament that have proved so disturbing? What are the prospects for a new reading when the text is still read and interpreted in a way not dissimilar to what was highlighted at the beginning of this book, with Old Testament passages such as Deuteronomy 7 taken literally as an operations manual for relations in Israel and Palestine and Israeli Prime Ministers assassinated on the basis of their *rapprochement* with Palestinians and perceived transgression of the command to not make any treaty/covenant with the "inhabitants of the land?"[30] No one can predict or completely guard against the misappropriation or abuse of the Old Testament. Its reception history underscores this point with countless examples and, as seen above, this is lamentably true of Deuteronomy 7.[31] However, if a Palestinian

---

29. For one such proposal see Jamal Khader and David Neuhaus, "A Holy Land Context for *Nostra Aetate*," *SCJR* 1 (2005–2006): 67–88.
30. Cf. the Introduction above and Georg Braulik, "Die Völkervernichtung und die Rückkehr Israels ins Verheissungsland: Hermeneutische Bemerkungen zum Buch Deuteronomium," 3–38 in *Deuteronomy and Deuteronomic Literature: Festschrift C. H. W. Brekelmans*, ed. Marc Vervenne and Johan Lust (Leuven: Leuven University Press, 1997), 3.

Christian begins with hermeneutics, as suggested in the previous chapter, and commits to respecting the voice of a text by listening to it long enough, he or she will actually hear and understand what it was intended to communicate. Such a reader will learn, among other things, that *ḥerem* was not practiced in the way suggested in Deuteronomy 7 and therefore cannot serve as a type or model to be emulated. *ḥerem* was in fact used in Deuteronomy 7 as a call for political and religious unity, beckoning the people of Israel and Judah, the former recent immigrants to Jerusalem following the destruction of the Northern Kingdom in 722 BCE, to unite as one עַם־קָדוֹשׁ (Deut 7:6).[32] If the chapter did serve to justify military action in some way before the exile, it was nevertheless clear to its contemporary hearers that it did not *really* sanction the annihilation of the land's native inhabitants. To use the words of Norbert Lohfink, it was rather a kind of "moral armament."[33]

In addition, readers will have learned that the meaning of Deuteronomy 7 did not remain static. They will have caught a glimpse of a practice in which the school of scribes responsible for Deuteronomy's composition incorporated and revised political and religious traditions in accordance with the needs of the context. They did this with an eye primarily on the text[34] and then with an eye on the "other"[35] so that they composed a new text, in rather "innovative"

---

31. For some examples of the reception history of the OT with regard to violence and war see Susan Niditch, *War in the Hebrew Bible: A Study in the Ethics of Violence* (Oxford: Oxford University Press, 1993). I anticipate with interest the forthcoming Blackwell Bible Commentary volume: Jonathon Campbell, *Deuteronomy*, BBC 5 (Oxford: Blackwell, forthcoming). This commentary series focuses on the reception history of the Bible.
32. See in chap. 6, "The Meaning of Deuteronomy 7 in Context."
33. Norbert Lohfink, "The Strata of the Pentateuch and the Question of War," 173–226 in idem, *Theology of the Pentateuch: Themes of the Priestly Narrative and Deuteronomy*, trans. Linda M. Maloney (Minneapolis: Fortress Press, 1994), at 194. Cf. Chapter 6, "The Meaning of Deuteronomy 7 in Context."
34. Cf. Samuel R. Driver, *Deuteronomy*, ICC (3d ed. Edinburgh: T & T Clark, 1969), lvi–lvii; *pace* Bernard L. Levinson, *Deuteronomy and the Hermeneutics of Legal Innovation* (Oxford: Oxford University Press, 1997), 6.

fashion, that is on the one hand faithful to the voice of the text and, on the other hand, true to the "face" of the "other." This practice was evident in the original composition of Deuteronomy 7 as well as in the subsequent editions of the book (exilic and post-exilic), each edition altering the meaning of Deuteronomy 7 for its constituency.[36]

This understanding of Deuteronomy 7 and the scribal practice behind Deuteronomy's composition has a number of important implications for Palestinian Christians and their approach to the Old Testament in the future. First of all, it underscores the need for a proper hermeneutic of the Old Testament. It highlights the "moral obligation" to listen to the voice(s) of the text first, the necessity of patience, and the hard work required to battle against misunderstanding. It shows that the use of the historical-critical method is indispensable to the proper understanding of a passage. It emphasizes that although Palestinian identity, Jewish-Christian *fraternité*, and tradition are important, they must nevertheless yield to the primary responsibility of understanding a given Old Testament text. As illustrated in the previous chapter, much of what would trouble a Palestinian Christian reading of Deuteronomy 7 is tempered considerably by the conclusions reached by the present author.

Second, this analysis is also significant for a Palestinian Christian understanding of the nature and authority of the Old Testament. The OT is not a "repository of static truths revealed in a unilateral manner without human involvement, but rather . . . a dynamic

---

35. Cf. The present writer on the political and religious reconciliation of the time and the manner in which the authors of Deuteronomy incorporated and contextualized traditions from the north. See in chap. 6, "The Meaning of Deuteronomy 7 in Context."
36. Ibid. The critical method that looks at this ancient practice is called "tradition history" or "tradition criticism" (*Traditionsgeschichte*). For an overview of tradition criticism and its recent developments see Walter E. Rast, *Tradition History and the Old Testament* (Philadelphia: Fortress Press, 1972); Douglas A. Knight, ed., *Tradition and Theology in the Old Testament* (London: SPCK, 1977); idem, "Tradition History," *ABD* 6: 633–38; idem, *Rediscovering the Traditions of Israel* (3d ed. Atlanta: SBL, 2006). This practice and its implications for a Palestinian Christian understanding of the nature and authority of the Old Testament will be discussed below.

collection of material that points to the ongoing human struggle for survival and meaning in real-life situations."[37] In other words, it is not "rarefied memory" but rather a collection of material that reveals a dynamic relationship between the community of faith and the traditional material, which the former applies to its own context and time.[38] As Douglas Knight explains, "In some instances [this process] can be carried out statically through very careful, even reverential transmission, avoiding the introduction of any changes in the wording of the traditions; in other cases persons in the line of transmission can be responsible—whether deliberately or accidentally—for alterations, expansions, omissions, and new combinations of the traditions."[39] It is this reality that was seen above and that must be born in mind when a Palestinian Christian considers the nature of the Old Testament.

This also has ramifications for how a Palestinian Christian views the authority of the Old Testament. More than anything else, it underscores Douglas Knight's assertion that "[w]e need to claim for humanity a more significant, active role in the revelatory process than is commonly done."[40] Whatever one's opinions on the matters of inspiration, revelation, canon, and, by extension, the authority of the Old Testament, Knight's comments rightly remind the reader of the active role played by the community of faith in the appropriation and

---

37. Knight, "Tradition History," *ABD* 6: 638.
38. As Walter Brueggemann explains, "behind every text, there was a moment of meeting; and out of that came a new affirmation and a fresh statement of faith. Out of each meeting the tradition was reshaped and faith took new form, a form it never had before." Walter Brueggemann, "Introduction: The Word in Its Particularity and Power," 11–12 in *The Vitality of Old Testament Traditions*, ed. Walter Brueggemann and Hans Walter Wolff (2d ed. Atlanta: John Knox, 1982), at 11. Tradition historians distinguish between the traditional material and the actual process of transmission with the Latin terms *traditum* and *traditio*. Knight, "Tradition History," 6: 634.
39. Knight, "Tradition History," 6: 634. For the caution employed by scribes in matters of textual intervention see Karel van der Toorn, *Scribal Culture and the Making of the Hebrew Bible* (Cambridge, MA: Harvard University Press, 2007), 146.
40. Douglas A. Knight, "Revelation through Tradition," 143–80 in idem, ed., *Tradition and Theology in the Old Testament*, at 168.

actualization (*Vergegenwärtigung*) of religious tradition. This reality does not invalidate the role of the Old Testament in the religious life of Palestinian Christians, but it does reposition it appropriately. For the message(s) of the Old Testament is/are never static. There is often continuity, but the claim these texts have on the relevant communities of faith is never beyond the "reaches of history" and the hands of its "tradents," that is, the individuals and groups responsible for passing on the tradition and reinterpreting it.[41]

The foregoing discussion of hermeneutics and the nature and authority of the Old Testament naturally leads to a third and final implication, namely, the role Palestinian Christians can play in actualizing the message(s) of the Old Testament for their own community.[42] As Knight wrote, the "creative process" behind the formation of much of biblical literature was both "collective" and "gradual."[43] The "collective" aspect of this process should raise the question: "Whose text is the Old Testament, and by what authority can a given passage be 're-presented' anew?"[44] The answer is that the Old Testament belongs to both Jews and Christians. The significance of this should not go unrecognized. With regard to Deuteronomy 7, Palestinian Christians should not be seen, or see themselves, as one of the seven nations, but as protagonists, authoritative "tradents" of

---

41. Walter Brueggemann, "The Continuing Task of Tradition Criticism," 115–26 in *The Vitality of Old Testament Traditions*, at 124; Knight, "Tradition History," 6: 636.
42. Robert Laurin laments what he believes was a result of the creation of the canon, namely, the "unfortunate freezing of tradition growth." This, he says, "inhibited later generations from participating in the struggle to ascertain authority for themselves and deadened the tradition to the letter of the law." Robert B. Laurin, "Tradition and Canon," 262–74 in *Tradition and Theology in the Old Testament*, at 271. This, however, is an inaccurate representation of the facts. As Brueggemann rightly points out ("The Continuing Task of Tradition Criticism," 122) the "traditioning process" did not cease when the Pentateuch reached its final fixed form, and neither did the prospect of new traditions cease with the close of the canon.
43. Knight, "Tradition History," 6: 637.
44. "Re-present" is the term used by James Luther Mayes to refer to *Vergegenwärtigung*, which means "actualizing in the present." Martin Noth, "The 'Re-Presentation' of the Old Testament in Proclamation," 76–88 in *Essays on Old Testament Hermeneutics*, ed. Claus Westermann; trans. James Luther Mayes (Atlanta: John Knox, 1979), at 80.

the text together with Jews and the church universal. Concomitantly, Palestinian Christians should take on board some of the recent developments in Jewish-Christian relations and not interpret the Old Testament in isolation from or in denigration of Jews. This process will undoubtedly be slow and gradual, but it is necessary if one is to do justice to the biblical text and the relevant communities, contexts, and perspectives discussed above.

I hope, finally, that this book will provide a significant and substantial resource for Palestinian Christians. Far from being a "will to power" or desire to "silence" their points of view, it has given voice to Palestinian Christians past and present.[45] It has provided a comprehensive overview of contemporary Palestinian Christian hermeneutics of the Old Testament, detailed the history and development of Palestinian Christianity from the middle of the nineteenth century to today, interacted with numerous perspectives on how the Old Testament should be read, and provided a way forward for Palestinian Christians in their reading of the Old Testament and Deuteronomy 7 in particular. It is my desire that this work will not only benefit Palestinian Christians but also provide a way forward for Jewish-Christian relations, a basis for furthering interreligious dialogue, and a point of reference for future scholarly research and action in reading the Old Testament in a way that is faithful to the voice of the text and the voices of the respective parties in the context described therein. I hope this marks the beginning of what J. R. R. Tolkien termed a "eucatastrophe."[46]

---

45. The phrase "will to power" comes from Edward Said's critique of Western writing on the Orient in *Orientalism*, 94.
46. J.R.R. Tolkien, *On Fairy Stories*, eds. Verlyn Flieger and Douglas A. Anderson (London: HarperColllins, 2014). Cf. J. R. R. Tolkien, "J. R. R. Tolkien to Christopher Tolkien," November 7–8, 1944, in *The Letters of J. R. R. Tolkien*, ed. Humphrey Carpenter (London: HarperCollins, 2006), 115–17.

Bibliography

1. Archival Material

1.1 Birmingham/UL:
University Library, Special Collections, Birmingham

Church Missionary Society Archives, Original Papers
(C M/O 1): Minutes of Conference of Local Committee of *CMS* in Palestine
(C M/O 2): Conferences of CMS missionaries in Palestine
(C M/O 8): Miscellaneous letters and papers to Secretaries at headquarters
(C M/O 9): Petitions to the Parent Committee
(C M/O 16): Seraphim Boutaji
(C M/O 20): Nicola Dabbak
(C M/O 36): Chalil Jamal
(C M/O 40): Michael Kawar
(C M/O 56): Cleardo Naudi
(C M/O 57): George Nyland
(C M/O 58): Nasir Odeh
(C M/O 71): Theodore Frederick Wolters
(C M/O 72): John Zeller

(CMS BV 2500): Register of Missionaries (Clerical, Lay, and Female), and Native Clergy, from 1804 to 1904

1.2 St. Antony's College, Oxford: Middle East Centre Archive

Blackburn, Donald (1902–1996): GB165-0378 (1 file and 22 photographs)

Blyth, Miss Estelle (1881–1983): GB165-0031 (1 box)

Dehqani-Tafti, Rt. Revd. Hassan Barnaba (b. 1920): GB165-0080 (2 boxes)

J&EM: Jerusalem and the East Mission: GB165-0161 (256 boxes)
    Palestine/Israel 1841–1976
       Boxes 1-3: Correspondence and papers of individual bishops in Jerusalem
       Boxes 4-7/4: Constitution and History of Bishopric/J & EM
       Boxes 7/5-16: General Correspondence 1915–1956
       Box 17: Religious affairs and religious liberty
       Box 18: Christians in Palestine
       Boxes 19-20: Eastern Churches 1913–1949
       Box 21: Palestine Native Church Council 1905–1957
       Boxes 22-24/3a: Missions 1847–1970
       Boxes 24/4-25: J & EM and America
       Boxes 26-29: Finance 1894–1969
       Box 30: Power of Attorney
       Boxes 31-32: Land, property, and donations 1941
       Box 33: St. George's Cathedral, Jerusalem 1890–1970
       Boxes 34-36: Property (Palestine) 1922–1963
       Education (Boxes 37-57)
       Boxes 37-38: General 1922–1961
       Boxes 39-47: Jerusalem Girls' College 1918–1963
       Box 48: Jerusalem Men's College 1917–1960

Box 49: British Community School, Jerusalem 1930–1947

Boxes 50-54: St. George's School 1900–1975

Boxes 55-56/1: English High School, Haifa 1923–1960

Box 56/2-4: St. Luke's School, Haifa 1920–1960

Box 57: St. Margaret's Home School, Nazareth

[…]

Boxes 60-72/2: Political 1929–1971

Boxes 72/3-74: Refugees 1929–1967

Boxes 75A-75Z: Minute books of various committees 1895–1974

[…]

Boxes 93-97: Jordan 1919–1975

Boxes 111-114/4: Jerusalem Bishopric 1928–1976

Boxes 114/5-122: J & EM, Central Organisation 1893–1976

Boxes 123A-B: *Bible Lands* magazines 1941–2011

[…]

Box 125: Minute books 1896–1921

Boxes 126-127: Bible Lands 1899–2006, PhD Thesis: Anglican Church & Egypt

Morgan, Miss Dorothy Blanche (b. 1906): GB165-0208 (2 boxes)

Tibawi, Abdul-Latif (b. 1910): GB165-0284 (4 boxes)

1.3 SOAS Archive–School of Oriental and African Studies, University of London

Jerusalem Christians Correspondence (1841–1979) – MS 380273 (1 file)

2. Palestinian Christians

2.1 Primary Sources

"A Moment of Truth: A Word of Faith, Hope, and Love, from the Heart of Palestinian Suffering." Accessed 10 Feb 2012: http://www.kairospalestine.ps/sites/default/Documents/English.pdf.

Abu El-Assal, Riah. "The Identity Crisis of the Arab Christian." *Reformed Journal* 36, no. 12 (December 1986): 10–15.

———."The Identity of the Palestinian Christian in Israel," 77–84 in *Faith and the Intifada: Palestinian Christian Voices*. Edited by Naim Ateek, Marc Ellis and Rosemary Radford Ruether. Maryknoll, NY: Orbis Books, 1992.

———."The Birth and Experience of the Christian Church: The Protestant/Anglican Perspective. Anglican Identity in the Middle East," 131–40 in *Christians in the Holy Land*. Edited by Michael Prior and William Taylor. London: World of Islam Festival Trust, 1994.

———. *Caught in Between: The Story of an Arab Palestinian Christian Israeli*. London: SPCK, 1999.

———. "Peace-making in Conflict Situations: Theological and Ethical Reflections." *Ecumenical Review* 53 (April 2001): 202–5.

Al-Liqa' Center for Religious Studies in the Holy Land. *Al-Liqa' Journal* 1–38 (May 1992–June 2012).

———. "Theology and the Local Church in the Holy Land." *Al-Liqa' Journal* 1 (May 1992): 93–107.

Ateek, Naim. "Gottes Verheissungen für die arabischen Völker," 50–58 in *Begegnung auf dem Ölberg: Die Referate einer jüdisch-arabisch-christlichen Begegnungswoche unter dem prophetischen Wort in Jerusalem (August 1975)*. Paulus-Paperbacks 8. Heilbronn: Paulus-Verlag, 1976.

———. "Three Bible Meditations: Hope in a Hopeless World." *Theological Review* 6 (April 1985): 47–57.

———, "An Arab-Israeli's Theological Reflections on the State of Israel after 40 Years." *Immanuel* 22–23 (January 1989): 102–19.

———. "Toward a Jewish Theology of Liberation: The Uprising and the Future." *Christianity and Crisis* 49 (December 11, 1989): 386–88.

———. "The Basic Principles of Dialogue in the Israeli-Palestine Conflict: Respect, Honesty, Sincerity, Humility," 59–73 in *Israel/Palestine*. Maryknoll, NY: Orbis Books, 1991.

———. "A Palestinian Perspective: The Bible and Liberation," 280–86 in *Voices from the Margin: Interpreting the Bible in the Third World*. Edited by R. S. Sugirtharajah. Maryknoll, NY: Orbis Books, 1991.

———. "The Emergence of a Palestinian Christian Theology," 1–6, and "Biblical Perspectives on the Land," 108–16 in *Faith and the Intifada: Palestinian Christian Voices* (1992).

———. "The Beginning of the Center." *Cornerstone* 1 (Spring 1994): 4–5.

———. "Herod & the Star." *Cornerstone* 2 (Winter 1994): 1–2.

———. "Whose Promised Land? An Interview." *Witness* 78 (April 1, 1995): 20–21.

———. "A Palestinian Theology of Jerusalem," 94–106 in *Jerusalem: What Makes for Peace! A Palestinian Christian Contribution to Peace Making*. Edited by Naim Ateek, Cedar Duaybis, and Marla Schrader. London: Melisende, 1997.

———. "What the Bible Teaches about Peace," 51–58 in *Seeking and Pursuing Peace*. Edited by Salim Munayer. Jerusalem: Yanetz Ltd., 1998.

———. "The Palestinian Story: An Interview with Naim Ateek." *Christian Century* 115 (June 1998): 608–12.

———. "Putting Christ at the Centre: The Land from a Palestinian Christian Perspective," 55–63 in *The Bible and the Land: An Encounter.* Edited by Lisa Loden, Peter Walker, and Michael Wood. Jerusalem: Musalaha, 2000.

———. "Zionism and the Land: A Palestinian Christian Perspective," 201–14 in *The Land of Promise: Biblical, Theological and Contemporary Perspectives.* Edited by Philip Johnston and Peter Walker. Leicester: Apollos, 2000.

———. *Justice, and Only Justice: A Palestinian Theology of Liberation.* Maryknoll, NY: Orbis Books, 2002.

———. "Suicide Bombers: What is Theologically and Morally Wrong with Suicide Bombings? A Palestinian Christian Perspective." *Studies in World Christianity* 8 (January 2002): 5–30.

———. "Suicide Bombers: A Palestinian Christian Perspective." *Voices from the Third World* 25 (June 1, 2002): 121–50.

———. "Suicide Bombings: A Palestinian Christian Perspective." *Church & Society* 94 (September 2003): 51–70.

———. "Introduction: Challenging Christian Zionism," 13–19 in *Challenging Christian Zionism: Theology, Politics and the Israel-Palestine Conflict.* London: Melisende, 2005.

———. "The Conflict over Palestine: A Palestinian Christian Response." *Quarterly Review* 25, no. 1 (March 1, 2005): 60–72.

———. "Sabeel—for justice and non-violence in Palestine." *Epworth Review* 32, no. 3 (July 1, 2005): 47–50.

———. "Jerusalem: From Brokenness to Wholeness." *Church & Society* 96 (September 2005): 136–39.

———. *The Forgotten Faithful: A Window into the Life and Witness of Christians in the Holy Land.* Jerusalem: Sabeel, 2007.

———. *A Palestinian Christian Cry for Reconciliation.* Maryknoll, NY: Orbis Books, 2008.

———. "Who is my Neighbor?" *Interpretation* 62 (April 1, 2008): 156–65.

———, and Jeremy Milgrom. "The Jews after Empowerment." *Christianity and Crisis* 49 (December 11, 1989): 386–91.

———, Marc H. Ellis, and Rosemary Radford Ruether, eds. *Faith and the Intifada: Palestinian Christian Voices* (1992).

———, Cedar Duaybis, and Marla Schrader, eds. *Jerusalem: What Makes for Peace! A Palestinian Christian Contribution to Peacemaking* (1997).

———, and Michael Prior, eds. *Holy Land, Hollow Jubilee: God, Justice, and the Palestinians.* London: Melisende, 1999.

———, Cedar Duaybis, and Maureen Tobin, eds. *Challenging Christian Zionism: Theology, Politics and the Israel-Palestine Conflict* (2005).

Awad, Bishara. "Speaking from the Heart: The Palestinians and the Land of Their Fathers," 177–85 in *The Bible and the Land: An Encounter* (2000).

Chacour, Elias. *Blood Brothers.* Grand Rapids: Chosen Books, 1984.

———. *We Belong to the Land: The Story of a Palestinian Israeli who Lives for Peace and Reconciliation.* New York: Harper Collins, 1992.

Corbon, Jean, George Khodr, Maître Albert Lahham, and Samir Kafity. Appendix, "A Memorandum by a Group of Middle Eastern Theologians (June 18, 1967)," 130–35 in Larry Ekin, *Enduring Witness.* Geneva: World Council of Churches, 1985.

Hanna, Atallah. "Pentecost and Jersualem," 5–7 in *Jerusalem: What Makes for Peace? A Palestinian Christian Contribution to Peacemaking* (1997).

Katanacho, Yohanna. "Christian Palestinian Arabs: Spreading Hope in the Middle East." *In the Gap: John Stott Ministries Newsletter* (Fall 2004): 1–2.

———. "Christ is the Owner of Haaretz." *Christian Scholar's Review* 34 (2005): 425–41.

———. "From Depression to Hope." *Cornerstone* 46 (Fall 2007): 16–17.

———. "Palestinian Protestant Theological Responses to a World Marked by Violence." *Missiology: An International Review* 36 (July 2008): 289–305.

———. "Approaches to the Bible." Paper presented at ICCJ–Kairos Consultation. Beit Jala, October 27, 2011.

———. "Jerusalem is the City of God: A Palestinian Reading of Psalm 87," 181–99 in *The Land Cries Out: Theology of the Land in the Israeli-Palestinian Context.* Edited by Salim J. Munayer and Lisa Loden. Eugene, OR: Cascade Books, 2012.

———. *The Land of Christ: A Palestinian Cry.* Bethlehem: Bethlehem Bible College, 2012.

Khoury, Geries. "The Palestinian Christian Identity," 71–76 in *Faith and the Intifada: Palestinian Christian Voices* (1992).

———. "Theology and the Local Church in the Holy Land: Palestinian Contextualized Theology." Accessed 18 June 2012: http://www.al-liqacenter.org.ps/p_materials/eng/theology.php.

Munayer, Salim J. "Relations between Religions in Historic Palestine and the Future Prospects: Christians and Jews," 143–50 in *Christians in the Holy Land* (1994).

———, ed. *Seeking and Pursuing Peace.* Jerusalem: Yanetz Ltd., 1998.

———. "The Theological Challenge the State of Israel Poses to Palestinian Christians." *St. Francis Magazine* 4, no. 3 (March 2008): 1–5.

———, and Lisa Loden, eds. *The Land Cries Out: Theology of the Land in the Israeli- Palestinian Context* (2012).

Raheb, Mitri. *Das reformatorische Erbe unter den Palästinensern: Zur Entstehung der Evangelisch-Lutherischen Kirche in Jordanien. Die Lutherische Kirche*. Gütersloh: Gerd Mohn, 1990.

———. "Biblical Perspectives on the Land," 108–16 in *Faith and the Intifada: Palestinian Christian Voices* (1992).

———. "Law, Power, Justice, and the Bible," 97–100 in *Faith and the Intifada: Palestinian Christian Voices* (1992).

———. "Biblical Interpretation in the Israeli-Palestinian Context," 109–17 in *Israel and Yeshua*. Edited by Torleif Elgvin. Jerusalem: Caspari Center for Biblical and Jewish Studies, 1993.

———. "The Spiritual Significance and Experience of the Churches: the Lutheran Perspective," 127–30 in *Christians in the Holy Land* (1994).

———. "The Prophet Micah and Jerusalem," 8–10 in *Jerusalem: What Makes for Peace! A Palestinian Christian Contribution to Peacemaking* (1997).

———. "Contextualising the Scripture: Towards a New Understanding of the Qur'an—An Arab-Christian Perspective." *Studies in World Christianity* 3 (January 1, 1997): 180–201.

———. "Mission in the Context of Fragmentation." *International Review of Mission* 86, no. 343 (October 1, 1997): 393–98.

———. *I Am a Palestinian Christian*. Minneapolis: Fortress Press, 1995.

———. "Sailing through Troubled Waters: Palestinian Christians in the Holy Land." *Dialog* 41, no. 2 (June 1, 2002): 97–102.

———. "Christ in the Palestinian Context: A Perspective from Bethlehem." *Church & Society* 94 (September 2003): 39–46.

———. *Bethlehem Besieged: Stories of Hope in Times of Trouble*. Minneapolis: Fortress Press, 2004.

———. "The Third Kingdom," 263–70 in *Challenging Christian Zionism: Theology, Politics and the Israel-Palestine Conflict* (2005).

———, ed., *The Invention of History: A Century of Interplay between Theology and Politics in Palestine*. Bethlehem: Diyar, 2011.

———. *Faith in the Face of Empire: The Bible through Palestinian Eyes*. Maryknoll, NY: Orbis Books, 2014.

———, Fred Strickert, and Garo Nalbandian. *Bethlehem 2000: Past and Present*. Heidelberg: Palmyra, 1998.

Sabbah, Michel. "The Significance of Jerusalem for Christians and of Christians for Jerusalem," xxiv–xxix in *Jerusalem: What Makes for Peace! A Palestinian Christian Contribution to Peacemaking* (1997).

———. "Christian Identity in the Holy Land," 9–16 in *Palestinian Christians: The Holy Land Guardians*. Jerusalem: Laity Committee in the Holy Land, 2006.

———. "Forgotten Christians in the Holy Land?" *Cornerstone* 43 (Winter 2007): 4–6.

———. *Faithful Witness: On Reconciliation and Peace in the Holy Land*. Hyde Park, NY: New City Press, 2009.

Sabeel. *Contemporary Way of the Cross: A Liturgical Journey along the Palestinian Via Dolorosa*. Jerusalem: Sabeel Palestinian Liberation Theology Center, 2005.

———. *Cornerstone* 1–61 (Spring 1994–Winter 2011).

———. "Purpose Statement." *Cornerstone* 61 (Winter 2011): 20.

Younan, Munib. *Witnessing for Peace: In Jerusalem and the World*. Minneapolis: Fortress Press, 2003.

———. "Religion and Politics." Lecture given at the WCC General Assembly in Porto Alegre, Brazil, Feb 2006. Accessed 7 Feb 2012: http://www.elcjhl.org/resources/younan/lecturestalks/lectures.asp.

2.2 Secondary Sources

"Al-Liqa' Center's Celebration of HB Patriarch Michael Sabbah's Golden Jubilee." *Al-Liqa' Newsletter* 30 (October 2005): 2–3.

"Bombs Hit Christian Bookstore, Two Internet Cafes in Gaza City." *Bulletin: Associated Christian Press* 451 (March–April, 2007): 25.

"Christ at the Checkpoint: Hope in the Midst of Conflict." Accessed 25 April 2012: http://www.christatthecheckpoint.com.

"Letter to Rev. Jerry Fallwell." Accessed 7 February 2012: www.saltfilms.net/issues/openletter.html.

"Palestinian territories profile." Accessed 3 August 2007: http://www.bbc.co.uk/news/world-middle-east-14630174.

"Persecution of Christians in Israel: The New Inquisition." *Journal of Palestine Studies* 8 (Autumn 1978): 135–40.

"Pope urges Middle East Christians not to leave their land." *Bulletin: Associated Christian Press* 450 (January–February 2007): 12–13.

"Reading the Old Testament in Bethlehem." Accessed 15 April 2009: http://www.comeandsee.com/modules.php?name=News&file=article&sid=974.

Abdel-Malek, Kamal. *The Rhetoric of Violence: Arab-Jewish Encounters in Contemporary Palestinian Literature and Film.* New York: Palgrave, 2005.

Abdul-Masih, Raed. *La Iglesia Local de Tierra Santa: 2,000 Años Continuous de Transmión y testimonio de la fe Cristiana.* Jerusalem: RAI: House of Art, 2005.

Anderson, Rufus. *History of the Missions of the ABCFM to the Oriental Churches.* 2 volumes. Boston: Congregational Publishing Society, 1872.

Andrew, Br., and Al Janssen. *Light Force: The Only Hope for the Middle East.* London: Hodder & Stoughton, 2004.

Angold, Michael, ed. *Eastern Christianity.* Volume 5 of *The Cambridge History of Christianity.* Cambridge: Cambridge University Press, 2006.

Antonius, George. *Arab Awakening*. London: Hamish Hamilton, 1938.

Arthur, Bryson. "Arab Christian Identity: 'Who am I?' (Part 1)." *Al-Kalima* 1 (January 2007): 4–5.

———. "Arab Christian Identity: 'Who am I?' (Part 2)." *Al-Kalima* 2 (September 2007): 4–5.

Badr, Habib, Suad Abou el Rouss Slim, and Joseph Abou Nohra, eds. *Christianity: A History in the Middle East*. Beirut: MECC, 2005.

Bailey, J. Martin. "The Palestinian-Israeli Conflict: A Lexicon." *The Link* 35 (April–May 2002): 2–14.

Barlow, Betsy. "Breaking the Silence: Michael Prior in the US." *Holy Land Studies* 3, no. 2 (November 2004): 141–43.

Bebbington, David. *Evangelicalism in Modern Britain: A History from the 1730's to the 1980's*. London: Unwin Hyman, 1989.

Bechmann, Ulrike, and Mitri Raheb, eds. *Verwurzelt im Heiligen Land: Einführung in das palästinensische Christentum*. Frankfurt am Main: Josef Knecht, 1995.

Belt, Don. "The Forgotten Faithful." *National Geographic* 215 (June 2009): 78–97.

Ben-Arieh, Yehoshua, and Moshe Davis, eds. *Jerusalem in the Mind of the Western World, 1800–1948*. With Eyes Toward Zion 5. London: Praeger, 1997.

Benedict XVI, "Apostolic Constitution *Anglicanorum Coetibus*: Providing for Personal Ordinariates for Anglicans Entering into Full Communion with the Catholic Church." Accessed 18 March 2015: http://w2.vatican.va/content/benedict-xvi/en/apost_constitutions/documents/hf_ben-xvi_apc_20091104_ anglicanorum-coetibus.html.

Benson, Arthur Christopher. *The Life of Edward White Benson: Sometime Archbishop of Canterbury.* 2 volumes. London: MacMillan & Son, 1899.

Bethlehem Bible College. "What We Believe." Accessed 12 August 2007: http://www.bethlehembiblecollege.edu/about/what-we-do.

———. "What We Believe." Accessed 8 February 2012: http://www.bethlehembiblecollege.edu/about/what-we-do.

Betts, Robert B. *Christians in the Arab East.* London: SPCK, 1979.

Blewett, Tim. "Bible, Land, Justice—The Challenge of Na'im Ateek and Palestinian Liberation Theology." *Theology* 96 (May 1993): 209–16.

Bloodgood, Francis J. "Palestine's Christian Remnant." *Christian Century* 66 (October 1949): 1226–28.

British Library. *The Christian Orient.* London: British Museum Publications, 1978.

Burge, Gary M. *Who are God's People in the Middle East?* Grand Rapids: Zondervan, 1993.

———. *Whose Land? Whose Promise? What Christians Are Not Being Told about Israel and the Palestinians.* London: Paternoster Press, 2003.

———. *Jesus and the Land: The New Testament Challenge to "Holy Land" Theology.* Grand Rapids: Baker, 2010.Burrell, David, and Yehezkel Landau, eds. *Voices from Jerusalem: Jews and Christians Reflect on the Holy Land.* Mahwah, NJ: Paulist Press, 1992.

Carmel, Alex. *Christen als Pioniere im Heiligen Land: Ein Beitrag zur Geschichte der Pilgermission und des Wiederaufbaus Palästinas im 19. Jahrhundert.* Basel: Reinhardt, 1981.

Chapman, Colin. *Whose Promised Land? The Continuing Crisis over Israel and Palestine.* Grand Rapids: Baker, 2002.

Christison, Kathleen. "Dilemmas of Arab Christianity." *Journal of Palestinian Studies* 22 (Autumn 1992): 117–19.

Christiansen, Drew. "Palestinian Christians: Recent Developments," 307–39 in *The Vatican-Israel Accords: Political, Legal, and Theological Contexts*. Edited by Marshall J. Breger. Notre Dame, IN: University of Notre Dame Press, 2004.

Church, Philip, Tim Bulkeley, Peter Walker, and Tim Meadowcroft, eds. *The Gospel and the Land of Promise: Christian Approaches to the Land of the Bible*. Eugene, OR: Pickwick, 2011.

Cleveland, William L. and Martin Bunton. *A History of the Modern Middle East*. 5th ed. Boulder: Westview Press, 2013.

Colbi, Saul. *Christianity in the Holy Land: Past and Present*. Tel Aviv: Am Hassefer, 1969.

———. *A History of the Christian Presence in the Holy Land*. Lanham, MD: University Press of America, 1988.

Cragg, Kenneth. *This Year in Jerusalem*. London: Darton, Longman and Todd, 1982.

———. *The Arab Christian: A History in the Middle East*. Louisville: Westminster John Knox, 1991.

Destani, Bejtullah D., ed. *Minorities in the Middle East*. 10 volumes. Slough: Archive Editions, 2007.

Dorman, David A. "The Artillery of Ideology: A Critique of Ussama Makdisi's *The Artillery of Heaven*. A Review Essay." *Theological Review* 30, no. 2 (November 2009): 233–34.

Du Brul, Peter. "The Crisis of Palestinian Christians," 118–58 in *Voices from Jerusalem: Jews and Christians Reflect on the Holy Land* (1992).

Dumper, Michael. "Faith and Statecraft: Church-State Relations in Jerusalem after 1948," 56–81 in *Palestinian Christians: Religion,*

Politics and Society in the Holy Land. Edited by Anthony O'Mahony. London: Melisende, 1999.

———. "The Christian Churches of Jerusalem in the Post-Oslo Period." *Journal of Palestine Studies* 31 (Winter 2002): 51–65.

Drury, Ben. "St. Paul's, West Jerusalem, Re-Dedicated." *Bible Lands* (Summer 2011): 5.

EAPPI (Ecumenical Accompaniment Programme in Palestine and Israel). *Theological Reflection on Accompaniment.* Geneva: Oikoumene WCC, 2005.

Eisler, Jakob, and Arno G. Krauss. *Nach Jerusalem müssen wir fahren.* Birsfelden: arteMedia, 2002.

Ekin, Larry. *Enduring Witness.* Geneva: World Council of Churches, 1985.

Elfar, Rana. "Dealing with the Scriptural Past: The Old Testament for Arab Christians Today," 95–106 in *The Bible and the Land: An Encounter* (2000).

Ellis, Marc H. "Jewish Theology and the Palestinians." *Journal of Palestine Studies* 19 (Spring 1990): 39–57.

———. *Toward a Jewish Theology of Liberation.* 3d expanded edition. Waco, TX: Baylor University Press, 2004.

Farah, Rafiq. *In Troubled Waters: A History of the Anglican Church in Jerusalem, 1841–1998.* Leicester: Christians Aware, 2002.

———. "Evangelical Missions and Churches in the Middle East: Palestine and Jordan," 727–34 in *Christianity: A History in the Middle East* (2005).

Fisher, Julia. *A Future for Israel? Christian Arabs Share Their Stories.* Milton Keynes: Authentic, 2006.

Foerster, Frank. "German Missions in the Holy Land," 183–95 in *Jerusalem in the Mind of the Western World, 1800–1948* (1997).

Frend, W. H. C. "Christianity in the Middle East: Survey down to A.D. 1800," 239–96 in Max Warren, ed., *Religion in the Middle East: Three Religions in Concord and Conflict*. Volume 1. Edited by A. J. Arberry. Cambridge: Cambridge University Press, 1969.

Gamble, Elizabeth Smith. "Indigenous Palestinian Liberation Theology: A Critical Examination of Current Literature." *Lexington Theological Quarterly* 27 (July 1992): 80–90.

Gilbert, Martin. *The Arab-Israeli Conflict: Its History in Maps*. London: Weidenfeld and Nicolson, 1981.

Gobat, Samuel. *Samuel Gobat, Bishop of Jerusalem: His Life and Work*. London: James Nisbet, 1884.

Gräbe, Uwe. *Kontextuelle palästinensische Theologie: Streitbare und umstrittene Beiträge zum ökumenischen und interreligiösen Gespräch*. Geneva: Erlanger Verlag, 1999.

Grafton, David D. "The Use of Scripture in the Current Israeli-Palestinian Conflict." *Word & World* 24 (December 2004): 29–39.

Green, Elizabeth, and Emily Hershberger. "'I never lose hope': An Interview with Palestinian Theologian Naim Ateek." *Sojourners* 34, no. 8 (August 2005): 26–31.

Gregerman, Adam. "Old Wine in New Bottles: Liberation Theology and the Israeli-Palestinian Conflict." *Journal of Ecumenical Studies* 41 (June 2004): 313–40.

Grieves, Brian J., and Naim Stifan Ateek. "A Journey of Justice, a Journey of Faith: An Interview with Naim Ateek." *Witness* 84, no. 9 (September 2001): 8–13.

Hanselmann, Siegfried. *Deutsche Evangelische Palästinamission: Handbuch ihrer Motive, Geschichte und Ergebnisse*. Neuendettelsau: Verlag der Evangelisch-Lutherische Mission Erlangen, 1971.

Hassan bin Talal, Prince of Jordan. *Christianity in the Arab World*. New York: Continuum, 1998.

Hassassian, Manuel. "The Influence of Christian Arabs in the National Movement," 308–30 in *Patterns of the Past, Prospects for the Future: The Christian Heritage in the Holy Land*. Edited by Thomas Hummel, Kevork Hintlian, and Ulf Carmesund. London: Melisende, 1999.

Heacock, Roger. "International Politics and Sectarian Policy in the Late Ottoman Period," 20–31 in *Patterns of the Past, Prospects for the Future: The Christian Heritage in the Holy Land* (1999).

Hechler, William. *The Jerusalem Bishopric*. London: Trübneck & Co., 1883.

Heldt, Petra. "Theological Significance of the Rebirth of the State of Israel: Different Christian Attitudes." *Immanuel* 22/23 (1989): 133–45.

———. "A Brief History of Dialogue between Orthodox Christians and Jews." *Immanuel* 26/27 (1994): 211–24.

Hewitt, Gordon. *The Problems of Success. A History of the Church Missionary Society 1910–1942*. London: SCM, 1971.

Heyer, Friedrich. *Kirchengeschichte des Heiligens Landes*. Stuttgart: Kohlhammer, 1984.

———. *2000 Jahre Kirchengeschichte des Heiligen Landes: Märtyrer, Mönche, Kirchenväter, Kreuzfahrer, Patriarchen, Ausgräber und Pilger*. Hamburg: LIT Verlag, 2000.

Hilliard, Alison, and Betty Jane Bailey. *Living Stones Pilgrimage: With the Christians of the Holy Land*. London: Cassell, 1999.

Hodder, Edwin. *The Life and Work of the Seventh Earl of Shaftesbury*. 3 volumes. London: Cassell, 1886.

Horne, Charles F., ed. *Source Records of the Great War*. 7 volumes. London: National Alumni, 1923.

Hosain, Samuel. *Israel Reassessed: A Christian Arab View*. Edinburgh: Handsel Press, 1988.

Hourani, Albert. *Arabic Thought in the Liberal Age: 1798–1939.* Cambridge: Cambridge University Press, 2003.

Hummel, Thomas. "Between Eastern and Western Christendom: The Anglican Presence in Jerusalem," 147–70 in *The Christian Communities of Jerusalem and the Holy Land: Studies in History, Religion and Politics.* Edited by Anthony O'Mahony. Cardiff: University of Wales Press, 2003.

———, Kevork Hintlian, and Ulf Carmesund, eds. *Patterns of the Past, Prospects for the Future: The Christian Heritage in the Holy Land* (1999).

Isaac, Jad, Marla Schrader, and Suheil Khalilieh. "The Colonization of Palestine," 122–34 in *Holy Land, Hollow Jubilee: God, Justice and the Palestinians* (1999).

Jaeger, D.-M. A., ed. *Papers Read at the 1979 Tantur Conference on Christianity in the Holy Land.* Studia Oecumenica Hierosolymitana 1. Jerusalem: Tantur, 1981.

Johnston, Philip, and Peter Walker, eds. *The Land of Promise: Biblical, Theological and Contemporary Perspectives.* Leicester: Apollos, 2000.

Jowett, William. *Christian Researches in the Mediterranean, from 1815 to 1820: In Furtherance of the Objects of the Church Missionary Society.* London: Seeley, 1822.

———. *Christian Researches in Syria and the Holy Land, in 1823 and 1824: In Furtherance of the Objects of the Church Missionary Society.* London: Seeley, 1826.

Kark, Ruth. "The Impact of Early Missionary Enterprises on Landscape and Identity Formation in Palestine, 1820–1914." *Islam and Christian-Muslim Relations* 15 (April 2004): 209–35.

Kassab, Najla. "A Middle Eastern Christian Approach to the Old Testament." *Theological Review* 13, no. 1 (April 1, 1992): 35–48.

Keith, Alexander. *The Land of Israel according to the Covenant with Abraham, with Isaac, and with Jacob*. Edinburgh: William Whyte, 1843.

Khader, Jamal, and David Neuhaus. "A Holy Land Context for *Nostra Aetate*." *Studies in Christian-Jewish Relations* 1 (2005–2006): 67–88.

Khalidi, Rashid. *Palestinian Identity: The Construction of Modern National Consciousness*. New York: Columbia University Press, 1997.

Khoury, Rafiq. "Palästinensische kontextuelle Theologie: Entwicklung und Sendung," 52–100 in *Zwischen Halbmond und Davidstern: Christliche Theologie in Palästina heute*. Edited by Harald Suermann. Freiburg: Herder, 2001.

Kildani, Hanna. *Modern Christianity in the Holy Land*. Translated by George Musleh. Bloomington: AuthorHouse, 2010.

King, Michael Christopher. *The Palestinians and the Churches, Vol. 1, 1948–1956*. Geneva: World Council of Churches, 1981.

Kuruvilla, Samuel J. "Radical Christianity in the Holy Land: A Comparative Study of Liberation and Contextual Theology in Israel-Palestine." PhD dissertation, University of Exeter, 2009.

———. *Radical Christianity in Palestine and Israel: Liberation and Theology in the Middle East*. London: Tauris, forthcoming.

Laird, Lance. "Meeting Jesus Again in the First Place: Palestinian Christians and the Bible." *Interpretation* 55 (2001): 400–12.

Lappin, Yaakov. "Christians: We'll Fight for Israel: Evangelical Delegates from around the world arrive at Knesset to express 'love for Israel.'" Accessed 7 Feb 2012: http://www.ynetnews.com/articles/0,7340,L-3309009,00.html.

Laqueur, Walter, and Barry Rubin. *The Israel-Arab Reader: A Documentary History of the Middle East Conflict*. 7th revised and enlarged edition. London: Penguin, 2008.

Lewis, Bernard. *The Multiple Identities of the Middle East.* New York: Schocken Books, 1998.

———. *The Middle East: A Brief History of the Last 2,000 Years.* New York: Scribner, 2003.

Lindén, Gunilla. *Church Leadership in a Political Crisis: Joint Statements from the Jerusalem Heads of Churches 1988–1992.* Uppsala: Swedish Institute of Missionary Research, 1994.

Löffler, Roland. "Aggravating Circumstances: On the Processes of National and Religious Identity within the Arab Lutheran and Anglican Congregations of Palestine during the Mandate Years," 99–124 in *Christian Witness between Continuity and New Beginnings: Modern Historical Missions in the Middle East.* Edited by Martin Tamcke and Michael Marten. Berlin: LIT Verlag, 2006.

———. *Protestanten in Palästina.* Stuttgart: Kohlhammer, 2008.

Lowe, Malcolm. "The Myth of Palestinian Christianity." Accessed 16 July 2012: http://www.gatestoneinstitute.org/2045/palestinian-christianity-myth.

Lückhoff, Martin. "Prussia and Jerusalem: Political and Religious Controversies Surrounding the Foundation of the Jerusalem Bishopric," 173–82 in *Jerusalem in the Mind of the Western World, 1800–1948* (1997).

———. *Anglikaner und Protestanten im Heiligen Land: Das gemeinsame Bistum Jerusalem, 1841–1886.* Wiesbaden: Harrassowitz, 1998.

Lutz, Charles P., and Robert O. Smith. *Christians and a Land Called Holy: How We Can Foster Justice, Peace, and Hope.* Minneapolis: Fortress Press, 2006.

Maalouf, Tony. *Arabs in the Shadow of Israel.* Grand Rapids: Kregel, 2003.

Macpherson, Duncan. *Pilgrim Preacher: Palestine, Pilgrimage and Preaching.* London: Melisende, 2004.

———. "Liberation Theologian and Peace Activist." *Holy Land Studies* 3, no. 2 (November 2004): 131–33.

———, and Michael Prior. *A Living Stone: Selected Essays and Addresses*. London: Living Stones of the Holy Land Trust, 2006.

Maïla, Joseph. "The Arab Christians: From the Eastern Question to the Recent Political Situation of the Minorities," 25–47 in *Christian Communities in the Arab Middle East: The Challenge of the Future*. Edited by Andrea Pacini. Oxford: Clarendon Press, 1998.

MacInnes, Rennie. "The Bishop's Quarterly Newsletter (May 12, 1918)." *Bible Lands* 77, vol. 5 (July 1918): 259–63.

Mandel, Neville J. *The Arabs and Zionism before World War I*. Berkeley: University of California Press, 1976.

Mann, Thomas W. "Israel and the Land : A Note from a Christian Perspective." *Theology Today* 35 (January 1979): 421–26.

Marsh, Leonard. "Palestinian Christianity: A Study in Religion and Politics." *International Journal for the Study of the Christian Church* 57 (July 2005): 147–66.

———. "Palestinian Christians: Theology and Politics in the Holy Land," 205–18 in *Christianity in the Middle East: Studies in Modern History, Theology, and Politics*. Edited by Anthony O'Mahony. London: Melisende, 2008.

———. "Whose Holy Land?" *Studies In World Christianity* 15 (January 2009): 276–86.

———. "Palestinian Christians and Liberation Theology," 69–91 in *Christianity and Jerusalem: Studies in Modern Theology and Politics in the Holy Land*. Edited by Anthony O'Mahony. Leominster: Gracewing, 2010.

Marten, Michael. *Attempting to Bring the Gospel Home: Scottish Missions to Palestine, 1839–1917*. London: Tauris Academic Studies, 2006.

Masalha, Nur. *The Bible and Zionism: Invented Traditions, Archaeology and Post-Colonialism in Palestine-Israel.* London: Zed, 2007.

———. "Reading the Bible with the Eyes of the Canaanites: Neo-Zionism, Political Theology and the Land Traditions of the Bible (1967 to Gaza 2009)." *Holy Land Studies* 8 (2009): 55–108.Masters, Bruce. *Christians and Jews in the Ottoman Arab World: The Roots of Sectarianism.* Cambridge: Cambridge University Press, 2001.

May, Melanie A. *Jerusalem Testament: Palestinian Christians Speak, 1988–2008.* Grand Rapids: Eerdmans, 2010.

McDermott, Dan. "Shaping the Church, Shaping the City." New Initiative for Middle East Peace, *Insights* 2 (Spring 2006): 44–54.

Merkley, Paul. *Christian Attitudes Towards the State of Israel.* Montreal: McGill-Queen's University Press, 2001.

Miano, Peter. "Professor Michael Prior and the Biblical Academy." *Holy Land Studies* 3, no. 2 (November 2004): 134–37.

Middle East Council of Churches. "Member Churches." Accessed 7 Feb 2012: http://www.mec-churches.org/member_churches/member_churches.htm.

Miller, Charles H. "Hermeneutical Problems for a Palestinian Catholic Reading the Old Testament and Current Pastoral Responses." Aram Society for Syro-Mesopotamian Studies, *ARAM* 18–19 (2006–2007): 307–24.

Mitri, Tarek. "Views on Arab Christians between Past and Present." *Islam and Christian-Muslim Relations* 9 (1998): 115–19.

Monhollen, Steven A. "Israel in Recent Mainline Protestant Thought and Practice: Alternative Views." *Lexington Theological Quarterly* 41, no. 2 (June 1, 2006): 149–67.

Moucarry, Chawkat. *Faith to Faith: Christianity & Islam in Dialogue.* Leicester: InterVarsity Press, 2001.

Muir, Diana. "A Land Without a People for a People Without a Land." *Middle East Quarterly* 15, no. 2 (Spring 2008): 55–62.

N.a. Review of Alexander Keith, *The Land of Israel according to the Covenant with Abraham, with Isaac, and with Jacob*. The United Secession Magazine 1 (April 1844): 187–92.

Neill, Stephen. *A History of Christian Missions*. 2d ed. Harmondsworth: Penguin, 1986.

Nerel, Gershon. "Spiritual *Intifada* of Palestinian Christians and Messianic Jews," 205–19 in *Israel: His People, His Land, His Story*. Edited by Fred Wright. Eastbourne: Thankful Books, 2005.

———. "Anti-Zionism in the 'Electronic Church' of Palestinian Christianity." *Analysis of Current Trends in Antisemitism* 27 (2006): 1–50.

———. "Between Palestinians and Israelis: The Church and the Media." Accessed 11 Feb 2011: http://www.youtube.com/watch?v=Mdxtm3me9Fg.

Newman, John Henry. *Apologia Pro Vita Sua*. London: Routledge, 1907.

Norman, Beryl, ed. *The Mountain of the Lord: Israel and the Churches*. London: Council of Christians and Jews, 1996.

Nothnagle, Almut, Hans-Jürgen Abromeit, and Frank Foerster, eds. *Seht, wir gehen hinauf nach Jerusalem! Festschrift zum 150jährigen Jubiläum von Talithia Kumi und des Jerusalemsvereins*. Leipzig: Evangelische Verlagsanstalt, 2001.

O'Brien, Conor Cruise. *The Siege: The Saga of Israel and Zionism*. London: Paladin, 1988.

O'Mahony, Anthony, ed. *The Christian Heritage in the Holy Land*. Jerusalem: Swedish Christian Study Centre, 1995.

———, ed. *Palestinian Christians: Religion, Politics and Society in the Holy Land* (1999).

———. "Palestinian Christians: Religion, Politics and Society, *c.* 1800–1948," 9–55 in idem, ed., *Palestinian Christians: Religion, Politics and Society in the Holy Land* (1999).

———, ed. *The Christian Communities of the Holy Land: Studies in History, Religion and Politics* (2003).

———. "The Vatican, Jerusalem, the State of Israel, and Christianity in the Holy Land." *International Journal for the Study of the Christian Church* 5 (July 2005): 123–46.

———, ed. *Christianity in the Middle East: Studies in Modern History, Theology and Politics* (2008).

Østerbye, Per. *The Church in Israel: A Report on the Work and Position of the Christian Churches in Israel.* Lund: Gleerup, 1970.

Pacini, Andrea, ed. *Christian Communities in the Arab Middle East: The Challenge of the Future* (1998).

Pappé, Ilan. "Michael Prior and the Struggle for Justice." *Holy Land Studies* 3, no. 2 (November 2004): 138–40.

———. *The Ethnic Cleansing of Palestine.* Oxford: Oneworld Publications, 2007.

———. "Calling a Spade a Spade: The 1948 Ethnic Cleansing of Palestine." *Cornerstone* 43 (Winter 2007): 10–11.

———. *The Forgotten Palestinians: A History of the Palestinians in Israel.* London: Yale University Press, 2011.

Parmenter, Barbara McKean. *Giving Voice to Stones: Place and Identity in Palestinian Literature.* Austin: University of Texas Press, 2004.

Parry, Ken, ed. *The Blackwell Companion to Eastern Christianity.* Oxford: Blackwell, 2007.

Pittman, Lester. "The Formation of the Episcopal Diocese of Jerusalem 1841–1948: Anglican, Indigenous and Ecumenical," 85–104 in *Patterns of the Past, Prospects for the Future: The Christian Heritage in the Holy Land* (1999).

Pleins, J. David. "Is a Palestinian Theology of Liberation Possible?" *Anglican Theological Review* 74 (March 1992): 133–43.

Prior, Michael. "Pilgrimage to the Holy Land, Yesterday and Today," 169–99 in *Christians in the Holy Land* (1994).

———. *The Bible and Colonialism: A Moral Critique*. Sheffield: Sheffield Academic Press, 1997.

———. "A Perspective on Pilgrimage to the Holy Land," 114–31 in *Jerusalem: What Makes for Peace! A Palestinian Christian Contribution to Peacemaking* (1997).

———. *Western Scholarship and the History of Palestine* (1998).

———. "The Moral Problem of the Land Traditions of the Bible," 41–81 in *Western Scholarship and the History of Palestine*. Edited by Michael Prior. London: Melisende, 1998.

———. *Zionism and the State of Israel: A Moral Inquiry*. London: Routledge, 1999.

———. "'You will be my witnesses in Jerusalem, in all Judaea and Samaria, and to the ends of the earth': A Christian Perspective on Jerusalem," 96–140 in *Palestinian Christians: Religion, Politics, and Society in the Holy Land* (1999).

———. "The Bible and the Redeeming Idea of Colonialism." *Studies in World Christianity* 5, no. 2 (January 1, 1999): 129–55.

———, ed. *They Came and They Saw: Western Christian Experiences of the Holy Land* (London: Melisende, 2000).

———. "Studying the Bible in the Holy Land," 104–27 in *They Came and They Saw* (2000).

———. "Zionist Ethnic Cleansing: The Fulfillment of Biblical Prophecy?" *Epworth Review* 27, no. 2 (April 1, 2000): 49–60.

———. "Confronting the Bible's Ethnic Cleansing in Palestine." *The Link* 33, no. 5. (December, 2000): 1–16.

———. "Israel-Palestine: A Challenge to Theology," 59–84 in *Faith in the Millennium*. Edited by Stanley E. Porter, Michael A. Hayes, and David Tombs. Sheffield: Sheffield Academic Press, 2001.

———. "Holy Places, Unholy Domination: The Scramble for Jerusalem." *Islamic Studies* 40 (September 2001): 507–30.

———. "A Moral Reading of the Bible in Jerusalem," 16–45 in *Jerusalem in Ancient History and Tradition*. Edited by Thomas L. Thompson. Sheffield: Sheffield Academic Press, 2003.

———, and Marianne Arbogast. "Christians and Zionism: an Interview with Michael Prior." *Witness* 86, nos. 3-4 (March 1, 2003): 19–22.

———. *Speaking the Truth about Zionism and Israel*. London: Melisende, 2004.

———. "Zionism and the Challenge of Historical Truth and Morality," 13–50 in *Speaking the Truth: Zionism, Israel, and Occupation*. Edited by Michael Prior. Northamptom: Olive Branch Press, 2005.

———. "Violence and the Biblical Land Traditions," 127–44 in *Challenging Christian Zionism: Theology, Politics and the Israel-Palestine Conflict* (2005).

———. "A Perspective on Pilgrimage to the Holy Land." *Church & Society* 96 (September 2005): 77–87.

———. "Reading the Bible with the Eyes of the Canaanite: In Homage to Edward H. Said," 273–96 in idem and Duncan MacPherson, *A Living Stone: Selected Essays and Addresses* (2006).

———, and William Taylor. *Christians in the Holy Land* (1994).

———, and Duncan Macpherson. *A Living Stone: Selected Essays and Addresses* (2006).

Racionzer, Leon Menzie. "Christianity in Modern Israel." *International Journal for the Study of the Christian Church* 5 (July 2005): 167–81.

Reitsma, Bernard. "Who is Our God? The Theological Challenges of the State of Israel for Christian Arabs: Faith and Ethnicity in the Middle East." *Faith and Ethnicity: Studies in Reformed Theology* 6 (2002): 180–202.

Richter, Julius. *A History of Protestant Missions in the Near East*. Edinburgh: Oliphant, Anderson & Ferrier, 1910.

Robert, Dana. *Christian Mission: How Christianity Became a World Religion*. Oxford: Wiley-Blackwell, 2009.

Ruether, Rosemary Radford. "Preface: The Conference and the Book," ix–xiv in *Faith and the Intifada: Palestinian Christian Voices* (1992).

———. "Israeli-Palestinian Conflict: How is God Present in History?" 69–80 in *God and the Nations*, Edited by Rosemary Radford Ruether and Douglas John Hall. Minneapolis: Augsburg Fortress, 1995.

———, and Herman J. Ruether. *The Wrath of Jonah: The Crisis of Religious Nationalism in the Israeli-Palestinian Conflict*. Minneapolis: Fortress Press, 2002.

Sa'ar, Amalia. "Carefully on the Margins: Christian Palestinians in Haifa between Nation and State." *American Ethnologist* 25 (May 1998): 215–39.

Sabella, Bernard, and Albert Aghazarian. *On the Eve of the New Millennium*. Christian Voices from the Holy Land. Jerusalem: Palestinian General Delegation to the United Kingdom Office of Representation of the PLO to the Holy See, 1998.

———. "The Emigration of Christian Arabs," 127–54 in *Christian Communities in the Arab Middle East: The Challenge of the Future* (1998).

———. "Socio-economic characteristics and challenges to Palestinian Christians in the Holy Land," 82–95 in *Palestinian Christians: Religion, Politics, and Society in the Holy Land.* (1999).

———. "Palestinian Christians: Historical Demographic Developments, Current Politics and Attitudes Towards Church, Society and Human Rights," 39–93 in *The Sabeel Survey on Palestinian Christians in the West Bank and Israel.* Jerusalem: Sabeel, 2006.

Sabra, George. "Two Ways of Being a Christian in the Muslim Context of the Middle East." *Islam and Christian-Muslim Relations* 17 (2006): 43–53.

Sahhar, George B., ed. *Palestinian Christians: The Holy Land Guardians* (2006).

Said, Edward. *The Question of Palestine.* New York: Vintage Books, 1979.

———. *Orientalism.* London: Penguin, 2003.

Sanders, Marthame, and Elizabeth Sanders. *Salt of the Earth: Palestinian Christians in the Northern West Bank.* Kentucky: Salt Films, Inc., 2005.

Segev, Tom. *One Palestine, Complete: Jews and Arabs under British Mandate.* New York: Metropolitan Books, 2001.

Sengstock, Mary C. "Traditional and Nationalist Identity in a Christian Arab Community." *Sociological Analysis* 35 (Autumn 1974): 201–10.

Sennott, Charles M. *The Body and the Blood: The Holy Land's Christians at the Turn of a New Millennium.* New York: Public Affairs, 2000.

Shenk, Calvin E. "The Middle Eastern Jesus: Messianic Jewish and Palestinian Christian Understandings." *Missiology: An International Review* 29 (October 2001): 403–16.

Shomali, Qustandi. "Arab Cultural Revival in Palestine," 283–307 in *Patterns of the Past, Prospects for the Future: The Christian Heritage in the Holy Land* (1999).

Sinno, Abdel-Raouf. *Deutsche Interessen in Syrien und Palästina 1841–1898: Aktivitäten religiöser Institutionen, wirtschaftliche und politische Einflüsse.* Berlin: Baalbek, 1982.

Sizer, Stephen. "The Theological Basis of Christian Zionism: On the Road to Armageddon," 59–75 in *Challenging Christian Zionism: Theology, Politics and the Israel-Palestine Conflict* (2005).

Šlajerová, Monika. "Palestinian Church Reads Old Testament: The Triangle of Ethnicity, Faith, Land, and Biblical Interpretation." *Communio* 47 (2004): 34–62.

Smith, Robert O. "Secular and Religious: ELCJHL Contributions to Palestinian Nationalism." *Currents in Theology and Mission* 32 (October 2005): 338–47.

Soudah, Romell. "Christians in the Holy Land: Across the Political and Economic Divide," 9–37 in *The Sabeel Survey on Palestinian Christians in the West Bank and Israel* (2006).

Stalder, William Andrew. "Palestinian Christians and the Old Testament: Hermeneutics, History, and Ideology." PhD dissertation, University of Aberdeen, 2012.

Stewart, Gordon. "The Old Testament: Friend or Foe of Palestinian Christians?" 103–20 in *The Gospel and the Land of Promise* (2011).

Stock, Eugene. *The History of the Christian Missionary Society.* 4 vols. London: CMS, 1899–1916.

Stockdale, Nancy L. *Colonial Encounters among English and Palestinian Women, 1800–1948.* Gainesville: University Press of Florida, 2007.

Stransky, Thomas. "Origins of Western Christian Missions,"137–54 in *Jerusalem in the Mind of the Western World* (1997).

Strickert, Frederick M. "I am a Palestinian Christian." *Currents In Theology and Mission* 25, no. 1 (February 1, 1998): 46–52.

Suermann, Harald, ed. *Zwischen Halbmond und Davidstern: Christliche Theologie in Palästina heute* (2001).

Thomas, David. "Arab Christianity," 1–22 in *The Blackwell Companion to Eastern Christianity* (2007).

Thompson, Thomas L. "The Politics of Reading the Bible in Israel." *Holy Land Studies* 7 (2008): 1–15.

Tibawi, Abdul L. *British Interests in Palestine, 1800–1901: A Study of Religious and Educational Enterprise.* Oxford: Oxford University Press, 1961.

———. *American Interests in Syria, 1800–1901: A Study of Educational, Literary, and Religious Work.* Oxford: Clarendon Press, 1966.

———. "Unpublished Letters on Protestant Missions in Palestine." *The Muslim World* 67 (October 1977): 258–65.

Tsimhoni, Daphne. *Christian Communities in Jerusalem and the West Bank since 1948: An Historical, Social, and Political Study.* London: Praeger, 1993.

———. "The Status of the Arab Christians under the British Mandate in Palestine." *Middle Eastern Studies* 20 (October 1984): 166–92.

Veiel, Friederich. *Der Pilgermission von St. Chrischona, 1840–1940.* Giessen: Brunnen, 1940.

Vila, David. "Information and Technology Resources for the Study of Arabic Christianity." *Journal of Religious and Theological Information* 6 (2005): 103–19.

Visser't Hooft, W. A., ed. *The Evanston Report: The Second Assembly of the World Council of Churches 1954.* London: SCM, 1955.

Wagner, Donald. *Dying in the Land of Promise: Palestine and Palestinian Christianity from Pentecost to 2000.* London: Melisende, 2001.

———. "For Zion's Sake." *Middle East Report* 223 (Summer 2002): 52–57.

Wessels, Antonie. *Arab and Christian? Christians in the Middle East.* Kampen: Pharos, 1995.

White, Malcolm. "Anglican Pioneers of the Ottoman Period: Sketches from the CMS Archives of Some Arab Lives Connected with the Early Days of the Diocese of Jerusalem." *St. Francis Magazine* 8, no. 2 (April 2012): 283–314.

Wild, Stefan. "Ottomanism versus Arabism: The Case of Farid Kassab (1884–1970)." *Die Welt des Islams* 28 (1988): 607–27.

Wilkinson, Paul Richard. *For Zion's Sake: Christian Zionism and the Role of John Nelson Darby.* Milton Keynes: Paternoster, 2007.

Ye'or, Bat. *The Dhimmi: Jews and Christians Under Islam.* Cranbury, NJ: Associated University Presses, 1985.

3. Old Testament (Hermeneutics/Biblical Studies/Theology/etc.)

Anderson, Bernhard W., ed., *The Old Testament and Christian Faith.* London: SCM, 1964.

Baltzer, Klaus. *The Covenant Formulary: in Old Testament, Jewish, and Early Christian Writings.* Oxford: Oxford University Press, 1971.

Barr, James. *Biblical Faith and Natural Theology: The Gifford Lectures for 1991 Delivered in the University of Edinburgh.* Oxford: Clarendon Press, 1993.

———. *History and Ideology in the Old Testament: Biblical Studies at the End of the Millennium.* Oxford: Oxford University Press, 2000.

———. "The Fundamentalist Understanding of Scripture," 70–74 in *Conflicting Ways of Interpreting the Bible.* Edited by Hans Küng and Jürgen Moltmann. Edinburgh: T & T Clark, 1980.

Barton, John, ed. *The Cambridge Companion to Biblical Interpretation.* Cambridge: Cambridge University Press, 1998.

Bathrellos, Demetrios. "The Eastern Orthodox Tradition for Today," 42–58 in *The Bible in Pastoral Practice: Readings in the Place and Function of Scripture in the Church*. Edited by Paul Ballard and Stephen R. Holmes. Grand Rapids: Eerdmans, 2005.

Bauckham, Richard. *The Bible in Politics: How to Read the Bible Politically*. London: SPCK, 1989.

Blenkinsopp, Joseph. "Deuteronomy," 94–109 in *The New Jerome Biblical Commentary*. Edited by Raymond E. Brown, Joseph A. Fitzmyer, and Roland E. Murphy. London: Geoffrey Chapman, 1990.

Boff, Clodovis. "Hermeneutics: Constitution of Theological Pertinency," 9–35 in *Voices from the Margin: Interpreting the Bible in the Third World*. Edited by R. S. Sugirtharajah. London: SPCK, 1991.

Braulik, Georg. *Deuteronomium*. 2 vols. Neue Echter Bibel 15, 28. Würzburg: Echter Verlag, 1986–1992.

———. "Die Völkervernichtung und die Rückkehr Israels ins Verheissungsland: Hermeneutische Bemerkungen zum Buch Deuteronomium," 3–38 in *Deuteronomy and Deuteronomic Literature: Festschrift C. H. W. Brekelmans*. Edited by Marc Vervenne and Johan Lust. Leuven: Leuven University Press, 1997.

———. "The Destruction of the Nations and the Promise of Return." *Verbum et Ecclesia* 25 (2004): 46–67.

———, and Ulrika Lindblad. *The Theology of Deuteronomy: Collected Essays of Georg Braulik, OSB*. Dallas: BIBAL Press, 1994.

Brekelmans, C. H. W. "Wisdom influence in Deuteronomy," 123–45 in *A Song of Power and the Power of Song: Essays on the Book of Deuteronomy*. Edited by Duane L. Christensen. Winona Lake, IN: Eisenbrauns, 1993.

Brueggemann, Walter. "Introduction: The Word in Its Particularity and Power," 11–12, and "The Continuing Task of Tradition Criticism," 115–26 in *The Vitality of Old Testament Traditions*. Edited by Walter Brueggemann and Hans Walter Wolff. 2d ed. Atlanta: John Knox, 1982.

———. *Theology of the Old Testament: Testimony, Dispute, Advocacy*. Minneapolis: Fortress Press, 1997.

———. *Deuteronomy*. Abingdon OT Commentaries. Nashville: Abingdon Press, 2001.

———. *The Land: Place as Gift, Promise, and Challenge in Biblical Faith*. 2d ed. Minneapolis: Fortress Press, 2002; orig. pub. 1977.

———, and Hans Walter Wolff. *The Vitality of Old Testament Traditions* (2d ed. 1982).

Buber, Martin. *I and Thou*. Edinburgh: T & T Clark, 1947.

Bultmann, Rudoph. "The Significance of the Old Testament for the Christian Faith," 8–35 in *The Old Testament and the Christian Faith*. Edited by Bernhard Anderson. London: SCM, 1964.

Burgess, Joseph F. "Lutheran Interpretation of Scripture," 101–28 in *The Bible in the Churches: How Various Christians Interpret the Scriptures*. Edited by Kenneth Hagan. 2d ed. Milwaukee: Marquette University Press, 1994.

Cairns, Ian. *Deuteronomy: Word and Presence*. Grand Rapids: Eerdmans, 1992.

Campbell, Jonathon. *Deuteronomy*. Blackwell Bible Commentaries 5. Oxford: Blackwell, forthcoming.

Carmichael, Calum M. *The Laws of Deuteronomy*. Ithaca, NY: Cornell University Press, 1974.

Carroll, Robert P. "Cracks in the Soul of Theology," 142–55 in *The Interpretation of the Bible in the Church*. Edited by J. L. Houlden. London: SCM, 1995.

Childs, Brevard S. *Biblical Theology of the Old and New Testaments.* London: SCM, 1992.

Christensen, Duane L. "Form and Structure in Deuteronomy 1–11." *BETL* 68 (1985): 135–44.

———, ed. *Deuteronomy 1–11.* Word Biblical Commentary 6a. Dallas: Word Books, 1991.

———. "Deuteronomy in Modern Research: Approaches and Issues," 3–17 in *A Song of Power and the Power of Song: Essays on the Book of Deuteronomy* (1993).

———, ed. *A Song of Power and the Power of Song: Essays on the Book of Deuteronomy* (1993).

———. *Deuteronomy 1:1–21:9.* Word Biblical Commentary 6a. 2d ed. Nashville: Thomas Nelson, 2001.

———. *Deuteronomy 21:10–34:12.* Word Biblical Commentary 6b. Nashville: Thomas Nelson, 2002.

———, and M. Narucki. "The Mosaic Authorship of the Pentateuch." *Journal of the Evangelical Theological Society* 32 (1989): 465–71.

Clements, Ronald E. *God's Chosen People: A Theological Interpretation of the Book of Deuteronomy.* London: SCM, 1967.

———. *Deuteronomy.* Sheffield: JSOT Press, 1989.

———. "The Deuteronomic Law of Centralisation and the Catastrophe of 587 B.C.E," 5–26 in *After the Exile: Essays in Honor of Rex Mason.* Macon: Mercer University Press, 1996.

———. "The Book of Deuteronomy," 269–538 in *The New Interpreter's Bible* 2. Nashville: Abingdon, 1998.

———. *The Book of Deuteronomy.* Peterborough: Epworth Press, 2001.

———. "The Origins of Deuteronomy: What are the Clues?" in "A Dialogue with Gordon McConville on Deuteronomy." *Scottish Journal of Theology* 56 (2003): 508–16.

Clendenin, Daniel B. *Eastern Orthodox Christianity: A Western Perspective*. Grand Rapids: Baker, 1997.

Collier, Gary D. "The Problem of Deuteronomy: In Search of a Perspective." *Restoration Quarterly* 26 (January 1983): 215–33.

Craigie, Peter C. *The Problem of War in the Old Testament*. Grand Rapids: Eerdmans, 1978.

———. *The Book of Deuteronomy*. New International Commentary on the Old Testament 5. 2d ed. Grand Rapids: Eerdmans, 1995.

Crump, Wayne. "Deuteronomy 7: A Covenant Sermon." *Restoration Quarterly* 17 (January 1974): 222–35.

Davies, Philip R. *In Search of Ancient Israel*. London: Sheffield Academic Press, 1992.

Davies, W. D. *The Gospel and the Land: Early Christianity and Jewish Territorial Doctrine*. Berkeley: University of California Press, 1974.

———. *The Territorial Dimensions of Judaism*. Berkeley: University of California Press, 1982.

———. *The Territorial Dimensions of Judaism: With a Symposium and Further Reflections*. Minneapolis: Fortress Press, 1991.

De Wette, W. M. L. *Dissertatio critico-exegetica qua a prioribus Deuteronomium Pentateuchi libris diversum alius cuiusdam recentioris auctoris opus esse monstratur*. Jena: Etzdorf, 1805.

Driver, Samuel R. *Deuteronomy*. International Critical Commentary. 3d ed. Edinburgh: T & T Clark, 1969.

Dutcher-Walls, Patricia. "The Circumscription of the King: Deuteronomy 17:16-17 in its Ancient Social Context." *Journal of Biblical Literature* 121 (2002): 601–16.

Earl, Douglas. "The Christian Significance of Deuteronomy 7." *Journal of Theological Interpretation* 3 (Spring 2009): 41–62.

Faber, Ben. "Ethical Hermeneutics and the Theater: Shakespeare's *Merchant of Venice*," 211–24 in *Hermeneutics at the Crossroads*. Edited by Kevin Vanhoozer. Bloomington: Indiana University Press, 2006.

Fishbane, Michael. *Biblical Interpretation in Ancient Israel*. Oxford: Clarendon Press, 1985.

Fitzmyer, Joseph. *The Biblical Commission's Document "The Interpretation of the Bible in the Church": Text and Commentary*. Rome: Pontifical Biblical Institute, 1995.

Florovsky, Georges. *Bible, Church, Tradition: An Eastern Orthodox View*. Belmont, MA: Nordland Publishing, 1972.

Frankena, R. "The Vassal Treaties of Esarhaddon and the Dating of Deuteronomy." *Oudtestamentische Studien* 14 (1965): 122–54.

García López, Félix. "'Un peuple consacré': Analyse critique de Deutéronome 7." *Vetus Testamentum* 32 (October 1982): 438–63.

Grabbe, Lester L., ed. *Can a 'History of Israel' be Written?* Sheffield: Sheffield Academic Press, 1997.

Greenberg, Moshe. "Hebrew *segulla*: Akkadian *sikiltu*." *Journal of the American Oriental Society* 71 (1951): 172–74.

Habel, Norman C. *The Land is Mine: Six Biblical Land Ideologies*. Minneapolis: Augsburg Fortress Press, 1995.

Hölscher, Gustav. "Komposition und Ursprung des Deuteronomiums." *Zeitschrift für die alttestamentliche Wissenschaft* 40 (1922): 161–255.

Horner, Barry. *Future Israel: Why Christian Anti-Judaism must be Challenged*. Nashville: Baker, 2007.

Houlden, J. L. ed., *The Interpretation of the Bible in the Church* (London: SCM, 1995).

Jeanrond, Werner. *Theological Hermeneutics: Development and Significance*. London: MacMillan, 1991.

Kaminsky, Joel. "Did Election Imply the Mistreatment of Non-Israelites?" *Harvard Theological Review* 96 (2003): 397–425.

Kang, Sa-Moon. *Divine War in the Old Testament and in the Ancient Near East*. Berlin: Walter de Gruyter, 1989.

Kline, M. G. *Treaty of the Great King: The Covenant Structure of Deuteronomy*. Grand Rapids: Eerdmans, 1963.

Knight, Douglas A., ed. *Tradition and Theology in the Old Testament* (1977).

———. "Revelation through Tradition," 143–80 in *Tradition and Theology in the Old Testament*. Edited by Douglas A. Knight. London: SPCK, 1977.

——— *Rediscovering the Traditions of Israel*. 3d ed. Atlanta: Society of Biblical Literature, 2006.

Knoppers, Gary N., and J. Gordon McConville. *Reconsidering Israel and Judah: Recent Studies on the Deuteronomistic History*. Winona Lake: Eisenbrauns, 2000.

Krašovec, Jože. "Is There a Doctrine of Collective Retribution in the Hebrew Bible?" *Hebrew Union College Annual* 65 (2001): 35–89.

Lapsley, Jacqueline. "Feeling Our Way: Love for God in Deuteronomy." *Catholic Biblical Quarterly* 65 (2003): 350–69.

Lash, Ephrem. "Biblical Interpretation in Worship," 35–48 in *The Cambridge Companion to Orthodox Christian Theology*. Edited by Mary Cunningham and Elizabeth Theokritoff. Cambridge: Cambridge University Press, 2008.

Laurin, Robert B. "Tradition and Canon," 261–74 in *Tradition and Theology in the Old Testament* (1977).

Levinas, Emmanuel. *Entre Nous: On Thinking of the Other*. New York: Columbia University Press, 1998.

———. "The Face," 85–92 in *Ethics and Infinity: Conversations with Philippe Nemo*. Pittsburgh: Duquesne University Press, 1985.

———. *Totality and Infinity*. Dordrecht: Kluwer Academic Publishers, 1991.

Levenson, Jon D. "Is There a Counterpart in the Hebrew Bible to New Testament Antisemitism?" *Journal of Ecumenical Studies* 22 (March 1985): 242–60.

———. *The Hebrew Bible, the Old Testament, and Historical Criticism*. Louisville: Westminster John Knox, 1993.

Levinson, Bernard L. "McConville's 'Law and Theology in Deuteronomy.'" *Jewish Quarterly Review* 80 (1990): 396–404.

———. *Deuteronomy and the Hermeneutics of Legal Innovation*. Oxford: Oxford University Press, 1997.

———. "The Hermeneutics of Tradition in Deuteronomy: A Reply to J. G. McConville." *Journal of Biblical Literature* 119 (2000): 269–86.

———. "The Reconceptualization of Kingship in Deuteronomy and the Deuteronomistic History's Transformation of Torah." *Vetus Testamentum* 51 (October 2001): 511–34.

———. "Reading the Bible in Nazi Germany: Gerhard von Rad's Attempt to Reclaim the Old Testament for the Church." *Interpretation* 62 (July 2008): 238–54.

Linafelt, Tod, ed., *Strange Fire: Reading the Bible after the Holocaust*. Sheffield: Sheffield Academic Press, 2000.

Lohfink, Norbert. *Das Hauptgebot: Eine Untersuchung literarischer Einleitungsfragen zu Dtn 5–11*. Analecta Biblica 20. Rome: Pontifical Biblical Institute, 1963.

———, ed. *Das Deuteronomium: Entstehung, Gestalt und Botschaft*. Leuven: Peeters, 1985.

———. "The Cult Reform of Josiah and Judah: 2 Kings 22–23 as a Source for the History of Israelite Religion," 459–76 in *Ancient Israelite Religion: Essays in Honour of Frank Moore Cross*. Edited by Patrick D. Miller, Paul D. Hanson, and S. Dean McBride. Philadelphia: Fortress Press, 1987.

———. "Der 'heilige Krieg' und der 'Bann' in der Bibel." *Internationale Katholische Zeitschrift "Communio"* 18 (January 1989): 104–12.

———. "Recent Discussions on 2 Kings 22–23: the State of the Question," 36–61 in *A Song of Power and the Power of Song: Essays on the Book of Deuteronomy* (1993).

———. *Theology of the Pentateuch: Themes of the Priestly Narrative and Deuteronomy* Translated by Linda M. Maloney. Minneapolis: Fortress Press, 1994.

———. "The Strata of the Pentateuch and the Question of War," 173–226 in idem, *Theology of the Pentateuch: Themes of the Priestly Narrative and Deuteronomy* (1994).

———. "The Reconceptualization of Kingship in Deuteronomy and the Deuteronomistic History's Transformation of Torah." *Vetus Testamentum* 51 (2001): 511–34.

———, and James G. Williams. "The Destruction of the Seven Nations in Deuteronomy and the Mimetic Theory." *Contagion: Journal of Violence, Mimesis, and Culture* 2 (Spring 1995): 103–17.

Luther, Martin. "Prefaces to the Old Testament." In *Luther's Works* 35. Edited by Helmut T. Lehman and E. Theodore Bachmann. Translated by Charles M. Jacobs. Philadelphia: Fortress Press, 1960.

Martínez, Florentino García, et al., eds. *Studies in Deuteronomy: In Honour of C. J. Labuschagne on the Occasion of His 65th Birthday.* Leiden: Brill, 1994.

McDonald, Nathan. *Deuteronomy and the Meaning of Monotheism.* Forschungen zum Alten Testament 2/1. Tübingen: Mohr Siebeck, 2003.

Marshall, Bruce D. "Christ and the Cultures: the Jewish People and Christian Theology," 81–100 in *Cambridge Companion to Christian*

Doctrine. Edited by Colin Gunton. Cambridge: Cambridge University Press, 1997.

Marshall, I. Howard. *Beyond the Bible: Moving from Scripture to Theology*. Grand Rapids: Baker, 2004.

Mayes, A. D. H. *Deuteronomy*. The New Century Bible Commentary. London: Oliphants, 1979.

———. "Deuteronomy 4 and the Literary Criticism of Deuteronomy." *Journal of Biblical Literature* 100 (1981): 23–51.

McBride, S. Dean. "Polity of the Covenant People: The Book of Deuteronomy," 78–93 in *A Song of Power and the Power of Song: Essays on the Book of Deuteronomy* (1993).

McCarthy, Carmel. *Biblia Hebraica Quinta, Fascicle 5: Deuteronomy*. Edited by Adrian Schenker, et al. Stuttgart: Deutsche Bibelgesellschaft, 2007.

McCarthy, Dennis J. *Treaty and Covenant: A Study in Form in the Ancient Oriental Documents and in the Old Testament*. Analecta Biblica 21a. Rome: Biblical Institute Press, 1978.

McConville, J. Gordon. *Law and Theology in Deuteronomy*. Sheffield: JSOT Press, 1984.

———. *Deuteronomy*. Apollos Old Testament Commentary 5. Nottingham: Apollos, 2002.

———. "A Dialogue with Gordon McConville on Deuteronomy III: A Response from Gordon McConville." *Scottish Journal of Theology* 56 (2003): 525–31.

———, and J. G. Millar. *Time and Place in Deuteronomy*. JSOTSup 179. Sheffield: Sheffield Academic Press, 1994.

McKenzie, Steven L. "The Theological Legacy of Deuteronomy," 28–43 in *Vergegenwärtingung des Alten Testaments: Beiträge zur biblischen Hermeneutik*. Edited by Christoph Bultmann, et al. Göttingen: Vandenhoek & Ruprecht, 2002.

Mendenhall, George E. "Covenant Forms in Israelite Traditions." *Biblical Archaeologist* 17 (1959): 49–76.

Merrill, Eugene H. *Deuteronomy*. The New American Commentary 4. Nashville: Broadman & Holman, 1994.

Miller, Charles H. *"As it is Written": The Use of Old Testament References in the Documents of Vatican II*. St. Louis: Marianist Communications Center, 1973.

Miller, Patrick D. "God the Warrior: A Problem in Biblical Interpretation and Apologetics." *Interpretation* 19 (January 1965): 39–46.

———."The Gift of God: Deuteronomic Theology of the Land." *Interpretation* 23 (October 1969): 451–65.

———. *The Divine Warrior in Early Israel*. Cambridge, MA: Harvard University Press, 1973.

———. *Deuteronomy*. Interpretation: A Biblical Commentary for Teaching and Preaching. Louisville: John Knox, 1990.

Moberly, W. L. "Toward an Interpretation of the Shema," 124–44 in *Theological Exegesis: Essays in Honor of Brevard S. Childs*. Edited by Christopher Seitz and Kathryn Greene-McCreight. Grand Rapids: Eerdmans, 1999.

Moran, William. "The Ancient Near Eastern Background of Love of God in Deuteronomy." *Catholic Biblical Quarterly* 25 (1963): 77–87.

Nelson, Richard D. "Ḥerem and the Deuteronomic Social Conscience," 39–54 in *Deuteronomy and Deuteronomic Literature*. Edited by Marc Vervenne. Leuven: Peeters, 1987.

———. *Deuteronomy*. Old Testament Library. Louisville: Westminster John Knox, 2002.

———. "Divine Warrior Theology in Deuteronomy," 241–60 in *A God So Near: Essays on Old Testament Theology in Honor of Patrick*

D. Miller. Edited by Brent A. Strawn and Nancy R. Bowen. Winona Lake: Eisenbrauns, 2003.

Nicholls, Benjamin Elliot. *Help to the Reading of the Bible*. London: SPCK, 1853.

Nicholson, Ernest W. "The Centralisation of the Cult in Deuteronomy." *Vetus Testamentum* 13 (1963): 380–89.

———. *Deuteronomy and Tradition*. Oxford: Basil Blackwell, 1967.

Niditch, Susan. *War in the Hebrew Bible: A Study in the Ethics of Violence*. Oxford: Oxford University Press, 1993.

Noth, Martin. *Überlieferungsgeschichtliche Studien 1: Die sammelnden und bearbeitenden Geschichtswerke im Alten Testament*. Tübingen: Max Niemeyer Verlag, 1957.

———. "The 'Re-Presentation' of the Old Testament in Proclamation," 76–88 in idem, *Essays on Old Testament Hermeneutics*. Edited by Claus Westermann. Translated by James Luther Mayes. Atlanta: John Knox Press, 1979.

———. *The Deuteronomistic History*. Sheffield: JSOT Press, 1981.

———. *The Chronicler's History*. Sheffield: Sheffield Academic Press, 1987.

O'Connell, Robert H. "Deuteronomy VIII 1-20: Asymmetrical Concentricity and the Rhetoric of Providence." *Vetus Testamentum* 40 (1990): 437–52.

———."Deuteronomy VII: 1-26: Asymmetrical Concentricity and the Rhetoric of Conquest." *Vetus Testamentum* 42 (April 1992): 248–65.

———. "Deuteronomy IX 7–X 7, 10-11: Panelled Structure, Double Rehearsal and the Rhetoric of Covenant Rebuke." *Vetus Testamentum* 42 (October 1992): 492–509.

O'Dowd, Ryan. *The Wisdom of Torah: Epistemology in Deuteronomy and the Wisdom Literature*. Forschungen zur Religion und Literatur des Alten und Neuen Testaments 225. Göttingen: Vandenhoeck & Ruprecht, 2009.

Oestreicher, Theodor. *Das deuteronomische Grundgesetz*. Beiträge zur Förderung christlicher Theologie 27/4. Gütersloh: Bertelsmann, 1923.

Oikonomou, Elias. "Scripture and Hermeneutics: An Orthodox View." *Immanuel* 26/27 (1994): 49–56.

Olson, Dennis T. *Deuteronomy and the Death of Moses: A Theological Reading*. Minneapolis: Augsburg Fortress Press, 1994.

Orr, James. *The Problem of the Old Testament*. New York: Charles Scribner's Sons, 1906.

Osborne, Grant. *The Hermeneutical Spiral: A Comprehensive Introduction to Biblical Interpretation*. Downers Grove, IL: InterVarsity Press, 1991.

Palmer, Richard E. *Hermeneutics: Interpretation Theory in Schleiermacher, Dilthey, Heidegger, and Gadamer*. Evanston: Northwestern University Press, 1969.

Pitkänen, Pekka. "Dr Jekyll and Mr Hyde? Deuteronomy and the Rights of Indigenous Peoples." *Political Theology* 11 (May 2010): 399–409.

Pontifical Biblical Commission. *The Interpretation of the Bible in the Church*. Boston: Pauline Books, 1993.

Poythress, Vern S. *Understanding Dispensationalists*. Grand Rapids: Zondervan, 1987.

Prokurat, Michael. "Orthodox Interpretation of Scripture," 59–100 in *The Bible in the Churches: How Various Christians Interpret the Scriptures* (1994).

Rast, Walter E. *Tradition History and the Old Testament*. Philadelphia: Fortress Press, 1972.

Rendtorff, Rolf. "Christological Interpretation as a Way of 'Salvaging' the Old Testament? Wilhelm Vischer and Gerhard von Rad," 76–91 in *Canon and Theology: Overtures to an Old Testament Theology*. Minneapolis: Fortress Press, 1993.

Rofé, Alexander. *Deuteronomy: Issues and Interpretation*. Edinburgh: T & T Clark, 2002.

———. "The Laws of Warfare in the Book of Deuteronomy: Their Origins, Intent and Positivity," 149–68 in idem, *Deuteronomy: Issues and Interpretation* (2002).

Rogerson, John. "An Outline of the History of Old Testament Study," 6–24 in *Beginning Old Testament Study*. Edited by John Rogerson. London: SPCK, 1998.

Ryrie, Charles. *Dispensationalism Today*. Chicago: Moody Press, 1980.

Schäfer-Lichtenberger, Christa. "Bedeutung und Funktion von Herem in biblisch-hebräischen Texten." *Biblische Zeitschrift* 38 (1994): 270–75.

———. "JHWH, Israel und die Völker aus der Perspektive von Dtn 7." *Biblische Zeitschrift* 40 (January 1996): 194–218.

Schleiermacher, Friedrich. *Hermeneutics and Criticism: And Other Writings*. Translated and edited by Andrew Bowie. Cambridge: Cambridge University Press, 1998.

Shearing, Linda, and Steven McKenzie, eds. *Those Elusive Deuteronomists: The Phenomenon of Pan-Deuteronomism*. Sheffield: Sheffield Academic Press, 1999.

Smith, George Adam. *Deuteronomy*. Cambridge: Cambridge University Press, 1918.

Sparks, Kenton L. *God's Word in Human Words: An Evangelical Appropriation of Critical Biblical Scholarship*. Grand Rapids: Baker, 2008.

Staerk, Willy. *Das Deuteronomium: Sein Inhalt und seine literarische Form: Eine kritische Studie*. Leipzig: Hinrich, 1894.

Steuernagel, Carl. *Der Rahmen des Deuteronomium*. Halle: J. Krause, 1894.

———. *Die Entstehung des deuteronomischen Gesetzes*. Halle: J. Krause, 1896.

———. *Deuteronomium und Josua und Allgemeine Einleitung in den Hexateuch*. Handkommentar zum Alten Testament 3. Göttingen: Vandenhoek & Ruprecht, 1900.

Strawn, Brent A., and Nancy R. Bowen, eds. *A God So Near: Essays on Old Testament Theology in Honor of Patrick D. Miller* (2003).

Stylianopoulos, Theodore G. "Scripture and Tradition in the Church," 21–34 in *The Cambridge Companion to Orthodox Christian Theology* (2008).

Thompson, John Alexander. *Deuteronomy*. Tyndale Old Testament Commentary. Downers Grove: InterVarsity Press, 1974.

———. *The Major Arabic Bibles: Their Origin and Nature*. New York: American Bible Society, 1956.

Tigay, Jeffrey H. *Deuteronomy*. JPS Torah Commentary. Philadelphia: Jewish Publication Society, 1996.

Tolkien, John Ronald Reuel. "J. R. R. Tolkien to Christopher Tolkien, November 7–8, 1944," in *The Letters of J. R. R Tolkien*. Edited by Humphrey Carpenter. London: HarperCollins, 2006.

———. *On Fairy Stories*. Edited by Verlyn Flieger and Douglas A. Anderson. London: HarperCollins, 2014.

Toorn, Karel van der. *Scribal Culture and the Making of the Hebrew Bible*. Cambridge, MA: Harvard University Press, 2007.

Townsend, Jeffrey L. "Fulfillment of the Land Promise in the Old Testament." *Bibliotheca Sacra* 142 (October 1985): 320–37.

Tucker, Gene M. *Form Criticism of the Old Testament.* Philadelphia: Fortress Press, 1971.

Von Rad, Gerhard. *Studies in Deuteronomy.* Translated by David Stalker. Studies in Biblical Theology 9. London: SCM, 1953.

———. *Deuteronomy.* London: SCM, 1966.

———. *The Problem of the Hexateuch and Other Essays.* London: SCM, 1984.

———. "The Promised Land and Yahweh's Land in the Hexateuch," 79–93 in idem, *The Problem of the Hexateuch and Other Essays* (1984).

———. *Holy War in Ancient Israel.* Grand Rapids: Eerdmans, 1991.

Walsh, Michael J. *Commentary on the Catechism of the Catholic Church.* London: Geoffrey Chapman, 1994.

Warrior, Robert Allen. "Canaanites, Cowboys, and Indians." *Union Seminary Quarterly Review* 59 (January 2005): 1–8.

Watson, Francis, ed. *The Open Secret: New Directions for Biblical Studies?* London: SCM, 1993.

Weinfeld, Moshe. "Deuteronomy—The Present State of Inquiry." *Journal of Biblical Literature* 86 (September 1967): 249–62.

———. *Deuteronomy and the Deuteronomic School.* Oxford: Clarendon Press, 1972.

———. "The Ban on the Canaanites in the Biblical Codes," 142–60 in *History and Traditions of Early Israel: Studies Presented to Eduard Nielsen.* Edited by André Lemaire and Benedikt Otzen. Leiden: Brill, 1993.

———. *Deuteronomy 1–11.* Anchor Bible 5. New York: Doubleday, 2006.

Welch, Adam. *Deuteronomy: The Framework to the Code.* Oxford: Oxford University Press, 1932.

Westermann, Claus. *Essays on Old Testament Hermeneutics.* Translated by James Luther Mays. Atlanta: John Knox Press, 1979.

Wevers, John Williams. *Notes on the Greek Text of Deuteronomy.* Atlanta: Scholars Press, 1995.

Whitelam, Keith. *The Invention of Ancient Israel: The Silencing of Palestinian History.* London: Routledge, 1996.

Wiseman, D. J. "The Vassal Treaties of Esarhaddon." *Iraq* 20 (1958): 1–99.

Wolff, Hans Walter. "The Kerygma of the Deuteronomic Historical Work," 83–100 in *The Vitality of Old Testament Traditions* (1982).

Wright, Christopher. "The Ethical Authority of the Old Testament: A Survey of Approaches, Part 1." *Tyndale Bulletin* 43 (May 1992): 101–20.

Wright, George Ernest. "The Book of Deuteronomy: Introduction and Exegesis," 311–30 in *The Interpreter's Bible* 2. Edited by George Arthur Buttrick. New York: Abingdon, 1952.

Wright, Jacob L. "Warfare and Wanton Destruction: A Reexamination of Deuteronomy 20:19-20 in Relation to Ancient Siegecraft." *Journal of Biblical Literature* 127 (September 2008): 423–58.

Würthwein, Ernst. *The Text of the Old Testament: An Introduction to the Biblia Hebraica.* Translated by Erroll F. Rhodes. London: SCM, 1980.

Younger, K. L. *Ancient Conquest Accounts: A Study in Ancient Near Eastern and Biblical History Writing.* JSOTSup 98. Sheffield: Sheffield Academic Press, 1990.

4. Jewish Studies/Israel/Jewish-Christian Relations

"Yad Hashoma: Biblical Village in the Judean Hills." Accessed 10 Feb 2011: http://www.yad8.com.

Berkhof, Hendrikus. "Israel as a Theological Problem for the Christian Church." *Journal of Ecumenical Studies* 6 (1969): 329–47.

Braverman, Mark. "Zionism and Post-Holocaust Christian Theology: A Jewish Perspective." *Holy Land Studies* 8 (2009): 31–54.

Cooper, Anthony Ashley. "State Prospects of the Jews." *Quarterly Review* 63 (January 1839): 166–92.

Crombie, Kelvin. *For the Love of Zion*. London: Hodder & Stoughton, 1991.

Croner, Helga. *Stepping Stones to Further Jewish-Christian Relations: An Unabridged Collection of Christian Documents*. London: Stimulus Books, 1977.

De Gasperis, Francesco Rossi. "Interreligious Dialogue in Jerusalem." Accessed 12 March 2012: http://www.etrfi.org/uploads/1/0/7/9/10798906/interreligious_dialogue_in_jerusalem.pdf.

Fischer, Eugene. "The Influence of Christian-Jewish Dialogue on Catholic Biblical Studies." *Studies in Christian-Jewish Relations* 3, Issue 1, Article 20 (2008).

Flannery, Edward. "Seminaries, Classrooms, Pulpits, Streets: Where We Have to Go," 128–48 in *Unanswered Questions: Theological Views of Jewish-Catholic Relations*. Edited by Roger Brooks. Notre Dame, IN: University of Notre Dame Press, 1988.

Gidney, W. T. *The History of the LSPCJ*. London: LSPCJ, 1908.

Goldberg, Louis, ed. *How Jewish is Christianity? Two Views on the Messianic Movement*. Grand Rapids: Zondervan, 2003.

Heldt, Petra. "A Brief History of Dialogue Between Orthodox Christians and Jews." *Immanuel* 26/27 (1994): 211–24.

———. "For Brothers to Dwell Together: Rethinking Christianity in Israel," 30–48 in *The Mountain of the Lord: Israel and the Churches*. London: Council of Jews and Christians, 1996.

———."Protestant Perspectives after 40 Years: A Critical Assessment of *Nostra Aetate*," 163–74 in *Nostra Aetate: Origins, Promulgation, Impact on Jewish-Catholic Relations*. Edited by Neville Lamdan and Alberto Melloni. Berlin: LIT Verlag, 2007.

———, and Malcolm Lowe. "Theological Significance of the Rebirth of the State of Israel: Different Christian Attitudes." *Immanuel* 22/23 (1989): 133–45.

International Conference of Christians and Jews. "An Address to the Churches (The Ten Points of Seelisberg)." Accessed 13 January 2011: http://www.ccjr.us/dialogika-resources/documents-and-statements/ecumenical-christian/567-seelisberg.

Kessler, Edward. *An Introduction to Jewish-Christian Relations*. Cambridge: Cambridge University Press, 2010.

Miller, Charles H. "Translation Errors in the Pontifical Biblical Commission's *The Jewish People and Their Sacred Scriptures in the Christian Bible*." *Biblical Theology Bulletin* 35 (2005):

Minerbi, Sergio I. *The Vatican and Zionism: Conflict in the Holy Land, 1895–1925*. Oxford: Oxford University Press, 1990.

Nerel, Gershon. "'Messianic Jews' in Eretz Israel (1917–1967)." *Mishkan: A Forum on the Gospel and the Jewish People* 27 (1997): 11–25.

———. "The Flagship of Hebrew New Testaments: A Recent Revision by Israeli Messianic Jews." *Mishkan* 41 (2004): 49–56.

———. "From Death to Life: The Restoration of Jewish Yeshua—Believers in the Land of Israel," 168–88 in *Israel: His People, His Land, His Story*. Edited by Fred Wright. Eastbourne: Thankful Books, 2005.

———. "'Post-mission' and 'Messianic Judaism'—Semantics and Reality (A Response to Dr. Mark Kinzer's *Postmissionary Messianic Judaism Three Years Later: Reflections on a Conversation Just Begun*)."

Accessed 10 Feb 2011: http://www.narkis.org/Archives/Lindsey%20Lectures/G.Nerel%20(Response%20to%20Kinzer)%202008.pdf.

Parkes, James. *Whose Land? A History of the Peoples of Palestine.* Middlesex: Penguin, 1971.

Perry, Yaron. *British Mission to the Jews in Nineteenth-Century Palestine.* London: Frank Cass, 2003.

Pontifical Biblical Commission. *The Jewish People and Their Sacred Scriptures in the Christian Bible.* Boston: Pauline Books, 2002.

Rosen, David. "The Jewish-Christian Relationship and the Middle East." Accessed 13 January 2011: http://rabbidavidrosen.net/Articles/Christian-Jewish%20Relations/The_Jewish-Christian_relationship_and_the_Middle_East_October_2010.pdf.

Synod of the Evangelical Lutheran Church of Saxony. "Declaration of Guilt Towards the Jewish People." Accessed 13 January 2011: http://www.ccjr.us/dialogika-resources/documents-and-statements/protestant-churches/eur/754-elcsaxony1948.

Van der Leest, Charlotte. "Conversion and Conflict in Palestine: The Missions of the Church Missionary Society and the Protestant Bishop Samuel Gobat." PhD dissertation, University of Leiden, 2008.

Wansbrough, Henry. "The Jewish People and its Holy Scripture in the Christian Bible." *International Theological Quarterly* 67 (2002): 265–75.

Wigoder, Geoffrey. *Jewish-Christian Relations since the Second World War.* Manchester: Manchester University Press, 1988.

Wright, Fred, ed. *Israel: His People, His Land, His Story* (2005).

World Council of Churches. "The Christian Approach to the Jews." Accessed 13 January 2011: http://www.ccjr.us/dialogika-resources/documents-and-statements/ecumenical-christian/737-wcc1948.

5. Interviews/Conversations/Meetings

Anonymous. "Justice and Reconciliation." Jerusalem, July 23, 2007.
Ateek, Naim. Jerusalem, July 28, 2007/Sheffield, May 26, 2012.
Katanacho, Yohanna. Nazareth, July 17, 2007.
Khader, Jamal. "The Church in Palestine: Crisis and Challenge." London: Heythrop College, June 24, 2009.
Raheb, Mitri. Bethlehem, July 25, 2007.
Ronecker, Karl-Heinz. Kirchzarten, April 7, 2010.

6. Maps and Pictures

"British Mandate of Palestine, 1920's." http://commons.wikimedia.org/wiki/File:BritishMandatePalestine1920.png, accessed March 18, 2015.

"Ottoman levant." http://en.wikipedia.org/wiki/Ma'an#/media/File:Ottoman_levant.png, accessed March 18, 2015.

Stalder, William Andrew, "Jerusalem: 40 Years of Reunification/Occupation." Photograph taken on June 24, 2007. © William Andrew Stalder.

"UN Partition Plan 1947 and UN Armistice Lines 1949, Map No. 3067 Rev.1, April 1983." Used by permission, United Nations Publication Board, New York.

Underwood & Underwood, "Palestine – Jerusalem: General Allenby's entrance into Jerusalem." Frank and Frances Carpenter Collection, Library of Congress. http://www.loc.gov/pictures/item/93513671/, accessed March 18, 2015.

Index

Abbas, Mahmoud (Palestinian President), xii, xvi, 179
ABCFM. *See* American Board of Commissioners for Foreign Missions
Abdul-Masih, Raed, 15n32, 18–19n68, 353
Abraham: covenant, 11n40, 46, 55, 56, 58, 63, 221, 229; dispensation, 47n176; person, 53, 54, 55, 56; promise to, 186–87, 189; son(s) of, 106
Abu El-Assal, Riah, 236n130
Adversus Iudaeos, 230n108
al-Aqsa: Intifada, 16; Mosque (Jerusalem), 203
al-Nahdah. 87–88
al-Nakba, 11, 26n86, 240. *See also* catastrophe

Alexander, Michael Solomon, 99, 101, 101n82, 102, 102n83, 102n86, 103, 104–5n94
Aliyah, 79n3, 80, 80n4
Allenby, Edmund (General), 83n10, 137, 137n1, 138, 148
Al-Liqa', 59n215, 59n216
American Board of Commissioners for Foreign Missions (ABCFM), 93, 93n49, 353
Amir, Yigal, xii–xiii
Ancient Israel, 57, 219, 221, 258, 323; history of, 212; invention of, 323; Israelites, 220; spiritual successors of, 221
Ancient Near East (ANE), 211, 253, 255–58, 260–61, 261n65, 262n72, 270, 272n120, 273n123, 274n136, 309
Anderson, Bernhard, 6, 7n23

ANE. *See* Ancient Near East

Anglican, 28, 95, 151, 159n79; Arab, 158n72, 160–66; bishop, 113, 148, 152n53, 183, 187n38, 328; bishopric in Jerusalem, 107–8, 151, 153–56, 157, 158n72; church/tradition/family, xiii, 20–21, 51n186, 106–8, 108n109, 114, 147, 151, 181, 235n129; Native Church, 153; Palestinian Anglican Church, 235; Palestinian priests, 133; person(s), 99; PNCC, 160–66; priest(s), 235n129; work of, 108n109, 323. *See also* Church of England

anti-Semitism, 68, 226, 230, 232

anti-Zionism, 233–34, 238n143

Antonius, George, 87–88

Arab(ism), 8n28, 23, 60, 87, 139; Christianity, and, 22 (*see also* Arab Christianity); countries, 10, 14, 175–76, 178–80, 184n27; Muslim(s), 124, 164 (*see also* Muslim); people, 10, 80–81, 144, 191n60; riots (1921), 239n145; riots (1928–1929), 144; Zionism, relation to, 81n8

Arab Anglicans (PNCC), 160–66

Arab Awakening, 13–14, 161n83

Arab Catholic, 166, 166n97

Arab Christian(s), xiv, 4, 8n28, 22–23, 27, 45, 74, 81, 81n8, 88–89, 89n36, 110, 112, 148, 150, 159, 184; Gershon Nerel's view of, 238; identity, 8, 89, 326, 328; leadership, 195n78. *See also* Palestinian Christian

Arab Christianity, xiv, 8n28, 22, 184; Orthodox, 67–69

Arab Evangelical Episcopal Community (AEEC), 157

Arab-Israeli, 9n29, 26nn85–86, 180n13; conflict, 38, 66, 74, 176, 179; war, 28n90, 145, 175, 178, 180n12

Arab Lutheran Church in Palestine, 157–59, 160, 166–72, 328

Arab nationalism, 10, 88–89, 136, 140, 143, 145, 159, 161, 164–65, 173

Arab Spring, 179

Arab-Zionist Conflict, 161n83, 172

Arabic culture/language, 12n44, 13, 13n45, 26n86, 30n101, 38, 87, 94, 97n67, 103n90, 112–13, 113n128, 114n132, 167, 167n104

INDEX

Armistice Agreements, 176; demarcation lines, 178, 178n6, 180n13
Assyrian Empire, 313–14
Assyrian Treaty, 257, 259–61, 310; Neo-Assyrian, 268
asymmetrical concentricity, 277n151, 286–94
Ateek, Naim, xiii, 13nn47–48, 27–38, 40, 43, 50, 65–66, 74, 236, 236n130, 236n134, 237, 249n19, 326, 332
Atiya, Aziz Sorial, 183
Audeh, Farid, 183
Auslegen, das (Explication), 4

Babylonian Empire: armies of, 264; destruction of Judah, 269n97
Babylonian Exile, 318, 318n317, 319, 321
Bachut, Hanna, 166–73, 182n20, 328
Balfour, Arthur James, 139–40
Balfour Declaration, 75, 139–40; Arab, response of, 142; CMS, response of, 151; PNCC, response of, 163–64
ban, xi, xiin4, xiii. *See also ḥerem*
Baptist: church/tradition/family, xiii, 20–21, 45, 51nn185–86, 52n188, 235; John the, 47n176; Naim Khoury, 45–50
Barclay, Joseph (Bishop of Jerusalem), 99, 105–6
Barnes, Albert, 113
Basler Missionsgesellschaft, 106
Bauckham, Richard, 32
Begin, Menachem, 27, 74
Beit Jala, 52n188, 59, 110, 188
Beit Sahour, 52n188, 166
believer, 35, 171, 222, 238; Arab, 45; Christian nations, 133; Jewish, 103; Old Testament, 58n212, 72
Benedict XVI (pope), 17, 229n105, 235n129
Berkhof, Hendrikus, 163
Berkhof, Louis, 58n212
Bethlehem, vii, 38, 44, 151, 214; Church, Evangelical Lutheran Christmas (*Weihnachtskirche*), 27, 39, 112n125, 167, 170; Church, First Baptist, 45, 51n185; Church, Young (*Junge Kirche*), 158, 167–68; International Center, 44; mission station of *Jerusalemsverein*, 105n94, 110; population of, 15n55; University of, 59

Bethlehem Bible College, 51–52, 52n189, 53, 56
Bible: abuse of biblical land traditions, 203; abuse (*Missbrauch*) of the Word of God, 169, 182, 337; authority of, 46, 51, 237, 339, 339n36, 340–41; Christian, 7; Christian reading of, 37, 61, 64; correspondence of relationships, 32–33, 332; de-judaization of, 235–37, 240n146, 336–37; Exodus, 256, 265n83, 272n116, 302, 311–12 (theme of, 34, 43n157, 206); gospel, 34, 42, 70, 74, 93n47, 104n91, 113, 114n134–35, 115, 115n140, 122, 134, 171, 191n60, 230; Gospel, Law and, 42; Gospels, 73; Hebrew, viii, 6n19, 7, 40, 71n259, 205, 317; Hexateuch, 206; historical records, 32; history of salvation, 61–63, 221; Holy Scripture, 37, 39, 40–42, 70, 129–30, 230–31; land traditions, 203–5, 207, 209, 211–2; New Testament (*see* New Testament); Old Testament (*see* Old Testament); Pentateuch, 206, 250, 252, 265n83; Pentateuch, Samaritan, 271n113, 273n128, 274n131, 274n133, 275n146; political readings of, 32–33, 35; prophecy (*see* prophecy); Tetrateuch, 317; Torah, 35, 204–5, 249n19, 264, 268n95, 274n134, 282–83, 283n177, 306, 316n306; witnesses of faith, 33

Bilu, 79, 81n8

Bishopric: Anglican, 107–8, 151, 153–56, 160; Protestant, 91n41, 94–95, 97, 99–107, 111–12, 112n126, 235n129; revival of, 107

Blyth, George (Bishop in Jerusalem), 99, 107–8

Boff, Clodovis, 32–33

Boston, Thomas, 113

Boutaji, Seraphim, 98, 123, 125–34, 327

Bowen, John, 112, 127

Braulik, Georg, 306, 319, 320, 337n300

Bridgeman, Charles, 154–55

Britain (Great). *See* Great Britain

British Mandate, 13, 15, 75, 80n4, 138, 141–46, 148–51, 153, 157, 160, 165, 165n94, 168n105, 173, 175, 327–28

Brown, George Francis Graham (Bishop in Jerusalem), 153, 155–56, 172n125
Brüderhaus, 110, 110n120, 111n121
Brueggemann, Walter, 36–37, 207, 207n23, 306, 340n38
Buber, Martin, 246
Bultmann, Rudolph, 7
Bunson, Christian Charles von, 100
Bunyan, John, 112

Camp David: Accords, 178n8; Summit, 179
Canaan, 203, 250, 266
Canaan, Bishara, 110, 112
Canaanite(s), 270, 271n109, 287, 290, 306, 312, 336. *See also* perspectives on Palestinian Christian Hermeneutics of the Old Testament: Michael Prior: "Reading with the Eyes of Canaanite"
canon (canonical): books, 6–7, 27, 70n257, 129, 207–8, 216n60, 238, 249n18, 324, 340, 341n42; law, 69, 180n109; non-canonical, 70n257
capitulation, 85, 149
Carroll, Robert P., 222–23

Cash, Wilson, 153
catastrophe, xii–xiii, 11, 25–26, 26n86, 45, 60, 74–75, 180n12, 267, 325, 327–28; day of, 175; destruction of Jerusalem (586BCE), 263; eucatastrophe, 342; faith, of, 27, 38, 38n131, 39, 45, 50, 58, 61, 66, 240. *See also* al-Nakba
Catechism of the Catholic Church, 64, 64n234
catechist, 114, 114n131, 118, 125–26
Catholic: Arab, 166, 166n97; Arabic-speaking, 60n219; Bible, 6n19; Catechism, 64n324; encyclicals (*see* Documents); Hebrew-speaking, 60n219; Hermeneutics, 62, 64–66 (*see also* Sabbah, Michel); interpretive tradition, 212–25, 215n57, 241, 336 (*see also* Miller, Charles); Latin Rite, 59n213; missions, 15n51, 20, 90n41, 95–96n60; Palestinian, 212, 220–22, 224; *Propaganda Fide*, 95, 95n59; protectorates, 86; schools, 88, 88n33; standards of interpretation, 213–25, 337 (*see also* Miller,

Charles); superiors general, Roman Cathlic, 14; Vatican Council, First, 130; Vatican Council, Second, 108n108
Catholic Church(es), xiii, 20–21, 85, 91, 95, 147, 214; Bethlehem, in, 214; Chaldean, 20n72, 21; conflict with Gobat, 103; Greek, 21, 112, 125–26; Eastern, 85, 166n97; Hebrew, 20n72; Jews, view of, 231; Latin, 21, 85; Melkite, 14; Nerel, views of, 226, 235n129, 239n143; Oriental, 20–21, 85; Protestant, views of, 104n91; Uniate, 20
Chacour, Elias, 14, 17, 18n67
Chafer, Lewis Sperry, 48
Childs, Brevard, 36
Christ, 21, 36, 51, 52n188, 63, 71, 112, 114n134, 122–23, 135, 152, 169, 171–72, 183, 189, 191, 327; authority (value) of, 35, 35n120, 237; death and resurrection of, 31, 230; Haaretz, owner of, 53–56; hermeneutical key, 36–38, 40, 43–45, 61, 64, 66; Jews, and, 133; Luther's view of, 43, 171; nationalism, and, 168; second coming, 99; Spirit of, 17, 230; time of, 15n51. *See also* Jesus
Christensen, Duane, 251n22, 258–59, 260, 265–66, 273n126, 274n134, 280–84, 293n201, 294, 305n246, 306
Christian(s): Western, 32; Eastern, 118, 154
Christianity, 6, 48, 137; Arab (*see* Arab Christian(s) and Arab Christianity); biblical, 32; carnival, 16; commandment of, 227; conversion to, 99–100, 102, 102n83, 152; Holy Land, in, 15; Jewish people, relationship to, 229n105, 234; primitive, 7; Protestant, 46, 100; revivalist, 92n47; sites of, 180; spirit of, 191n60; value of, 164; Western, 23, 238
Christison, Kathleen, 22–23
Church Missionary Society (CMS), 91n41, 94–98, 103n90, 105–8, 108nn108–9, 109–10, 113n130, 134, 151–53, 155, 155n61, 157; Boutaji and Kawar, 125–28, 128n84, 133; Jamal, and, 116, 118–20, 122–24; PNCC, and, 160–61, 163, 166

INDEX

Church of England, 98, 100–101, 123, 126–28; Articles of Religion, 128, 133; Palestinian Clergy, relationship with, 98, 126–28, 128n184, 129, 131; PNCC, relationship with, 162, 165 (*see also* PNCC); Protestant Bishopric in Jerusalem, 94; United Evangelical Church in Prussia, joint venture with, 94, 100–101; Tractarians (High Church Party), 104n93, 106. See *also* Anglican; missions and institutions

Church(es): Arab Anglican, 160–66; Arab Lutheran, 143n19, 157–59, 160, 166, 166–73; Baptist (*see* Baptist); electronic, 233; Evangelical Lutheran, 27, 39, 228; German Protestant, 92, 92n47, 104n94, 109–12, 112n126, 147; Greek Orthodox (*see* Greek Orthodox); Lutheran Arab Church of Bethlehem, The (*Die evangelisch-arabischen Gemeinde zu Bethlehem*), 158–59; Palestinian Anglican Church, 235; Palestinian Lutheran Church of Jerusalem, The, (*Die palästinensisch-evangelische Gemeinde Jerusalem*), 158–59; Palestinian Protestant, 104, 105n94; Uniate, 20, 86; Young, 157–58, 158n71, 159

Churchill, Winston, 140n10, 142n17

Clayton, Gilbert, 161

Clements, Ronald, 250n22, 252n26, 262, 263–65, 266–67, 268n95, 306, 314

Clendenin, Daniel B., 70n257

CMS. *See* Church Missionary Society

Colbi, Saul, 151

concentric design or structure, 282, 284, 284n181, 286, 292–93, 293n198–99, 307. See *also* concentricity

concentricity, 286. See *also* assymetrical concentricity

conquest: Arab (638 CE), 15, 164; biblical, 206, 306, 313, 313n290; paraenesis (Deuteronomy), 286, 289, 293; Zionism, discourse of, 205; Zionist, of Palestine, 210

conversion, 20, 23n77, 63, 91, 94n9, 99, 152, 183n26

401

Cooper, Anthony Ashley, 99. *See* Shaftesbury, 7th Earl of
covenant: Abrahamic, 11n40, 46, 63, 221; Davidic, 63, 221; grace, of, 58, 58n212; heuristic images of, 221; Israel, with, 237; League of Nations, of, 141n12, 142n14, 146n36; Mosaic, 63, 68, 73, 221; new, 63, 229, 324; Noah, 221; old, 63, 72, 73; Old Testament, 230; Palestinians and Israelis, relevance for, 61; theology (theologian), 47n174, 48, 56, 58. *See also* Deuteronomy
Cragg, Kenneth, xiv, xvii, 8n28, 25, 88, 138–40
Craigie, Peter C., 259n55, 276n147, 306
Crimean War, 84n18

Damascus, 138–39
Danby, Herbert, 154
Davies, Philip R., 206, 211, 323, 336
deacon, persons ordained as, 102n83, 105n95, 114, 125–26
Delitzsch, Franz, 233
denomination(s), 19, 21, 103, 235. *See also* non-denominational
destruction, 45, 275n143, 318; buildings, of, 264; devote (dedicate) to, 271, 271n107, 287, 290, 296, 299, 300n229, 301; Northern Kingdom (722 BCE), of, 338; Palestine, of, 26n86; peoples, of, 204, 296, 299, 300n229; religious paraphernalia, 299, 301; Temple (586 BCE), of, 265, 267, 267n93, 319. *See also* ban, *ḥerem*
Deuteronomic Code, 251, 252n26, 276, 279
Deuteronomist, 298n219
deuteronomistic: author, editor, 317; editing, 297, 297n214; historian, 252; idealism, 266
Deuteronomistic History (DtrH), 268n96, 269, 304, 317, 318n313, 318n317, 319, 319n318, 321
Deuteronomy, 120; amphictyony, 256, 278; author of (Dtr) (*see* Dtr [author of Deuteronomy]); centralization of the cult, 257, 264, 267; Decalogue, 251, 252n26, 261n68, 276, 279–80, 280n167, 298n218, 301, 303, 305, 305n247; Hezekiah, 257, 262–63, 265, 269, 279, 313–15,

333; Josiah, 257, 258n48, 262–63, 265, 269, 279, 313–15, 333; law (civil, cultic, criminal), 250–52, 252n26, 254n34, 256, 261, 262n72, 264, 267–68, 277, 277n152, 278–80, 298, 298n216, 299, 299n224, 307–8, 308n267, 309, 309n270, 310, 315, 317–18; legal innovation, 264, 267, 270n99; literary forms, 253–56; monarchy, 264–65; Moses (Mosaic Authorship), 250, 250n21, 251–52, 255, 257, 259, 264–65, 265n83, 270, 271n112, 277, 282, 299; origins, 257–69; paraenesis, 251, 254, 286, 289, 293, 299; rhetorical purpose, 269–70; scribes (scribal tradition), 259, 262–63, 268–70, 279, 295n205, 316, 316nn306–7, 321, 338–39, 340n39; text and translation, 270–76; title and contents, 250–53; traditions (*see* tradition); *Urdeuteronomium*, 252, 252n23, 319; wisdom writers, 262–63

Deuteronomy 7, xi–xiii, xv, 249; hortatory introductions, 276; literary forms, 276–80; literary structure, 280–94; meaning, 311–21; message, 305–10; text and translation, 270–76; traditions, 294–305

Deutsche Christentumgesellschaft, 108

dhimmi, 83–84, 84n15, 89

diachronic, 57, 57n210, 216n60, 334

dialogue: culture, with, 223; fraternal, 230; interreligious, 68–69, 193, 336, 342; Jewish-Christian, 68–69, 231–32, 234; Jewish-Palestinian Christian, 333; Palestinian-Western Christianity, 238; religion and politics, 245; strains of loyalties, and, 245

Diocese, 14, 19, 59–61, 69n251, 127, 154, 157n70, 160, 181n16

Dispensationalism, 46–47, 47nn174–75, 48, 58

Dispensationalist, 47, 47n173, 47n175, 48–49, 52n188

documents: *Declaration of Guilt towards the Jewish People* (ELCS), 228; *Dei Verbum*, 62, 62n224, 66n241, 209, 215n56; *Divino Afflante Spiritu* (papal encyclical), 215, 215n55, 215n57, 216; *Fundamental*

Agreement between the Holy See and the State of Israel, The, 226; *General Pastoral Plan, The,* 214, 217, 220, 224; *Le peuple juif et ses Saintes Écritures dans la Bible chrétienne (The Jewish People and their Sacred Scripture in the Christian Bible),* 214, 217–21, 223, 231n111; Memorandum by a Group of Middle Eastern Theologians, A, 187–89; *Nostra Aetate* ("Declaration on the Relationship of the Church to Non-Christian Religions"), 66, 217n68, 229–30, 230n108, 231, 231n110; *Notes on the Correct Way to Present Jews and Judaism in Catholic Preaching and Teaching,* 232; *Providentissimus Deus* (papal encyclical), 214–15; *Reading the Bible Today in the Land of the Bible,* 59–60, 65–66, 216–17, 220; *Report on the Christian Approach to the Jews* (WCC), 228; *Ten Points of Seelisberg,* 226, 226n96

Doddridge, Philip, 113

Dome of the Rock (Jerusalem), 203

Driver, S. R., 252, 254, 254nn34–35, 265n83, 271n106, 273n127, 275n139, 280, 306

Dtr (author of Deuteronomy), 317, 317n310, 318–19

Eastern Orthodox, 20–21, 85

ecclesiology, 115, 122, 133, 160

Eisler, Jakob, 108

Ekin, Larry, 184n27, 187n38

election, 43n157, 61, 187–88, 189n48, 190n58, 213, 217, 228–29, 237, 269, 272n117, 288, 291, 306, 332–33

EMOK. *See Evangelische Mittelostkommission*

Epstein, Yitzhak, 80

Erlöserkirche, 112

evangelical, xiii, 18, 20–21, 46, 51–58, 91, 93n47, 99, 106–7, 125–26, 153, 160–61, 235, 330, 333–34, 334n20. *See also* Churches

Evangelical Synod of Syria and Lebanon, 183

Evangelische Mittelostkommission (EMOK), 193, 194n72

evangelist, 110, 114, 116, 122, 228

exile: Babylonian, 263, 318, 318n317, 319–21, 332–33, 338;

Jews (nineteenth century CE) in, 79; period of (exilic), 267–68, 317–19, 321, 339; period of (post-exilic), 263–64, 266–68, 319–20, 339; period of (pre-exilic), 268, 316, 319, 321

Exodus: book, 256, 265n83, 272n116, 302, 311–12; event, 289; theme, 34, 43n157, 208

Farah, Rafiq, 105n94, 105n97, 147n39, 156
Fenn, C. C., 126, 128
Fischer, Eugene, 230n108, 231–32, 232n113
Fisher, Julia, 45, 51n185
Fisk, Pliny, 93
Flannery, Edward, 230
Fliedner, Theodor, 105n94, 109, 109n113
Florovsky, George, 71, 71n263, 72
Francis (pope), xi, xvi
fraternité. *See* Perspectives on Palestinian Christian Hermeneutics of the Old Testament, Gershon Nerel: "Reading with the Eyes of Jewish-Christian *fraternité*"
Frederick William IV (King of Prussia), 99–101, 101n80, 104n91

French Mandate, 141
fundamentalism: Christian, 46, 46n171, 51n186; Islamic, 13

Gasperis, Francesco Rossi de, 228, 239
Gaza, xi, 17n63, 52n188, 178–79, 180n13
Gobat, Samuel (bishop of Jerusalem), 94n51, 95, 96n62, 97–98, 98n70, 99, 103, 103n90, 104, 104n91, 104nn93–94, 105, 105n94, 106n100, 108, 108n108, 109, 109nn112–13, 109n115, 110, 114, 124, 126, 155n61
God: Creator, 31; Father, 42; gift of, 62; glory of, 48; goodness of, 17; Holy Spirit, 5n9, 46, 51, 62, 62n224, 63, 71n259, 126, 132, 132n195; justice (of), 30–31, 34, 42; kingdom of, 63, 232; love of, 309n270, 310n274; Palestinian Christian views of, xiv, 27, 29, 31, 35–36, 39, 42, 44, 50n185, 52n189, 53–56, 237, 249; people of, 49, 132n195, 205, 230–31, 308, 314; plan of, 219; promises of, 46, 50, 205, 332; purpose of, 48; Son, 219 (*see*

also Jesus and Christ); will of, 47; wisdom, 51; word of (Bible), 35, 46, 51, 51n185, 51n187, 56–58, 61–62, 65, 70, 112, 118, 118n152, 122, 125–26, 130–34, 169, 182, 259; Yahweh, 255n35, 263n74, 268–69, 278n157, 298n219, 318, 318n317

Gospel, 34, 42, 70, 73–74, 93n47, 104n91, 113–14, 114n135, 115, 115n140, 122, 134, 171, 191n60, 230

Gräbe, Uwe, 182n19, 187, 190n58, 192–94, 195n78, 329

Grand Palestinian Revolt, 143. *See also* Great Arab Revolt (1936–39)

Great Arab Revolt (1936–39), 144, 144n27, 163

Great Britain, 10, 10n38, 91, 94n52, 99n74, 101, 101n81, 138–41, 144–45, 150, 164, 173n126

Great War, the, 141, 147–48, 152, 157, 158n71

Greek Orthodox: Church, 39, 45–46, 66, 68, 73–74, 84, 187n37, 335; Patriarch, 97; persons, 18. *See also* Hanna, Atallah

Greek Orthodox Patriarchate of Jerusalem, 21

Haaretz, 54–56
Haddad, Schedid Baz, 165n93, 167, 173n126, 328
Haifa, 14, 67, 112, 147n39
Hanna, Atallah, xiii, 28, 66–74, 326, 335
Hanselmann, Siegfried, 92n47, 109
Harcourt, Hugh, 190, 190n58
Hauptachse, 307. *See also* virtual axis
Heldt, Petra, 69, 69n251
ḥerem, 224n90, 285, 307–8, 310–13, 313n294, 315, 315n304, 319–21, 338. *See also* ban
Hermeneutics, 3–8, 244–48, 326–29, 330, 337–42. *See also* Palestinian Christian Hermeneutics of the Old Testament (PCHOT)
Herzl, Theodor, 26, 225, 231
ḥesed, 373n127, 285
historical-critical method, 5, 215, 220–23, 241n147, 248n17, 330, 332, 334n20, 336–37, 339
history: ancient Israel, 206, 212; anti-Semitism, of, 68; Arab-

Israeli conflict, 176; Bible, and, 41, 119, 122–23, 135; biblical, and, 32, 41; God, working in, 58, 64; Islamic, 8n28; Israel, of, 25n80, 60, 63; Jews (Jewish people), 37; mission, 92n45, 92n47, 93n49, 94n55, 95n57; Old Testament, of, 6n14, 156; Palestine (Palestinian), 9, 12, 60, 323; Palestinian Christianity, 79–197; PCHOT, 181–95; PNCC, 165; reception, 204, 207, 337, 338n31; redemption, 121; salvation (*see* salvation history); subject of, 119; tradition, 339n36. *See also* Deuteronomy

Hittites, 256, 270, 287

Holladay, William, 190, 190n58

Holocaust, 8n26, 68, 226, 228, 228n103, 239

Holy Land, xvi, 14–16, 18, 22n73, 92n47, 100–101, 109n114, 110, 110n116, 111, 172, 195n78, 209

Holy War(s), xiv, 39, 112, 271n108, 278–80

Hooft, Visser't, 183

Hummel, Thomas, 94, 104n91, 105

ICCJ. *See* International Council of Christians and Jews

ICE. *See* International Christian Embassy

identity: Arab, 89, 158; Arab Christian, 8, 8n28; biblical figures, 236; Christian, 221; churches, 101n80, 159n79; cultural, 12; Deuteronomy, in, 315; Jewish, 11; land, 13n45; language, 13; Palestinian, 11–12, 67, 186, 339; Palestinian Christian (*see* Palestinian Christian identity); Palestinian national, 9, 11–12, 14, 73; race, 12; religion, 13

ideology, 201–2, 243, 255, 268, 304, 313n290, 329–30

independence, 9–10, 84, 89, 107n102, 139, 145, 175; catastrophe, or, 25; Day of Independence, 175; ecclesiastical, 101n80, 165n94, 173, 331; literary (biblical), 271–72n114, 299; missionary societies (CMS), of, 108nn108–9; PNCC, of, 160, 162–63; War of Independence, 145n34, 175

injustice, 16, 61, 164, 186, 191n60, 207, 245n7. *See also* justice innovation, 304; legal, 264, 267, 270. *See also* Levinson, Bernard L.

International Christian Embassy (ICE), 22

International Council of Christians and Jews (ICCJ), 226, 231n111

International Messianic Jewish Alliance, 233

interpretation: Arab Lutheran, 172; biblical, 36, 43, 62, 66, 120, 185–86, 186n33, 187, 191–92, 194, 196, 231, 326, 329–30, 335; Catholic, 214–16, 222–23; critical methods of, 221, 331; evangelical, 56–57; fundamentalist, 221; grammatical, 120; illumination, necessity of, 134; Jewish, 216; literal, 48; Middle Eastern models of, 190; misinterpretation (*Missbrauch*), 52, 172, 204, 245, 336; Neo-Marcionite, 190n58; Old Testament, of, 3, 209, 326; Orthodox, 70, 190, 335 (*see also* Greek Orthodox); Palestinian Christian, 238, 330; Protestant, 70, 168; Quranic literalist, 221; theological, 71; typological, 40, 72; western models of, 190, 196; Zionist, 191n60, 221. *See also* Deuteronomy

Intifada: Aqsa, Al-, 16; first, 13n47, 29n94, 179, 195–96; second, 13n47, 16, 179, 179n10; spiritual, 234–35

Isaac, Munther, ix, 333

Islam, 8n28, 16, 83, 137, 154

Islamic, 23, 53n192, 74, 150n46; fundamentalism, 13; history, 8n28

Israel: ancient (*see* ancient Israel); anti-, 234–35, 238–40 (*see also* anti-Zionism); biblical, 48, 237; history of, 79–90, 137–46, 175–80; Jewish State of, 11, 23, 37, 189; modern State of, xii–xv, 8n26, 10–12, 23, 25–28, 28n90, 38, 38n131, 48, 50, 50n185, 53–54, 58, 66–69, 73–75, 80, 156, 175–80, 181–82, 185, 195, 203, 217, 226, 238, 240, 245n7, 325, 327–28, 331, 333, 336; new (true), 72. *See also* Arab-Israeli Conflict; Arab-Israeli War; catastrophe; Day of Independence; Deuteronomy; Israelite; Jewish immigration to

Israel/Palestine; relations, Arab-Israeli; relations, Palestinian-Israeli; treaty, Egypt-Israel Peace Treaty; *Verus Israel*; War of Independence

Israelite, 54, 204, 206, 213, 219–20, 251, 263, 278, 303, 310, 315, 320

Jamal, Chalil, 98, 112–25, 126, 128, 128n184, 132–35, 327

JEM. *See* Jerusalem and East Mission

Jerusalem, vii, 12n44, 18, 22n73, 24, 33n112, 49, 50n185, 53, 59, 67, 83, 112–14, 123, 134, 151, 180n13, 225, 232, 324; Allenby's entry in, 83n10, 137; Anglican Bishopric in, 153–56, 161, 162n86, 183, 328; Arab Lutheran Church in, 158–59, 166–67; Arab Patriarch of, 67; biblical, 236n134, 264–65, 314, 338; Bishopric Fund, 108; East, 179; Fall of (586 BCE), 267, 318, 321; Greek Orthodox Church of, 66; Greek Orthodox Patriarchate of, 21, 86, 91n41; heavenly, 64n234; holy places in, 84n18; Israeli policies in, 52n188, 68n249; Jews (biblical) in, 227; Latin Patriarch of, 17, 59, 66, 195; Latin Patriarchate of, 21; Nebi Musa Riots in, 143; new, 63; Old City, 45, 178; Protestant Bishopric in, 94, 97, 99–108, 111, 235n129; religious work in, 108n109, 110–12, 113n130; *sanjak* of, 83; Sabeel Center in, 37; St. George's Cathedral in, 27; Tantur Ecumenical Center, 59n215; Temple, 267, 267n93; theological term, as, 191; West, 22, 46

Jerusalem Day, 24

Jerusalem and East Mission (JEM), 108, 154–55

Jerusalemsverein, 105n94, 109–10, 110n116, 166

Jesus, 14, 27, 30n101, 34–37, 42, 46, 50n185, 51n185, 63–65, 114n134, 117n149, 121, 133, 168, 169, 209, 225, 227, 236, 236n134, 327

Jew(s), 54, 100, 124, 144. *See also* Messianic Jew

Jewish, 42, 44, 68, 79, 168, 170; Bible, reading of, 37; Chalil Jamal's views of, 123–25; converts to Christianity, 101–2, 102n87; Home

409

(Homeland) in Palestine, 26, 79, 139–40, 142, 142n13, 144–46, 150–52, 155, 163, 168n105; identity, 11, 26; immigration to Israel/Palestine (*see Aliyah*); Israel, perspective of, 25; Michael Prior's view of, 205; Michel Sabbah's view of, 66; Naim Khoury's view of, 45–47, 50; non-Jewish communities in Palestine, 10, 139–40, 142, 144, 146; Orthodox Christian view of, 69, 73; Palestinian Christian views of, 74; people, 170, 187–89; people, history of, 37; Pius X (pope) views of, 225–26; population in Palestine, 11, 81, 87, 94; question, 26, 79; Rennie MacInnes' view of, 154; revolts (Bar-Kokhba), 12n44; state, 11, 23, 37; Temple, 12; Yohanna Katanacho's view of, 54, 64. *See also* Jewish-Christian relations; Muslim, Muslim-Jewish conflict; nationalism, Jewish; Perspectives on Palestinian Christian Hermeneutics of the Old Testament, Gershon Nerel: "Reading with the Eyes of Jewish-Christian *fraternité*"; *Yishuv*; Zionist

Jewish-Christian relations, 219, 225–32, 238–39, 241, 335, 337, 342

Jizya, 83

John Paul II (pope), 95n59, 217, 222

Josiah, 257, 258n48, 262–63, 265–66, 269, 279, 313–15, 333

Jowett, William, 96, 96nn62–64

Judaism, 36, 48, 137, 154, 168, 187, 227, 230, 232, 238, 282, 327

justice, 30, 30n101, 31, 33n112, 34–35, 38, 38n131, 42–43, 54, 60, 65, 84, 164, 192–93, 244n6, 247–48, 264. *See also* injustice

Kairos Palestine Document, 19

Kaiserwerth Diakonissen (Deaconesses of Kaiserwerth), 109, 109n113

Kallai, Zecharia, 53

Kassab, Farid, 81n8

Kassab, Najla, 245, 245n7

Katanacho, Yohanna, xiii, 22, 28, 35n121, 51–58, 326, 333–34, 334nn19–20

Kawar, Michael, 98, 123, 125–34, 327
Kessler, Edward, 228, 228n103
Khalidi, Rashid, 10, 10n38, 11
Khodr, George, 69, 69n251, 187n38, 190–91
Khoury, Geries, 59
Khoury, Naim, xiii, 28, 45–50, 51, 51n185, 52n188, 74, 326, 333, 333n18
Khoury, Rafiq, xvi
Klein, F. A., 113, 113n130
Klostermann, August, 277, 277n152, 278–79
Knesset, 50n185
Knight, Douglas, 340–41

land, xii, xiv, 12–13, 13n45, 14, 15n51, 16–17, 18n67, 23, 27, 29, 34, 38n131, 39, 44, 50, 50n185, 52, 52n189, 53, 53n191, 54–55, 61, 65, 80–81, 93, 102, 121, 124, 131, 138, 142, 142n13, 145n31, 148, 148n41, 166, 168, 179, 184, 190–91, 203, 205–6, 209, 249, 299, 306, 309, 320–21, 326; Canaan, of, 250; inhabitants of, xiii, 138, 142, 148, 148n41, 312, 320, 337; Israel, of, 38n131, 50n185, 79, 178, 236–37; land without a people . . . , 11, 11n40; Palestine, of, 10, 12, 83, 236; promise of, 187–89, 191, 204, 207n23, 217, 221, 237, 328; Promised, 46, 205–6, 266, 306, 310; purchase (sale) of, 67n247, 143, 145, 146n37. *See also* Bible, abuse of biblical land traditions; Bible, land traditions; Deuteronomy; Holy Land; Jewish Home (Homeland) in Palestine; occupation
Latin Patriarch. *See* Jerusalem, Latin Patriarch of
Latin Patriarchate of Jerusalem. *See* Jerusalem, Latin Patriarchate of
Latin. *See* Catholic
Lawrence, T. E., 138
League of Nations, 141, 143, 149
Lemche, Niels, 206, 211, 336
Letter Commendatory, 103, 104n91
Levant, 10, 100n76, 110
Levenson, Jon D., 6–7
Levinas, Emmanuel, 246–48
Levinson, Bernard L., 255n39, 265–66, 266n86, 268, 268n95
Levites, 256, 262n71

Lewis, Bernard, 9, 12, 12n44, 83, 85, 89, 89n36
Liberation Theology. *See* Palestinian Liberation Theology (PTL); Palestinian Theology of Liberation (PTL); theology
liturgy, 29, 62, 69, 73, 184, 188, 213, 258
living stones, 17, 18n67
Löffler, Roland, 143, 146n38, 158n71, 158n75, 159, 159n79, 161, 161n83, 162n85, 163, 166nn97–98, 172
Lohfink, Norbert, 266, 271n108, 280, 283, 284–86, 291, 293–95, 300–301, 302, 304–5, 307, 307n265, 307n267, 313, 315, 338
London Society for Promoting Christianity amongst the Jews (LSPCJ), 94, 94n53
López, Felix García, 306
LSPCJ. *See* London Society for Promoting Christianity amongst the Jews
Lückhoff, Johann, 22
Lückhoff, Martin, 106n100
Luther, Martin, 43, 167–68, 170, 170n114, 170n116, 171–72

Lutheran. *See* Arab Lutheran Church in Palestine; Bethlehem, Evangelical Lutheran Christmas Church; Church(es), Arab Lutheran; Church(es), Evangelical Lutheran; Church(es), The Lutheran Arab Church of Bethlehem (*Die evangelisch-arabischen Gemeinde zu Bethlehem*); Church(es), The Palestinian Lutheran Church of Jerusalem (*Die palästinensisch-evangelische Gemeinde Jerusalem*); interpretation, Arab Lutheran; Jerusalem, Arab Lutheran Church in

MacDonald, James Ramsay (Prime Minister), 143–44
MacInnes, Rennnie (Bishop in Jerusalem), 148, 152n53, 153–55, 155nn60–61, 160–61, 162n86
Mallik, Charles, 183
Mandate. *See also* British Mandate
Mandel, Neville J., 81n8
Marcionism (neo-Marcionism), 42, 184, 188, 190n58, 238n140, 328
Marshall, I. Howard, 56

Marten, Michael, 91
Mayes, A. D. H., 250n22, 254n35, 271n114, 282n173, 295, 297–300, 301, 301n233, 302, 304–6
McConville, J. G., 259–60, 265–66, 273n126, 280, 293n201, 300, 300n229, 305–6
McDermott, Dan, 67
McGrath, Alister E., 65n241
MECC. *See* Middle East Council of Churches
Melanie, May, 19n71, 324
Merrill, Eugene H., 259n55, 306
Messianic: Age, 205; expectation, 63; interpretation, 209; Jew, 20–21, 233
Messianic Jewish Alliance of Israel, 233
Middle East, vii, 10, 12, 17, 19, 20, 20n72, 26n85, 38, 45, 47n173, 66n243, 86–87, 89, 179, 181n16, 183, 185–87, 187n37, 188–89, 192, 194, 194n71, 197, 229n105, 239, 245, 331
Middle East Council of Churches (MECC), 20, 20n72, 189n51, 192–93, 194n72, 197
Miller, Charles H., xv, 202, 212–25, 240, 241n147, 248n17, 249, 329–30, 335–37

millet, 84, 84n16, 89, 150, 150n46
minority, 87; Bible, in, 42; Christian, 15, 18, 81, 88, 89, 150, 153, 173, 193; double-minority, 51n185; Jewish, 81, 172n125
Mishnah, 267n93
missions and institutions: basis and motivations of, 91–93; American Board of Commissioners for Foreign Missions (ABCFM), 93–94; London Society for Promoting Christianity amongst the Jews (LSPCJ) (*see* LSPCJ); Church Missionary Society (CMS) (*see* CMS); German, 108–12. *See also* Anglican/Protestant Bishopric; PNCC
Moran, W. L., 273n123, 308, 309n270
Muhammad (Prophet), 8
Munayer, Salim, 333
Muslim, 8n28, 13, 13n47, 38n131, 44, 51n185, 53n192, 58, 81, 84–85, 88–89, 93, 96–97, 115, 124, 150, 150n46, 152, 156, 164, 173, 234, 240; countries, 89n36; militants, 17n63; Muslim-Christian relations, 53,

53n192; Muslim-Jewish conflict, 17; ruler, 83, 85; state, 83

Nahdah, al-. *See* al-Nahdah
Nakba, al-. *See* al-Nakba
Napoleon, 95, 95n60
national home, 139–40, 142, 144–46, 150–52, 155, 163, 168n105
nationalism, 10n35, 16, 168, 236; Arab, 10, 88–89, 140, 161, 164, 164n91, 165; Jewish, 138, 140; Palestinian, 10, 11–12, 163
Naudi, Cleardo, 95
Nazareth, 14, 59, 112, 126–27
Near East Council of Churches (NECC), 184n27
Nebi Musa riots, 143
NECC. *See* Near East Council of Churches
Nelson, Richard, 293n201, 306, 313n290
Nerel, Gershon, xv, 202, 225–41, 249, 329–30, 335–37
New Testament, 7, 31, 36, 37–39, 42, 46, 51, 58n212, 61n223, 64, 66, 116, 121–22, 129, 155, 165, 169–70, 170n116, 171, 188, 208–9, 218–19, 227, 238, 267, 331; authority of, 51; fulfillment in, 122, 135, 209; Hebrew, 233; Old Testament, relationship to, 6–7, 37, 61, 71–72, 171, 218–19, 232; theology of, 36n123. *See also* Bible
Nicholls, Benjamin Elliot, 113, 113n128, 116n142, 118, 120–25, 133
Nicholson, E. W., 252n23, 267
non-denominational, 92
Northern Kingdom, 270n104, 314, 338
Noth, Martin, 317, 317nn309–10, 318, 318n317, 319
Numeruswechsel, 297, 300–301, 304

O'Brien, Conor Cruise, 176
O'Connell, Robert, 277, 277n151, 284n181, 286–94, 304, 307
O'Mahony, Anthony, 20n72, 84, 141n13, 150n46
occupation, 13, 16, 24–25, 29, 39, 95, 148, 178–79, 205, 318, 324
Odeh, Nasir, 128n184
Oikonomou, Elias, 70–71
Old Testament: authority of, 35, 51, 129, 237, 339, 339n36, 340–41 (*see also* Bible, Scripture, and New Testament,

authority of); hermeneutics of the, 3–8. *See also* believer, Old Testament; Bible, Hebrew; covenant, Old Testament; Deuteronomy; History, Old Testament; Interpretation, Old Testament; New Testament, relationship to the Old Testament; Palestinian Christian Hermeneutics of the Old Testament (PCHOT); Perspectives on Palestinian Christian Hermeneutics of the Old Testament; prophecy, Old Testament; Scripture(s), Hebrew; Theology, Old Testament

Operation Cast Lead, 179

Oriental Orthodox, 20–21, 85; CMS views of, 97–98

Orr, James, 134

Orthodox, xiii, 6n19, 20–21. *See also* Greek Orthodox; Eastern Orthodox; Oriental Orthodox

Oslo Peace Accords, xii, 60

Ottoman: armed forces, 137; authorities, 90; Christians, 86; Empire, 10, 81, 83, 83n12, 84, 84n16, 84n18, 85, 85n19, 85n24, 86, 88–89, 98, 99n74, 139, 146, 149, 150n46; government, 84, 86; internal affairs, 85; *millet* system, 150, 150n46; period, 80; politics, 88; powers, 89; rule, 83, 83n10, 89, 148; Turks, 139

Packer, J. I., 57

Palestine: history of (British Mandate), 137–46; history of (Dawn of Zionism), 79–90; history of (modern State of Israel), 175–80

Palestine Liberation Organization (PLO), 178

Palestine Native Church Council (PNCC), 95, 98, 99n73, 151, 155, 157, 157n68, 160–66, 170, 173

Palestine Problem, 145, 187, 192, 192n64, 196

Palestinian Christian. *See* Palestinian Christian identity

Palestinian Christian Hermeneutics of the Old Testament (PCHOT): elements of, 3–27, 326; examples of (contemporary), 28–75, 326, 332–35; PCHOT (1917–1948), 159–73; PCHOT (1948–1967), 182–85; PCHOT (1967–1975), 185–91; PCHOT

415

(1975–1982), 191; PCHOT
(1983–1987), 191–94; PCHOT
(1987–Present), 195. *See also*
Perspectives on Palestinian
Christian Hermeneutics of the
Old Testament, "Prescription
for a Palestinian Christian
Hermeneutics of the Old
Testament, A"

Palestinian Christian identity, xiii,
8–9, 27, 74, 159, 166–67, 194,
196, 235n128, 328, 331

Palestinian Christianity: history of
(British Mandate), 146–59;
history of (Dawn of Zionism),
90–112, 146–59; history of
(modern State of Israel),
180–81

Palestinian Liberation Theology
(PLT), 29–38, 249n19, 332. *See
also* Palestinian Theology of
Liberation (PTL)

Papademetriou, George C., 68

Pappé, Ilan, 26n86, 180nn12–13

Parsons, Levi, 93

PBC. *See* Pontifical Biblical
Commission

PCHOT. *See* Palestinian Christian
Hermeneutics of the Old
Testament

Peel Commission, 144

Peres, Shimon (Israeli President),
xi, xvi

Perspectives on Palestinian
Christian Hermeneutics of the
Old Testament: Michael Prior:
"Reading with the Eyes of
Canaanite," xv, 202–12,
240–41, 243, 248, 329–30,
335–37; Charles Miller:
"Reading with the Eyes of
Tradition," xv, 202, 212–25,
240–41, 248, 329–30, 335–37;
Gershon Nerel: "Reading with
the Eyes of Jewish-Christian
fraternité," 225–40, 241, 248,
329–30, 335–37

Philistines, 12, 12n44

Pike, James A., 184n28

Pike, John Gregory, 113

Pilgermissionsgesellschaft, 109

Pius X (pope), 225–26, 231

Pius XII (pope), 215

Pizzaballa, Pierbattista, xvi

PLO. *See* Palestine Liberation
Organization (PLO)

PLT. *See* Palestinian Liberation
Theology

PNCC. *See* Palestine Native
Church Council

pogrom, 79

polyphonic, 36–37

Pontifical Biblical Commission (PBC), 214, 215n66, 217, 217nn67–68, 218–20, 335, 335n24
Poythress, Vern, 49
Prior, Michael, xv, 202–12, 240, 249, 329–30, 335–37
Propaganda Fide, 95, 95n59, 96n60
prophecy: Israel as fulfillment, 48–49, 99; Jews, preservation of, 151; Jews, suffering of, 125; Old Testament, 168–72, 333; Old Testament, abrogation of, 155
Propst, 111–12
proselytism (proselytize), 68, 97, 104n91, 107
Protectorate, 85–86
Protestant. *See* Bishopric, Protestant; Catholic Churches, Protestant views of; Christianity, Protestant; Church of England, Protestant Bishopric in Jerusalem; Church(es), German Protestant; Church(es), Palestinian Protestant; interpretation, Protestant; Jerusalem, Protestant Bishopric in; Scripture, Protestant understandings of

Protestant Evenings, 167–68, 170, 328
PTL. *See* Palestinian Theology of Liberation

Qleibo, Ali, 12, 12n43

Rabin, Yitzak (Prime Minister of Israel), xii–xiii
Rad, Gerhard von, 54, 240n146, 253–54, 254n34, 255–56, 258–59, 259n57, 262, 271n108, 277n152, 278, 278n157, 279–80
Raheb, Mitri, xiii–xiv, 8, 27, 38–45, 50, 61, 65–66, 69, 74, 104n94, 109n112, 110n117, 158n71, 158n74, 159, 168, 168n105, 237, 326, 332–33
rapprochement, 12, 225, 226n96, 337
redaction (criticism), 254n35, 295n203, 297–99, 299n224, 301, 302n238, 319n318
Reformation, 70, 100, 167, 170
refugee(s): Jewish, 184n27; Palestinian, 54, 180n12, 184n27
Reinicke, Carl, 111n123, 112
relations: Arab-Israeli, 178; Catholic-Jewish, 217, 229–32;

church-state, 73, 181n13;
ecumenical, 19; Jew-Arab, 80;
Jewish-Christian (*see* Jewish-Christian relations); Muslim-Christian (*see* Muslim-Christian relations); Muslim-Jew (*see* Muslim-Jewish conflict); Palestinian-Israeli, 61, 178–80
reunification, 24–25
Revelation, 47, 51, 57, 61–62, 64, 65n241, 69–71, 168, 219–20, 229, 298, 334, 340
Roman Catholic. *See* Catholic
Rosen, David (rabbi), 229n105
Rothschild, Walter (2nd Baron), 139
Ruether, Rosemary Radford, 10, 10n35, 30n100
Ryrie, Charles, 47, 47n175, 48–49

Sabbah, Michel, xiii, 14–15, 15n55, 17, 19, 28, 28n90, 59–66, 195–96, 213, 216, 217n64, 220–21, 224, 326, 334–35, 335nn24–25
Sabeel, 27, 30, 30n101, 37
Sabella, Bernard, 15n56, 181n14
Said, Edward, 9, 210, 323, 342n45
salvation, xiv, 48–49, 51, 58, 62, 62n224, 63–64, 67, 92, 115, 122, 129–35, 189, 189n48; history (of), 53, 55, 61–62, 64, 191, 221; plan (of), 135, 169
Sanjak, 83
Schleiermacher, Friedrich, 4, 4n6, 5n9, 244–45
Schneller, Johann Ludwig, 39, 105n94, 108–11, 111n122
Scofield, C. I., 47, 47nn175–76, 49
Scripture(s), 5, 45, 51; authority of, 46; Boutaji and Kawar's view of, 126–34 (*see also* tradition); Catholic understanding of, 64–65; Chalil Jamal's view of, 114–24 (*see also* tradition); Christian, 36, 208; dispensations in (*see* Dispensationalism); distribution of, 98; evangelical understanding of, 56–58; George Khodr's view of, 191; Hanna Bachut's view of, 167–72; Hebrew, xiv, 27, 30–31; holy, 37, 39–42, 70, 230–31; Jewish, 208; Luther's understanding of, 42–43; Orthodox understanding of, 69–70; Protestant understanding of, 330–31; sacred, 61, 61n223, 62, 65, 207; tradition, and (*see* tradition);

translation of, 97; unity and continuity of, 71. *See also* Palestinian Christian Hermeneutics of the Old Testament (PCHOT)
Second World War, 145, 226, 238
Sennott, Charles, 16
Shaftesbury, 7th Earl of, 99–100, 100n76, 102. *See* Cooper, Anthony Ashley
Shamir, Yitzhak, 27
Sharon, Ariel, 179
Shechem(ite), 256, 264, 267, 303, 315n301
SICSA. *See* Vidal Sassoon International Center for the Study of Anti-Semitism
Six Day War, 28, 39, 45, 178, 180n12, 185, 187, 189, 328, 331, 335
Smilansky, Ze'ev, 80
Smith, George Adam, 251n22, 270n104, 295–96, 304, 306
Spittler, Christian Friedrich, 108–10, 110n120
St. Chrischona, 103n90, 110
St. George's Cathedral, 27, 108, 154, 156n66, 184
St. Paul's (native Arab) Church, 114n132, 147n39, 158nn72–73

Stewart, Weston Henry (Bishop in Jerusalem), 153, 156, 183
Stock, Eugene, 95, 95n57, 97n67, 98n70, 122
strain of loyalties, 74, 245, 247
Strauss, Friedrich Adolf, 110
Suez Crisis, 178, 178n6
supersessionism, 231
synchronic(ally), 57, 57n210, 216n60, 334
Syrische Waisenhaus (Syrian Orphanage), 110–11, 111n22, 166

Talitha Kumi, 109, 109n115
Tantur, 30, 59n215, 203
Tanzimât, 83n12, 84, 85n19
theology (of): anti-Jewish, 234; Arab, 237; covenant, 47n174, 58; Dispensational, 47–49, 333n18; Jewish Liberation, 203; Jews, significance of, 190; liberation, 33–34; martyria, 38n131; Old Testament, 36, 36n123; oppression, 203; replacement, 46n170, 50, 69. *See also* Palestinian Liberation Theology (PLT)
Thompson, Thomas L., 206, 211, 336

Tibawi, Abdul, 88, 88n33, 94n52, 96, 97n66, 99n74, 104n91, 107n105
Tigay, Jeffrey H., 274n136, 280n167, 306, 308n268
Tolkien, J.R.R., 342
Torah, 204–5, 263n74, 268n95, 274n134, 282–83, 283n177, 306, 316n306
Torah-oriented traditions, 35, 249n19
Townsend, Jeffrey, 53
Tradition (tradition): actualization of, 315n304 (*see also Vergegenwärtigung*); Assyrian, 255n38; Boutaji and Kawar's views of, 129–31, 133–34; Chalil Jamal's views of, 115, 115n140, 123; Christian, 7, 15n51, 17–19, 39, 46, 69, 91, 93n47, 158n72, 166n97, 327, 333, 336; criticism/history (*Traditionsgeschichte*), 339n36, 340nn38–39, 341, 341n42; Deuteronomic, 303; Deuteronomy 7, of, 294–305; Egyptian, 255n38; Gilgal, 303, 305; and Hanna Bachut, 167, 170, 172–73; Masoretic, 258; Palestinian Christian, emergence of, 323–35; PNCC, and, 165–66; Schechemite, 256, 303; Scripture, and, 62, 65, 70n257, 129, 330–31, 334; theories of, 65n241. *See also* Perspectives on Palestinian Christian Hermeneutics of the Old Testament, Charles Miller: "Reading with the Eyes of Tradition"
Transjordan, 141, 251
treaty: Ancient Near East, 257–58, 260–61, 261n55; Assyrian, 257, 259, 261, 310; Deuteronomy 7, xi, xiii, 262, 272n120, 337; Egypt-Israel Peace Treaty (1979), 178, 178n8; Hittite, 259, 310; Suzerain-vassal, 261
Tsimhoni, Daphne, 148, 150, 150n45, 181n15

understanding (misunderstanding). *See* hermeneutics
United Nations, 145, 179; Partition Plan (1947), 178

Vergegenwärtigung, 341, 341n44
Verus Israel, 238
Victoria (queen), 100

Vidal Sassoon International Center for the Study of Anti-Semitism (SICSA), 233
Vilayet, 83, 83n12
virtual axis, 291–92, 307. *See also Hauptachse*

Waddy, Stacy, 154
Warrior, Robert Allan, 210
WCC. *See* World Council of Churches
WCCP. *See* World Conference of Christians for Palestine
WCSF. *See* World Student Christian Federation
Weihnachtskirche, 167, 170
Weinfeld, Moshe, 53, 252n25, 255, 255nn38–39, 256, 258, 258n48, 260–63, 265, 269, 271n109, 271nn111–2, 272n114, 272n116, 272nn119–20, 273n121, 273n123, 273nn126–27, 274n132, 275n139, 276n147, 277, 279, 279n163, 180, 295, 300, 301–5, 306, 307n265, 308n268, 309–10, 310n274, 312, 314, 314n297
Weizmann, Chaim, 143, 154
Welch, Adam, 295, 296–97, 304, 306, 312n284

West Bank, 26n85, 45, 52n188, 178–79, 180n13, 203
Wette, W. M. L. de, 257, 257n48, 258
Whitelam, Keith, 25n80, 206, 211, 323–24, 325n8, 336
White Paper: British Government, the, 145, 145n31; Churchill, 142, 142n17; Passfield, 143; Zionist reaction to, 145n32
William I (Kaiser), 106
Wolff, Hans Walter, 318n317
World Conference of Christians for Palestine (WCCP), 189–90
World Council of Church (WCC), 184n27, 185–86, 186n32, 189, 192–93, 197; Amsterdam (1948), 228; Evanston (1954), 182–84; Porte Alegre (2006), 22n73
World Student Christian Federation (WSCF), 189
World War I, 10. *See also* Great War
World War II. *See* Second World War

Yishuv, 80, 80n4, 81
Yom Kippur War, 178
Younan, Munib (Bishop), 22n73, 38n131, 236n130

zero-statement, technique of, 320
Zion, 49, 79, 100
Zionism, xii, 10–11, 75, 79–81, 143; anti-Zionism, 233–4; Christian, 70, 72–73; Christian views of, 153–56, 190, 190n58; Michael Prior's view of, 205; Palestinian Christian conflict with, 165n94; Palestinian Christian views of, 168, 187; Vatican and, 225
Zionist(s), 28, 80, 142n17; anti-Zionist, 235, 238–40; Christian, 11n40; claims to Palestine, 156; Congress, 81n8, 142n17; Federation, 139; Israel, state of, 23, 191n60; Jewish, 11n40, 35, 139; leaders, 143; Michael Prior's views of, 205, 210; movement, 10n38, 40, 81n8; party, 140; policies in Palestine, 154–55; program, 79; religious, 34; views of, 191n60. *See also* Arab-Zionist Conflict

www.ingramcontent.com/pod-product-compliance
Lightning Source LLC
Chambersburg PA
CBHW071144070526
44584CB00019B/2656